Civilization in Islam

Civilization In Islam

M. Abbas

Reference Press

4831/24, Ansari Road
Darya Ganj
New Delhi-110 002
Phone: 51563444
Fax: 51563334
E-mail: info@essessreference.com
url: http://www.essessreference.com

First Published 2005

ISBN: 81-88583-89-8

Rs.800/-

Published by:
Reference Press
4831/24, Ansari Road, Darya Ganj,
New Delhi-110 002.
Phone: 51563444
Fax: 51563334
E-mail: info@essessreference.com
url: http://www.essessreference.com

Printed in India at:
Mehra Offset Press, New Delhi

Contents

Preface

Islam is not only a religion or faith. It's a way of life. Islam has given the world a new and rich civilization. The Arabs among all the great nations of the world, which have contributed to the building of human civilization, perhaps, have wielded the sword and the pen with equal success for several centuries. The success of Arabs in the intellectual areas was no less remarkable than their success in the battle field, and the teaching of the holy Prophet infused a spirit of civility, culture, piety, justice and forbearance into a savage race and inspired their hearts with love of knowledge.

The Teachings of the Holy Prophet of Islam knitted together into Islamic brotherhood the warring tribes of Arab, who, thus formed into an irresistible force, swept over the whole world, weeding out corruption and evils, wherever they went, founded a wealthier society based on equality, fraternity and justice. The nomadic Arabs, who rose from their desert tents, founded in a remarkably short time, the mightiest Empire of the medieval period, which stretched from the shores of the Atlantic in the west to the highlands of Palmir in the East. In fact they brought about the greatest revolution in the history of mankind— a revolution which embraced almost all branches of human activity.

The book in your hands touches upon all aspects of Islam. It begins with the evolution, struggle, fundamentals of Islam, values, polity and concludes at the present state of Islamic society. The book also presents the critical and comparative review and analysis of the faith.

The author has heavily drawn upon from the books of other writers and a lot of research papers. He owes his debt and gratitude to all of them. The motive of this book is to make people understand the culture, laws and basic principles of Islam.

The undersigned is confident enough that the present book will give a clear vision to its readers about the Civilization of Islam, with its remarkable historical background.

Author

1

Almighty's Commands

Divine Law

The idea of a future existence—of an existence after the separation of the living principle of our nature from the mortal part—is one of the most wonderful phenomena of the human mind. It is so generally shared by races of men otherwise utterly distinct from each other, that it has led to the belief that such an idea must be one of the first elementary constituents of our being. A more careful examination of facts connected with the infancy of races and tribes, would lead us to the conclusion that the conception of a future existence is also the result of the natural development of the human mind.

The wild savage has scarcely any idea of a life separate and distinct from that which he enjoys on earth. The Dhanger, the cannibal Andamanese, look upon death as the end of existence. Then comes a later stage, when the mind of man has passed out of its savage state, and when its hopes and aspirations are not bounded by an earthly death, when it anticipates another course of existence after the course here has been fulfilled. But even in this stage, the human conception does not rise out of the groove of daily life. Life after death is a mere continuation of life on earth, though with fewer famines to fear, with more to live upon. This idea of a continued life beyond the grave, must have been developed from the yet unconscious longing of the human soul for a more extended sphere, where the separation of dear friends, so painful to both savage and civilised man, should end in reunion.

The next stage is soon reached; man comes to believe that present happiness and misery are not, cannot be, the be-all and end- all of his existence; that there will be another life, or that there is another life after death, where he will be happy or miserable in proportion to his deserts.

Now we have reached a Principle and a Law.

Principle and Law : The mind of man goes no future towards developing the idea of future existence. The nihilistic philosopher makes no discovery, asserts no new position. He is only treading in the footsteps of our savage ancestors, whose field of vision was restricted to this life and this along. Human thought, at least here, runs in a cycle!

It is a well-authenticated fact, however, that all those ideas which represent the various stages, from a subjective point of view, exist simultaneously not only among different nations, but even in the same nation, in different combinations, according to the individual development.

Egyptians First : The Egyptians are said to have been the first to recognise the doctrine of a future life; or at least to base the principles of human conduct on such a doctrine. With an idea of metapsychosis they joined an idea of future recompense and punishment. Man descended into the tomb only to rise again. After his resurrection he entered on a new life, in company with the sun, the principle of generation, the self-existent cause of all. The soul of man was considered immortal like the sun, and as accomplishing the same pilgrimages. All bodies descended into the lower world, but they were not all assured of resurrection. The deceased were judged by Osiris and his forty-two assessors. Annihilation was often believed to be the lot of those adjudged guilty. The righteous, purified from venial faults, entered into perfect happiness, and, as the companions of Osiris. were fed by him with delicious food.

We might naturally expect that the long stay of the Israelites in Egypt would introduce among them some conception of a future life with its concomitant idea of rewards and punishments. But pure Muslim (or the teachings which pass under that name) does not recognise a state of existence differing from the present. The pivot on which the entire system of Mosaic legislation turns, consists of tangible earthly rewards and punishments. The vitality of the laws is confined within a very small compass. The doctrine of a resurrection, with the ideas arising from it which appears in later Judaism—especially in the writings of Daniel and Ezekiel—is evidently a fruit of foreign growth, derived from Zoroastrian sources. Even the descriptions of Sheol, the common sojourn of departed beings, equally of the just and unjust, which appear in comparatively early writings, do not seem of true Hebraic origin, so utterly do they differ from Semitic conception. In Sheol man can no longer praise God or remember his loving kindness. It is a shadow realm, a Jewish counterpart of the heathen Hades, in which the souls lead a sad, lethargic, comfortless existence, knowing nothing of those who were dear to them on earth, mourning only over their own condition.

Strongest Faith : But later Judaism is full of the strongest faith in a future life. Tradition reveals in the descriptions of the abodes of bliss, or of the horrors of the damned. Zoroastrianism thus acted on the Hebraic race in a double way. It not only developed in them a purer and more spiritual conception of a future existence, but later Mago-Zoroastrianism strongly coloured the Rabbinical beliefs with materialistic ideas of punishments and rewards here after.

Vividly Recognised : It was, however, among the Aryan nations of the East that the doctrine of a future life after visible death, was distinctly and vividly recognised. In one branch of the Aryan family it took the shape either of an eternal metapsychosis, a ceaseless whirl of births and deaths; or of utter absorption after a prolonged probation in Absolute Infinity or endless, unfathomable Space or Nothing. In the other branch, this doctrine was clothed in the shape of a graduated scale of rewards and punishments, in the sense in which human accountability is understood by the modem Christian or Muslim. Whether the Zoroastrians from the beginning believed in a corporeal resurrection, is a question on which scholars are divided. Dollinger, with Burnouf and other, believes that this notion was not really Zoroastric, and that it is of later growth, if not derived from the Hebrews.

Developed Conception : However this be, about the time of the Prophet of Arabia the Persians have a strong and developed conception of future life. The remains of the Zend Avesta, which have come down to us expressly, recognise a belief in future rewards and punishment. The Zoroastrianism of the Vendidad and the Budesheh, enlarging upon the beliefs of the Avesta holds that after a man's death the demons take possession of his body, yet on the third day consciousness returns. Souls that in their lifetime have yielded to the seductions of evil, cannot pass the terrible bridge Chinevad, to which they are conducted on the day following the third night after their death. The good successfully pass it, conducted by the Yazatas (in modem Persian, Ized), and, entering the realms of bliss, join Ormuzd and the Amshaspands in their abode where, seated on thrones of gold, they enjoy the society of beautiful fairies [Harun-i-Bihisht], and all manner of delights. The wicked fall over the bridge or are dragged down into the gulf of Duzakh where they are tormented by the Daevas. The duration of this punishment is fixed by Ormuzd, and some are redeemed by the prayers and intercessions of their friends. Towards the end of the world a Prophet is to arise who is to ride the earth of injustice and wickedness, and usher in a reign of happiness. After this a universal resurrection will take place, and friends and relatives will meet again. After the joys of recognition there will follow a separation of the good from the bad. The torments of the unrighteous will be fearful. Ahriman will run up and down Chinevad over whelmed with anguish. A blazing comet falling on the earth, will ignite the world. Mountains will melt and flow together like liquid metal. All mankind, good and bad alike, will pass through this glowing flood, and come out purified. Even Ahriman will be changed, and the Duzakh purified. Evil thenceforth will be annihilated, and all mankind will live in the enjoyment of ineffable delights.

Such is the summary, as given by the great scholar of the East and the West, of a religion which has influenced the Semitic faiths in an unmistakable manner, and especially the eclectic faith of Muhammad.

About the time when Jesus of Nazareth made his appearance, the Phoenicians and Assyrians had passed away. The Hellenised Roman ruled the world, checked in the East, however, by triumphant and revived Mago-Zoroastrianism.

The Jew had lost his independence for ever. A miserable sycophant occupied the throne of David. A mightier power than that of the Seleucidae kept in subjection his spirit of unruliness. Like every nation animated by a fierce love of the country, creed and individuality, the Jews, as their fate grew darker and darker, became more and more inspired with the hope that some Heaven-commissioned ministrant, like Gideon or Maccabeus, would restore their original glory, and enable them to plant their feet on the necks of their many oppressors. The appearance of a Messiah, portrayed in vivid colours by all their patriotic Seers, the Jewish Bards, was founded on one grand aspiration—the restoration of the Kingdom of Israel. Under the influences of the Mago-Zoroastrians in the East, among some classes of society specially among those whom the hellenising tendencies of Herod had withdrawn from the bosom of Israel—the belief in a personal Messiah was either faint and indistinct or a mere echo from the vulgar masses. But, as Milman beautifully observes, the Palestinian Jews had about this time moulded out of various elements, a splendid though confused vision of the appearance of the Messiah, the simultaneous regeneration of all things, the resurrection of the dead, and the reign of Messiah upon earth.

All these events were to take place at once, or to follow close upon each other. The Messiah was to descend from the line of David; he was to assemble all the scattered descendants of the tribes, and to expel and destroy their hateful alien enemies. Under the Messiah, a resurrection would take place, but would be confined to the righteous of their race. Amidst all this enthusiasm and these vague aspirations, the hopes of eternal life and future bliss were strangely mingled. The extremes of despair, and enthusiastic expectation of external relief, always tend to the development of such a state of mind among the people. One section appears to look forward to an unearthly kingdom, a reign of peace and law under divine agency, as an escape from the galling yoke of brute force; the other looks forward to the same or cognate means for securing the kingdom of heaven by the blood of aliens and heathens.

The Messianic prophecies commence with the calamities of the Jews. All prophecies of a Deliverer have a similar origin. And all such prophecies end, or, as we ought perhaps to say, are fulfilled in some Person who accomplishes the duty providence appears to impose upon him, according to the dictates of his conscience, but departs more or less from the vague predictions held out to the masses in the outpourings of loyal hearts, grieving over the moral and social ruin of their people, and which are cherished by the latter as the only source of consolation under degradation and despair.

Kingdom of Heaven : The traditions which record the sayings of Jesus have gone through such a process of elimination and selection, that it is hardly possible at the present moment to say which are really his own words and which are not. But taking them as they stand, and on the same footing as we regard other religious documents (without ignoring their real spirit, yet without trying to find mysterious meanings like the faithful believer), we see that throughout these traditional records, the notion of an immediate advent of a new order of things—"of a kingdom of heaven" is so predominant in the mind of Jesus as to overshadow all other ideas. The Son of Man has appeared; the kingdom of God is at hand; such is the theme of every hopeful word. This kingdom was to replace the society and government which the Prophet of Nazareth found so imperfect and evil. At times, his words led the disciples to conclude that the new Teacher was born to lead only the poor and the famished to glory and happiness, that, under the hoped-for theocratic regime these alone would be the blessed, and would constitute the predominating element for "woe" is denounced in awful terms against the rich and the well-fed. At other times, the realm of God is understood to mean the literal fulfillment of the apocalyptic visions or dreams connected with the appearance of the Messiah.

Sometimes, however, the kingdom of God is a realm of souls, and the approaching deliverance is merely a spiritual deliverance from the bondage of this mundane existence. All these conceptions appear at one period to have existed in the mind of Jesus simultaneously. But the fierceness and bigotry of the dominant party and the power of the Roman eagle made any immediate social change impossible. As every hope of present amelioration died away, hopes and aspirations of a brighter future took possession of the heart. Jesus felt the present state could not last long; that the time of mankind was at hand, when he himself would appear in the clouds of heaven, clothed in divine garments, seated on a throne, surrounded by angles and his chosen disciples. The dead would rise from their graves and the Messiah would sit in judgment. The angels would be the executors of his sentence. He would send the elect to a delightful abode prepared from the beginning of the world, and the unrighteous into everlasting fire prepared for the devil and his angels where there will be weeping and gnashing of teeth. The chosen, not numerically large, would be taken into an illuminated mansion, where they will partake of banquets presided over by the father of the race of Israel, the patriarchs and the Prophets, and in which Jesus himself will share. That the inauguration of the new regime with the second advent of Jesus and the resurrection of the human race was considered not to be distant is apparent from the words of the noble Prophet himself, when he impresses upon his hearers the approach of the kingdom of God, and the utter futility of every provision for the occupations and exigencies of the present life.

The words of the Teacher, acting in unison with the state of mind engendered by the circumstances of the age, had sunk deep into the hearts of his disciples; and all looked forward with a vividness of expectation hardly surpassed in the annals of human beliefs, to the literal fulfillment of the prophecies concerning the millennium.

If the first generation of the Christians had a profound and constant belief, it was that "the world was approaching its end, and that the great revelation of Christ was to happen soon." It is only when the Christian church becomes a regular organisation that the followers of Jesus expand their views beyond the Judaic world, and forgetting their millenarian dream they pass into the Greek and Roman system, and extend the empire of their creed over untold legions of barbarians fresh from their forests, who looked upon Jesus and his mother as the counterparts of their own Odin and Freya worshipped in their primeval homes.

But ever and anon, the Christian world has been agitated in moments of convulsions and disasters by the millenary excitement and a fierce expectation of the apocalyptic appearance of the great Prophet of Nazareth. The idea, however, of the realm of God has, with the lapse of ages and progress of thought, taken either a spiritual shape or utterly faded away from the mind; or, where it has been retained, derives its character from the surroundings of the individual believer.

Such was the state of belief with regard to a future existence among the various religionists of the earth prior to the teachings of Muhammad.

Respecting a Future Life : The chief and predominating idea in Islam respecting a future life is founded upon the belief that, in a state of existence hereafter, every human being will have to render an account of his or her actions on earth, and that the happiness or misery of individuals will depend upon the manner in which they have performed the behests of their Creator. His mercy and grace is nevertheless unbounded and will be bestowed alike upon His creatures. This is the pivot on which the whole doctrine of future life in Islam turn, and this is the only doctrinal point one is required to believe and accept. All the other elements—whether evolved from the genius and intuition of the inspired Teacher or caught up and syncretised from the floating tradition of the races and peoples of his time—all these other elements, whatever their ultimate significance, are mere accessories. Setting aside from our consideration the question of subjectivity involved in all ideas of future rewards and punishments, we may say, in all ideas of a life after death, we must bear in mind that these ideas have furnished to the moral teachers of the world, the most powerful instrument for influencing the conduct of individuals and nations. But though every religion, more or less, contains the germ of this principle of future accountability in another state, all have failed to realise thoroughly its nature as a continuous agency for the elevation of the masses. Virtually for its own sake, can only be grasped by minds of superior development for the average intellect, and for the uneducated, sanctions more or less comprehensible will always be necessary.

To turn now to the nature of these sanctions, it must be remembered that it is scarcely ever possible to convey an idea of spiritual pleasure or spiritual pain to the apprehensions of the generality of mankind without clothing the expression in the garb of tangible personalities or introducing sensible objects into the description of such pleasure or pain. Philosophy has wrangled over abstract expressions undressed in tangible phraseology. Such expressions and conceptions have seen their day; have flourished and have died without making themselves felt beyond a small restricted circle of dreamers, who lived in the indefinable vagueness of their own thoughts.

Addressing the World Around : Muhammad was addressing himself not only to the advanced minds of a few idealistic thinkers who happened to be then living, but to the wide world around him engrossed in materialism of every type. He had to adapt himself to the comprehensions of all. To the wild famished Arab, what more grateful or what more consonant to his ideas of paradise, than rivers of unsullied incorruptible water, or of milk and honey, or anything more acceptable than unbounded fruits, luxuriant vegetation, inexhaustible fertility? He could conceive of no bliss unaccompanied with these sensuous pleasures. This is the contention of that portion of the Muhammadan world which, like Sannai and Ghazzali, holds that behind the descriptions of material happiness portrayed in objects like trees, rivers and beautiful mansions with fairy attendants, lies a deeper meaning; and that the joy of joys is to consist in the beatific visions of the soul in the presence of the Almighty, when the veil which divides man from his Creator will be rent, and heavenly glory revealed. In this, they are upheld by the words of the Quran as well as the authentic sayings of the Prophet "The most favoured of God," said Muhammad, "will be he who shall see his Lord's face (glory) night and morning, a felicity which will surpass all the pleasures of the body as the ocean surpasses a drop of sweat."

One day talking to his friend Abu Hurrayrah, the Prophet said, "God has prepared for His good people what no eye hath seen nor ear heard, nor hath it entered into the heart of any one" and then recited the following verse of the Quran:—"No soul knoweth the joy which as secretly prepared for it as a reward for that it may have wrought." Another tradition reports that Muhammad declared the good will enjoy beautific vision of God, to which reference, he said, is made in the following verse of the Quran:—"And God inviteth unto the Dwelling of Peace... For those who do good, there is excellent reward and superabundant addition."

As to the parabolic nature of the Quranic expressions, this school of thinkers bases its convictions on the following passage of the inspired Book:—"It is He who hath sent down unto thee the Book' Some of the signs (verses) are firm (i.e. perspicuous or clear to understand); —these are the basis (or fundamental part) of the Book; —"and others are figurative."

Another section looks upon the joys and pains of the hereafter as entirely subjective. It holds that as extreme mental pain is far more agonising than physical pain, so is mental pleasure of the higher type far more rapturous than any sensuous pleasure; that as, after physical death, the individual Soul merges ('returns', in the Quranic expressions) in the Universal Soul, all the joys and pains, portrayed in vivid colours by the inspired Teacher to enable the masses to grasp the truth, will be mental and subjective. This section includes within its bosom some of the greatest Sufis or Mysitics of the Muslim world.

Another, and by far the largest class, however, believe in the literal fulfillment of all the word-paintings of the Quran.

Without venturing to pass any opinion on these different notion, we may take this occasion to state our own belief with regard to the Quranic conception of future rewards and punishments.

A careful study of the Quran makes it evident that the mind of Muhammad went through the same process of development which marked the religious consciousness of Jesus. Muhammad and Jesus are the only two historic Teachers of the world, and for this reason we take them together. How great this development was in Jesus, is apparent not only from the idealised conception towards the end of his earthly career regarding the kingdom of heaven; but also from the change of tone towards the non Israelites. Thoroughly exclusive at fist, with a more developed religious consciousness, wider sympathies awaken in the heart.

As with Jesus, so with Muhammad : The various chapters of the Quran which contain the ornate descriptions of paradise, whether figurative or literal, were delivered wholly or in part at Mecca. Probably in the infancy of his religious consciousness Muhammad himself believed in some or other of the traditions which floated around him. But with a wider awakening of the souls, a deeper communion with the Spirit of the Universe, thoughts which bore a material aspect at first became spiritualised. The mind of the Teacher progressed not only with the march of time and the development of his Religious Consciousness, but also with the progress of his disciples in apprehending spiritual conceptions. Hence, in the later suras, we observe a complete merging of the material in the spiritual, of the body in the soul. The gardens "watered by rivers," perpetual shade, plenty and harmony, so agreeable to the famished denizen of the parched, shadeless, and waterless desert, at perpetual discord with himself and all around him,—these still form the groundwork of beautiful imageries; but the happiness of the blessed is shown to consist in eternal peace and good will in the presence of their Creator.

"But those," says the Quran, "who are pious shall dwell in gardens, amidst fountains; (they shall say unto them) Enter ye therein in peace and security; and all rancour will we remove from their bosoms; they shall sit as brethren, face to face, on couches; weariness shall not affect them therein, neither shall they be repelled thence for ever.

Perfect Standards

What can be nobler or grander in its conception or imagery, or give a better idea of the belief in Muhammad's mind (at least towards the latter period of his career) concerning the nature of the present and future life than the following passage:—"It is He who enableth you to travel by land and by sea so that ye go on board of ships, which sail on with them, with favourable breeze, and they rejoice therein. But if a tempestuous wind overtake, and the waves come on them from every side, and they think they are encompassed there with, they call on God, professing unto Him sincere religion; (saying) wouldst thou but rescue us from this, then we will ever be indeed of the thankful. But when we have rescued them, behold! they commit unrighteous excesses on the earth. O men! verily the excesses ye commit to the injury of your own souls, are only for the enjoyment of this earthly life; soon shall ye return to us, and we will declare unto you that which ye have done. Verily, the likeness of this present life is not otherwise than the water which we send down from heaven, and the productions of the earth, of which men and cattle eat, are mixed therewith, till the earth has received its beautiful raiment, and is decked out; and they who inhabit it imagine they have power over it! (But), our behest cometh unto it by night or by day, and we make it as if it had been mown, as though it had not teemed (with fertility) only yesterday. Thus do we make our signs clear unto those who consider. And God inviteth unto the Abode of Peace, and guideth whom He pleaseth into the right way. For those who do good is excellent reward and superabundant addition of it; neither blackness nor shame shall cover their faces. These are the inhabitants of paradise; therein do they abide for ever. But those who have wrought evil, shall receive the reward of evil, equal thereunto; and shame shall cover them,—(for there will be none to protect them against God), as though their faces were covered with a piece of the night of profound darkness."

Then again the following passage, in its solemn grandeur, its sublime dignity and the purity of its aspirations, not to say its practical depth, is surpassed by nothing in the history of the moral world. "Who fulfil the covenant of God, and break not their compact; and who join together what God hath bidden to be joined; and who fear their Lord, and dread an ill-reckoning; and who, from a sincere desire to please their Lord, are constant amid trials, and observe prayers and give alms, in secret and openly, out of what we have bestowed on them; and turn aside evil with good for this is the recompense of that Abode, gardens of eternal habitation, in to which they shall enter, together with such as shall have acted rightly from among their fathers, their wives and their posterity; and the angels shall go in unto them by every portal, (saying) Peace be with you! because ye have endured with patience.' Excellent is the reward in that Abode!"

Enough has been said to show the utter falsehood of the theory that Muhammad's pictures of future life were all sensuous. We will now conclude this chapter with the following passage from the Quran, to show the depth of spirituality in Islam, and the purity of the hopes and aspirations on which it bases its rule of life:

> "O thou soul which art at rest, return unto thy Lord, pleased and pleasing Him enter thou among my servants; and enter thou my garden of felicity."

2

Ideal Character

Model of Morality

The facts stated above give briefly an idea of the difficulties and hardships the Prophet (PBUH) had to face in the proclamation of his prophethood, propagation of his teachings and protection of all those taking to his teachings.

In a country where there was no government and law and order. Where murder and blood shed was in the days work, whose citizens might be resembling ravenous beasts and worse than cattle in ignorance and total absence of discernment and rationality, putting up a claim, queer to the entire country, and fomenting trouble and opposition among all the tribes, was not so easy. Again, this claim gaining favour under conditions of the unlimited opposition of millions of people, bent on wiping it out with all their might, hearts and minds, and means at their disposal, persistently for years together, is certainly a vivid proof of the Divine Aid.

In connection with the events related earlier, the morals, excellence, attributes and laudable deeds outshine like pure gold in sand and dirt. And it is these events that bring to light the fact that in the totally opposite conditions of oppression and helplessness and power and majesty, existence with the same simplicity can be the accomplishment of one whose heart has been totally possessed by the Divine Law. When it has been purged of the worldly involvements.

The blessed events of the Prophet's (PBUH) life are a model and an example for every country, every class, both for individuals and groups and parties.

Instead of the perfections of the prophethood and characteristics of the Prophet, only those simple natural good habits, good disposition, amiability and extremely good manners shall be taken up which a fortunate person of a docile nature can take as a model of moral perfection:

> Ye have indeed in the Messenger of Allah an excellent example. Al Quran XXXIII: 21

Our leader, Muhammad (PBUH) was unlettered. And upto the time of his being raised a Prophet, had not had the company of any learned person.

Archery, horsemanship, use of lance in fighting, poetry, panegyric or laudative poetry, geneology were those arts and skills of that period which every young man of a noble family did pick up for the sake of fame and prestige, and without which no one had any chance of coming to a position of honour or distinction in his community. The Prophet had not learnt or picked up any of these from any body as a student. Nor did he ever shown any interest in learning them.

French Professor Cideo writes about the Prophet (PBUH):

> "He had a smiling countenance, sociable, mostly quiet (a man of few words), remembering God most of the time, far removed from absurdity, abhorring frivolity and had the most appropriate opinion and wisest (among those around him)."

"In the matter of doing justice, he never made any distinction between the far and near (close to him or present before him and a stranger or one absent). He loved the indigent and was happy among the poverty stricken. He never meted out a degrading treatment to a poor person because of his lack of means. He captivated the hearts of his associates and patiently put up with the uncouthness or objectionable conduct of the ignorant. He never parted with any one talking to him until he himself left him. He loved his companions most. He had no hesitation in sitting on the ground if nothing to cover it was available. He himself repaired his own shoes and put patches on his clothes. Met even his enemies and unbelievers with a cheerful countenance."

Hujjah-al-Islam Ghazzali writes:

> The Prophet offered green fodder to the cattle himself, tied the camels, cleaned the house, milked the goat, took his food with his servant or slave, gave a helping hand to the servant in his work, went to the market for purchase of the necessities of life and himself brought these things home. He was always the first to greet (say salam) to every one young or old, high or low (never allowing them precedence over himself). Whoever accompanied him, he walked hand in hand with him.

He never made distinction between master and man, Abyssinian and a Turk. He had the same attire for the day and night wear. However lowly a person invited him to dine with him, he accepted without reserve. And whatever was offered to him, he took it cheerfully. He was not given to saving for the morning from the night's rituals, nor from the day's food for the night contentment and real trust in Allah. He was good natured, of a generous disposition and cheerful countenance (smiling face) but never laughed (loudly). He was mostly full of anxiety for one reason or another but not ill-tempered. He was meek but without meanness. He was awe-inspiring but not a harsh countenance. He was generous but not prodigal. He was merciful to one and all but expected nothing from anyone. He mostly kept him head bent.

Shah Wali-al-Allah writes:

> Whoever happened to confront him suddenly he became awe-inspired and whoever sat with him for a while became devoted follower and admirer.

He was particularly kind to his kinsmen and those serving him. Anas (R) served him for ten years but never heard even 'ugh!' or hunh'! from him. Never a foul word or abuse befouled his pure clean tongue, nor he ever cursed any one. He showed remarkable patience in face of distress from others. He showed profound mercy to the people in general. None ever suffered at his hand or by his tongue. Reform of his family and the community received his first attention. He was aware of every body and everything. His attention was focused on the Kingdom of Heaven.

In Sahih Bukhari it has been said:

> The Prophet (PBUH) gave glad tidings to the obedient and warned the disobedient and transgressor. Allah's servant and His Messenger offered asylum to the uninformed. Leaving everything to Allah (after doing what was his own due). Neither harsh in behaviour nor in speech. Never raised his voice in speaking, nor tit for tat in dealings. Those seeking forgiveness, he readily forgave (if it was not a transgression against God). He forgave the sinner also. His mission was to correct the crookedness in religions. His teachings gave eyes to the blind, ears to the deaf and lifted the curtains from the hearts of the negligent. The Prophet's (PBUH) character was decorated with every excellence and qualified with all the finest attributes. Peace and tranquillity was attire and doing good his distinctive sign, taqwa, (piety), his conscience, wisdom his speech, justice his conduct, His Shariah wholly uprightness and his millat (Belief and Faith). Guidance in his guide. He removes misguidance, elevating the position of the lowly and making the little known outstanding, changing minority into majority and the want or destitution into richness.

Silence and Speech : The Prophet as a matter of habit remained silent never speaking needlessly. The Prophet (PBUH) was extremely sweet spoken and eloquent. His speech was not at all affected. His words were so captivating that they went to the listener's heart and soul. This quality of his speech was such as compelled even the adversaries to admit it. And again, it was this marvel of his speech which the ignorant attributed to sorcery.

The continuity of his speech was such that, in word or purport, there was no fault. He used words with such precision and order that if the listener liked, he could count them.

Smiling and Weeping : The Prophet never laughed loudly, nor did he burst into laughter on his own. His laughter was limited to a serene smile. However, in the pre-down prayer (Tahajjud) he burst into tears at times. At other times, the death of a sincere associate (companion) or kinsman his eyes welled up with tears.

His infant son, Ibrahim, had died while yet a suckling. When he was put into the grave, it was too much for a loving father and mercy for mankind and brought tears to his eyes. He said:

> "The eyes manifest grief, the heart is grieved too, but we say only what our Lord and Sustainer loves to hear from us: O Ibrahim thou in thy parting caused us grief.

On another occasion he happened to lift on to his lap his grand daughter, Zainab's (R) dying daughter. His love for the child and in death pangs, proved too much for him and it brought tears to his eyes. Saad (R) asked him about this phenomenon and was told that it was due to those tender chords in the human heart that are touched. It is God-given mercy. And Allah too will be merciful only to those of his servant that are kind-hearted and show mercy to fellow-beings.

Once Abdullah Ibn Masood (R) was reciting Quran before the Prophet (at his bidding). When he came to the verse:

> How then if we brought from each people a witness and we brought thee as a witness against these people.
> (Q.IV: 41)

> He said to him: "That's enough." Ibn Masood (R) lifting his eyes saw tears running down the Prophet's (PBUH) eyes.

The Diet : The Prophet (PBUH) advised people not to go to sleep on a hungry stomach (missing the night meal) and pointed to it as a sign of senility. He also advised them against going to sleep immediately after supper.

He used to persuade people to be sparing or at least moderate in eating. He used to say to them that they should keep one third of the stomach for food, another one third for water and the last one third for the stomach itself (meaning that the stomach should not be fully stuffed to cause it pain or at least inconvenience and hardship).

He used to take fruits and vegetable with their correctives.

To be cautious against certain diseases and the healthy to be careful were his orders.

Sick persons were advised by him to get treated by a physician clever at his job and also stressed abstention. He forbade a novice and a quack to practise medicine and held him responsible for damage to people's health. He also forbade use of prohibited things as medicines and said: "Allah has not kept healing properties in the prohibited things for you."

Visiting the Sick : Whoever among the companions fell ill, he used to visit him. He used to sit very close to the sick person and tried to console him. He used to encourage him saying: "Allah willing you shall be all right, there is no cause for worry." He also asked the patient if he desired anything, and if it was not harmful to him, he would arrange it for him. A Jewish boy who used to wait on him, fell ill and the Prophet visited him in his sick bed and it is reported also asked him to embrace Islam and after approval of his father, he did.

Treatment of Diseases : When suffering from any ailment, he himself used medicine and advised others also to do the same saying:

> "O ye servants of Allah! Do take medicine, since Allah has appointed a cure for every malady, save one disease. People asked him which is that? He said: "It is extreme old age (decrepitude). (When the body reaction to inherent deterioration as well as foreign invaders becomes minimum or totally absent).

Speeches (Harangues) : He used to harangue people standing on the floor or from a pulpit or on camels back, beginning from bearing witness to the unity of Allah and concluded with asking Allah for forgiveness. Something from the Quran was a must as part of it and the Islamic principles were taught (preached) in it.

> "All those things were explained in the speeches (of the Prophet) which were the need of the hour for the Muslim community and according to the time and its demand everything was covered in them.
>
> (Zad-al-Maad Vol. I, P. 49)

These harangues were not limited to Friday congregations, but whenever he felt there was need for it he would speak with the Word of God to support his own. At the time of speaking, he held in his hand a club, a bow on which, if need be, he would temporarily support himself. But there is no instance of his ever holding a sword in his hand when speaking to an audience nor he ever used it as a body support.

Allamah Ibn-al-Qayyim says: "The ignorant are often heard saying that the Prophet (PBUH) took the pulpit sword in hand, pointing to the (most erroneous) belief that Islam was propagated at the point of sword." The 'Allamah goes on to say, (is of the opinion) that this common belief of the ignorant masses is totally wrong.

1. Supporting himself on a sword has no proof.
2. Harangues started in Medina and had been conquered with the force of the Quran and not the might of the sword. Again, the

Allamah also goes on to add that the Islamic Faith was established with the Heavenly revelation.

Charity and Gifts : He never used anything coming as Sadaqah (charity). However, he had no objection to accept gifts.

The gifts from sincere companions (R) as well as Christians and Jews were accepted and in turn gifts were sent to them. But those from the polytheists were rejected outright.

He rode the mule sent by Maquqas, the king of Egypt, and in the battle of Hunain that same mule was under him. But he rejected outright the horse sent by 'Amir bin Malik and plainly stated, "We do not accept gifts from a polytheist."

The precious gifts coming to the Prophet (PBUH) were usually given to his companions.

His Own Praise : Any such laudation of his that would bring any other prophet lower, he disapproved, and used to say:

> Never resort to a mode in relation to the prophet's attributes which lowers one than any other.
>
> He attended a marriage ceremony where girls of a very tender age were singing the songs of laudable deeds of their encounters. They also sang in praise

of the Prophet (PBUH) that they had among them a Prophet who can tell you today of the happenings of tomorrow. The Prophet stopped them from saying those words and asked them to continue with their songs of ancestors.

Correcting an Erroneous Belief : Death occurred of the Prophet's son Ibrahim. And that also happened to be the day of solar eclipse. People started talking. The sun too is mourning the death of Ibrahim. It is eclipsed. The Prophet addressed those present there: Solar and Lunar eclipses are not due to anybody's death.

Regard for the General Expediency : When the Quraish renovated Kaaba during the pre-Islamic period it was not raised on the old foundation. They left out some covered area outside, with a plinth so high that ladder was needed to enter the enclosure and with only one door. The Prophet one day commented on it addressing 'Aishah (R).

"Your community (Quraish) have embraced Islam only lately, otherwise I would have demolished their structure and made certain necessary alterations. Kaaba needs two doors, one for entry and another for departure."

When the mischievous activities of the hypocrites crossed all limits of decency and humanity, 'Umar Farooq (R) suggested that they should be put to the sword. The Prophet said to him: "No. People will adversely comment: "Muhammad has started killing his friends."

Humanness and Apostleship : The Prophet always tried to show his commands emanating from him as an Apostle separate from those he issued as a human being:

1. Once he said: "I am after all human and conflicts and quarrels are put up before me. Someone of you can express himself and put up his case better than the other which gives a notion of his truth, and I decide the case in his favour. So if a Muslim gets anything from his Muslim brothers share, he should clearly understand that it is a part of fire, it is up to him to take it or leave it."
2. He pleaded the case of Mughith and intercessed with Baridah a slave girl, his, (Mughith's) wife. She had separation from him after freedom. Baridah asked the

Prophet (PBUH): Is that your command to me?" The Prophet replied:? No. It is my intercession on his behalf." To this she said: "I have no need of Mughith."

The Medinites, on the basis of experience used to sprinkle the pollen dust of male date palm trees on the female tree's flowers. The Prophet once casually remarked: "Where is the need of this operation?" The owners of date palm groves gave up the practice, with the result that due to scanty pollination by natural agencies like wind alone, fruit that year was scanty too. The date palm growers brought this phenomenon to the Prophet's (PBUH) notice. He owned it without reserve that they knew their worldly affairs better than he did. "Follow me unstintedly with certainty only in those things I order you relating to your Faith," he concluded.

Affection for Children : Passing by the children on his way, he greeted them initially with the Islamic salutation (As-Salam-u-Alaikum, peace be on you). He placed his hand on their heads and at times lifted one on to his lap.

Kindness to the Aged : After the conquest of Mecca, Abu Bakr Siddiq (R) brought his old decrepit blind father to the Prophet (PBUH) for Bahia (oath of fealty). The Prophet (PBUH) said to Abu Bakr, "Why did you give all this trouble to an old man (in this state of disabilities)? I would have myself visited him."

Honour and Prestige of the Excellent : Saad bin Muaz (R) who (came by a severed artery of the arm at Uhud which could not be sealed and ultimately caused his death), had been named by the Banu Quraiza Jews to pronounce his decision in their case (of high treason) and called to the scene of action. When he had come to the mosque, the Prophet (PBUH) asked his companions of Aus tribe to pay their respects to him by advancing to receive him, saying "Greet and receive your leader." And his tribesmen (Aus) did the Prophet's bidding.

1. Hassan bin Thabit composed couplets lauding Islam and most effective retorts to the adversaries. As a recognition of his services to Islam, a pulpit was laid in the mosque for his recital.

Prayer for the Person Engaged in Service to Allah : Anas bin Malik (R) served the Prophet for ten years in Medina. During this long period he never took him to task. One day he prayed for him: "O Allah! confer on him plentiful wealth and progeny and also bless them for him."

Respect and Regard for Others and Hospitality

1. The Prophet never sat with extended feet (legs) in company.
2. Whoever met him on the way, he had precedence in greeting him.
3. He also had precedence in shake-hand.
4. He called his companions by their patronymic appellations. (This was the mode of calling people honourably in Arabia)
5. He never interrupted anybody talking.
6. If he was offering supererogatory prayer and somebody happened to come to see him, he would shorten it and after meeting his need continued the prayer.
7. He was smiling most of the time.
8. One of the she camels (dromedaries) of the Prophet (PBUH) was called 'Asba. It was swift footed and never allowed any camel to get and advance over her. A bedouin Arab coming along on his mount surpassed 'Asba and the Muslims so to say, took it ill, but the Prophet said:

   The sunnah of Allah in this world is that if He exalts any, He also brings him low.
9. There came a person who called the Prophet (PBUH) the best (superior most) of the created beings. The Prophet (PBUH) said to him: "That title befits only the Prophet Ibrahim (PBUH)."
10. Somebody came to see the Prophet (PBUH) and was awe-inspired. He, however, reassured him saying: "Be at ease. I am not a king. I am the son of a poor woman of Quraish who used to take dried meat."

Holiest Model

Affection and Clemency : 'Aishah Siddiqah (R) says:

1. Nobody in sweet nature and politeness came close to the Prophet (PBUH). Whether a companion called him or a member of his own house his usual answer was "I am here."

2. Supererogatory devotional acts were always performed in seclusion so that the Ummah may not be overburdened in his pursuit.
3. When there appeared two alternatives before him, he would resort to the simpler or easier one.
4. He entered a contract with his Lord that whomsoever he called a bad name or cursed, Allah should make it an atonement for his sins and a means of His Mercy, forgiveness and closeness.
5. He had instructed that they should not talk about one another in my presence. I want to leave this world without any ill opinion about any one.
6. Once on the occasion of solar eclipse, in the special congregation, he wept and prayed like this:
   (A) O my Lord and Cherisher! Thou hast promised me that my ummah shall not be the recipient of any visitation from Thee, (1) So long I am Here with them, and (2) As long as they are beseeching Thee for their forgiveness.
   (B) And at present My Lord, I am among them and they are all seeking Thy forgiveness.

For every prophet, there was a specific prayer and they invoked that and it was blessed with response. As for the specific one for me, I have kept it for the Last Day.

Justice and Compassion : If two persons fell out of each other he meted out justice to them. If however, he had a personal complaint against anybody he would always forgive.

1. A respectable lady of Quraish, Fatima bint-Mazan, was found guilty of theft. The tribe wanted to save her from the prescribed punishment of this crime, chopping of the hand. So as an "effective" measure they made Osamah bin Zaid a favourite of the Prophet (PBUH), her intercessor at the court of the Shariah. The Prophet (PBUH), in spite of his indulgence, disapproved Osamah's involving himself in the case, saying: "Dare you intercess in a limit set by Allah? Listen to me, If Fatimah bint Muhammad committed theft, I would have her hand chopped off."

2. Sawad bin 'Umar relates that one day he went to the Prophet (PBUH) gaudily dressed. The Prophet (PBUH) disapproved of it and patted my abdomen with the stick he had in his hand. I said to the Prophet (PBUH): "I shall avenge myself." The Prophet bared his abdomen, said to him: "You are welcome to it." (But all that he did was kissing the seal of prophethood).

Clemency to the Enemies

1. A severe famine struck Mecca, until the starving lot was compelled to subsist on carrion and bones. Abu Sufyan (one of the arch enemies of Islam and Muslims) came to the Prophet (PBUH) and addressed him thus: "Muhammad! You preach kind treatment of kinsmen. Your community is at the doorstep of total annihilation. Kindly pray to God, which the Prophet most graciously did and in response brought heavy rains.
2. Thamamah bin Athal stopped supply of food grains to Mecca (after his embracing Islam) as a sign of goodwill to the Muslim community against their deadly enemies. However, the Prophet (PBUH) prevented him from persisting with it.
3. In Hudaibiah, the Prophet was offering prayer with the Muslims when seventy or eighty persons quietly came down the Tanim mount with the evil intent of taking a heavy toll of Muslim lives while they were engaged in prayers. But they could not succeed in their satanic design and were taken prisoners. But the Prophet granted them their freedom without any ransom or punishment.

Generosity and Benignity

1. He never turned away a beggar (anyone asking for help). Flat refusal was almost a taboo with him. If he was unable to do anything for him, he would put up an excuse as if he were requesting to be forgiven for a shortcoming.
2. Somebody came to him asking for alms. The Prophet (PBUH) said to him that he had nothing to give him just then. He could, however, borrow in his name which he would meet later. 'Umar Faruq (R) said to him (the Prophet

(PBUH)) that Allah had not compelled him to go beyond his means to help people. The Prophet kept quiet, evading his objection. An Ansari sitting close by spoke out: "O Apostle of Allah why not respond to him saying, Allah, the Master and Lord of the Throne is our Sustainer and as such there is no fear of poverty and destination." The Prophet smiled and his face was aglow with delight and he said: "You are right. I have these commandments from Him (My Master, Lord and Sustainer)."

3. Once he gave an indigent person half a 'wasaq' of grain borrowed from some one. The creditor turned up later for recovery of his loan. The Prophet ordered payment of full one wasaq of grains to this creditor, half that he had loaned and an additional half from us as a gesture of generosity and reward for a good deed (helping a destitute).
4. He used to say and had almost declared it as a matter of policy that the assets of the dead is the share of the inheritors and the debts the liability of the Islamic state if he died a destitute.

Modesty and Bashfulness

1. Abu Saeed Khudri (R) says that the Prophet (PBUH) was more modest than a purdah observing bashful girl. Whenever something disgusting came before him in people's mutual talk, his face showed that disgust from his facial expression.
2. 'Aishah Tayyibah (R) has stated that if the Prophet did not like any deed or word of any person, he did not object to and forbid it pointedly but in a general way showed his disapproval of that word or deed (to avoid embarrassment of the guilty.)
3. In day-to-day affairs and dealings, he would take upon himself the greatest burden but would not order anyone else to undertake it or offer a helping hand, out of modesty.
4. Whenever some repentant person begged to be excused, the Prophet (instead of scolding or lecturing him from a superior stand according to the way of people) modestly hung his head.
5. 'Aishah Tayyibah (R) reports that she never saw him naked.

Excellence of Leaving Inheritance for the Survivors

It is better for you to leave your inheritors independent rather than leaving them penniless beggars.

Example of the Finer Sex and Humouring them for Agreeable Relationship

Woman is like a rib (curved normally) which can be broken in an attempt to straighten it out. But it is possible to make use of it curved as it is. (Cleverly handling a woman in as much as letting her have her own way according to her particular bent of mind, harmlessly, she can cooperate and help a lot in running a household and bringing up children nicely).

Woman's Position in Household : A woman is the ruler in her husband's house and over her offspring.

Deep Knowledge of the Quran : A person who has gone deep into the Quran pondering (over) its words, meanings, the background and the broad principles about the nature of this scripture, will be with the revered chosen and virtuous messengers (angels).

Most Pleasing Words in the Sight of Allah : These are just two words so dear to Rahman, easy to pronounce but heavy on the scales (evaluating men's deeds):

> Glory to Allah and Praise for Him, Glory to Allah (who is free from all faults they ascribe to Him), (Allah), the supreme (in Glory).

The Glorious Quran : If a learned person were to write about the life of the Prophet (PBUH) the chosen of Allah, in great detail, he will have to discuss the Quran, revealed to him. But even if somebody, like me writing in a simple and brief manner his biography, he too will find himself compelled to present a sample of the Quranic teachings, though leaving out the finer point demanding detailed discussions. To my mind, the life history of the Apostle of Allah without any mention of the Quran with samples, is incomplete, sadly tacking in this most important aspect. Somebody had asked 'Aishah Siddiqah (R) about the morals of the Prophet (PBUH), she had replied: "The Quran is his (sublime) morals."

It is our sacred belief that every word of the glorious Quran is the word of Allah. (It is known by the name of the Word of God).

But it was the Apostle of Allah (PBUH) who introduced this word of Allah to the world. It was revealed to Muhammad, the Apostle of Allah (PBUH) in twenty three years. It exists in those very words in which he recited it and gave to the world. It has been preserved intact by Allah and shall remain so to the end of days. It is in our hearts and minds pervading them and on our tongues having the marvel of memorization, seen nowhere else in the world with any other scripture existing today.

This pure and clean Word of God exist every where in the world, even the remotest corners which Muslims have found access or non Muslims have embraced Islam. Millions of men all over the world recite different portions of it in their five times daily prayers.

Since its revelation its propagation has been on the increase. From the moment, the mother of the believer, Khadijah Al Kubra (R) heard from the Prophet (PBUH) the first ever revelation in Hira cave, day-by-day, rather every moment the number of its votaries is on the increase. No country, no particular period customs and manners, the favourable or adverse condition of its followers or antagonists, can become an impediment in its progression.

In many countries and languages faulty translations to misguide the world were put forth and its true and clear teachings were confused with misleading explanatory foot notes, but none of these satanic devices could bring down its greater and greater publication and distribution with the time.

Unlike other scriptures, the Holy Quran is extant in the language it was revealed and the world has access to it everywhere. Not an iota got changed during a millennium and a half. But the other holy books like Torah (the old Testament) and Injil (The Gospels) and the epistles of the saints, Vedas and Zand and Pazand can not claim to be the original versions and free from tampering, so much so that it becomes difficult to believe that their greater part could be the revealed scriptures. In fact no religious book save the Quran could escape perversion. Even the languages in which they are said to have been revealed exist today nor any copy of the original to be seen. The earliest Gospel is the Greek version of Injil and not the original Aramic.

Since the Quran itself relates all those objections levelled against it or the false accusations brought forth against the Prophet about the origin of Quran, it is its own true history, showing both sides of the picture clearly. The Glorious Quran due to its truth and unassailable position has demonstrated that boldness which no other scripture in the world can claim for itself (and for obvious reasons).

The Quranic teachings have that undeniable truth in them that those religious communities and nations that did not acknowledge it openly, yet claimed that their religious books too had those truth in them, which either preceded the Quran or followed it. How true is the word of Allah:

> No falsehood can approach it from before or behind it. It is sent down by one Full of Wisdom. (Q. XLI: 42)

What have put forth as claim in the above lines will become manifest to you, reader, when you will study the conditions extant in the pre-Quranic period of Judaism, Christianity, Zoroastrianism, Buddhism, and Sanatan or Aryah Dharm of Hinduism (their social and political orders) and then come to study their progress in all walks of life to date, considering at the same time that long before this revolution in this country, the teachings of the Quran were in usage in most spheres of life if not all.

Now whether any religious or ethnic group acknowledges the blessings and bounties of the Glorious Quran, as do the founders of Brahmo Samaj, or Martin Luther, the rebel of the Roman Catholic Church as he stands accused of his strong learnings to be derivations from the Quran, by the orthodox Catholics, or those who find it repugnant to acknowledge even that much remotely derived benefit as many religious sects that have definitely though stealthily borrowed Quranic teachings, are going on borrowing as problems arise which Quran alone has solved. (Some of them openly praise Islamic laws minus the courage of adoption, like our prime minister who recently lauded the Muslim Divorce Laws beside other things that appeal to him and many others of that bilk from time to time). (There is a big flow in this type of thinking of people like Gandhiji. He held the rule of Abu Bakr (R) and 'Umar Faruq (R) as his ideal but was either ignorant of or deliberately over lacking the very common principle that laws divorced from an ideology, the driving force of action, are not effective at all or very little).

The Glorious Quran is the only scripture with the glad tidings:

> This day have I perfected your religion for you completed my favour upon you. —Al Quran V: 3

The Truth

Discernment of the Divine Entity

1. In the name of Allah, the Beneficent, Most Merciful.
2. No vision can grasp Him. But His grasp is over all vision. (Q. 6: 103)
3. There is nothing whatsoever like unto Him. But He is the One that hears and sees. —Al Quran XLII: 11
4. Allah is the Protector of those who have faith: from the depths of darkness He leads them forth into light. (Q. II: 257)
5. Allah! There is no god but He,— the Living, the Self-Subsisting, Supporter of all, no slumber can seize Him, nor sleep. His are all things in the heavens and earth. Who is there can intercede in His Presence except as He permitteth? He knoweth what (appeareth to His creatures as) Before or After or Behind them. Nor shall they compass aught of His knowledge except as He willeth. His Throne doth extend over the heavens and the earth, and He feeleth no fatigue in guarding and preserving them, for, He is the Most High, the Supreme in Glory. —Al Quran II: 255
6. He hath inscribed for Himself (the rule of) Mercy. (Q. VI: 12)
7. Say: He is Allah, the One, Allah, the Eternal, Absolute, He beqetteth not, nor is He begotten; and there is none like unto Him. —Al Quran CXII: 1-4

The Definition of True Faith

1. The nature in which Allah has made mankind. No change (there is) in the work (wrought) by Allah: that is the true Religion, but most among mankind know not. (Q. XXX: 30)

2. (Our religion) takes its true from Allah and who can give a better true than Allah. —Al Quran II: 138

3. The same religion has he established for you as that which He enjoined on Nuh—the which We have sent by inspiration to thee—and that which we enjoined on Ibrahim Moses and Jesus, namely that you should remain steadfast in Religion, and make no divisions therein:
—Al Quran XLII: 13

What for Does Allah Want Good Deeds From Man

It is not their meat, their blood, that reaches Him:
(Q. XXII: 37)

Shariah was Meant to Perfect Man's Humanity

1. Allah doth not wish to place you in difficulty, but to make you clean, and to complete His favour to you, that ye may be grateful. —Al Quran V: 6

2. —— For, prayer restrains from shameful and evil deeds; and remembrance of Allah is the greatest (thing in life) without doubts. —Al Quran: XXIX: 45

The Duties of the Prophet

1. A similar (favour have ye already received) in that We have sent among you a Messenger of your own, rehearsing to you Our Signs, purifying you and introducing you in scripture and wisdom, and in new knowledge.(Q H: 151)

2. For he commands them what is just and forbids them what is evil; he allows them as lawful what is good (and pure) and prohibits them from what is bad (and impure); he releases them from heavy burdens and from the yokes that are upon them. (Q. VII: 157)

Retribution both Here and Hereafter

1. If the people of the towns had but believed and feared Allah, we should indeed have opened out to them (all kinds of) blessings from heaven and earth, but they rejected (the truth) and We brought them to book for their misdeeds.
—Al Quran VII: 96

2. If only they had stood fast by the Torah, the Gospel, and

all the revelation that was sent to them from their Lord, they would have eaten both from above them and from below their feet. —Al Quran V: 66

3. Whatever misfortune happens to you is because of the things your hands have wrought, and for many (a sin) He grants forgiveness. —Al Quran XLII: 30
4. Now no person knows what delights of the eye are kept hidden (in reserve) for them —as a reward for their (good) deeds.

The Divine Sunnah Alters Not

1. No change will thou find in Allah's Way (of dealing).
2. No turning off will thou find in Allah's Way (of dealing). —Al Quran XXXV: 43
3. He Who created the seven heavens one above another. No want of proportion will thou see in the creation of the Most Glorious. So turn thy vision again, seest thou any flaw. Again turn thy vision a second time: (thy) vision will come back to thee dull and discomfited, in a state worn out. —Al Quran LXVIL3-4

Only Personal Effort can be Fruitful

1. That man can have nothing but what he strives for; Q. LIII: 39
2. Verily this (the bounties in Heaven) is a reward for you. (from Allah) and your Endeavour is accepted and recognized. —Al Quran LXXVI: 22
3. That was a people that hath passed away. They shall reap the fruit of what they did and ye of what ye do! —Al Quran 141

The Lofty Position of Patience and Piety

1. If ye persevere patiently and guard against evil, then that indeed is a matter of great resolution.—Al Quran III: 186

The Position of Wisdom

1. And he to whom wisdom is granted receive indeed a benefit over-whelming. —Al Quran 32:.24

The Fruit of Patience

1. And We appointed from among them, leaders giving guidance under Our command, so long as they persevered with patience. —Al Quran 32: 24

Cutting Oneself off from Greed

1. Nor strain thy eyes in longing for the things We have given for enjoyment to parties of them. (Q. XX: 131)

Not to Consign to Oblivion the Hereafter in the Luxuriance of Life Here

1. Nor forget thy position in the world but do thou good.

Guard against Self Destruction

1. And spend of your substance in the cause of Allah, and make not your own hands contribute to (your) destruction. —Al Quran II: 195

Forging Falsehood is Inimical to Belief

1. It is those who believe not in the Signs of Allah, it is they who forge falsehood. It is they who lie. —Al Quran XVI: 105

Absolutely Prohibited Things

1. Say: The things that my Lord hath indeed forbidden are: indecent deeds whether open or secret: sins and trespasses against truth or reason, assigning of partners to Allah for which he hath given no authority: and saying things about Allah of which ye have no knowledge.—Al Quran VII: 33

Worship of Allah is Divine Baptism

1. (Our religion) takes its true from Allah and who can give a better hue than Allah. It is He Whom we worship. —Al Quran II: 138

Pen and Writing Praise Worthy

1. Nun. By the Pen and by the (Record) which men write. —Al Quran LXVIII: 1

Signs of Allah for the Wise

1. Behold! In the creation of the heavens and the earth, in the alternation of the Night and the Day, in the sailing of ships through the ocean, for the profit of mankind, in the

rain which Allah sends down from the skies, and the life which He gives there with, to an earth that is dead; in the beasts of all kinds that he scatters through the earth; in the change of winds and the clouds which they trail like their slaves between the sky and the earth. (Here) indeed are Signs for a people that are Wiser. —Al Quran II: 164

Swearing Prohibited

1. Obey not every mean swearer. —Al Quran LXVIII: 10
2. And make not Allah's (name) an excuse for your oaths. (Q. II: 224)
3. Keep to your oaths. —Al Quran V: 89

Call to Total Peace (Islam the Religion of Peace)

1. O ye who believe! Enter into Islam whole heartedly; and follow not the footsteps of the satan, for he is to you an avowed enemy. —Al Quran 11: 208

Mutual Reform

1. Make peace between persons. —Al Quran II: 224
2. And keep relations straight between yourselves. (Q. VIII: 1)

Teaching Forgiveness and Overlooking Faults

1. Let them forgive and overlook. Do you not wish that Allah should forgive you? For Allah is Oft-Forgiving, Most Merciful. —Al Quran XXIV: 22

True Teachings Manifest Themselves

1. Soon will We show them in the (furthest) regions (of the earth), and in their own souls, until it becomes manifest to them that this is the Truth. —Al Quran XLI: 53

The Principles

Judges Must be Learned

And remember David and Solomon when they gave judgement in the matter of the field into which the steep of certain people had strayed by might: We did witness their judgement. To Solomon, We inspired the right understanding of the matter to each (of them) —Al Quran XXI: 78-79

Mischief Prohibited

Do not mischief on the earth, after it hath been set in order. —Al Quran VII: 56

Iniquity Brings Destruction

How many were the towns We utterly destroyed because of their iniquities and setting up in their places other peoples. —Al Quran XXI: 11

Righteousness Gives Stability

Nor would thy Lord be the One to destroy the towns unjustly while their people are righteous.(Q. XI: 117)

To Avoid War Preparedness is the Only Way

Against them make ready your strength to the utmost of your power, including steeds of war, to strike terror (into the hearts of) the enemies of Allah and your enemies. —Al Quran VIII: 60

To Conduct the Affairs of the State Consultation is a Must

1. And consult them in affairs (of moment). Then when thou hast taken a decision, put thy trust in Allah.(Q. III: 159)
2. Who (conduct) their affairs by mutual consultation: —(Quran XLII: 38)
3. She said: "Ye chiefs! Advise me in (this) my affair: no affair have I decided except in your presence." (Q. XXVII:32)

Scholarly Learning

Listening to Wisdom, Pondering over Them and Adopting the Best

So announce the Good News to My servants — those who listen to the Word, and follow the best of it: those are the ones whom Allah has guided, and those are the ones endued with understanding.
—Al Quran XXXIX: 17-18

Acquiring Knowledge from Aliens

Say: 'Have you any certain knowledge? If so produce it before us. —Al Quran VI: 148

3

The Fundamentals

The basic philosophy of Islam revolves round a set of beliefs and concepts. The Unity of God, Prophethood and the Hereafter are the irreducible fundamentals of this creed. These concepts are rooted in the basic awareness of man and the realities of human experience.

Human awareness springs from a sense of being which is inherent to man and his contemplation of the physical universe. The Quran dwells on the reality of human consciousness generated by an interaction of the inner self of man and the outer world of nature. Sura Zariyat states:

> "On earth, and in yourselves, there are signs for firm believers. Can you not see? Heaven holds your sustenance and all that you are promised. I swear by the Lord of heaven and earth that this is true, as true as you are speaking now" (51:20-23).

The cardinal beliefs of Islam are not figments of imagination made sacrosanct by supernatural sanctions but emanate from deeper levels of human thought and experience.

As man delves into his own self and contemplates about his whereabouts he is irresistibly drawn towards four basic realisations which point to the reality of God. The universe is a vast mechanism of infinite complexity but it is perfectly ordered and regulated. Man has a limited vision and potentialities.

The Comprehension

There are many areas of life and dimensions of the universe which defy his understanding. Man cannot comprehend the universe as a whole, much less control it. Sura Yunus states: "The unbelievers ask: Why has no sign been given him by his Lord? Say: Allah alone has knowledge of what is hidden. What if you will: I too am waiting. It is he who guides you by land and sea. You embark and as you set sail, rejoicing in a favourable wind, a raging tempest overtakes you. Billows surge upon you from every side and you fear that you are encompassed by death. You pray to Allah with all fervour. Deliver us from this peril and we will be truly thankful. Yet when he has delivered you, you commit evil in the land and act unjustly. Men, it is your own souls that you are corrupting" (10: 20-23).

Beneath the complex exterior of the universe lies a design, a pattern, a system. The Quran dilates on the impeccable order of the universe as a sign of divine being who presides over it. This is described being who presides over it. This is described as Hikmat Sura Yasin says:

> "Let the once-dead earth be a sign to them. We gave it life and from it produced grain for their sustenance. We planted it with the palm and the vine and watered it with gushing springs, so that men might feed on its fruit. It was not their hands which made all this. Should they not give thanks?

The night is another sign for men from the night We lifted the day—and they are plunged in darkness.

The sun hastens to its resting place: its course is laid for it by the Mighty One, the All-Knowing, We have ordained phases for the moon, which daily wanes and in the end appears like a bent and withered twig.

The Sun is not allowed to overtake the moon, nor does the night outpace the day. Each in its own orbits runs" (36: 36-43).

The Universe provides for man and caters to his purposes and requirements. This fact is epitomised by the Quranic term *Raboobiyat Sura Qaf* cogently states:

> "We spread out the earth and set upon it immovable mountains. We brought forth in it all kinds of delectable plants. A lesson and an admonition to penitent men. We send down blessed water from the sky with which We bring forth gardens and the harvest grain, and tall palm trees laden with clusters of dates, a sustenance for men; thereby giving new life to some dead land. Such shall be the Resurrection." (50: 7-11).

The universe holds out many benefits to man which are not accidental but form part of the cosmic design. This aspect of universal experience is embodied in the Quranic term *Naymat.* The mercy of God who has made the universe as the abode of man is not only unlimited but also continuous. The boundless mercy and munificence of God is described as *Rehman* while its continuity and timelessness as *Rahim. Sura Waqiah* states:

> You surely know of the first creation. Why, then do you not reflect? Consider the seeds you grow. Is it you that give them growth or We? If We pleased We could turn your harvest into chaff.

Consider the water that you drink. Was it you that poured it from the cloud or We? if We pleased We could turn it bitter. Why then do you not give thanks?

> Observe the fire which you light. Is it you that create its wood or We? We have made it a reminder for man (56: 58—74).

The awareness generated by human contemplation of the universe underpins the reality of God. Deep down the recesses of human psyche lies the evidence of a reality higher than man himself. The objective universe offers many hints and clues for the existence of a mighty power.

The concept of Prophethood flows from the concept of God with irresistible logic. God, who is the creator and sustainer of man enjoins upon him a certain way of life. The values and principles of life which God has framed for the salvation of man are communicated through revelation. The prophets are the messengers of God and teachers among men. They convey by word and deed the infallible message of God. The message of God was conveyed to man gradually. Islam marked the perfection of Divine communication and its apostle Muhammad (peace be upon him); embodied the finality of prophethood.

Although the fundamental beliefs of Islam are rooted in the introspective reaches of human personality and the many splendoured reality of physical universe, there are many queries and questions which agitate the mind and require a satisfactory answer. The prophets disabused the minds of men of erratic beliefs and mistaken notions. Apart from this, history bears proof of many societies which were so sunk in abysmal ignorance and superstition as to disallow any opportunities of contemplation. The prophets admonished such people to the right path and exposed their misconceptions.

Almighty's Truth

The prophets drew the attention of ignorant and confused men to the reality of God and offered for human weal a full-fledged system of life. They were not day-dreamers but men of action who braved with courage and steadfastness the opposition of the uninformed. They were dynamic persons who changed the destiny of man by conviction and consistency. They were not closeted away from the ordeal and challenge which their environment posed. The prophets brought despairing men a message of hope and infused them with a noble purpose. Sura *Araf* states:

> Whenever, there come to you apostles from amongst you rehearsing my signs unto you. Those who follow them will be rewarded and those who reject them will be punished.

Sura Mujadala bears out the dignity and stature of the prophets:

> Believers, when you converse in private, do not speak with wickedness and enmity and disobedience towards the apostle, but with justice and piety. Have fear of Allah before whom you shall be brought together. Believers, when you confer with the apostle, give alms before such conference. That is best and purest for you. But if you lack the means, know that Allah is forgiving and merciful. (58:9-10).

How would the prophets be recognised? The Quran states that the first man on earth was a prophet, therefore, he needed no proof of himself. Thereafter, every prophet foretold the signs of his successor. Jesus told his people that he was the messenger of God as proclaimed to them by Moses. The Bible contained many hints and references about the advent of the Prophet (peace be upon him). The chapter of New Testament captioned Matthew makes many statements about the prophet who would follow Jesus. Prophesy reached its perfection and came to fulfilment in Muhammad (peace be upon him).

Almighty Supreme

The Quran guarantees the triumph of good represented by Prophet (peace be upon him) over evil embodied in ignorant persons whom he confronts with the divine message. The prophets overcame by faith in God and personal resilience the storm of opposition raised by vested interest they sought to abolish. Those who persisted in evil despite the warning and admonition of apostle were exterminated from the face of earth by natural calamity. The Quran is unambiguous on this fact.

Those that oppose Allah and His Apostle shall be brought low as have been before them. We have sent down clear revelations. A shameful punishment awaits the unbelievers.

> Do you see those that have befriended people with whom Allah is angry? They belong neither to you nor to them. They knowingly swear to falsehood. Allah has prepared for them a grievous scourage. Evil indeed is that which they have done. They use their faith as a disguise and debar others from the path of Allah. A shameful scourage awaits them (58.5: 14— 16).

Akhrat (Hereafter) is another cardinal concept of Islam. It has a basis in sound human experience. Man has limitless desires and aspiration. His self craves for the infinite. He has a natural urge to transcend the confines of time and space and rise above the transitoriness of life. The belief in *Akhrat* fulfils human promptings for and eternal life; it provides a point of certainty in flux and unending change.

Secondly, human beings live in communities. Social life entails a system of rights and responsibilities. No society exists in a perfect form. Here men are being deprived of fundamental rights and there responsibilities are being shrugged aside. Exploitation of man by man is a fact of life. The short span of life and human ways of doing things preclude the possibility of dispensing perfect justice. How can a person responsible for massacre be punished in this life? These facts provide a rational basis for belief in the Hereafter.

Bounty of God : Picking up threads from the concept of God discussed above, emphasis was laid on the bounty of God. If God has offered men certain benefits and privileges, why should man not be accountable for it? *Sura Naba* recounts the gardens of luxurious growth given to man and draws attention to the day of sorting out. The Quran dwells on the concept of *Akhrat* at great length:

> About what are they asking?
>
> About the fateful tidings—the theme of their disputes.
>
> But they shall know the truth; before long they shall know it.
>
> Did we not spread the earth like a bed and raise the mountains like pillars?
>
> We created you in pairs and gave you rest in sleep.

We made the night a mantle, and ordained the day for work. We built above you seven mighty heavens and placed in them a shining lamp. We sent down abundant water from the clouds, bringing forth grain and varied plants, and gardens thick with foliage.

Fixed is the Day of Judgement. On that day the Trumpet shall be sounded and you shall come in multitudes. The gates of heaven shall swing open and the mountains shall pass away like vapour (78: 1-12).

The *al-Qiyamah* is variously described by the Quran as Day of Judgement, Day of Reckoning, Day of Sorting Out.

A rational interpretation of fundamental beliefs of Islam has been attempted. The Quran makes a cogent and convincing statement of how concepts like unity of God, Prophethood and the hereafter are rooted in human observation and experience. It rejects the view that religion is based on the instinct of fear latent in man and demonstrates that the roots of religious faith in positive aspects of human life.

Islam has made unique contributions to human civilisation; and among these is the concept of the dignity of man. According to the Holy Quran man is the noblest of God's creation, as it says; "Certainly, We created man in the best make". (95: 4). At another place the Holy Quran declares: "And surely We have honoured the children of Adam and We carry them in the land and the sea, and We provide them with good things, and We have made them to excel highly most of those whom We have created". (17: 70). Man was made Allah's vicegerent on earth, and he was destined to rule everything around him. The Holy Quran says: "And when thy Lord said to the angels, I am going to place in the earth one who shall rule in it". (2: 30).

The idea of man being the ruler of the universe is repeated in many verses of the Holy Book: "And He has made subservient to you whatsoever is in the heavens and whatsoever is in the earth, all, from Himself. (45: 13). "Allah is He Who made subservient to you the sea that the ships may glide therein by His Grace, and that you may give thanks". (45: 12). "He has made subservient to you the sun and the moon; each pursues its course till an appointed time". (31: 29). "And He has made subservient to you the night and the day and the sun and the moon. And the stars are made subservient by His command. Surely there are signs in this for a people who understand" (16:12).

According to Islam, man's position in nature was that of a conqueror. He was created to control all the forces of nature and to rule in the earth and not to bow before them. But man degraded himself to the utmost when started worshipping the earth, rivers, trees, fire, the sun and the moon and the stars, and all those objects of nature which were made subservient to him. He even worshipped unhewn stones, and sometimes carved out idols with his own hands and worshipped them as if they were Divine, or as if they controlled good or evil for him. As the Holy Quran says: "Do you worship that which you knew not? And Allah has created you and what you make" (37: 95-96). And as Ibraham asked his Sire:

"Why dost thou worship that which neither hears, nor sees, nor does it avail thee in the least" (19:42).

The gravest of sins, according to the Holy Quran is *Shirk* or associating others with Allah. This is not due to feeling of jealousy on the part of Allah, but because *Shirk* demoralises man, while Divine unity brings about his moral elevation. That is why Islam has laid so much emphasis on *Tauheed* or oneness of God, which is the most fundamental principle of the Islamic faith.

Man was endowed with vast capabilities for attaining knowledge. In the first place, he was given knowledge by Allah as the Holy Quran says: "And he gave Adam knowledge of all things" (2: 31). The Arabs were an illiterate people, and reading and writing was so rare among them that it may be said not to have existed at all. The Holy Prophet (peace be upon him), himself did not know reading and writing and is called Unlettered Prophet (peace be upon him), as stated in the Quran: "And thou didst not recite before it any book, nor didst thou transcribe one with thy right hand (29: 48). Yet the first Divine message received by him was about reading and writing. As the Quran says: Read in the name of thy Lord who created. Creates man from a clot. Read and thy Lord is most bounteous, Who taught to write with the pen. He taught man what he knew not". (96: 1-5).

Read and write, was thus His first message; and to these two means of gaining knowledge of things, the faculty of observation was also granted to man. The Holy Quran has repeatedly invited the attention of man to the creation of this universe and the various phenomena working around him. He asked to observe and reflect. To quote one instance from the Quran: "In the creation of the heavens and the earth and the alternation of the night and the day, there are surely signs for men of understanding. Those who remember Allah standing and sitting and (lying) on their sides and reflect on the creation of the heavens and the earth. Our Lord, thou hast not created this in vain"; (3: 189-90). The process of observing and reflecting convinces man that every thing made by God is perfect. He sees no incongruity in Allah's creation, and this naturally leads him to His glorification. "Glorify the name of the Lord, the Most High; Who creates things, then makes them complete: And who makes things according to a measure then guides them to their goal". (87: 1-3).

Man, before Islam, was at the lowest ebb of human civilisation. He was just a slave of nature's forces. The Holy Prophet (peace be upon him) raised him to the dignity of the master and the ruler, and it was due to this realisation of man's position to the universe that the Muslims in their very early history took vigorous strides towards the expansion of knowledge and the advancement of the sciences. Reading and writing was within a few years spread throughout the whole of Arabia and other countries which came under the influence of Islam and the Muslim State so encouraged the pursuit of study and scientific research, that centres of learning and universities sprang up throughout the empire of Islam.

According to Islam, every child is born in a state of sinlessness; and it is afterwards in life, that a person becomes a Jew or a Christian or anything else by following the religion of his parents. The Holy Prophet (peace be upon him) said: "Every child that is born conforms to the true religion (Allah's *fitrat;* and it is his parents who make him a Jew or a Christian or a Magian" *(Bukhari,* 32: 79). Every child is, thus, recognised by birth to be a Muslim, and the purity of human nature is not affected by his being born of non-Muslim parents. The Holy Prophet (peace be upon him) once related a vision in which he had seen the Prophet Ibraham in paradise with children all around him, and he added that those children were all the children that had died in the state of nature, i.e. before they attained the age of discretion. Some of the companions of the Holy Prophet (peace be upon him) asked him if the children of the polytheists were also included? The Holy Prophet (peace be upon him) replied: "Yes, the children of those who set up gods with God *(mushrikeen)* as well" *(Bokhari,* 91:48). The doctrine of the sinlessness of man by birth is an aid to his leading a sinless life. If a man does good and avoids evil, he is true to his nature. It further strengthens him to overcome sin, because he knows that nature had fitted him for this task. And step by step he can further rise to very high spiritual levels.

Not only that no impurity is attached to man by birth, but he also partakes of the Divine nature, for it was the Divine Spirit that was breathed into man, into every human child. As the Holy Quran says: "Who made beautiful everything that He created, and He began the creation of man from dust. Then He made his progeny of an extract of worthless water. Then He made him complete and breathed into him of His spirit" (32: 7-9). The Divine Spirit spoken of here is something distinct from the animal soul. It shows a mystic relation of the spirit of man with the Divine Spirit, and refers to the higher life of man. The destiny of man, according to Islam, is thus higher than mere conquest of nature, it is to seek union with the Divine Spirit. The goal of life is "Liqa Allah", or the meeting of God. In the language of the Holy Quran: "O man; thou must strive hard striving (to attain) to thy Lord until thou meet Him" (84: 6).

Human Behaviour

Islam encompasses entire human conduct. Justice is the *sine qua non* of Islam. Like other religions Islam is not satisfied with just transformation of the moral viewpoint of the individual or society, leaving man to his own sweet whim of what to obey and what not to obey as per the dictates of his convenience.

Islam is concerned with all sides, all sectors and all levels. As such, it aims at making a compact, homogenous, steel-cast *'Millat'* with definite laws of do's and don'ts and, what is more important, with a sovereign enforcing authority backed by all powers of reward and punishment. It gives laws in all sectors of human conduct at levels of family, society and polity, trade, politics, social manners, citizenship, agriculture, industry, foreign relations, health, public finance, public works, education, civilisation and what not. And it gives justice to see that they are practically enforced.

After declaration of prophethood, for full 13 years in Mecca, the Prophet of Islam (peace be upon him) preached the best principles of individual and social conduct, presented the best logic and arguments, demonstrated the best powers of oratory and persuasion, gave the best specimens of personal virtues, quoted the commandments of the Holy Quran, discussed the life-after-death. More than 95 per cent of the inhabitants of Mecca and of the places around remained infidels showing intenser enmity towards the Holy Prophet (peace be upon him), his Companions and Islam. When, however, the scene changed to Medina with Islam becoming a state, a government, a political and military force, new people came within its fold and Islam could set up a model in all sectors for all times and climes.

At Medina, the Prophet (peace be upon him) blended the ever-warring tribes into one compact fraternity, changed hearts, values and viewpoints, reformed society and polity, created an atmosphere of dependable safety, peace and goodwill and overthrew the governments of oppression and tyranny whose game was to play one set of people against another.

The Holy Quran puts all emphasis on the suppression of oppression and enforcement of justice.

"Verily Allah orders you to give the due to whomsoever it belongs and when you sit in judgement, be just and upright—" (4: 58).

"O people of *Eimman* (Faith) give all support and perseverance to the cause of justice in the way of Allah. And do not trespass for fear of this nation or that. And catch full hold of justice as it is close to *Taqwa.* And fear none but Allah. Verily He knows every action of yours". (5: 8).

"Tell them, O Prophet, that your Allah has commanded justice."

"Sure, we have sent to you this Book of Rights so that you may pronounce judgements between peoples as per the commandments of Allah. And do not be among those who unjustly take sides" (4: 105).

Only 227 verses of the Holy Quran discuss laws and they pertain to no more than 11 sectors of human activity. Of course, this is the core and kernel, the nucleus. All the remaining parts of the structure of the Islamic polity have been furnished by the *Sunnah,* the sayings and doings of the Prophet (peace be upon him).

As regards the two evil courses of bribe and recommendations the Holy Prophet (peace be upon him) said that he who gives and he who takes bribe will both go to Hell. He has cursed the giver and taker of bribe.

True Judge : The Holy Prophet (peace be upon him) had to deal with hundreds of cases between persons belonging to erstwhile opposite camps. The least favour or disfavour on his part would have broken the oneness and unity of *Millat.* But it was his impartial justice that gave no loophole of criticism to anyone that kept the *Millat* intact, that is the model par excellence to all posterity.

He has prescribed the special qualifications of the judge, the *Qadi.* Once he said: "Judges are of three kinds-one of which will go to Paradise, recognises the right of one *vis-a-vis* another and pronounces judgements accordingly. The other is one who recognises the rights but due to any worldly consideration does not act accordingly. And the third kind is one who does not care to recognise the rights and acts unjustly".

"When a judge does his best to know the truth from untruth and finds the truth, he would get two rewards. But one who does not find the truth in spite of his best efforts would get one reward only."

As regards the court-procedure, he said: "None is to pronounce judgement if he is in wrath and anger."

"Both the parties are to be present before the judge."

"I am but a human being. I try legal disputes. It is possible that one of the party is more adept in presenting his side of the case and under the impression of his being rightful, I judge in his favour. So if a party secures such a favour by trampling the right of another party, the former is taking nothing but a piece of Hellish Fire. It is for him to take it or leave it."

He has ordered the judge to hear equally attentively both the parties and to deliver judgement only when the truth comes out. Similarly, the Holy Prophet (peace be upon him) has laid down the essential qualifications of the court witness. He had refused to accept the evidence of (1) person guilty of breach of trust, (2) person guilty of immoral sex; (3) person who has previously been inflicted with court punishment; (4) person who harbours feelings of revenge or hate against his brother, including the party in question; (5) person who has been guilty of giving false evidence; (6) person who is related to or in service of one of the parties or is a flatterer to one of the parties.

He said that giving false evidence is equivalent to committing *Shirk.*

The Holy Prophet (peace be upon him) while awarding judgement took full notice of the condition of health, of finance and of other factors of the guilty and gave relaxations accordingly. He always pardoned whenever it could be. He always arranged for compromise and *Qasas* whenever it could be. He gave punishment only when it had to be.

Islam considers the whole humanity as one family and treats mankind as one community. The Holy Prophet (peace be upon him) was first to demolish narrow visions of geographical and political nationhood, and taught the lesson of broad-mindedness and international brotherhood to the world at large.

Paying his tribute to the Holy Prophet (peace be upon him) the French poet Lamartine wrote: "Muhammad is the one great man without whom the world would appear incomplete. Truly, Muhammad stands to this day, and for all time to come, at the peak of humanity.

Every nation at sometime or other, in its history, had its superman, the luminary who gave it light, the reformer who inspired it with noble ideals, and the Prophet who raised it morally, intellectually and spiritually on a high pedestal. But no other prophet of any religion has exercised so deep and lasting an influence in the religious, historical and social history of mankind as the Prophet of Islam (peace be upon him).

As a prophet and reformer, entrusted with the noble mission of raising mankind from the depths of degradation and the dungeons of moral, political, social and religious bankruptcy and decadence into which it had fallen in the sixth century, Prophet Muhammad (peace be upon him) could not be otherwise than a revolutionary in the fullest sense of the term. The lofty ideals he preached not only brought about a complete change in the political situation but also had an equally important and a more enduring bearing on the social conditions of the people.

To consider that the advent of the Holy Prophet (peace be upon him) on the Arab horizon merely heralded the birth of a politically unified Arabia is to pay but poor tribute to him and confess shocking ignorance of the implications of the message and his dynamic personality which ushered in a revolution of considerable magnitude in the thought and actions not only of the Arabs but of mankind itself.

Nation in Islam

Islam, the religion the Holy Prophet (peace be upon him) preached, introduced the conception of the nation as a unit and a vital stage in the organisation of human society. It is lofty in the conception of the relationship of man to God and noble in its doctrine of duty of man to man to the lower creation. It was the first religion that preached and practised democracy in its true sense.

It was Islam which for the first time proclaimed liberty to mankind, and introduced universal brotherhood in humanity. It does not recognise differences of class, caste, race, nation, or geographical and political boundaries and territories of the world. No one in Islam is better because of creed or colour. "An Arab has no superiority over a non-Arab, nor a non-Arab over Arab except piety". Islam laid down the ideal that nobility depends not in belonging to a particular family or tribe but upon being noble in personal conduct and character. The Divine Message has come down to us in the form of the Holy Quran which is the basic source of guidance for humanity.

It is a great charter of the freedom of humanity. As a book of ethics, and a code of conduct, clear, concise and simple in terms, there is no other sacred book in the world to replace it. It is "a stupendous monument of solitary legislation", to quote the words of Washington Irving. No wonder it has exercised a most potent and powerful influence over mankind throughout the ages.

Islam's institutions are unique: they do not compromise with materialistic dogmas. They stand firm on individual piety and individual freedom a close-knit family devoted to the welfare of a classless, benevolent society.

The principle of equality and brotherhood, justice and freedom which the Holy Prophet (peace be upon him) defined as integral elements of faith have engendered a righteous character and a noble spirit in society.

Distinguishing the essence of piety from the mere form of ceremony of righteousness, the Holy Prophet (peace be upon him) made faith in Allah and benevolence towards man the essential features of religion. He brought to perfection the grand idea of unifying the whole human race and gathering it together under one banner.

His was "a life consecrated, from first to last, to the service of God and humanity". He preached that a true Muslim is one from the danger of whose tongue and hands all Muslims are immune and that the best occupation is service to mankind, that knowledge is a valuable legacy, manners and courtesy the various ornaments, and carefulness a clear and transparent mirror and that spiritual virtue consists in adoring Allah.

The Prophet of Islam (peace be upon him) denounced vehemently meanness and slander, hypocrisy and untruthfulness, superstition, gambling, drinking, oppression of the weak by the strong and other evils, and gave new light and guidance to mankind.

The supreme place he gave in the faith to the duty of alms-giving and charity to the poor is another praiseworthy feature of religion he preached. He told us that every good act is a charity, an exhortation to your fellowmen to do virtuous deeds is equal to alms-giving; guiding the wanderer to the right path is charity; assisting the blind in crossing the street is charity; removing stones and thorns and other obstructions from the road is charity; giving water to the thirsty is charity, and so on. There is hardly a religious duty which is more sacred and benevolent to the Muslims than that of charity to the poor. The Holy Prophet (peace be upon him) preached that true poverty is not merely lack of wealth but lack of desire for wealth.

Eternal Religion

The strict observance by the Muslims of the daily prayers for five times is another testimony to the value of a living faith and the spirit of universal brotherhood. One should also witness the congregational prayers offered by the faithful to see for himself the atmosphere of equality, brotherhood and love. In the presence of Allah, all stand shoulder to shoulder, the rich and the powerful with the poor and the lowly, the master and the servant offering prayers and bowing themselves before Allah in abject submission. Can there be any more levelling influence in the world?

The Holy Prophet (peace be upon him) upheld the dignity of

women and gave them an honoured place in society. The economic and cultural position of women was raised to a high status, and recognition of women's right to property marked the beginning of a new era, which is now the recognised feature of every civilized society. With his far-sighted vision, the Holy Prophet (peace be upon him) laid down a complete social system containing minute regulations for man's conduct in all circumstances of life.

His love for, and human treatment of, animals are too well-known. According to a *Hadith,* the Holy Prophet (peace be upon him) is reported to have said: "If you behold three mounting an animal, stone them until one descends".

The Prophet of Islam (peace be upon him) will for ever remain the symbol of the most exemplary human conduct. All his efforts were aimed at elevating man's mind and soul, and giving him an exalted position. He preached righteousness and toleration, and in his own self presented the most accomplished model of his teachings. In his own lifetime he moulded the character of his fellowmen, reformed them, changed their thoughts, put new ideals before them, elevated them to a higher plane and let them onwards, towards the path of progress and to the fullness of a better and nobler life.

With the passage of time, Western writers, in spite of their ignorance and prejudice, began to assess the position of the Holy Prophet (peace be upon him) and the revolution brought about by him. In the case of some honest and fair appraisal and objective considerations have been dominant. A case in illustration is that of Dozy where truth found to favour: "We see then that the Arab conquests of the seventh century have continued to play an important role in human history, down to present day. It is this unparalleled combination of secular and religious influence which I feel entitles Muhammad (peace be upon him) to be considered the most influential single figure in human history". (The 100*: A ranking of the Most Influential Persons in History*— Michael H. Hart). In this list the name of the Holy Prophet (peace be upon him) is on the top. Jesus Christ is number three.

Lamartine in his *"History* de *La Turquie",* Vol. II, says about the Holy Prophet (peace be upon him):

> "No person in the world had ever willingly or unwillingly, independently or under duress kept before him an object or goal higher than the goal of Muhammad (peace be upon him)."

This goal was much higher than general human level, much above human intellect. What was this goal? To do away one by one with the curtains of superstition that were hung between God and man to fill the heart of man by his presence and dye man in colours of God's attributes, to present in the crowd of false deities the sacred and reasonable concept of God free of any defect. Up to now no man has dared to undertake such a stupendous and grand task, which is beyond human reach and then its sources should be so limited. This is so because neither when he conceived the idea of this responsibility, nor when practical steps were taken to implement it, he had only his person or a few residents of a corner of the desert at his disposal. There were no sources, no support, nor necessary arrangements. With this sort of paucity of resources, no man in the world, up to now, has brought about such a glorious and splendid revolution.

"A revolution of such dimensions that within two hundred years, Islam practically as a religion ruled over Arabia. In the name of God, it had conquered Iran, Khurasan, Western India, Syria, Egypt, Ethiopia, territory of North Africa known at that time, many islands of Mediterranean and Spain. If the loftiness of the goal, absence of resources and brilliancy of results is the criterion of human genius, then where is the man who can dare present any other human being to compete with Muhammad (peace be upon him). Great men in the world have piled arms, codified laws and ruled over extensive empires. At the most they created material powers and resources which in most cases were reduced to ashes. But this man did not shake only the armies and battalions, legislative assemblies, big empires, nations and families but also the hearts of millions of people living in one-third area of the known world of that time.

"And more than that. This personality shook places of sacrifices, deities, religions and rituals, conceptions and convictions and as a matter of fact shook the very souls of men. On the basis of a book, whose every word has a legal significance, he built up a community which in its turn fused different languages and races into one single nation. This everlasting nation, rebellion and hatred against false gods and overflowing love for one God are the legacies of this great personality. In the midst of a plethora of false gods the proclamation of conception about one God in itself was such a miracle that as soon as these words were uttered by him all places of worship of false gods were destroyed. One-third of the world was set on fire.

"His life, his devotion, his relentless efforts against superstition and the great courage to scoff at the fury and anger of false gods is known. His life at Mecca and thirteen years' tribulations and severe opposition were met with supreme fortitude and courage. He gladly bore the ridicule and denial of the opponents. All these troubles and then migration by him, his continuous preaching and invitation, his supreme efforts, his full confidence in the success of his mission and in unfavourable circumstances his supernatural calm and collected disposition at the time of victory and success, amnesty and forgiveness not for the sake of statecraft, but for the success of his divine goal and object. His wishes and hopes in the world of deep stance, his regular prayers, his supplications, secret contacts with his God, his life, his death and his popularity and influence after his demise, all these facts provide evidence for what kind of life? Do these facts show a life of a deceitful fabrication or the life of a person who had unshakable confidence and trust in his claims. It was his this very ironclad confidence and faith generated in him a very strong current on power and strength by which he made his belief ever-living and everlasting. What was this belief?

"First Oneness of God and the second to explain what God is not. This *"illa"* and the other *"illa"*. One part to wipe away the false gods in the world (even use of sword if pressed by necessity) and the other part to lay out the carpet of one true God's majesty. A great thinker, orator of a high order, prophet law-giver, military leader, victor of beliefs and convictions, responsible for presenting correct ideology of life with reason and clarity of vision; the founder of a system, in which false gods cannot enter man's mind; twenty worldly states and above them the sovereignty of One God. This is Muhammad (peace be upon him).

"Bring all of your criteria, all of your tests by which the greatness of human beings is checked and measured and then reply if the world has produced any man greater than him?"

The views of another Western author, viz., Pringle Kennedy should be taken into consideration. After dealing with the subject of social, religious and cultural condition of the world he says: "It is a matter of surprise that this new culture was born in Arabia at a time when it was urgently needed.

"For those among us who think man is everything, Muhammad (peace be upon him) is a great example of what a man can do. Those who believe that changes and revolutions in history are not the result of one man's efforts but are more dependent on the peculiarities of environments and the ability of human mind to accept them cannot deny that if a revolution had to come (as it came in Arabia) it could not take place without Muhammad (peace be upon him) and would have remained pending for an indefinite period". (Pringle Kennedy— *"In Arabian Society at the Time of Muhammad").*

The Eclipse of Christianity in Islam by L. E. Brown bears testimony to the fact that: "Due to influence of Muhammad (peace be upon him), Arab clannish pride and exclusiveness came to an end. They became members of a brotherhood which they never knew. This link was the faith of Oneness of God. If brought them to a centre and conquests followed easily.

Hitti opines in his book *"History of the Arabs"* as under: "This was the first time that the Arabs were brought together not in the name of blood-relationship but in the name of religion. Allah was the supreme sovereign of this state. The Prophet (peace be upon him), throughout his life was His representative and ruler of the country. For this reason Muhammad (peace be upon him) in addition to his spiritual responsibilities, directed the affairs of the state like state officials. In his nation after forsaking all tribal preferences and old relationship became brothers."

The Reverend Stephenson is of the opinion: "It must be freely admitted at first that for his nation the personality of Muhammad (peace be upon him) was the source of many and great benefits. He was born in a country where political set-ups, reasonable beliefs and ethical behaviour were unknown. He brought about these three things. Through his mature intelligence, he reformed ali these three simultaneously. In place of different tribes he made them one nation, similarly he preached the Unity of God in place of deities and gods. All the major unwholesome practices were done away with. As Islam flowed out of old Arabia, barbarians were gathered in its fold and they became the possessors of the benefits of Islam. Islam is an instrument to lead human beings from darkness to light and from *Satan* to God.

The Reverend Bosworth Smith observes: "On account of such a good fortune which has not parallel in history, Muhammad (peace be upon him) is the founder of three elements. One nation, one state and one religion. The founder himself was unlettered but he gave the world a Book which has poetic and musical stance in it as also complete code of conduct and law. This is the miracle of Muhammad (peace be upon him), permanent miracle and actually a miracle."

Revolutionary Effects

They all write about an unprecedented revolution not only political but social, religious, moral, ethical and in short all matters covering life of man. They all pay tribute to Quran. At this stage it is necessary we should know what was there in the world at that time that was swept away to make room for higher and bright set up and a new world was created.

Pringle in his *"Arabian Society at the Time of Muhammad"* (peace be upon him) says that at that time it seemed that the grand edifice of civilisation which had been built during the last 4,000 years, was about to collapse and human beings were about to revert to the same barbaric state wherein every tribe was deadly enemy of the other and nobody had any knowledge or regard for institutions and regulated existence. Ancient tribal values had been lost, and on the lines of old methods kingship could no longer flourish. The institutions which Christianity introduced they did not inculcate spirit of discipline or unity but were being the cause of disunity estrangement and destruction. Time had come when all-round there was gross indiscipline, bloodshed and there was no horizon of man's life. It had gone down to the level of beasts of jungle. The tall tree of civilisation whose green and flourishing branches provided shadow and comfort to the world and were laden with the golden fruits of art, science and literature was shaking about to fall. It no longer received the moisture of respect and attachment. Only the outer crust remained. The holocaust of wars and battles cut it down to pieces and these pieces were supported by old customs and ceremonies. It was feared that they would fall down any time. Was it possible under these conditions to create or introduce emotional culture which could bring round humanity to one central point and save civilisation. This culture had to be of a new pattern because all old customs and usages had finished and to resurrect them needed centuries.

Says Carlyle: "The humanity like a dry jungle was waiting for a spark. That spark of electricity appeared in the form of that great personality and ignited the universe."

This is the evaluation of great revolution brought about by the Holy Prophet (peace by upon him). They could not go further for two reasons. Firstly, the prejudice and opposition generated by Pope Urban II (1042—1099) who initiated the crusades. This prejudice still exists. Secondly, the West is devoting all its energy and deploying all scientific discoveries to destroy opponents besides exploiting the weak. Deadly arms are being manufactured and sold. Humanity today stands at the brink of mass destruction. For these reasons, the West has not been able to turn its attention towards higher values, and sanctity of human life.

Historic March : Islam has always faced challenges on its historical march. It faced its first crisis when the Holy Prophet (peace be upon him) passed away from this earthly scene. This was very close to the rise of Islam as a historical force. When the Holy Prophet (peace be upon him) died, the crucial point was whether there should be any Islamic history at all. Some of the then Muslims (e.g. the Beduins) felt that the affair was now over: they had taken a vow of fidelity to a leader, he was no more, and that was the end of the affairs. Others felt the need for restoring status quo and emphasising the recognition of urban and tribal realities. Besides, it was presumed that new religious faith should take its course on those basis. But this was rejected and it was decided that to keep the followers of the Holy Prophet (peace be upon him) united as a socio-political economic unit and as one that marches forward in the world to enforce and spread as unit the message of Islam. This decision was taken not without opposition which was finally crushed and silenced. This decision was of immense significance for the later history of Islam.

The decision to keep the community intact and choose a leader for itself in place of the Holy Prophet (peace be upon him) appeared to be more pertinent than the issue (which has received immeasurable attention) of who that leader should be. Then emerged the issue of the actual development of Islamic history on earth, having understood the significance of its last success and homogeneity. The early Muslims took the whole burden and opportunity of government as well as cultural creation in the widest sense. They completed this task significantly so that when they could presently look at this society that they had constructed, they felt satisfied that it led the world. God had enjoined upon men the way to live; those who followed the path were visibly receiving His blessings.

Great Debacle : History, however, has its own inner logic. Muslims feel it to be will of God on earth.

But this period of Islam's earthly glory did not last long. The early period of Islam primarily comprised Arab elements, it lost its vigour after spending its inherent force with the fall of Baghdad in 1258, the successful Arab rule came to its formal end. The Mughal invasion gave a death blow to the Arab ascendency of Islam. Many millions were massacred; whole cities were laid waste and political rules passed into the hands of infidel barbarians. This ended the classical period of Islamic history.

This was a first great crisis of Islamic history. With the demise of the Arab Empire, Islamic history seemed to have lost its driving force. It appeared as if divine purpose as conceived by Islam was faltering, if it has not actually failed.

Great Survival : Despite this debacle, Islam on earth survived this crisis and it re-appeared in a new and rather different mould. With the drawing to a close of the European Middle Ages, Islam's mediaeval period—between its classical and modern eras—set in motion. Historians of Islam—whether Muslims or Westerns have taken much less interest in this mediaeval phase of Islam than that of the classical. In spite of it, there were new aspects which were not without significance. This phase of Islam produced constructive answers to the issues raised.

Later Events

On the religious side, *Sufism* was a new major development. The *Sufi* or mystic interpretation of Islam has its germs even in the classical period. Yet at the time it was confined to an insignificant minority, comprising an elite of the pious withdrawn from the main stream of Islamic march. The mediaeval period bolstered its immensity throughout the Muslim world. The movement took an institutional form and gained popularity. There were additions also in interpretation; as for example, the *Masnavi* of Jalaluddin Roomi which was produced after the fall of Baghdad.

Besides, Islam converted the conquerors. After imposing on the Muslim alien rulers for 50 years, the Mughal dynasty which had subjugated the Muslim world, itself embraced Islam as a historical force soon asserted itself in Persian and Turkish forms. These forms were different from the preceding ones. New forms were different from the old in the government structure, social organisation and in cultural and aesthetic values. In this new era, Islam again began to march as a political force.

After its nadir in the Thirteenth Century, Islam began to touch a new zenith in the Sixteenth; which could be put forth as the Islam's greatest century uptil now. Then the Ottoman Empire was a most powerful state on earth; Europe shivered before its apparently unending series of conquests. At the same time, *Safuids* had established a family based on imperial power in Iran, the Mughals then had firmly entrenched themselves in India and constituted the greatest rule the subcontinent had seen for many a long time.

This second revival of Islam was confined not only to the building of Empires, but it was a new expansion also in geographical and spiritual senses. The second great wave of military expansion and missionary fervour brought for Islam new converts: in the Northern Asia Minor and the Balkans and Central Asia, in the South Negro Africa and in the East Indonesia. Thus, classical Islam was doubled in area and numbers. Once again, it was evident that historical Islam was a power to be reckoned with.

However, the second flowering of Islam, with the possible

exception of the Turkish, has not been generally regarded by the Muslims as fully consistent with the classical Islam. What the Muslims accomplished in it is not so keenly regarded as a complete example of Islam at work in the world, moulding into a divine pattern the flux, of historical development. But this tendency should not be overemphasised. The classical version of Islam has always remained official, and its social importance cannot be minimised. But even in this period Muslims never grudged to extol any individual who either successfully defended Islamic domain or extended it. Even then, there were many Muslims in the world who regarded conquest of Constantinople in 1453 as an example of God's power as well as Sultan Muhammad's effort.

However, it is a fact that in the sixteenth century Muslim World was again a mighty force having wealth and splendour. Whatever opinion one may hold up of it, the Muslims of this period were victorious in a history expansive and successful.

But even this success did not last long. The second wave of Islamic Revival was more short-lived than the first. The advance of Muslim society ceased and by the eighteenth century it entered a period of decline. Its military and political power underwent serious reverses; its commercial and economic life enfeebled, its intellectual efforts stagnated, its artistic talent lost lustre and religious vitality ebbed. The writings of great masters were confined to commentaries and classical systems were used to congeal mental faculties rather than as an impetus for opening up new horizons of thought. On the *Sufi* side, the orders degenerated from mystic perception to exploitable superstition.

Besides, it is a strange coincidence that this decay coincided with a new upsurge of Europe. At about the same time, Western civilisation set about its greatest venture of expansion that human history has ever seen. It accumulated vitality, skill, and power on a vast scale; with them the West was then refashioning its own life and soon the life of the globe.

Opposite Powers

The force of the West which was imbued with exploratory restlessness met the Muslim World in decline and subdued it. By 1800, the West subjugated such centres of Muslim power as remained on many areas and imposed its rule. During most of the nineteenth century many Muslim countries lost their freedom. The Dutch entrenched them in Indonesia; Iran and the Ottoman Empire, though formally independent, lost their freedom to act. Muslim society, once dignified was now everywhere despondent in spirit and prey to outside forces.

Muslims uphold that Islam essentially is a religion, and as such deeply personal and also conclusively surpassing all particularities and limits of this existence and all its affairs; despite this, it has the distinction of having a deep concern for these affairs. It was essential for a true Muslim to carry out in this world the divine obligation as to how mankind, individually and collectively, should live. If this is seen from another angle, it appears that Muslims should see how that ideal society is built. In short, Islamic history is the fulfilment, under divine guidance, of the purpose of human history.

It is a fact that actual Islamic history, for some centuries, approximated to this ideal. We have also observed that in actual fact, periods of decay and regeneration in Islamic history have alternated. Besides, we have also noticed that the mediaeval period of Islamic history has ended in disorder. Although, many Muslim countries had gained independence after World War II and their economic plight has considerably improved, yet the basic problem has persisted; and the issue of internal cohesion and fear of foreign interference remained. In this age of Super Power contention for the domination at the cost of the other, fears of foreign interference and internal disorder have not vanished and then a challenge to Islam's will to carve history according to its dynamism.

The basic malady of modern Islam lies in perception that something has gone wrong with Islamic history; hence the fundamental problem of modern Muslim is how to restore that history; and set it working in full vigour again so that Islamic society may again be luxuriant as a divinely-guided society. In the twentieth century the basic spiritual crisis of Islam results from the realisation that something is discordant between God-ordained religion and the historical development of the world controlled by God. Muslims have failed to establish any tangible interconnection between these two factors—otherwise they would have long subjugated the contemporary historical situation to the requirements of their faith.

This is not to say that the Muslims have ignored this problem. Of course, men like Abdul Wahab Najdi (1703-1887), Jamaluddin Afghani (1839-1897), Shah Waliullah (1703-1762), and many others have tried to analyse and solve this problem. Their efforts in this direction have immense value. But the problem still persists and the Muslim world despite its area, numerical strength and potential wealth had failed to shake of fears of internal disruption and foreign interference.

This is not to say, that the Muslims did not try to adopt suitable devices for the transportation of its worldly condition. Many attempts have been made to solve the problem; firstly, liberalism was tried, but it failed. From the late nineteenth century to the First World War, European liberalism was in great vogue in many Muslim countries, but Muslims soon realised that this internal Westernising of the Islamic community constituted subtler and more dangerous version of the same threat; subversion from within. Its inherent threat to Islamic history and society was enough to alarm those who fervently cherish the realisation and embodiment of classical divine precepts as the goal of Muslim endeavour. This attitude to Westernisation has in recent decades reappeared with new vigour and vehemence.

Above all, there has been despair in the particular ties between Islam and Western liberalism itself. In the early stages of contact of Muslim world and the Western liberalism, Muslims hoped that Western liberalism could assist them in their basic enterprise of reconstructing the Islamic society, and thereby setting Islamic history on road to progress. The resulting disenchantment had led Muslims to seek new ways of fulfilling Islamic mission on earth as the Islamic Revolution in Iran, the shift in Pakistan to a new search for Islamic solution of problems and revival of Islam-oriented parties in many Muslim countries. But behind this new trend lurks the danger of an emerging new dogmatism which in its old form severely blocked the progress of Muslims for centuries. The need remains for reconciling Islam with rational modes of thought and behaviour to reconstruct Islamic society.

4

Roots of Wisdom

Sacred Intellect

The political character of Islam has been a subject of gross misrepresentation by the followers of the rival creeds. Politically Islam conferred more benefits on mankind in the few years which its Founder spent at Medina, than centuries of vague theorizing by the followers of the Portico or the Academy, or by the hangers-on in the anterooms of the Jurisconsults of Rome. It gave a code to the people and a constitution to the State, enforced by the sanctions of religion. It limited taxation; it made men equal in the eye of the law; it consecrated the principle of self-government. It established a control over the sovereign power by rendering the executive authority subordinate to the law,—a law based upon religious sanctions and moral obligation. The excellence and effectiveness of each of these principles," says Urquhart, "(each capable of immortalizing its founder) gave value to the rest; and all combined endowed the system which they formed, which a force and energy exceeding those of any other political system. Within the lifetime of a man, though in the hands of a population wild, ignorant, and insignificant, it spread over a greater extent than the dominions of Rome. While it retained its primitive character, it was irresistible."

A Sea Change : A change came immediately over every country which the Moslems entered. Cities sprang into existence;

order took the place of anarchy. The short government of Abu Bakr was too fully occupied with the labours of pacifying the tribes of the desert to afford time for the regulation of provinces, which the hostility of the Byzantines threw into Muslim hands. But with the reign of Umar commenced that sleepless care for the welfare of the subject nations, which characterised the government of the early Caliphs. The battle of Kadessia, which threw Persia into the hands of the Moslems, was the signal of deliverance for the downtrodden subjects of the Chosroes. The Jew, whom the Magozoroastrians massacred from time of time, the Christians, whom they deported and exiled, "breathed freely," says M. Gobineau, "under the authority of a Prophet who declared them true believers, though incomplete, and exacted a nominal impost in consideration of exemption from military duties." The peasantry and petty landowners trampled under foot by an insolent oligarchy, and regarded with contempt by the priesthood, hailed the Moslems as the forerunners of their salvation. So with other countries. Nations, which till then had slumbered rapt in the apathy of wretchedness, woke into new life and new energy, under the auspices of the Prophet of Arabia. The people everywhere received the Moslems as their liberator. Wherever any resistance was offered, it was by the priesthood and the aristocracy.

An examination of the conditions of the Moslems under the first four Caliphs, brings to view a popular government based on a definite code, and administered by elective chiefs with limited powers. The chiefs of the States were controlled by public opinion, and were open to the censures of their meanest subjects. Uthman was obliged to render every day an account of the public money; and Ali appeared before the ordinary tribunals of justice as accuser of a Christian thief. The decisions of the judges were supreme; and the early Caliphs could not assume the power (as later usurpers did) of pardoning those whom the regular tribunals had condemned. The law was the same for the poor as for the rich; for the man in power as for the labourer in the field.

The importance which Islam attaches to the duties of sovereigns toward their subjects, and the manner in which it promotes the freedom and equality of the people, and protects them against the encroachment of their rulers, is shown in the erudite work of the celebrated publicist Imam Fakhr-ud-Din Fazi (of Raghes, Rai), on the Reciprocal Rights of Sovereigns and Subjects, written barely more than a hundred years after the time of the Prophet.

Exemplary Laws : The laws of the Moslems based on equitable principles and remarkable for their simplicity and precision, did not demand an obedience either difficult to render or incompatible with the intelligence of mankind. "And if," says M. Oelsner, "the law which regulates the right of succession be regarded as the most important institution for the internal peace and welfare of society, to the Moslems must be conceded the honour of possessing a code surpassing in this respect all ancient legislation."

Those countries where the Moslems established themselves remained exempt from the disastrous consequences of the feudal system and the feudal code. Admitting no privilege, no caste, their legislation produced two grand results that of freeing the soil from factitious burdens imposed by barbarian laws; and of assuring to individuals perfect equality of rights.

"A happy mixture of simplicity and energy, of disinterestedness and good faith, of modesty and bravery, of piety, and of love for universal humanity, made the charm," says M. Oelsner, "of the manners of the early Moslems." The sobriety of life imposed by the precepts of the Prophet, preserved the general mass of Moslems from those wild outbursts which disgraced the lives of the followers of other religions; the sanctity of speech and the respect for law and property formed a safeguard for the world against oppression.

Augustus of Arabs : Abdullah al-Mamun has been deservedly styled the Augustus of the Arabs. Abul Faraj cosine instead of the chord in astronomical and trigonometrical calculations.

Love of Learning : The love of learning, which characterised the Abbassids and the Fatimides, was handed down to the dynasties which succeeded them. The Samanides in Transoxiana (Ma-war-un-Nahr); the Buyides (al-Buwaih) in Persia, and at Baghdad in the capacity of mayors of the palace; the Ghaznavides at Ghazni, vied with each other in the cultivation of learning and patronage of the learned. The Seljukides—Tughral, Alp Arslan, Sanjar and Malik Shah—were not only remarkable for their grandeur, their clear comprehension of what constituted the welfare of the people, but were equally distinguished for intellectual gifts and unbounded enthusiasm in the cause of learning.

The hordes of the devastator Chengiz, swept like overwhelming torrents over Muslim Asia. Wherever they went, they left misery and desolation. But the moment the wild barbarians adopted the religion of the Prophet of Arabia, a change came over them. From the destroyers of the seats of learning and arts they were transformed into the founders of academies, and the protectors of the learned. Sultan Khoda-Bendah (Uljaitu Khan), the sixth in descent from Chengiz was remarkable for his attainments and patronage of the sciences. Even Halaku, the grandson of Chengiz, and the destroyer of Baghdad, protected the astronomer-philosopher, Khwaja Nasir-ud-din of Tus.

Under the Buyides flourished Abul-wafa, who introduced the use of the secant and the tangent in trigonometry. "But this was not all," says M. Sedillot, "struck by the imperfection of the lunar theory of Ptolemy, he verified the ancient observation, and discovered independently of the equation of the centre, a third inequality, which is no other than the variation determined six centuries later by Tycho Brahe."

Flourishing Scholars : Under Mahmud, the celebrated conqueror, and his successor, flourished the philosopher, mathematician, and geographer al-Beruni (Abu Raihan)—Firdousi, the prince of poets—Dukiki, Unsuri and Sanai. The intercourse which had about this time sprung up between India and the Muslim Empire of Ghazni, enabled the Moslems to amalgamate with their discoveries the hitherto jealously hoarded knowledge of the Indians.

Calendar Reformed : Under the Seljukide dynasty, especially under Maiek Shah and Sanjar flourished some of the mightiest intellects of Islam. The astronomical observations executed under Maiek Shah led, in 1079-1080, to a reform in the calendar, which preceded by six centuries the Gregorian reform in the west. The astronomer-poet, Umar Khyam, whose work has been translated both into French and English, and the beautiful singer, Anwari, flourished under Sanjar.

Under the Muslim successors of Chengiz, the light of knowledge irradiated all parts of the Eastern world, penetrating even to China.

The astronomical tables of Ibn Yunus were translated in 1280 by the Chinese, and thus what is attributed to the ancient civilization of China, is only a borrowed light from the Moslems.

Promotion of All Sciences : It was, however, not only astronomy which the Moslems cultivated and improved. Every branch of higher mathematics bears traces of their genius. The Greeks are said to have invented algebra; but among them, as M. Oelsner has ably remarked, it was confined to furnishing amusement "for the plays of the goblet." The Moslems applied it to higher and nobler purposes, and thus gave it a value hitherto unknown. Under Mamun, they discovered the solution of equations of the second degree and very soon after, they developed the theory of quadratic equations.

The cultivation of the physical sciences was no less diligently pursued by the Moslems. Chemistry. Botany, Geology, Rural Economy, the Science of Agriculture and Natural History, exercised the powers and intellect of the greatest men. But the Moslems certainly deserve the gratitude of the modern world, for having introduced the method of experimentation in the domains of the exact sciences in place of the theorizing of the Greeks.

Chemistry as a science is the undisputed invention of the Moslems. Abu Musa Jafar of Kufa (the Geber of Christian writers) is the true father of Muslim Chemistry. "His name is memorable in chemistry, since it marks an epoch in that science of equal importance to that of Priesley and Lavoisier."

In the knowledge of anatomy and pharmacy, the Moslems left all their predecessors far behind and developed those branches of learning into positive sciences. Botany, they advanced far beyond the state in which it had been left by Dioscorides and enriched the herbalogy of the Greeks by the addition of two thousand plants. Regular gardens existed both in Cord ova and Baghdad, at Cairo and Fez, for the education of pupils, where discourses were delivered by the most learned in the science.

Aldemri is famous in the Muslim world for his history of animals,—a work which forestalled Buffon by seven hundred years.

Geology, which had been claimed by a European science, was cultivated under the name of Ilm-e-Tashrih-ul-Ardh, the science of the anatomy of the earth.

But of all the sciences cultivated by the Arabs and the Moslems, agriculture was the one in which they made the greatest progress. "No civilized nation of their times," says an European writer, "possessed a code of husbandry more judicious or more perfect." In metallurgy, no nation of the world has surpassed the Moslems. The blades of Toledo, Damascus and Granada have been scarcely matched by the best productions of the modern world. Numismatics was not unknown; and the work of Makrizi serves as a model to the scholars of all ages.

Superiority in Architecture : The superiority of the Moslems in architecture requires no comment. Their development of the science of political economy is too well-known to need more than a bare mention. But their backwardness in two of the greatest of the fine arts, sculpture and painting, has furnished Christian writers with a subject for a great display of rhetoric. This backwardness has been charged to the prohibition of images by the Quranic laws,—a prohibition similar in nature to the Levitical commandment. This charge is made without due knowledge of the significance of the prohibitive law, or of the circumstances which induced its promulgation. Probably to the first Moslems, preeminent iconoclasts, painting and statuary were odious as leading to idolatry. That this view was not contrary to fact is made evident by history. Their scruples indeed saved them from the fate of other races and religionists who drank to the dregs the cups of polytheism and fetish-worship, and marked out for them a distinguished place in the universe. But the moment the Moslems secured themselves from the attacks of faithless enemies, the moment they applied themselves to the cultivation of the arts of peace, they became aware of the historic significance of this prohibitory law. They perceived at once that it was special in its application, and was directed only against the making of similitudes or images for worship. Hence throughout the Muhammadan world, a taste for painting and sculpture arose simultaneously with the progress of literature and arts. The palaces of the Caliphs, both of the East and of the West, the mansions of the princes who followed in their footsteps, and the houses of the grandees, were invariably decorated with pictures and sculptures. We read in the Tales of the Thousand and One Nights, (the Arabian Nights, those faithful representatives of Muslim life and manners under the Abbassids)—that Harun-al-Rashid had fitted up special picture galleries in his palace. Mamun and his successors, the princes of the house of Buwaih, the Sefavian sovereigns of Persia, were all remarkable for their love of paintings. Islam does not interfere with the progress of the fine arts. Certainly, in the decoration of mosques, no figure of animated beings is allowed to enter.

The achievements of the Moslems in the field of general literature were as glorious as those in any other department of knowledge. In rhetoric, in philology, in poetry, in history, in romance, many of the grandest monuments of human intellect exist in the languages of the Moslems, and especially in that of the Arabs.

No nation—not even the Greeks—excelled the Arabs in eloquence or in rhetoric, the laws of which they formulated with the precision of a Quintilian.

The Great Book : The division and jealousy of the tribes, which had prevented the assimilation and fusion of their several dialects, had nevertheless conduced to the enrichment of the national language, as spoken in Hijaz. The annual conflux of people at Okadh, with the periodical contests of the poets, imparted to it a regularity and polish. But it was the Quran:

> "a book, by the aid of which the Arabs conquered a world greater than of Rome, and in as many tens of years as the latter had wanted hundreds to accomplish her conquests by the aid of which they, alone of all the Shemites, came to Europe as kings Whither the Phoenicians had come as tradesmen, and the Jews as fugitives or captives, came to Europe to hold up, together with these fugitives, the light to "Humanity : they alone, while darkness lay around, to raise up the wisdom and knowledge of Hellas from the dead, to teach philosophy, medicine, astronomy, and the golden art of song to the West as to the East, to stand at the cradle of modern science, and to cause us late epigoni for ever to weep over the day when Granada fell"

It was this book which fixed and preserved the Arabic language on a systematic foundation. Remarkable for the simple grandeur of its diction, the chaste elegance of its style, the variety of its imageries, the rapid transitions like flashes of lightning, which show the moralist teaching,—the philosopher the osophizing,—the injured patriot denouncing fervid expressions the immorality and degradation of his people, and withal the God of the Universe proclaiming through the man, the fundamental truths which govern the moral world. Such is the Quran. And the awe and veneration with which the greatest poets of the day listened to its teachings, show how deeply it must have moved the people. Possessing little homogeneity, delivered at different times—in moments of persecution and anguish or of energetic action, or delivered for purposes of practical guidance. There is yet a vitality, an earnestness and energy in the Quran, which show that the Prophet spoke with an inspired tongue. It has been the fashion of late, at least in the Western world, to deride the merits of the Quran, and to place it as a literary achievement below the tritest Greek or Latin work. Lest it should be thought that our opinion is actuated by prejudice, we quote the words of Mr. Deutsch.

"Those grand accents of joy and sorrow, of love, and valour, and passion, of which but faint echoes strike on our ears now, were fulltoned at the time of Muhammad; and he had not merely to rival the illustrious of the illustrious, but to excel them; to appeal to the superiority of what he said and sang as a very sign and proof of his mission .... The poets before him had sung of love...Antrara, himself the hero of the most famous novel, 'the ruin, around which ever hover lovers' thoughts, of the dwelling of Abla, who is gone, and her dwelling-place knows her not; it is now desolate and silent. Amr-ul-kais, the standard bearer of poets, but on the way to hell' as Muhammad called him, of all things praises his fortune which women, chiefly Oneisa, and in brilliant, often Helnesque, verse sings of the good things of this world, until his father banishes him on account of an adventure wherein he, as usual, had been too happy. And of a sudden, in the midst of a wild revel, he hears that his father had been slain, and not a word said he. But higher and louder waxed the revel, and he drank deep, and gamed till the grey dawn, when he arose of a sudden and swore a holy oath that neither wine nor woman should soothe his senses until he had taken bloody vengeance for his father... . They sang of valour and generosity, of love and strife and revenge, of their noble tribe and ancestors, of beautiful women, ... of the valiant sword, and the swift camel, ...or of early graves upon which weeps the morning's clouds, and the fleeting nature of life, which comes and goes as the waves of the desert sand, and as the tents of a caravan, as a flower that shoots up and dies away—while the white stars will rise and set everlastingly, and the mountains will rear their heads heavenwards, and never grow old.... . Muhammad sang none of these. No love-minstrelsy his, not the joys of this world, nor sword nor camel, not jealousy or human vengeance, not the glories of tribe or ancestors, nor the unmeaning, swiftly and never extinguished existence of man, were his themes. He preached Islam, and he preached it by rending the skies above and tearing open the ground below, by adjuring heaven and hell, the living and the dead."

Excellent Poetry : In Poetry, the Muslim genius had not been surpassed, as regards fertility of intellect, by that of any other nation in the world. In every branch of poetry, lyric, didactic, elegiac, idyllic or epic, the Muslim poets may be numbered by hosts.

The drama is said to have been neglected by the Moslems. But the reason of this apparent neglect is not difficult to find, and has been already grasped by several European writers. The Arabs and the Persians who undertook dramatic compositions never considered it necessary that the work should be written entirely in verse. Descriptions, similitudes, reflections, and many of the speeches they expressed in numbers, but the narrative part was, with greater perception of the exactness of circumstances, written in prose. Many of the tales of the Thousand and One Nights" are composed in this mixed manner.

Most Splendid Proof : In History, the Moslems have given to the world the most splendid proofs of their genius. The bibliographical encyclopaedia of Hajj khalif (the Kashf-uz-zunun) bears a glorious testimony to the fecundity of the Muslim mind. But in one department of the science of history, the Moslems, or more properly the Arabs, might justly lay claim to the merit of originality. The science of historic evidence, unknown or at least unappreciated in Europe till the middle of the last century, was perfectly known to the Moslems. The mass of conflicting traditions with which they had to deal, regarding the life and history of their great master, rarely gave rise to the science of sifting the credibility of historical documents.

Such were the glorious achievements of the Moslems in the field of intellect; and all arose directly from the teachings of one persecuted man, flying from the sanguinary attacks of remorseless enemies. Called by his voice, from the abyss of barbarism and ignorance in which they had hitherto dwelt, with little hope of the present, with none of the future—they went out into the world, not to slaughter like the Israelites of old, but to teach and elevate, to civilise and refine. Afflicted and downtrodden humanity awoke to new life. Whilst the barbarians of Europe, who had overturned an effete empire, were groping in the darkness of absolute ignorance and brutality, the Moslems were occupied in the task of civilisation.

During centuries of moral and intellectual desolation in Christian Europe, Islam led the vanguard of intellectual progress. In an Indian story we read of a land enshrouded in darkness, to which the demons of the air bar all access. It is not a fanciful land. Christianity had established itself on the throne of the Caesars, but it had utterly failed in the object of regenerating the nations of the earth. From the fourth century, the darkness of Europe grew deeper and deeper. During these ages of ignorance Ecclesiasticism barred every access through which the light of Knowledge, represented latterly by Muslim civilisation, could stream in. But though jealously shut out from this land of fanaticism, the benignant influences of Islam in time made themselves felt in every part. From the court of the Norman princes of Sicily, from that of the great Frederick II, from sunny Andalusia, from the dark palaces of the Isaurian sovereigns, from the dark places of the Isaurian sovereigns of Constantinople, Islam spoke to the benighted inhabitants of Europe.

The wars of the Gulfs and Ghibelines; the contests of the Iconoclasts of Byzantium with orthodoxy, partially represented the grand battle of Rationalism with Patristicism, of Muslim Civilisation with Barbarism, of Islam with Ecclesiasticism. From the schools of Salerno, of Baghdad, of Damascus, of Granada, of Cordaova, of Malaga, the Moslems taught the world the gentle instructions of philosophy and the practical teachings of stem science. Popes came to their universities to listen to the sweet accents of learning.

Balanced View

The first outburst of Rationalism in the West, occurred in the province most amenable to the power of Muslim civilisation. Ecclesiasticism crushed this fair flower with fire and with sword, and threw back the progress of the world for centuries. But the principles of the Liberty of Thought, so strongly impressed on Islam, had communicated their vitality to Christian Europe. Abelard, the impulsive lover of Heloise had felt the power of the genius of Averroes, which was shedding its light over the whole of the Western world. Abelard struck a blow for free thought, which his successors were not loth to follow up. Avenpace and Averroes were the precursors of Descartes, Hobbes and Locke.

The influence of Abelard and of his schools soon made itself felt in England. Wickliffe's originality of thought and freedom of spirit took their rise from the bold conceptions of the former thinkers. The later German reformers, deriving their notions on one side from the iconoclastic advocates of Constantinople, and on the other side from the movement of the Albigenses,—the Wickliffites, and even from the Gulfs,—preeminently represented the Islamic ideas, only in a Teutonic garb. Luther, in who, as Hallam, justly thinks, there existed a vein of insanity, tried to repudiate all obligation to Islam, by using harsh epithets with regard to Muhammad, in his translation of the Quran. But can any one doubt that he was influenced by it? Melancthon and the other German reformers were all deeply read in Muhammad's teachings.

To come again to the point whence we started: while Christian Europe had placed learning under the ban of persecution, while the Vicar of Christ set the example of stifling the infant lispings of Free thought, while the priests led the way in consigning to the flames myriads of inoffensive beings for mere aberration of reason or simple differences of opinion regarding the nature of some bread and wine; while Christian Europe was exercising demons and apothe osizing and worshipping rags and bones, learning flourished under the Muslim sovereigns, and was held in honour and veneration as never of old. The Vicegerents of Muhammad allied themselves to the cause of civilisation, and assisted in the growth of Free thought and Free-enquiry—originated and consecrated by the Prophet himself. Persecution for the sake of faith was unknown and whatever the political conduct of the sovereigns, the world has never had superior examples, in their impartiality and absolute toleration of all creeds and religions. The cultivation of the physical sciences,—that great index to the intellectual liberty of a nation,—formed the daydream of the whole life of the Moslems.

Three great evils have befallen the human race; three great disasters, which have materially retarded the progress of the world, and put back the Hour Hand of Time for centuries. The first is the failure of the Persians in Greece; the second is the unsuccessful siege of Constantinople by the Saracens under Muslemah in the eight century; and the third is the unfortunate result of the battle of tours between the Moslems under Abdur Rahman Fehri, and the wild hordes of Charles, duke of Acquittance, summoned by the Christians, Mortal. Each of these events has prevented either the growth of progress of civilisation. If the Persians had succeeded in bringing Greece within the circle of their dominion, the influence of the Hellenic genius would have been far greater, and would have extended over a wider area than was possible under the factious jealousies of petty states, many of them smaller than the smallest municipality in India or England. The Persians under the Kyanian (Achaemenian) sovereigns carried on their war with a far-seeing policy. They always allowed the states which became subject to them to retain a certain degree of independence and autonomy. The principle on which they proceeded arose not from a desire of rapine and conquest, but rather from a well-devised policy of federation. Had Persia succeeded in amalgamating Greece with herself, the result only partially attained by the Hellenic upheaval under Alexander, the son of Philip of Macedonia, would have been attained centuries earlier.!

So the two failures of the Moslems, one before Constantinople, and the other in France, retarded the progress of the world for ages. Had the Arabs been less remiss at Tours, had they succeeded in driving before them the barbarian hosts of a barbarian chief, whom the ecclesiastics themselves afterwards condemned to everlasting perdition, the history of the darkest period in the annals of the world would never have been written. The Renaissance, civilisation, the growth of intellectual liberty would have been accelerated by seven hundred years. We should not have had to shudder over the massacre of the Albigenses, which a Pope instigated nor of the Huguenots, for which a Pope returned thanks. We should not have had to mom over the fate of a Bruno or of a Servetus, murdered by the hands of those who had revolted from their mother-church. The history of the autos-da-fe, of the murders of the inquisition, of the massacres of the poor Aztecs and Incas; the tale of the Thirty year's War, with its manifold miseries, all this would have remained untold. Above all Spain, at one time the favoured haunt of learning and arts, would not have become the intellectual desert it now is– bereft of the glories of centuries. Who has not mourned over the fate of that glorious race, which the mad bigotry of a despot of the Escurial exiled from the country of its adoption, which it had made famous among nations? Justly has it been said, "In an ill-omened hour the cross supplanted the crescent on the "toworo of Granada." The shades of the glorious dead, of Averroes and Avenpace, of Valadeta and Aishah, sit weeping by the ruined haunts of their people—haunts silent now to the voice of minstrelsy, of chivalry, of learning, and of art,—only echoing at times the mad outcries of religious combatants, at times the fierce sounds of political animosities. Christianity drove the descendants of these Muslim Andalusians into the desert, sucked out every element of vitality from beautiful Spain, and made it a synonym for intellectual and moral desolation.

If Muslemah had succeeded in capturing Constantinople—the capital of Iran, the warm advocate of orthodoxy and cruel murderess of her own son, the dark deeds which sully the annals of the Isaurians, the Comneni, the Palaeologi, the terrible results which attended the seizure of Byzantium by the Latins, above all, the frightful outburst of the unholy wars in which Christian Europe tried to strangle the nations of Asia, would probably never have come to pass. But one thing is certain, that if Constantinople had fallen into the hands of the Moslems, the iconoclastic movement would not have proved altogether abortive; and the reformation of the Christian Church would have been accomplished centuries earlier. To use an oft-repeated expression, Providence willed otherwise. The wave of Free thought which had reached the Isaurian emperors from the Islamic regions, broke upon the rocks of ignorance, superstition, and bigotry; its power was not felt, until the combined action of the schools of Salerno and Cordova,— the influence of Averroes, and perhaps of some Greeks who had imbibed learning at the Saracenic fountain-head—had broke down the rampart of Ecdesiasticism.

Shining Instances

Islam thus introduced into the modern world civilisation, philosophy, the arts and the sciences, everything that ennobles the heart and elevates the mind. It inaugurated the reign of intellectual liberty.

It has been justly remarked, that as long as Islam retained its pristine character it proved itself the warm protector and promoter of knowledge and civilization—the zealous ally of Intellectual freedom. The moment extraneous elements attached themselves to it, it lagged behind in the race of progress.

Let us hope that the time is approaching when Islam, freed from the blind idolatry of letters and apotheosis of dead men, will regain her true character and, joining hands with Christianity of the devoted Prophet of Nazareth, will march on together in the work of Civilisation. Islam and Christianity both aim at the same results,— the elevation of mankind. The gain of the one is gain of the other. Why, then, should the two be hostile to each other? Why should not the two harmonize? Islam had done no evil to the world, nor has Christianity. Both have conferred the greatest benefits on mankind. Why then should not the two, mixing the waters of life treasured in their bosom, form the bright flowing river which would bear our race to the most glorious fields of Humanity? Everything that elevates the heart of man is true; everything that leads to goodness and purity in action and in thought is true. Why not then henceforth adopt the words of the Prophet of Arabia, as the motto of Humanity:

> 'Try to excel in good works, when ye shall return unto God, He will tell you as to that in which ye have differed."

5

The Basis

Historic Charter

Introduction to the Charter : The word, 'constitution' in its legal sense is of recent origin. A modern writer defines constitutions as "codes which aspire to regulate the allocations of functions, powers and duties among the various agencies and offices of the government...." When we apply it, to a document which was signed within a few months of the Hijrah of the Prophet (PBUH), fourteen hundred years ago, we do not get the exact sense and meaning given to it by either the Prophet (PBUH) himself or those to whom the document was being given. He had called, the document under study, as:

"A Writing from Muhammad, the Prophet of Allah."

Basis of Future Statutes : It could also mean a letter and a document, the last being the most appropriate. This settles one thing. It was neither a 'treaty' nor an agreement, because it was "From Muhammad, the Prophet of Allah," and not an agreement between him and others. They had not—no objection in receiving it as a Charter laying down the Code of Life for Yathrib. They also accepted his position as "The Prophet of Allah," even though some of them desired to retain their attachment to the religion they already professed. They had, as a matter of fact, no option, but to accept it or else live in Yathrib as aliens.

A few points need to be borne in mind while studying this document. First, that the document must be placed chronologically before any of the other objects is studied. This is necessary, because of two reasons. The first reason is that unless its period is determined it will not be possible to determine the object for which it was promulgated.

We have referred elsewhere to the immediate object of this document. The document is of a permanent nature. There must, therefore, have been other reasons which are of a lasting nature. The Constitution, if we consider it as such, of the first Islamic State, brought into existence by the Prophet (PBUH) himself has to remain, in most respects, if not all, a model Constitution for all states established by Muslims. We, therefore, feel that it needs studying from a number of angles.

Dictated by Prophet : It is important to bear in mind that the document was dictated by the Prophet of Allah (PBUH). He had been receiving Sublime Guidance, for thirteen years, from Allah. A person of his calibre would not issue a document of this nature without an adequate and a set purpose. Furthermore a person of his knowledge, experience and capabilities would not issue a self contained document piece meal. If a document is issued by installments it loses consistency and results in being misunderstood. His actions subsequent to the issue of this document have also great relevancy.

They show, if he was in the habit of tackling problems in a consistent or a disjointed manner. It must be kept in mind that he is The Law Giver and laws given by him have stood the test of time. Persons who create and promulgate laws have to consider problems from all angles, otherwise their laws fail to receive such reception as desired. There has to be logic and consistency in the words and actions of men placed in the position he occupied. Written documents become out of date if they are void of consistency. Lastly it has to be borne in mind that this document was issued under certain conditions. Therefore, to gauge its proper importance we must bear in mind all the time, the circumstances which necessitated its issue. These have been discussed briefly.

We have referred to the document as a Constitutional Charter.

"The form and nature of a constitution are dictated by the relationship prevailing among the various sections or classes of people." There was no organized group with whom the Prophet (PBUH) could have executed a treaty or an agreement. Hence we find that it was neither a treaty nor an agreement. It is important to bear in mind its heading, which also forms the very first Clause.

The heading needs to be given in full.

"This document (writing) is from Muhammad The Prophet of Allah (PBUH) to Quraish and Yathribite believers and Those who will follow them and fight alongside with them. They will form *One Ummah* to the exclusion of others."

Primarily the document has been issued to administer the affairs of *Muhajir* and *Ansar* believers. Its jurisdiction is then extended to those who live and fight *Jihad* under the leadership of these *Muhajir* and *Ansar* believers. Leadership has been given to the entire Muslim community. The Prophet (PBUH) has not spoken of his leadership. This point has great significance for future generations of believers.

The manner of promulgation of the Charter may also have a bearing on the circumstances at the time of its issue and the keenness of the recipients to be favoured by inclusion in the *Ummah*. From the wording and placing of concessions to various tribes, it creates the impression, that the dictation of the Charter took place in an open *Darbar*, and as the Arab custom was and still is, those to whom a clause did not apply they spoke up to be included and at once another clause was dictated for inclusion.

The document was issued within a few months of the Hijrah of the Prophet (PBUH) which took place in July or August 622 A.C. This is the period when, "a few years earlier, the reign of the grandson of Nushirwan was extended to the Hellespont and the Nile, the ancient limits of the Persian monarchy; the Christians of East were scandalized by the worship of fire and the impious doctrine of the two principles; the Magi were no less intolerant than the bishops, and the martyrdom of some native Persians, who had deserted the religion of Zoroaster, was conceived to be the prelude of a fierce and general persecution. The oppressive laws of Justinian, the adversaries of the Church were made the enemies of the state; the alliance of the Jews, Nestorians and Jacobites, had contributed to the success of Chosroes, and his partial favour to the sectaries, provoked the hatred and fears of Catholic clergy."

The Persian monarch was so full of arrogance that, as his predecessors used to carry away the gods of the defeated, back to Persia, he carried away to his capital the Holy Cross from Jerusalem. The situation, however, altered, within a few years as predicted in the *Quran*. Byzantium, "rallied under Heraclius, who had led his troops in 624 A.C., into the heart of Iran. Chosroes was deposed and executed by his own subjects, and Heraclius recovered the Cross".

A Great Deal : It meant a great deal for the prestige of the Emperor. To have brought back Holy Cross, the symbol of true Christianity, to Jerusalem, where the Jews were supposed to have been instrumental in having Jesus Christ crucified, was a great achievement. Syria, at that time, was a truly Christian land. "In fact this is the only period in which Syria has been a fully Christian country. Not only was the country Christian, but the age was an ecclesiastical age".

It was in this age of persecution, religious prejudices, taboos, ethnical differences, and acute hatred resulting in mass killings, when this document was dictated to an assembly of believers, *Mushrikeen* and Jews, not far from a totally Christian land, where at about the same time controversies raged, which ended in a, "sentence of excommunication on the tomb of St. Peter ; the ink was mingled with the sacramental wine, the blood of Christ and no ceremony was omitted that could fill the superstitious mind with horror". It was the same period, when in India, Harsha ruled and according to a Chinese pilgrim, "The penalty of imprisonment, inflicted after the cruel Tibetan fashion, which left the prisoner, to live or die, was freely awarded, and mutilation was often adjudged".

In spite of it all, we are told that in every one of these lands their particular civilization was at its peak and yet man was in bondage and writhed at the feet of other men. Man had forgotten that he and other men were all descended from Adam and Adam had been created from clay:

"He it is Who hath created you from clay". 6:2

How unnatural that men should be regarded as unequals and yet inhabit the same planet. Many prophets had come and tried to teach men and women, that they were equal as human beings, but it was left to the Last Prophet of Allah to establish complete equality in those who believed in Allah and him as His Messenger and Servant.

While he was dictating this document of great consequence he was observing the principle of equality. It would take centuries for mankind to realise the effect and importance of this principle.

The ultimate destination of mankind, while on this planet, is the mastery of elements of nature. He has to achieve vast knowledge of nature of things and elements to an extent that very few can imagine. Acquisition of knowledge at the level of entire humanity demands peace, justice and equality among mankind. This will come about when mankind rises above the level of present ignorance and becomes One Ummah. This is the most important lesson taught by the Last Prophet of Allah, while dictating this unique document. Universal peace will be achieved when the principle of equality of man is universally accepted. The Prophet (PBUH) when dictating this document brought the level of all men on an equal pedestal. Jews who, at the time, were looked down upon, except may be in Iran, were given equality with Arabs of Quraish and *Ansar* origin. Equality of man appears to be one of the main features of his Mission, and, "It is difficult to portray the events of the life of the Prophet (PBUH) unless we first understand the nature of the Mission entrusted to him".

This Mission, according to the *Quran* is complete guidance of mankind in all walks of life. Man has to enter Islam completely.

> "O ye who believe! Come, all of you, into submission".
> 2:208

And the Prophet has to bring mankind into Islam-submission to the Will of Allah.

> "(This is) a Scripture which We have revealed unto thee (Muhammad) that thereby, thou mayst bring forth mankind from darkness unto light, by the permission of their Lord, unto the Path of the Mighty, the Owner of Praise". 14:1.

Eternal Message : The Eternal Message of Allah happens to be placed in a world which, in certain respects, alters with changes in time and geography. And yet this Eternal Message guides men to the straight path. "The glory of Islam is that it distinguishes the universal from the changing particulars".

If we study the *Quran* and try to locate Eternal Commandments we will find that these happen to be all in respect of those aspects of human life and nature, which remain constant and are not subject to any great changes as a result of time and place. Those aspects of life whether at the level of an individual or at the collective level of society, which are subject to changes due to change in surroundings, have been left to the individual or the society, as the case may be, to find the best solution as long as no other Commandment is violated in the process. This means that no restrictions have been placed on "the changing particulars."

It is the same with the *Sunnah* of the Prophet (PBUH). He has set precedents in all walks of life, but restrictions were placed only in the field of universals and particulars left to be decided by the individual and the society, as the case may be. He was the Messenger of the Code of Life Revealed by Allah. He was not sent as a military commander and yet he demonstrated the "why, when and how" of war, because the Ummah needed guidance in it. He was not a statesman and yet he demonstrated how justice tempered with mercy was to be administered in a society of equals. He led his army to many a battlefield, keeping in view the principles of war and compulsions of strategy and tactics dictated by geography and other factors and demonstrated all the qualities of a great commander.

His critics fail to keep his mission in view when commenting on his activities as a soldier or as a statesman because their view of a Way of Life is limited to acts of prayers only. To say that, "Muhammad (PBUH) himself was not a warrior and had few military gifts. In battle, he invariably followed behind the front line, never, if avoidable, himself engaged in hand to hand fighting", amounts to disregarding his role as a guide of commanders. The writer forgets that commanders do not engage, normally, in hand to hand fighting. They have to direct, control and deploy troops as the situation may demand. This vague statement of a British general does not mention those qualities of martial nature, which in his opinion were absent in the Prophet (PBUH). He would have probably liked to see in him qualities displayed by British generals like Kitchener, who, "sword in hand and Bible in pocket he enjoyed a career of spectacular warfare in Russia, China, India, and Africa...." Kitchener's enjoyment of war amounted to perversity, when he had defeated Mehdi's Army he arranged a victory parade, on 10th of April 1898, in which, he treated the captured enemy commander Amir Mahmud in the most cruel manner. "Dragging chains which were riveted round his ankles, and wearing a halter round his neck the defeated army commander was made to walk, and sometimes run, behind the cavalry. His hands were bound behind his back, and he was driven forward by Sudanese guards, who lashed him with whips when he stumbled. Kitchener rode on a white horse in triumph". What a spectacle of British chivalry and martial excellence during the closing years of nineteenth century when European civilization was at its height.

This British general of whom many generations spoke with admiration, gave orders, that the tomb of Mahdi be razed to the ground and his bones to be cast into the Nile. Mahdi's skull which was unusually large was kept aside to be used as ink-stand. One suggestion was to use it as a drinking cup. He had ordered Wantage, another famous British soldier, to "loot like blazes. I want any quantity of marble stairs, marble pavings, iron railings, looking glasses and fittings, doors, windows, furniture of all sorts". A victorious general who pardoned his life-long enemies must have appeared to General Glubb, to lack martial qualities common among European generals and conquerors. The objective of the Prophet (PBUH) was to establish peace as a precedent for believers until the end of time. He had to demonstrate what was an ideal life. This included both war and peace.

It included the life of a labourer and also that of a ruler. He demonstrated the life of a man of all walks of life, when he was being persecuted and we find no change in the way he lived, when he was the ruler of entire Arabia and his army had a successful round of exchange of arms with the Byzantine Imperial Army, at the battlefield of Mowta. As a general his strategy was not only to win the war, but to succeed in the days after the war as well, and his war stands alone in the annals of military history, which brought happier days both for the winner and the vanquished although a winner in earlier battles he had accepted armistice on the enemy's terms.

It has been recorded by his biographer "When there was peace and war was abolished and men met in safety and consulted together none talked intelligently about Islam without entering it. In these two years double as many or more than double as many entered Islam as before".

Throughout his life he was keen to use all his resources to bring about peaceful atmosphere in which his Message could be understood and accepted. Today, fourteen centuries after him, the world has accepted the point of view that peace alone can solve mankind's problems. A modern writer has said, "In an age of Total War we will need Total Peace". War, however, has to be catered for." Wars do not break out of themselves, but they may change the course of history and the fate of mankind.... War has, therefore, become the greatest of social problems". For him and for Islam war had become the greatest of not only social, but also political problem. He gave to the world, Islam—The Message of Peace— when war had been brought to his doorstep.

This document is of great consequence as it gives an answer to a multinational *Ummah,* as to how they should face an aggressor and survive. One of the outstanding features of this document, which cemented the citizens of Yathrib was Justice with Equality for all. Peace within communities and, at international level, cannot be established without equality and equal status to men and groups of men—the nations. This equality was not acceptable either within Arabia or at the international level at that time. The Arabs of Mecca, steeped in the idea of racial superiority, their minds clouded with racial prejudices, and having a class ridden society, were in no mood to accept equality between Abu Jehl, the high born Quraish chief and Bilal the Negro slave.

Equality of Men : It was the principle of equality of man which evoked the animosity of the two neighbouring mighty empires of Iran and Byzantium, towards Islam and Muslims. The ruling classes of both these empires were securely entrenched as the high born elites, who held the birth right of princely and regal positions. The birth of an Ideology of "Equality before the Eyes of Allah," both in this and the next world, was a revolutionary reality which had to be nipped in the bud. The rest of the world was to array itself on the side of these two Empires, one after the other. The prophesy of Abbas bin Ubada was fulfilled soon enough, but it was to continue being fulfilled for ever.

It was during the Second *Bayah* at Al-Aqaba that Abbas bin Ubada-al-Ansari, said to the *Ansars* who were swearing allegiance to the Prophet (PBUH), "O men of Khazraj, do you realise to what you are committing yourselves in pledging your support to this man? It is to war against all and sundry. If you think that if you lose your property and your nobles are killed you will give him up, then do so now, for it would bring you shame in this world and the next. But if you think that you will be loyal to your undertaking even if you lose your property and your nobles are killed, then take him for by God. It will profit you in this world and the next".

The men from Khazraj and many others who followed their footsteps are still being challenged by the enemies of Justice and equality for all. It is, outwardly, that people oppose Islam, while their real opposition is against the principle of equality of man, by those whose vested interest are in danger of being jeopardised. It was a question of life and death in that age. Religion during that age made men of religion oblivious of cruelties perpetuated in the name of religion. Minor differences or even suspicion of minor differences led men to throw others into flames. As has been remarked, "It remained for the Medieval Church, however, to put cruelty and burning and gruesome public executions on the firm popular basis of exalting religious spectacles".

There can be no peace in the world unless the world led by Muslims observes laws relating to *Jihad* in the Path of Allah and in conducting their foreign affairs as ordained in the *Quran.* This document was the first writing, directing towards the principles and the policy according to which human societies should conduct their affairs. It has been universally accepted that in the world of today there is no International Law, relating to the conduct of states in matters of conflict or mutual interest, obligations and the making and breaking of treaties. There have been usages in various parts of the world, which have been overlooked more often than not and in all conflicts national interests have prevailed. "International Law, so called, is in reality national law regulating international relations of those states".

Islam has a complete Code of International Law. It, however, operates at the level of the *Millah* of Islam, on the principle that believers are an *Ummah* when considered with respect to the rest of humanity. If Muslim States, observe in their interstate relations, the Commandments of the *Quran,* the super powers will find it difficult to drive humanity in World Wars, as they have done twice during twentieth century. These Quranic Injunctions dictate relations between Muslim states and also between Muslim states and others. Islamic Law is the only Law which forbids states to undertake aggression of any kind; not even for the spread of religion.

This document, apart from being the Constitutional Charter of the state of Yathrib was at the same time the document on the authority of which this state had come into existence. The person proclaiming the coming into being of this new state was Prophet Muhammad (PBUH), the last of the line of prophets, who had received Revealed Word of Allah. As a result of the contents of this document, the state of Yathrib received all those elements which add up to the formation of a state. "A state exists as soon as the four formal elements (a people, a territory, a government and the characteristics of sovereignty) can be found in it and that recognition by other states merely recognizes the social fact", and non-recognition does not alter its status.

The newly created state of Yathrib was, however, recognized soon after its establishment. The Prophet (PBUH), immediately after the promulgation of this document went out of Yathrib, stayed with various tribes, each of which held sovereign status within its tribal territory, and executed friendly treaties with them. Apart from establishing treaty relations" with neighbouring tribes, these journeys of the Prophet (PBUH) fixed approximate limits of the territory of Yathrib. The boundaries of an Islamic State, cannot be a permanent feature. Islam cannot have and does not have fixed boundaries. Islam attracts people because of principles of justice and equality. It spreads and with its spreading are extended its boundaries. Islam has not remained static even during its days of political eclipse. The spread of Islam in Africa has been when a greater part of Africa had been occupied by European Colonial powers.

By Way of Persuasion : In Malay Archipellago Islam was spread by Muslim merchants at a time when Spain held sway over the area. "They did not come as conquerors, like the Spanish in the sixteenth century, or used the sword as an instrument of conversion; nor did they arrogate to themselves the privileges of a superior and dominant race so as to degrade and oppress the original inhabitants".

It is said of Al-Mamun that when a certain Yazdanbakht a leader of the Manichaean sect came on a visit to Baghdad and held a disputation with the Muslim theologians, in which he was utterly silenced, the caliph tried to induce him to embrace Islam. But Yazdanbakht refused saying, "commander of the faithful, your advice is heard and your words have been listened to but you are one of those who do not force people to abandon their religion".

It was the same in Eastern Europe where, "The Calvinists of Hungary and Transylvania, and the Unitarians of the latter country, long preferred to submit to the Turks rather than fall into the hands of the fanatical house of Hapsburg ; and the Protestants of Silesia looked with longing eyes towards Turkey ...," The writer speaks in the same vein of other countries and other lands. "Even in Italy there were men who turned longing eyes towards the Turks in the hope that as their subjects they might enjoy the freedom and the toleration they despaired of enjoying under a Christian government".

As said earlier, this toleration of Muslims, in all the then known lands of the Globe, was the result of magnanimity shown by the Prophet of Islam (PBUH) when dictating this document in Yathrib, at the time, when the first state of Yathrib was coming into existence. The Muslims have honoured the spirit of this document throughout these fourteen centuries, which is not a mean achievement. In spite of it, and may be because of it and the resulting popularity of Islam, it "Inspires perfidy of the Balkans, the hate of the Jews, the apprehension of the Hindus and the animosity of the Russians".

The remarks of Abbas bin Ubada Ansari have been referred to above. His prediction continues to come true and may continue much longer. The basic reason for this opposition is the fear of loss of vested interests of the ruling classes and the religious hierarchy, of many faiths which upholds these classes and are a hindrance towards universal equality of man and the resultant justice and fair-play for the masses.

The tenacity with which Muslims have held on to the principle of equality is due to the fact that, they believe staunchly in the Sovereignty of Allah, which is the core and basis of all Islamic teachings. Islam stands for the Sovereignty of Allah alone and of none else. This, in practice, means that the Eternal Laws enjoined by Allah cannot be altered. If this principle was accepted by the ruling classes they would, after that, not be able to frame laws as and when it suited their vested interests. They desire to keep the framing of laws in their own hands and thus they and their institutions set aside for framing and promulgating laws retain Sovereignty in their own hands.

The law assures, that Parliament is omnipotent and paramount. It can make or unmake laws on any matter whatsoever.... The power and jurisdiction of parliaments, says Sir Edward Coke, is so transcendent and absolute, that it cannot be confined, either for causes or persons, within any bounds.... It hath sovereign and uncontrollable authority in making, confirming, enlarging, restraining, abrogating, repealing, reviving and expounding of laws, concerning matters of all possible denominations, ecclesiastical or temporal, civil or military, maritime or criminal. This fact is contained in their Constitutions, whether written or based on practice, precedence and legal judgements. Speaking of the Constitution of England (which included English possessions in Scotland, Ireland and Wales) Dicey, an eminent lawyer, has mentioned "three leading characteristics in the existing Constitution of England ; they are now generally designated as the Sovereignty of Parliament, the rule of law and the convention of the constitution".

If a similar analysis was to be made of the Constitutional Charter of Medina, its leading characteristics, that would emerge would be firstly, the "Sovereignty of Allah and His Prophet (PBUH), secondly, 'The Rule of Law' and thirdly, 'The Equality of Man. As composed to the Sovereignty of Parliament which means sovereignty of man made laws, and Convention of the Constitution, these characteristics certainly carry more weight. Mankind has, time and again, failed to convince itself that it can successfully conduct its affairs, without Guidance from Allah. Mankind, in nearly every land, "has been the victim of disastrous illusion—the illusion of our ability to emancipate ourselves from natural laws". Whether we call them as Natural Laws, (Revealed to prophets of earlier eras) or openly admit that they are Laws given by Allah who alone is our Creator and Sustainer and Knows our needs far better than us, makes no difference.

These are laws which are based on Truth from Him, who has set a destination for mankind which cannot be arrived at except by conducting ourselves in accordance with these Laws. Man has been given knowledge and intelligence, but both these qualities are limited as compared to the knowledge and Power of Allah. "It is evident that human intelligence has not increased simultaneously with the complexity of the problems involved." Today, as much as in the past, civilized humanity has shown itself incapable of directing either its individual or collective affairs. The modern world, like the Quraysh of Mecca, needs to be bold and pay homage, to the basic principle of the acceptance of the Sovereignty of Allah.

This document, The Constitutional Charter of Medina, laid down, in no uncertain terms, that Allah alone wielded Supreme Power and that the method of invoking that power is Allah Himself and His Prophet (PBUH) is the interpreter of His Laws. This document also lays down priorities to be adopted for the security and defence of states established by Muslims. The test of Constitutions whether they are capable of meeting the needs of their respective states has been suggested by a modern American writer as follows:

> "How effective is the constitution in enabling us to come to grips with periodic crises? What are the principle objectives of our national institutions? What service do they render? What are the rights and obligations of American citizenship"?

The Constitutional Charter of Medina, as a document, is

fourteen hundred years old. If modern constitutions are examined in the light of the above mentioned questionnaire it would clearly come out that human mind has not made any perceivable advance in this respect. The history of events in Medina, subsequent to the issue of this Constitutional Charter, has been recorded in greatest possible detail. We can, as a result of its perusal, say that the periodic crises that occurred in Medina, after the promulgation of this document, were conveniently solved through actions based on it.

Unanimous Acceptance : There is no doubt about the fact that at the time of its promulgation, the entire population of Yathrib had rejoiced about it and had unanimously accepted to live under its protection and abide by its laws.

This document, "brought into existence a voluntary association of all sections of Medinites—Muslims and non-Muslims, emigrants and locals, principals and clients,..." Aus and Khazraj, the two Arab tribes, were the only people who could claim that Yathrib belonged to them. They had been at war with one another, but had settled their differences, lately. An agreement had been reached tentatively that in order to give the place semblance of an organized community they should choose a king. Abdullah bin Ubay the leader of Khazraj was being talked of as the future king of Yathrib when Bayate Aqba Thani took place. Soon after this, *Muhajirs* started arriving in Yathrib. They and the *Ansars* were a far more organized group, than any tribe could be, and Abdullah bin Ubay's crowning ceremony was soon forgotten.

There were Jews also in Yathrib. They were all engaged in trade and commerce and being rich had built themselves strong forts outside the main city of Yathrib. The Jews, however, did not either own or belong to the place. A number of theories have been advanced, but the most plausible theory is that they were immigrants from Syria as a result of one of purges that used to be carried out from time to time, to rid the Holy Land of them. They were living under the protection of various sub-tribes of Aus and Khazraj. They did not possess any right other than what the *Haleef*-protecting tribe—cared to allow them.

Status Changed : This document had completely altered their social and political status. They were being raised to the status of citizens of Yathrib like any other person from amongst the tribes of Aus and Khazraj. This was a great elevation in their status. They were no more aliens or emancipated slaves. They would, henceforth be able to speak up to the Arabs as equals and the word Jew would soon loose the sense of inferiority which it had, hitherto, carried all the world over.

The Prophet (PBUH) was allowing them a further concession, which would soon make them a political force to be reckoned with. He was, on certain conditions, inviting them to become a part of the *Ummah* of believers. This invitation happened to be under Divine Guidance and was, therefore, all the more attractive. Although this invitation was also given to the Christians, but they were so few in Arabia that the Jews would have been certain to overshadow them always. This invitation, however, had one point which in the end was likely to be unacceptable to them. It was that they had first to accept the Sovereignty of Allah. The invitation being the result of an *Ayah* of Quran must have made them hesitate but they do not seem to have shown any such hesitation in the beginning. The Words of this *Ayah* of *Quran',* are:

> "Say: O People of the Scripture! Come to an agreement between us and you: that we shall worship none but Allah, and we shall ascribe no partner unto Him, and that none of us shall take others for lords besides Allah. And if they turn away, then say: Bear witness that we are those who have surrendered
> (unto Him)". 3:64

The Prophet (PBUH) was trying to create a multinational Ummah which was to form a coalition of all those who believed in Allah and thus were being asked to form a united front against the godless. He had advocated an idea, which the West have taken up lately, but not with the intention of finding a united platform for all religions, but, to find out means of accelerating Christian Missionary activities in Africa and South East Asia. What would have been the shape of a society, in which, all those who believed in Allah, were to form *One Ummah,* and yet continue calling themselves by their old denominations, would be difficult to imagine.

Hijrah of the Prophet (PBUH) had brought about a fundamental change in the society of Yathrib. There were, in Yathrib, Mushrikeen, who were pagan Arabs and did not follow any set rules, which could fall under the heading of Laws of a Religion. There were, as mentioned earlier, Jews, who, at least in principle, followed the law of Moses (May Allah's Blessings be on him). Because of being the followers of a Revealed religion, they considered themselves as superior to the pagan Arabs, although they lived under their protection. There were some Arabs who had adopted the law of Moses, but their position was strangely unidentifiable. They lived among their own families and observed Arab customary law, but considered themselves as possessing a higher intellectual creed. If they were asked to choose one of the two camps, in case of a quarrel, they would have joined their particular tribe and not gone to the Jewish camp.

The arrival of the Prophet (PBUH) altered the social structure of Yathrib completely. In fact, it had started undergoing a change since the Bayate Aqba Thani. The Prophet (PBUH) had appointed twelve leaders from among the Medinites who had come to Mecca to embrace Islam. The Prophet (PBUH) had told the gathering, "Bring out to me twelve leaders that they may take charge of their people's affairs.' They produced nine from Al-Khazraj and three from Al-Aus". This was the beginning of Muslims bringing into existence an organized Islamic Society. "With the appointment of these twelve leaders an organized Islamic Society came into being". On their return to Yathrib, these twelve leaders conducted the affairs of Medinite Muslims, until the arrival of the Prophet (PBUH).

The Jews had not been able to set up any communal life with the few Arabs who had accepted the *Shariah* of Prophet Moses. The Prophet of Islam was inviting not only Arabs but Jews, Christians and all others to share with the believers, higher values of the activities of a community organized on the basis of Sovereignty of Allah and equality of man-His most Balanced creation. The result was that, even when the believers were in a small minority, the social life of Yathrib, due to their presence, had started taking its direction from the Muslims and adopted Islamic values in an imperceptible way. The Prophet (PBUH) and the small band of his

Companions set the pace and texture of social life and thus became the centre of all communal activities. Whenever any issue demanded Allah's commandment for its settlement or the prophet's own verdict in the matter, the Muslims did make all possible efforts to arrive at the authentic views of Islam on the basis of these two sources. The earlier Revelations of the *Quran* of Medina period are all relating to laws regarding various aspects of life. Many of them resulted from questions asked at these gatherings where the Prophet (PBUH) invited people to embrace Islam.

He is known to have gone to a Jewish school to preach Islam to them. If there passed a group of people, by the road, he would stop and join them to invite them to Islam, even though they disliked it.

The Structure

A new social structure based on the Sovereignty of Allah and equality of man was taking shape. A new culture was emerging out of this social structure. Man was being given, for the first time in his cultural life, the proper place in the scheme of things, and man's mind was awakening to his place in this universe. One can find no better key to the internal logic of a society than its conception of man and his place in nature. This high position had been bestowed upon man by Allah himself, in His Eternal Code of Life. The result was that the social and cultural trends of life in Yathrib, at a time when the believers were in a small minority, took a turn towards adoption of Islamic values, and life became centralised around the personality of the Prophet (PBUH) and his Companions.

As mentioned earlier the Constitutional Charter of Medina has importance for more than one reason. It is the earliest written document of the Government and State of Medina. Later documents like the Peace Treaty of Hudaybiya, the Victory Proclamation of Khayber, and the overlordship Gazette Notification of Aila granted to the Christian population of that place, were all of the nature of proclamation of cessation of hostilities due to one or the other reason. This document stands in a different position. It established a state and a government in order to meet aggression. Invasion by Quraysh of Mecca had to be stopped. Defence of a society cannot be assured without first organizing that society. When a society is organized it takes the shape of a state. The state must have law and it must also lay down as to what was the source of law and who in future would be entitled to amend or add to this law. All these steps were being finalised through the Constitutional Charter of Medina.

This process has been explained in modern terminology in the following words. "Peace among men and a civilized society, which are one and the same thing, are imaginable only within a legal order equipped with institutions to give effect to principles and norms in the form of law..." The Prophet (PBUH) was laying down that the final authority in Islam would be Allah, through revelations to him. Arabian society was losely governed by custom. There was no written law. Absence of law was a great hindrance to the establishment of a progressive and stable society. The Charter was removing this imbalance. "Whenever men group together and approve of a given standard morality, they must speak finally in terms of a law. Law permits morality to grow and as it grows the standard of law is elevated and morality is further advanced, for the two have reciprocal influence".

In this case, although hostilities had not started, war had been declared and arrangements had to be made to face the enemy. Allah had also Commanded.

> "O ye who believe! Take your precautions, then advance the proven ones, or advance all together". 4:71

It is beyond doubt that the document was promulgated to bring into existence the State of Medina so that it could be defended against the impending attack by the Quraysh of Mecca. Discussion leading to the declaration of its contents, if any, are conspicuously absent from both the *Seerah* and *Hadith* literature.

Totally Authentic : Its authenticity is, however, above doubt of any kind. It cannot be a spurious document. Once Islam and the Muslims had emerged as victorious, not only within Arabia, but had also liquidated the two strongest empires of the then civilized world, there was no need for them to concoct a document of the early period when Muslims were very few and not very strong. In actual fact once they stepped out of Arabia, they paid no particular attention to it. It is genuine both from external evidence and from the inner evidence of its contents. The idea that it is the sum total of a number of agreements arrived at on a number of occasions is so illogical that it should be ignored completely. As is well known, the events which took place after the promulgation of the Charter, developed with such rapidity, and in such an unforeseen manner that a situation had arisen where there was no need of fresh terms being issued, or new agreements gone into with any party.

The idea that the document in its present shape is the result of numerous agreements is the result of the basic misconception, that it was an agreement. One may ask "agreement between whom, because the document was being issued with the heading "From Muhammad, The Prophet of Allah." Its contents were Legal Orders and not paragraphs of an agreement. A charter from some one in Power can be amended or additions made to it by the authority issuing the original charter. From Badr onwards the Prophet (PBUH) did not have to issue new instructions to any one in Yathrib. The Jews were getting weaker every day and signs of rebellion on their part had developed immediately after Badr. They had not "followed the believers and not fought along with them." They had not, therefore, qualified for any of the concessions granted to them through the Charter. If anything, any fresh document, would have curtailed concessions granted to them from the incidence of rebellious behaviour of the Jewish tribe, Banu Qainuqua, immediately after Badr, the Jews were not in a position to request for a reappraisal of their relations with the ruling party.

The arrival of ultimatum from the Quraysh of Mecca was a serious affair. They were a powerful tribe and had the influence which leaders of thought possess in a society. They exercised the sole authority of laying down the religious ceremonies and the Arab Way of Life. They held the monopoly of carrier trade between southern Arabia and the flourishing market of Middle East, and were very rich as Compared to the rest of Arabia. An attack by them, against Yathrib, would wipe out this small agricultural town of Najd. War in any case, "is not a pass time. It is a serious means for a serious object". The Meccan object was very serious. Muhammad (PBUH) had "mocked their Way of Life," and taken refuge in Yathrib. To save their Way of Life they had to destroy him completely. They had awoken to the danger from the time of the second Bayah of Aqba. As already mentioned when some of the Companions started migrating to Yathrib they, "assembled in their council chamber, the house of Qusayy bin Kilab, where all their important business was conducted, to take council what they should do in regard to the Prophet (PBUH), for they were now in fear of him." It was suggested that "they should put him in irons behind bars." This was objected "on the ground that news would leak out that he was imprisoned, and immediately his followers would attack and snatch him away: then their numbers would so grow that they would destroy the authority of the Quraysh altogether".

After some further discussion Abu Jehl came out with a new plan. This was "that each clan should provide a young, powerful, well born, aristocratic warrior ; that each of these should be provided with a sharp sword; then that each of them should strike at him and kill him. The Banu Abdu Manaf could not fight them all and would have to accept money which they would all contribute". Having failed to kill him they were not able to liquidate Islam in Mecca. They could not, however, let it prosper in Yathrib. They were afraid, as they said, that "Their numbers would so grow that they would destroy the authority of Quraysh altogether". They decided not to permit their numbers to grow and decided to act quickly. They knew of the disappointment of Abdullah bin Ubay. His people had made a sort of jewelled diadem to crown him and make him their king, when Allah sent His Prophet (PBUH) to them; so when his people forsook him in favour of Islam he was filled with enmity realizing, that the Prophet (PBUH) had deprived him of his kingship. However, when he realised, that his people were determined to go over to Islam, he went too, but unwillingly, retaining his enmity and dissimulating".

Declaration of War : The Quraysh sent a letter to the people of Yathrib, but addressing it to Abdullah bin Ubay. The letter was, in fact, a declaration of war. It said, "you have given protection with you, to our men. You should kill these people or turn them out of Yathrib. We swear by Allah, that if you do not do that, we will all attack you and having destroyed you, will capture your womenfolk". This was a very good excuse for him to use force and turn the

Prophet (PBUH) and his *Muhajir* Companions from Yathrib. He was the head of a very powerful tribe, which appears to have been numerically stronger than others. Its members were alive to the needs of religious revival. Out of twelve leaders chosen to look after the affairs of Muslims of Yathrib, nine belonged to his tribe. He decided to use force if the occasion demanded to kill the Prophet (PBUH) and the few Muhajir Companions.

The Prophet (PBUH) heard of his decision and went to him. Very little of the conversation between them is recorded. Abdullah bin Ubay was confronted with a new reality. Islam, although a religion of peace, denoted complete submission to the Will of Allah. It meant the acceptance of the Sovereignty of Allah which in practical life was demonstrated by obeying the Laws of Allah. This is what is meant by:

> "I created the Jinn and humankind only that they might worship me". 51:56
>
> And one of the Commands of Allah is that He has Ordained righting for the believers.
>
> "Warfare is ordained for you". 2:216

The occasion for which this Commandment has been primarily Ordained is when some other group fights against you. It says:

> "Fight in the Way of Allah against those who fight against you, but begin not hostilities". 2:190

It has to be remembered that this *Ummah* is One:

> "Verily this Ummah of yours is One Ummah". 23:52

The Prophet (PBUH) brought home to Abdullah bin Ubay in these words:

> Do you realise that if you use force the Muslims from Yathrib will fight alongside the *Muhajir* Muslims and you will be shedding blood of your tribe on both sides.

He realised the mistake he was making and decided not to use force against the Prophet (PBUH) and his companions. His change of attitude was the result of his fear of being defeated at the hands of determined fighters. History is replete with instances, where people have had recourse to peace for fear of being hurt, in the end. The philosophy of Ahimsa—non violence—is also the product of such logic, because the same people believe in Kali Devi, the goddess, which quenches its thrust from blood of gory murders. Peace accepted by him was of this kind. When we could not use force he resorted to mischief and remained a hypocrite and a tool of the Jews until his death.

History books are silent on further details of the conversations, that took place between the Prophet (PBUH) and Abdullah bin Ubay, it would be correct to assume that the latter must have asked the Prophet (PBUH) the way Yathrib was to be defended against the Meccans. The details of the Charter lead us to the conclusion that the Prophet (PBUH) must have replied that the Muslims would defend Yathrib and if the others would like to share that responsibility the believers would permit them to join in this great honour. It could also be said that, as a result of the urgent need to defend Yathrib, the Prophet (PBUH) formulated the plan of establishing the state of Yathrib, giving it a Constitution, and laying down the responsibility of defence on believers. Abdullah bin Ubay could not help accepting this plan. The next event mentioned in history books is the Constitutional Charter itself.

Shadow of War : The Charter was dictated under the shadow of an impending war of extreme intensity. Its defence paragraphs must belong to the same period. The concessions granted to the Jews are linked with defence paragraphs and must belong to the same period. The paragraphs covering general administration were also the demand of the time. There are no further events in the history of Yathrib, which could have resulted in the issue of further documents. The division of the document of Professor Sergeant in A, B, X, Y, etc, amounting to eight different documents can certainly be called a futile effort, made merely to create doubts and with no fruitful object. The war that was visualised when dictating this document lasted for nine years and had, before ending, embroiled the largest Empire of that period in it, thus initiating the longest war of history—The war between the Crescent and Cross—which is raging even today, fourteen centuries after the Charter came into force, and is no where near its end as yet. Islam until then had laid greater stress on the building of character of individuals.

The Charter ushered in the collective life of the *Ummah.* The principle that Muslims formed a nation by themselves even when they lived in surroundings, which were not purely Islamic, was given prominence by the Charter. The contents of the Charter make it clear that even when living as a numerical minority, believers take over the administration of the society on condition, that the principle of the Sovereignty of Allah is being acted upon. As mentioned earlier, as far as details are concerned, when dictating the Charter, greater emphasis has been paid to matters relating to the defence of the state, than to other matters.

The Prophet (PBUH) as a result of the wisdom and insight granted to him by Allah, kept his mind centered on the period after the war, when need would arise for rehabilitation of people. In the words of a modern military thinker, "The true national objective in war lies in the 'after war'. If the civilized world is to be saved from collapse, there is urgent need to produce true grand strategists to replace the blind exponents of mass destruction". He argues that "If you concentrate exclusively on victory, with no thought for the after effect, you may be too exhausted to be profited by the peace, while it is certain that the peace will be a bad one, containing the germs of another war". The author is speaking from experience of two World Wars. Britain won both of them but lost the peace that followed.

The experience of modern world over the last two centuries has shown that the war to end war has yet to be fought, unless laws of war laid down by Allah are observed in total. The war that was initiated by the Quraysh of Mecca and won by the Prophet (PBUH) ended, as far Arabia was concerned, because the Prophet (PBUH) keeping the after-war period in view had done nothing, during and at the end of war, which could keep alive the hatred generated by war. Modern wars have tended to increase hatred to a point, when, a rapprochement becomes impossible. We need, therefore, to study his life, his teachings, his foreign policy and the manner in which he fought his war and then magnanimously pardoned his enemies. It will show a pattern of human behaviour unparalleled in the annals of human history.

The Prophet (PBUH) had accepted the responsibility of defending Yathrib against the threatened attack, when Yathrib had yet no state, no government and no army. He and his Companions were the total force available for this onerous task. There were no armaments, no provisions, no transport animals and no finances to provide all these instruments of war. He had, however, men, who were prepared to lay down their lives in the Path of Allah. He had trained them to such unchartered heights of Belief in Allah, that no weapon could force them to abandon their positions.

He also knew his enemies. They were resourceful. They were rich merchants and could furnish their army with the most sophisticated weapons. They also had the means to last them during a long drawn war. They had friends among Arab tribes.

They could, as a result widen the zone of war and have him surrounded and they had the means and facilities to make the blockade permanent, but his Belief in Allah outweighed those considerations. It is true that "once war begins, no one can tell how it will go. There are some who urge, that we should abolish all armaments, and refuse to fight on any pretext. If this view is put forward on religious grounds, I will not deal with it beyond saying, that it does not seem to me in accordance with the Bible... If on the other hand its advocates believe that it would make for peace, it is inconsistent with recent events. China offered little or no resistance to Japan, yet that did not save her from the loss of territories as large as Europe, and the slaughter of some thousands of her citizens" .

The position of believers, at the time of declaration of war by Mecca, was far more precarious than any community of peaceful and peace-loving people, who are threatened by a neighbour, who does not approve of their Ideology and their Way of Life. The enemy was the same, who had persecuted them in Mecca, ignoring relation of blood and friendship. A small number, a little over seventy had migrated to Habsha, and now less than fifty males had reached Yathrib and found a place, where they hoped to live according to Allah's given Way of Life, and they were being threatened with war and possible extermination. They had no alterative but to accept war. If they decided to avoid war, where could they go. They would have become stateless. The result would have been that the Islamic Society, which was visualised by the Prophet (PBUH) as a result of Revelations to him, from Allah, would not have been possible to be established. Allah's Promise was, that they would be uppermost if they were believers, was enough for them:

> "It is a promise from Allah in truth; and who can be more truthful than Allah in utterance"? 4:122

And:

> "(It is) a Promise of Allah. Allah faileth not His Promise". 39:20

And Allah has promised that:

> "Faint not nor grieve, for ye will overcome them if ye are (indeed) believers". 3:139

> "And verily Our word went forth of old unto Our bondmen sent (to warn) that they verily would be helped, And that Our host, they verily would be the victors". 37:171-173

They were indeed believers in its fullest meaning. No group of any *Ummah,* of days gone by, had reached heights, of belief in Allah, which they had proved to have reached, and were yet to prove on many an occasion.

Not in Vacuum : Documents of this nature are not issued in a vacuum. There is always a background and a pressing need for them. In fact, pressing necessity, for the execution and enforcement of such documents alone made them acceptable to people. Such documents, whether they are named as agreements, treaties, charters or constitutions, are promulgated because the very existence of those societies depends on bringing into existence means of laying down the pattern of communal life, and such documents provide and guarantee a disciplined life of the-community. Apart from rights and duties of individuals and groups such documents lay down restrictions and penalties for the breach of rules of conduct, expected of those for whose guidance they are issued. Preparations to meet the threat of war are taken in hand, when the danger is real and the entire society recognises it. War cannot be taken lightly because it "is a social phenomenon too complex to be governed by any simple formula".

Except the Prophet (PBUH) himself no one was either qualified nor was there anybody who had the moral strength to accept the responsibility of making the decision to defend Yathrib or when the decision had been taken to take defensive preparations in hand and then conduct the war.

To accept the duty of defending a state and its people is a decision of great moral character. An ill prepared nation is in serious danger of losing its war. To lose a war means to surrender the "right of freedom of thought" and to lose freedom of thought means to lose the right to live according to one's chosen Way of Life, which includes one's mode of worship. The Muslims could not afford to lose the war. They had chosen the Islamic Way of Life of their free will. It was being challenged by the people, who had persecuted them for nearly thirteen years. They were determined, that if they could not win the war they would fight to the last man. The battles fought by the believers for the defence of Yathrib were all fought with the determination, that they would fight until each one of them had achieved Shahadah. The Prophet (PBUH) had trained his Companions to wish for Shahadah, and he was certain, that they will come up to his expectations. His historic words, just before the attack of Meccan Army started at the battlefield of Badr are a testimony of the believers having absorbed this philosophy. He had said:

> O Lord!
>
> If this little band of believers
>
> Is wiped out today
>
> There shall be none left
>
> To obey your Commandments
>
> Until the Day of Judgement.

There had been wars before and there were to be wars in future as well, but this war was different both in conception and the manner in which it was expected to terminate. Both sides were fighting to defend their respective Way of Life. It could end in not only the defeat of one army or the nation it belonged to, but it was to end with the end of the Way of Life to which the loser belonged. It was a war aimed at the extermination of the Muslim's Ideology and Way of Life. The idea, that all wars are fought for differences, which can be solved peacefully, does not appear to be applicable to this war. Normally it can be said that, "Just how senseless and futile an expedient it really is, can usually best be judged by those who lose rather than by those who have won". In this case it was not applicable because the losers were to forego the freedom of living in accordance with their chosen Way of Life.

Sovereignty of Allah : This document had been dictated keeping in mind this Philosophy of War, that to remain a believer in Allah was only possible when Sovereignty of Allah could be proclaimed and life was led in accordance with His Commandments. To achieve that it was essential, that land occupied by believers had to be defended to the last. It was, therefore, necessary, that Yathrib had its Basic Law—its Constitution—promulgated in a manner that its defence preparations could be taken in hand legally and constitutionally. Hence the correct heading of the document can be "The Constitutional Charter of Yathrib... Medina".

It was not an agreement with the Jews as Allama Shibli Nomani calls it. He says "The Prophet (PBUH) sent for *Ansars* and Jews and dictated an agreement which was accepted by both parties". Another eminent writer Jalal-ud-Din Jaffery writes, "When the Prophet (PBUH) arrived in Medina, he had an agreement written between the *Ansars* and the Jews". Naeem Siddiqui, the only one out of all Urdu writers, has shown a different approach to the problem. He writes, "The Prophet (PBUH) created an organization for the arming of the State of Medina, through which he integrated the Muslims, the Jews and the unbelievers, into a new society. He had a written document of the nature of an agreement, prepared. The nature of this document was of a proper constitution and it can be correctly called as the first written constitution".

Nearly all writers of *Seerah* in Urdu have called the "Charter" as an "Agreement," between either the Prophet (PBUH) and the Jews, or between the believers and the Jews. An eminent learned man like Syed Abul Hassan Nadvi has termed it as an agreement of peace with the Jews. Having correctly said that, "The Prophet (PBUH) on this occasion gave a writing to the *Muhajirs* and *Ansars,* "he adds "which contained an agreement of peace with the Jews". Another eminent historian writes, "On arrival at Medina, the Prophet (PBUH) during the very first year of Hijrah considered it appropriate to execute an agreement with all nationalities on the principle of internationalism so that a national solidarity should continue in spite of the ethnic and religious differences". Khalid Alvi, referring to the Jews writes, "He (the Prophet (PBUH) made an agreement with them".

It could be that the word agreement has crept in because of absence of a proper equivalent of the term "Charter," in Urdu. The mistake dates back to Ibne Hisham, due to absence of a technical term for "Charter" in that age. He has used the word *Aahadahum* which has been translated as "covenant." The sentence as a result reads " the covenant between the Muslims and the Medinians and with the Jews".

Muslim and non-Muslim writers of *Seerah* in English, who belong to the present age, have also relied on Ibne-Ishaq, in more or less the same manner as Urdu writers. Abu Bakr Sirajuddin (Martin Ling) who has written with great devotion says, "and the prophet (PBUH) now made a covenant of mutual obligations between his followers and the Jews of the Oasis".

A non-Muslim writer of Pakistan origin says that before the signing of the agreement a thorough exchange of views had taken place. This may be correct, but no work of early period seems to mention a thorough exchange of views. He writes, "After a thorough exchange of views, an agreement was reached and was reduced to writing".

Muir while translating the document uses the words "Charter of Muhammad the Prophet" instead of "Charter from Muhammad," but in introducing it writes, "It was natural that Muhammad, holding these sentiments should desire to enter into a close and binding union with the Jews, and this he did in a formal manner shortly after reaching Medina. He associated them with himself by a treaty of mutual obligation drawn up in writing,...".

The Distinction : The difference between an agreement and a Charter is very vast. An agreement is between two equals and a Charter is given from one to others. An agreement can be rescinded by either party. A Charter can be altered, amended or cancelled only by the authority which promulgated it. Apart from the heading given to the document its contents alone can guide later researchers to give their verdict on it, whether it was a treaty, an agreement or a Charter.

Treaties are between states and usually the heading says so. For instance, "Security Treaty between Australia, New Zealand and United States of America". Similarly Pacts are between independent sovereign states. For instance, "Pact of Mutual Cooperation (CENTO)" was signed between a number of states including Pakistan, Turkey and Iran. Recently a new name for mutual treaties has appeared. This is called a "Convention." For instance, "Convention regarding the Regime of the Straits".

Let us, once again, look at Meethaq-e-Medina in a little greater detail, particularly its heading. It says:

> "This document (writing) is from Muhammad, The Prophet of Allah (PBUH.)."

It is clear that it is neither an agreement nor a treaty because it is not between Muhammad (PBUH) and some others. It is from him and he is the Prophet (PBUH) of Allah. Those receiving the document are being told that the person issuing this document is doing so in his capacity as the Prophet of Allah. Then it goes on to say that it is being given "To Quraysh and Yathribite believers."

Believers whether from Mecca or from Yathrib were all his followers known as his Companions. No group of people in the history of mankind have shown their devotion to their leader as was shown by his Companions to Muhammad (PBUH) the Prophet of Allah. When marching out to the battlefield of Badr, the leader of Ansars of Yathrib, Saad bin Muadh said, "We believe in you, we declare your truth, and we witness, that what you have brought is truth, and we have given you our word and agreement to hear and to obey; so go forth where you wish, we are with you; and by Allah, if you were to ask us to cross the sea and you plunged into it, we would plunge into it with you; not a man would stay behind. We do not dislike the idea of meeting your enemy tomorrow. We are experienced in war, trustworthy in combat."

Whatever else description or name may be given to this document it cannot be called an agreement between the Prophet (PBUH) and his followers. It was being given by him to them and they were all included in it, both the *Muhajirs* from Mecca and the *Ansars* of Yathrib.

There were others as well. They were:

"those who will follow them and fight alongside them."

It would be applicable to others as well, provided these others followed the lead of his followers, the believers, from Mecca and Yathrib. Apart from following the believers they had to take part in fighting alongside the believers to qualify themselves as recipients of this august document.

This heading ends with a brief last remark, "They will form *One Ummah* to the exclusion of others." It means that if the others qualified as recipients of the document, then they and the believers, the Companions of the Last Prophet of Allah, will form an Ummah, apart from the rest of humanity. It was a great honour, that was being bestowed on them, but the price was also very high. They had to accept the believers as their leaders and continue to follow them by joining in war with them against their enemies.

Thus the document was primarily issued as the Basic or Fundamental Law, The Constitution of Yathrib, so that defence arrangements could be taken in hand, on behalf of the entire population. The believers, being the group which had sworn allegiance to him as a result of the *Bayah* formed the manpower of his army. The march to the battlefield of Badr proved this fact. None others were prepared to sacrifice themselves for a cause, in which they did not believe.

Next Charter

History has recorded one more Charter given by the head of a state. This was King John of England. This Charter, however, was taken by force by the barons of the realm, because, "King John was very unwilling to grant it. This was on the 15th of June 1215 A.C., that the Great Charter was sealed with the king's great seal. He agreed that 24 barons shall be appointed to see that he kept the promises which it contained. He agreed only because he was compelled.... He never meant to keep the promises that it contained, and he did not keep them. He sent to France for soldiers and when they came he made war on his own people. He asked his friend the Pope for help and the Pope helped him by ex-communicating all barons, by London under Interdict, and by telling John that he had no need to keep his promises". The surprising part of the whole story is, that, there was not much in the Charter, which an honest ruler of an average society need to have objected to.

It may seem strange that the Pope of all the people, should have advised a Christian ruler to go back on his promises. It was, however, not the first time, nor the last time, that the head of Church had advised a prince to go back on his promises. In one case, "the Pope, who PBUH his plans being nullified, by this (peace treaty) initiated the Magyars to break the peace; oaths sworn to infidels not being binding".

The Charter given at Yathrib was in the spirit of Islam, the New Way of Life. It had to be in accordance with all ethical, moral and legal principles laid down by Allah, for believers in Him and His Prophet (PBUH). The time of its issue was the most critical period in the history of Islam—a time when the threat against Islam and Muslims was the greatest. This fact must be kept in mind while studying the Clauses of the Charter.

The position in which the Muslims were placed at this time has been misrepresented by some Western writers. Preparations for defence of Yathrib have been interpreted as aggressive designs against the Meccans. A well known British historian writes that "Muhammad had now, as it were, thrown down the gauntlet, which the Meccans could not but pick it up. He had effectively challenged them to a full scale trial of strength". It appears that after writing a few more sentences he remembered that it was the Meccans who had declared war. He adds; "The Meccan belief Muhammad would avoid them rested on a misappraisal of the relative strength and fighting qualities of the two parties". He has avoided to give the source on which he has based the superior strength of the Muslim Army.

General Directions

Clause 6.

> "All parties will redeem their prisoners with kindness and justice according to practice among believers".

We have already looked at this Clause under Laws pertaining to defence matters. It would not be out of place to examine it under Laws or Directions of general nature. The matter deals with humane treatment of members of the Armed Forces. It would, therefore, clarify matters, if it was examined from the point of view of the individual in a Muslim society.

Islam, complete submission to the Will of Most Kind and Benevolent Allah, enjoins kindness amongst its members and expects mutual help and consideration between groups, which comprise the *Ummah.* When war takes place through the invasion of any part of the *Ummah, Jihad* becomes a Duty of all groups:

> "Warfare is ordained for you, though it is hateful unto you". 2:216

Even when the persecuted happen to be unbelievers Allah expects, that believers in His Benevolent Sovereignty, must go to their help:

> "How should ye not fight for the cause of Allah and of the feeble among men and of women and the children who are crying: Our Lord! Bring us forth from out this town of which the people are oppressors! Oh give us from Thy presence some protecting friend". 4:75

When war takes place, some achieve the highest honour of becoming martyrs, some get wounded and there is a possibility that some may be taken prisoners by the enemy. They had gone to war for the common cause of the *Ummah.* Therefore, it is the collective duty of the *Ummah,* that these prisoners are redeemed with Islamic kindness, which means, as early as possible and without any thought of how high the cost may be. Until the advent of Islam, and particularly until this Constitutional Charter was dictated by the Prophet (PBUH) of Islam, the redeeming of prisoners was not a statuary obligation in any known law of either any civilised society or of barbarians. In it the believers were ordered to redeem their prisoners with kindness and justice, which is the hall mark of believers. The others, which meant the Jews and idolators, were given a chance to live under the guidance of believers and to fight alongside them, in the Path of Allah. If they availed of this option, they were expected to show the same kindness to their brothers and to come up to the same standard of justice, which was common among the believers. They were, therefore, bound by law to redeem their prisoners, under this Clause. If this is the standard expected of allies of a Muslim state, it would be correct to assume, that a, "Muslim state has of necessity to be a welfare state .... particularly with reference to economic justice."

Man seems to have had a rebellious trait, developed in him, as a result of the persuasions of Satan, which he, at times, is unable to control. Prophets sent by Allah have tried and have achieved varying results, but those who are disposed to rebellion, have reverted to the path of selfish and shortsighted policies. These rebellious elements, who on most occasions are only a small minority, create enough mischief to upset the general peace of society. Men of influence in all denominations have warned mankind of the dangers hidden in following the path of mischief with different results. A modern writer has sounded warning of the same nature by saying, "I feel sure that man faces the worst half millennium in his terrifying history. For man, today, must quickly learn who and what he is and how he is governed in nature, or else bring upon himself wars rebellions." Another writer has warned that science has, so far, failed to give directions, leading to peaceful communal life, "The tragedy of our times is that the science of destruction has run amuck. And the problem is how to synchronize the science of life with the science of death."

The Prophet (PBUH) was teaching mankind the way to a communal life of peace, love and justice. He knew that mankind would not give up war unless and until Islam had become the Universal Way of Life. Until then war had to be discouraged, but steps had to be taken that the miseries of war were minimised as much as possible. He was leading mankind to that Way of Life which would eventually lead to the synchronization of the science of life and science of death.

Clause 18.

"The enemies of Jews will not be helped."

We have touched on this question, under Laws governing Jews only. We would like to add a few words here that this neutrality between the enemies of Jews and the state of Yathrib was to be resorted to in case the Jews did not accept the leadership of believers and did not take part in war alongside with them. If, however the Jews followed the believers and fought alongside with them, then, they were to become a part of the *Ummah* and enemies of Jews were to be enemies of believers. In case the Jews did not desire to become a part of the *Ummah* then a neutral position was to be maintained with the enemies of Jews. This appears to be the beginning of Laws of Neutrality. Modern writers call it the theory of "Neutral Law." It has been said that, "Modern theory has paid tribute to the doctrine of neutral law for their contribution to the so-called "modern system of International Law."

This Clause and a few others, establish the fact that this was the first document in the legal history of human efforts in the International Field. It must be remembered that the directions contained in this Charter, under general rules, are meant for the Guidance of entire mankind. Minorities will exist, among all nations, for a long time to come. There must, therefore, by some universal understanding with regard to the treatment to be meted out to minorities. This Charter shows a way towards those basic concessions to be provided to minorities.

Today, fourteen centuries after the dictation of this Charter by an unlettered Prophet of Allah (PBUH), we notice that there are still people in this world who refuse to their minorities the right to exist. This only happens in those countries, where the Sovereignty of Allah is being denied.

Clause 27.

> "If any unbeliever, kills a believer, without good cause, he shall be killed in return, unless the next of kin are satisfied. All believers shall be against such a wrong-doer. No believer, if he believes in Allah and the Last Day, will be allowed to shelter such a man. Who ever shelters such a man, on him will be punishment of Allah on the Day of Judgement."

Law and order had to be maintained in this newly established state. Severest punishment was being declared for breaking a Fundamental Law of the land. Believers were the party, which was running the state as the Government Party, which had accepted the responsibility of the defence of the territories of the state of Yathrib. If a member of the ruling party was murdered without good cause it was important that the culprit should be punished. It was, however, laid down that if the next of kin desire to pardon the culprit no punishment will be meted out to him. The society being a mixed society, it was possible that the culprit was a close relative or a friend of one of the believers.

The state was new and young. It did not have time to lay down procedures of litigation. In any case this Charter was the Fundamental Law and procedural rules are not included in such documents. Hence no punishment was specified for this crime.

Clause 28.

> "When you differ on anything the matter shall be referred to Allah and Muhammad (PBUH)".

The point to note is that in *multi-Ummah* society the highest authority to arbitrate is being named Allah and His Prophet Muhammad (PBUH). The Jews were to remain as Jews and the *Mushrikeen,* though not specifically mentioned, were to continue in their belief as before. In spite of it Allah was being accepted the final authority, which meant that His Laws as conveyed to them by Muhammad (PBUH) was being accepted as the Law of the Land. It speaks volumes about the manner in which the Prophet (PBUH) and his few Companions must have conducted themselves, during the very short time, that they had been living among Yathribites since Hijrah. The conduct of *Ansar* Muslims, who had invited the Prophet (PBUH) and the change brought in their conduct and character since becoming Muslims, must have had a tremendous influence on the others. The spread of Islam in Indonesia and various parts of Africa has been the result of similar influence of Muslims penetrating into the interior.

This Clause leads to the conclusion that the Prophet (PBUH) was able to impress on Yathribite non-Muslims, that what was being revealed to him, was from Allah and in exactly the same manner as had been revealed before him to other Prophets like

Ibrahim and Moosa. In other words, they had accepted Sovereignty of Allah to be exercised through him.

This meant that Laws of Islam were to be the Law of the state of Yathrib, and all customs and traditions in operation were to become ineffective and illegal, if they contravened any Laws Revealed to Muhammad (PBUH).

The final authority in a state, whether it is a monarch or a house of representatives is the authority which has the right and prerogative to make law. Hence it is called the sovereign authority. Acceptance of Laws Revealed to the Prophet (PBUH) by Allah, amounted to the acceptance of Sovereignty of Allah in practice, but without acknowledging it in verbally.

Clause 32.

"Loyalty gives protection against treachery."

The declaration of war by the Quraysh of Mecca had made it essential, that every body should be warned against treachery at this time of grave danger to the entire population of Yathrib. We have dealt with this Clause under Laws pertaining to Defence, but, being a Law of general nature affecting the very existence of the realm and of such a nature that it will affect Muslim countries for ever it must be studied in greater detail keeping in view conditions faced by Muslim *Ummah* today and are likely to continue to affect for a considerable period in the near future.

The greatest danger to Muslim lands from treacherous activities is from the followers of pseudo-prophets, produced by European influence, during the nineteenth century. The followers of these new religions claim to be Muslims, while holding beliefs contrary to Islam. These non-Muslims going about with Muslim names and observing some of the practices of Islam will act as secret agents on behalf of foreign powers. They will play the part of Kaab-bin-Ashraf and Abdullah bin Ubay without a moments hesitation.

It so happens that these non-Muslims, happen to be nationals of a number of Muslim countries, which, until some years ago, happened to be British colonies. The governments of these countries have to be vigilant. They must pay special attention to the security of their plans particularly in matters of defence. They have been directed not to employ such people in appointments of trust. Allah has Ordained:

"Do not take in trust accept yourselves." 3:118

The military position of Yathrib, as compared to Mecca was even worse than a small Muslim country of today, when compared to one of the super powers. The effort to defend against Mecca could not be given up. The consequences of defeat could not be imagined. It meant complete annihilation. Consideration of terms for existence at the end of an unsuccessful battle was out of question. It is an old axiom that, "Similarity between opponents creates laws of warfare, while dissimilarity leads to unlimited or absolute warfare," which in the sixth century meant complete annihilation. Normal rules of warfare are not observed, where the weaker side is so weak that it cannot proclaim its opposition openly. The Prophet (PBUH) had decided that Yathrib should have no weak spot on the home front. Only then could he hope to face the enemy with all available strength.

Loyalty is a quality which has in itself the quality to furnish defence against treachery. None dare accuse a loyal person of a crime connected with or the result of treachery. The loyalty of Companions of the Prophet (PBUH) was above suspicion. It was this loyalty of theirs, which kept the internal cohesion of Yathrib intact. The first successor of the Prophet (PBUH), Abu Bakr was known for his loyalty to the Prophet. It has been said that, "The secret of Abu Bakr's strength was his faith in Muhammad (PBUH) Abu Bakr had no thought of self aggrandisement.

Endowed with sovereign and absolute power, he used it simply for the interest of Islam and the people's good. He was too shrewd to be himself deceived, and too honest to himself to act the part of a deceiver. To the last moment of his life he had the betterment, contentment and freedom of the population, uppermost in his mind, who had entrusted themselves into his hands. His will was symbolic of the manner he looked at his responsibilities. "To him who shall succeed, give it as my dying request, that he be kind to the men of this city, which gave a house to us and to the faith. And the Jews and Christians, let him faithfully fulfil the covenant of the Prophet (PBUH) with them." Muir, like other writers, refers to the Charter a covenant. With Companions like Abu Bakr and Umar there could not flourish many disloyal men around.

Clause 33.

> "The freedmen of *Thaalba* will be afforded the same status as *Thaalba* themselves."

This decision was in conformity with the spirit of Islam. Islam encourages people to set free their slaves, so that a free society comes into existence. A slave, is no better than an animal. He has no stakes in the preservation of the society in which he lives. A free citizen of a society of equals does not surrender, because, surrender makes him slave of the victor. Nations who lost their battles two hundred years ago remained slaves for two centuries. Even when they gained political freedom they continued to be economic slaves of the erstwhile masters. They have suffered because their grand parents surrendered to foreigners. This Clause shows the path to equality and freedom of man and was dictated to make certain that those who were freed and were slaves no more should be really free and prove themselves as honourable asset to the society in which they lived.

Clause 36.

> "Anyone who kills another without warning amounts to his slaying himself and his household, unless the killing was done due to a wrong, being done to him."

Murders and killings upset and unbalance the smooth running of a society. Killings without warning possess an element of deceit and treachery, particularly when the killing is not to avenge a wrong already done by the culprit.

The warning, that such a killing amounts on the part of the murderer make to himself liable to killing and other members of his household were appropriate to the times. To avenge one murder, people of that age, were apt to kill entire family of the culprit. Murders are the worst of crimes in any society, and when their numbers increase the sense of security, and living among reliable human beings disappears.

"Clause 41.

"A man will not be made liable for the misdeeds of his ally."

It had been said in Clause 3 and 5 that prisoners will be redeemed with kindness and justice was common among believers. This was a clause which proved, that justice was kept uppermost in the Laws promulgated in a society, led by believers. Clause 34 had referred to alliances but no person could be made responsible for the misdeeds of his ally. This Law appears to be the fore-runner of the following *Ayah* of *Quran:*

"And no burdened soul can bear another's burden".
35:18

The allies of Jews had been given the same status as the Jews themselves, but this could not make them liable for the misdeeds of their allies.

Clause 42.

"Anyone, who is wronged must be helped."

Kindness and justice had been declared as the common practice among believers. The Basic Law being given to believers had to come upto the standard of justice expected of believers. If a wronged person was not aided by the Law itself and law enforcing authorities, in a society composed of believers, then it could be said, that justice was a common practice among believers.

Clause 45.

"A stranger, who has been given protection will be treated as his host, while doing no harm and is not committing any crime."

Protection could be given by any one of the nationals of Yathrib. It was, however, being assured, that the protected will be treated at par with his host. He could not expect a higher reward than the person who gave him protection. It was the right of the host, that his guest received the same treatment, which he was entitled to.

This protection, however, became null and void if he committed a crime. The case of Kaab bin Ashraf should be examined keeping this Clause, as well, in view.

Clause 46.

> "Woman will be given protection only with the consent of her family"

This was a social matter, but if handled carelessly it could develop in a long drawn war. Women are considered a protected trust to be honoured by men of that family or tribe. If a woman is forcibly carried away or given protection against the permission of her family, the act will amount to destroying honour, prestige and respectability of that family and tribe. To avoid any such trouble with the neighbouring tribes, a law was enacted that no one will give protection to a woman, unless the family of that woman had given permission to her to seek protection in Yathrib. Women of all tribes, inside and outside the state of Yathrib, were being given the honour they deserved.

Clause 47.

> "In case of any dispute or controversy, which may result in trouble the matter must be referred to Allah and Muhammad (PBUH). Allah will accept any thing in this document, which is for bringing piety and goodness."

This Clause declares in no uncertain terms, the place where power rested in this newly established state of Yathrib. It means that the Fundamental Law of the land revolved around the belief in the Sovereignty of Allah. This Clause further reiterates this belief. It means that differences and disputes must be resolved in the light of *Shariah.* As *Shariah* is the result of interpretation of revelations from Allah, the decision, therefore, rested with the Prophet (PBUH).

All those present in the assembly were recognizing the Sovereignty of Allah and His Prophet (PBUH) even though they may not have accepted Islam in Total. They were thus, Constitutional Muslims for having accepted the Constitution based on *Shariah*—which gave the last Way of Life—Islam.

Clause 51.

> "Every one, will have his share, in accordance with which party he belongs to."

As it happens in the case of political parties, the individual member, in case he differs with the official views of the party, cannot evade responsibility for the decision of the party. It was the same in tribal system. The views of the individual carried weight until such time as the decision was made. Once the decision had been taken by the tribe or the sub-tribe, all individuals had to abide by it. Their rewards or responsibilities had to be decided in relation to the party, to which the individual belonged.

It was only fair that individual's responsibility should be in accordance with that of his tribe. To avoid future complications, it was best to have the principle accepted and announced through the Charter.

Clause 53.

> "Anyone who acts loyally or otherwise does it for his own good."

People knew of the impending war. They knew, that it would be a fight to the end. If the invasion came all were likely to suffer equally. The Meccans were not likely to show compassion to those, who did not take part in fighting. When a place is destroyed or looted the invader does not look round for those, whom he would like to spare or those who would like to be spared. The decision to follow the leadership of believers was being taken up voluntarily and after consideration of the result of accepting the responsibility or evading it. It was neither a favour nor act of grace towards the believers. Loyalty to this cause, in future, was also to be for their own good.

Clause 54.

> "Allah approves this document."

This Clause has to be viewed keeping the occasion, of the dictation of the document in view. The background, in which the dictation was being made, has been surveyed in earlier pages. The Hijrah, the construction of the mosque, the declaration of war by Mecca, the decision to defend Yathrib, were all incidents connected with the purpose of the dictation of this Constitutional Charter.

The contents of the Charter studied so far have also to be borne in mind. The document opened with the words "From

Muhammad, Prophet of Allah (PBUH)" This was accepted by all those present including the Jews and unbelievers. The superior status of believers had been established. The Sovereignty of Allah and His Prophet had been categorically explained and accepted. In matters of dispute the final arbitrator was to be the Prophet himself. Now finally the seal of Allah's approval was being put on to the document. It was not a part of the *Quran* — not a clear Revelation — but a document issued by Muhammad (PBUH) His Messenger — to which His consent had been obtained, and this Consent of the Almighty was being announced in open Court.

From Hijrah to the dictation of the Charter, the Prophet (PBUH) had given guidance and conveyed his decisions in the light of the Training and Guidance received by him from Allah. He does not appear to have received any clear cut Ordnance from Allah as to the nature of the State and Government of Yathrib. He had to establish the Deen — Way of Life — of Islam, which was based on the full, complete and unadulterated Sovereignty of Allah, but the details of his Constitutional Charter were to be filled in by Muhammad himself. As Hafiz Ghulam Sarwar has said, "Although Muhammad (PBUH) was inspired, as to what Allah wished him to do, the ways and means of carrying out His Message were left to Muhammad (PBUH). This was his part of the work. Allah would show him the path, but Muhammad (PBUH) himself had to walk it."

His was a great responsibility. There was a time, when he did not know, what were the responsibilities of a prophet of Allah. He had been "Quite unaware of the fact that he was to be Commissioned by Allah as the Last of the Prophets. We do not find any hint, direct or indirect, that his mind was preparing blue prints of any religious adventure." We have, therefore, to be content with the exact situation. The document was from him and not a Revelation from Allah, but it had His Approval.

Allah's approval was given, because it was for the good of humanity. It laid down, that matters were to be conducted in accordance with kindness and justice of the highest standard — the standard which had been placed before the best *Ummah* so far created amongst mankind (3:110). It has been unfortunate, in fact a tragedy, that this document has been overlooked by statesmen, both Muslim and non-Muslims, of the past centuries. As a result the world has drifted towards man made totalitarianism, which is the product of human mind in its totality. Its authors have also realised the dangers to which it is leading humanity. "It is only now, when Western humanity is faced with the appalling result of its work of destruction, that it is beginning to realise, what has happened and to look back on the road it has travelled. Yet it has not reached the point of admitting, that this totalitarian state is not the invention of a handful of criminals in the grand style, but its own product, the incalculable consequence of its own positivism, a position void of faith and inimical to metaphysics and religion. It will not yet believe, that it is the incontrollable result of man's loss of faith in the Divine Law, in an Eternal justice," justice which is the main theme of Islam, justice which alone can keep society free from internal intransigence.

Clause 55.

> "This document will not protect anyone, who is unjust or commits a crime."

Defence of the realm is a commendable action. To have joined the defenders of Yathrib and agreed to abide by the contents of this Constitutional document was an honourable undertaking, but it did not give a license to commit injustice or any act contrary to Law. On the contrary it demanded greater care to behave in an honourable manner and administer justice of the standard Commanded by Allah.

The king can commit no crime. It may be justifiable in societies, where the king is the source of Law. In Islam the source and fountain of law is Allah himself. No man, therefore, can be above law and as such membership of this document also carried added responsibilities, but no immunity.

Clause 57.

> "Allah is the protector of the good people and those who fear Allah; and Muhammad (PBUH) is the messenger of Allah."

This is a statement of fact, an annunciation of the after tried and experienced Omnipotent Protection of the Most Merciful Allah. Allah is Good and protects His good servants, who fear Him and abide by His Laws. These Laws have been Revealed by Him to His Prophet and Messenger Muhammad (PBUH).

This document laid the Foundations of Revealed Law of Allah. This document at the same time Commissions Muhammad (PBUH) to interpret, explain, promulgate, administer and live according to the Law of Allah, so that his action can serve as the practical demonstrations of His Law until Time comes to an end.

> "And in the day when the Hour riseth the unrighteous will despair". 30:12

6

Faith as a Force

Shariah: Valuation of Need : The obligation of a believer to the Islamic Law is a derivative of the truism that Islam is a code of life. From another viewpoint, definition of a civilized society, or the social organization of high order, is the prestige accorded to law in it. The Islamic Law can be envisaged to attain a high degree of prestige in society and, hence, can become a factor for its civilization. Unlike the Canon Law which was not intended for the actual organization of society, Islamic Law's orientation is particularly focused upon this objective. The Gospel confirmed the validity of secular principles by its famous allusion to Caesar, the Islamic Scripture extolled the requirement of benefiting from the original sources of law. The religious duty towards the obedience of law plays an important role in establishing the authority of the law and ensuring its observance. A particular type of human undertaking, religious law offers rewards in morality of aspiration and excellence in social life.

Shatibi distinguished between two intentions of the lawgiver: Creational predestined intention in which human will was not assigned any role, and imperative legal intention wherein Divine Will did not impose itself upon human volition. The response to the query, why has the law to have a religious basis, by Fazlur Rahman, was that the concept of Lawgiver denoted an excellence of the knowledge of deducing the conditions of practical intelligibles and of actualizing them in peoples and states. Additionally, the theoretical excellence available in, and the interests of public weal served by, religious law are the other attributes. In the opinion of Ibn Taymiyya, revelation of laws through Prophets was an expression of Divine religious, moral and legal intention or will, and the revelation of laws by instituting them in nature comprised the Divine scheme of physical laws, social habits and human natural instincts and capacities." As an important deduction then, the rules of Shariah should conform to the laws of human nature and social behaviour. This logically leads to the conclusion that for the religion to continue to be a reflection of the real world, the factor of human ingenuity is indispensable. If this perspective is cogently suited to the continuity of the Islamic juristic principle of Ijtihad, then, the critical differentiation between an evolved religion and the religion that is situated at a low rung of evolution is marked by that reflection. With this in view, the long-standing pursuits of the science of law, devoted to discovering the principles of just law for many centuries, are appreciable, so that, such principles conform to the Will of God, to nature and to reason." The fact that such a criteria has already been demonstrated for the Islamic religious law does not represent a simple coincidence. On similar, if not the same, grounds the some what daunting and seemingly unresolvable problems faced by humankind, as a consequence of socio-political complexities in the present age, the adherence to the legal positivism is yielding to the enthusiasm in the revival of natural law.

Religious Law-Advantages : Multiple advantages that accrue from the religious law should emphasize the significance of Islamic legal system. Theoretical excellence as an attribute and the interest of public weal as the accompaniment of the law with religious basis have been already observed. In support of these benefits emanating from religious law, and the fact not well recognized, that Aristotle and Plato formulated actual theories of state and law on the basis of religion, is citable. On other occasions, the search for the maximization of the efficiency of law has pointed to religious and moral codes. In religious laws the association of obligatory aspect of legal rules with feelings of obligation exists, which is not the situation in legislated laws otherwise. And in order to achieve the excellence of respective capabilities among the observers of a law, the assistance of religion is always complementary.

Morality : Religion is incomplete without a moral code and it is a matter of general agreement, but not without contention, that between law and morality, there is a "necessary" connection. Law and morality are not synonymous, and Hart has isolated four features of morality which distinguish it from law, however, according to his concept of law, morality constitutes an indispensable component of necessary and sufficient conditions for the existence of a legal system." The explanation for this connection resides in the commonness of purpose that exists between the two, for proximate nexus of actual human weal is discernible in both instances. On this basis, the viewpoint appears valid that an interaction between the two is recognized, with the implication of effecting the contents mutually. For law to be founded upon a sense of moral obligation, or on the conviction of the moral value of the system, is a matter of general consent, since this proves exclusive of the personal arbitrariness. The superior criteria of legal validity have come to rely upon the scrupulous conformity with justice and substantive moral values. From a practical standpoint, a legal synthesis of law and morality, and such an opportunity is available in religion, is achievable, so that, moral obligations are transformable into positive legal requirements.

Morality and Society : In view of the determinants of the fundamental moral outlook of a society, not unlike those of an individual, and the correlation that exists between law and society in terms of the former being the reflection of its soul, religion occupies a prominent place. Ideals and morality in a society perform a recognized role in the development of law, and religion functions as their rich source. The concept of Islamic morality resides in the upper reaches of human excellence and in the highly dedicatory ideas of duties, such as are epitomized by the religious notions of "inwardness of sin" and "martyrdom," respectively. The subject of justice is universal as a centerpiece of invariably all major legal systems, however, the duty to be just in personal sense is identifiable with sublime moral and religious codes. Similarly, the legal notion of liberty may be enshrined in many a political constitution, but the aspiration to individual freedom is not fully subscribed without the impact of the systematized belief system of an evolved religion. Understandably then the view of "good life" remains essentially incomplete without a moral basis, which is regularly available in an evolved religion. This concept of the morality of *excellence,* translatable in the complete realization of human potentials, as suggested by the Islamic scriptural idea of the "best community," cannot remain without leaving its desirable impact upon the law. It is appropriate to quote a modern legist in this respect: "As sound laws cannot be in contravention of the moral dictates in a social set-up, therefore, the legal validity of laws necessarily requires the criterion of consonance with moral reference and, as its extrapolation, the legal system is in need of conformity with moral precepts being adhered to in society."

Positive Aspects

The aspect of religious obligation to support a "comparable" legal system notwithstanding, various benefits that accrue from the Islamic legal system to the society, underscore the necessity for its institution. The *sine* qua *non* of an authentic political society in the present-day world is the exercise of its own law. Any society which has entertained aspiration in order to make manifest its separate identity as a paradigm of socio-political organization, or even to maintain its independent distinction, for it to lay claim to its legal personality is an indispensable requirement. The set of rights and the legal apparatus for their satisfactory fulfillment, more than the complex of duties, are regarded as a distinctive feature of a society. Within the meanings of Islam being a code of life, religion as the source of Islamic Law, and the latter-day legal concept of fundamental rights, it is apparent that Islam is a "nomocracy" and the "rule of law" is the foremost fundamental right. This legal notion of "rule of law," in the context of Islamic fundamental right, is definable as the political rule in the society according to the requirements of Islamic Law as an antecedent to the securing of public interest from the infringement of political authority, and it is typified in a pivotal Quranic verse. Realization is due to the observation of critical legal significance that the freedom of individual is absolute within the confines of "rule of law."

The Islamic legal system, to apprehend its significance in the organization of a society, or in the political life of a civilization, cannot reliably be introduced without entertaining the vision of the "unity of purpose" as embodied in the Quranic concept of "best community." In this perspective, the legal system cannot remain without undergoing a transformation to become scientific, realistic and ascendant. For the development of the science of law or jurisprudence, rather than allowing the system to simply function as the means of legal dispensation, the retention and enhancement of the capacity for legal adaptability according to the evolved methodology, and devising of juristic means for the system to enter the ranks of major legal systems in the world, are a necessity.

The lessons offered by history are fecund with invaluable instructions concerning the preeminence of Islam in the past, and the role played in it by the legal acumen of Muslim jurists in the framing of legal system. And from a more proximate age, the considerations, in opting for a particular type of legal system by another society, proffer inferences which can find analogous application in the Muslim society. During the eighteenth century, with improvement in colonial living conditions and changes in the economy and political ideas in North America, the need was felt for a more developed law.

The negative orientation towards the viewpoint of Common Law, to have been made by and for a feudal society, underwent change and gradually the law was seen in a different light. To use it as a bulwark to protect civil liberties against royal absolutism was realized, and its utility as a link between all that was English in America, in the face of the menace constituted by Louisiana and French Canada, was recognized. On the other hand, due to the natural orientation toward methods out of favour with colonial jurists, the increasingly popular idea of an autonomous national law was in harmony with the new American political independence. These political determinants, in the wake of lessons furnished by the French Revolution, were to result in the American constitutional document. The distinguishing features of this constitution were the indissoluble association of the idea of liberty with the natural law, and the inclusion of the natural rights of the citizens as the subject of legal guarantees, with the granting of special legal priority to their adjudication.

The present internal as well as external imperatives concerning the security of society, and to repose aspirations in the future, are some of the more important factors that constitute convincing reasons for the adoption of Islamic legal system, especially when viewed in the light of preceding outlines of historical occurrences. In more specific terms, the American constitutional document as the basis of future legal system was adopted primarily due to political considerations, which were the product of concern for the national security, in opposition to natural tendencies. This was notwithstanding of the fact that the political identity of the society remained at the time in want of completion without a distinguishing legal dimension. The subsequent success of the constitutional document is explainable on the basis of the observation regarding the importance of human agency in the building of political institutions, and the selection of a particular system of law then acquires a subsidiary significance.

According to the Marxian theory of dialectical materialism, the material productive forces of society conditions the progress of social, political and spiritual life. The social foundational basis or "infrastructure," according to Marx, was constituted by the material production and, hence, superiority of the principles of political economy was established over those of private law, a view also subscribed by Saint Simon. The material foundation was assigned the role of acting as the determinant of social classes, institutions and political power in the society. The "superstructure" of society, in contrast, comprised of non-material entities and included law as well as religion, and it was viewed to be contingent upon the material production.

Now, on this analogy of economic determinism, Islamic legal system is the foundational entity in the society with a preponderant role over other social entities, including economic production. The Marxist argument, that without control of wealth and the pattern of its distribution, the genuine scope for equality and individual initiative remains extremely limited, is a profound observation, no doubt. However, with the facility of Islamic legal system in a Muslim society, the social benefits and the desirable economic objectives mentioned in the Marxist idea, are significantly enhanced and credibly facilitated in attainment, respectively. The development of fundamental principles relating to economics in primary Islamic source of law carries the potential of providing wide scope to the fulfillment of socio-economic ideals in Islam. The prospects for the formation of original systems, as a consequence of the organization of Islamic Legal System, should be to the equal satisfaction of an ideologue or a jurist, and a reformer or a statesman, for the political rewards of ideological originality are attainable in the form of ascendant social order.

Faith in Practice

The concept of law is not separable from its sound ideological character, for it partially at least is determinant of the world-view and the interrelationship of man with the society in all its important manifestations. The religion is of recognized value in the definition of these parameters and in accordance with this viewpoint, it maintains ideological character. Any law, with its foundations upon religious principles, can be deemed to fulfill these ideological requirements more suitably, and Islamic Law is no exception in this respect. In this view, the law is not just the means of resolving disputes, but it is the proper instrument for creating a distinct society. The primary function of the Marxist Law was not the expression of a certain concept of justice based upon tradition, but the organization of the national economic forces, and the transformation of the behaviour and attitude of its citizens. Antedating the Marxist revolution, the law in the Russian society was not considered to be the basis of social order.

It is an ideological imperative to consider law as the basis of social order and the transformation of society is held to necessitate the change in law. This description of the dynamic nature of the functions of law is eminently suited to the law developed with a religious framework. Islamic Law, with a precedent to its distinction in the past and with an original formulation of a legal methodology for the future, has the capacity for the reconciliation of superior requirements of religious legal doctrines and existential realities to an ascendant outcome. According to the ramifications of the material dialecticism, the infrastructure comprising the means of production, retained a primary significance in relation to law and consequently the Marxist Law maintained an economic pre-occupation, while "bourgeoise" law was viewed to concern itself with order and morality. Now any law in its ideological sense is describable as the means of guiding and transforming a society towards its adopted ideals, but this observation is nowhere more naturally applicable than upon Muslim law in relation to the Islamic ideals. On the other hand, Common Law which has come to establish itself as one of the major law system in the world, in the opinion of C. S. Wade, et al it does not ensure the social and economic well-being of the citizen, nor the effective legal remedies or legal limits upon the legislator's power to infringe upon human rights are secured, and Common Law is subject to modification by the legislature. In comparison, the legal principles available in the original source of Islamic Law are distinctly oriented towards the socio-economic weal of the individual in specific, and the law, as the instrument for the completion of Islamic socio-political ideal of "best community," is legitimately concerned with that well-being of the individual in society, in general. Further, these fundamental Islamic legal principles are deemed immune from legislative modifications under any pretext. And, finally, law is acknowledged to exercise a guiding influence upon the way of thinking in a society, and in conjunction with the historical observation that law is a reflection of a civilization, the Islamic legal system remains an antecedent of Islamic identity of the society.

The philosophy of Islamic Law had the objectives of law as its basic doctrine. This doctrine is a continuation and development of the concept of "Masla" as expounded in pre-Shatibi period. The legal thought in that era centered upon the concept of the unity of Islamic Law, a subject which was, perhaps, the natural consequence of independent schools of law. Aside from being the unity in its origin, the unity of Islamic Law had a more emphatic implication of the unity of the intent of law, whose establishment necessitated the expounding of the doctrine of the end of law to be the good and welfare of human-beings. In the modern legal terminology, the juristic assertion of "law is not what it is, but what it does shifts the emphasis about law from its nature and reallocates it upon the functional results of law. With this in view, then, and an insight into the object of religion as the purpose for its revelation, which is none other than the "falah" or success of mankind, the object of revealed law in Islam is definable as the organization of the "best community," in the language of the Quranic ideal, through comprehensive network of acts, rights and obligations. At this juncture, recognition is due to the fact that a position of fundamental significance is reserved for Islamic Law in the scheme of socio-political order, and this treatise propounds a formulation for the establishment of Islamic legal system as an essential initial measure for the law in the attainment of its objective. In this perspective, a comparison with the objective of Marxist Law is meaningful in the instance of Islamic Law.

Justice : The definition of justice notwithstanding, justice in the Islamic sense is a religious value, that is, a stipulated purpose or aim for the attainment of success ("falah"). A religious value may either function as means or an end itself, on the analogy of the values in the utilitarian concept wherein liberty is considered to function towards the garnering of happiness as an end. In the classification of various values, a hierarchical arrangement appears necessary, for some values function as means to the attainment of higher values which contribute to the ultimate value. In the "attainment system" of Islam, the concept of "success" as an ultimate value at the individual level corresponds to the idea of "best community" at the level of society. Realization is due to the inference that the notion of ultimate value has the important implication of subordination of all other values. The Platonic conception of justice involved the best of abilities in each sphere of life and as a value it was assigned a place at the summit of the moral realm. Hobbes has sought to treat all laws as just by definition, but this view proved untenable in the light of legal empiricism.

Subscription to the view that every legal system represents a set of values which the law comes to reflect, is of assistance in the delineation of certain Islamic values in relation to the concept of justice. The Islamic conception of justice represents a constellation of values and, hence, its description is multifaceted. Justin known in history as the "lawgiver," defined justice as "giving to each man his due," and the referred verses from the Quranic revelation convey the same idea. Moreover, the attainment of equality is treated by the moral and legal philosophers as the vital function of justice. The values reflected from the Quranic verse, dealing with the subject of polygamy, substantiate this particular notion of justice. But, more importantly, the same revealed verse is illustrative of the "equality of treatment for those in the same category according to a classification," and is describable as "result-oriented," in distinction from "process-oriented" type of, equality. This vital Islamic notion of equality is intellectually apprehensible by keeping the comparison between the formal and substantial categories of justice in view. The categorization of justice in its formal and substantial types relies upon the criteria of the existence of rules, their generality and impartial application for the identification of the former type, and the justness of the content of law is the attribute of the latter. This particular concept of equality in practical legal terms is translatable as "equality before law." Application of law in all situations and upon all persons, in present juristic terms, is considered to be the embodiment of justice. On the other hand, equality before law shares several legal features in common with supremacy of law. The last legal value is the practical essence of Islam; it is an evident truth which is as evidently forgotten, and this vital legal notion is conveyed in the revealed verse of central significance that typifies this connotation of Islam, wherein the ruler is directed to uphold the revealed law.

Added features of the legal value of justice are illuminated if viewed in the light of its opposite. Application of a law in want of just content, or the partial application of a law in contrariness to the requirements of its just content, produce the same end-result of legal injustice. Now, as an important issue related to the evaluation of legal history and to the higher consideration of juristic values, imperfect legal development in the constitutional definition of the political authority in Islam, as a result of the misapplication of "just content of the law" in relation to the supremacy of law, is notice worthy. Similarly, misunderstandings regarding the Islamic social values were caused as well as perpetuated due to the omission in the legal application of the provision related to the "equality of treatment" in connection with polygamy, which is an instructive instance of the "misapplication" or "partial application" of the "just content of law." Not without a grave sense of historical irony, it is indicated that, more due to unwillingness for the convenience of social customs than due to inability for the reasons of judicial acumen, the omission in the fine understanding of this value and, hence, in the incorporation of the corresponding interpretation of the legal rule in Islamic Law, not only legitimised but also identified polygamy with the sublime name of Islam. Thus, even for the reasons of the legal values that Islamic Law represents, as exemplified by the value of justice provided in the revealed law, a persuasive viewpoint in support of the development of Islamic legal system is available. And the legal formulation, described in this monograph, outlines an approach towards the attainment of this objective.

Social Functions : Due to the religious origin of Islamic Law, it is viewed as a suitable instrument to regulate the most varied aspects of social relations. In contrast with the law in other societies, it is assigned the primal position in the social order. The conceptual necessities related to Islamic Law allow it to maintain a unity with religion, which affords a delineation of universal principles underlying all the relevant rules. Such principles exercise harmonizing influence upon the legal rules and religious precepts.

Islam is essentially a religion of law and Gibb, the famous orientalist, observed that Islamic Law was the most far-reaching and effective agent in moulding the social order and community life of the Muslim peoples and it held the social fabric of Islam compact and secure through all periods of political fluctuations. And it was further maintained by the same author that the influence of the Islamic Law was felt in almost all aspects of social and economic life. According to Bergstrasser, the Islamic Law is the epitome of true Muslim spirit and the most decisive expression of Islamic thought. The needs of society that Islamic Law tends to satisfy are pointed out by Shatibi in the enumeration of five objectives of its protection: Din, aql, mal, nafs and nasl. In the language of present day knowledge, the protective functions of the law in relation to social needs are translatable as the interests of the Faith, the Quranic attitude of reason and rationality in Islam, economic resourcefulness, social identity, and propagation of civilization. This approach accords a preference to the functions of Islamic Law rather than to its consideration as an entity. For it is only in this way, that the law can genuinely reflect the aspirations of a society.

Special Needs of Society : A society having no fundamental basis or higher ideals is normally caught in a state of flux by being at the demands of mundane motives and exigencies. It tends to ignore the demands of morality and justice and creates mutually contradictory systems which are in need of frequent adjustments and replacements.

This background provides the justification for ideological pursuit and socio-political systems to be based upon compatible ideals.

Without an Islamic Legal System, such an objective of the compatibility of ideals pertaining to various social systems in a Muslim society is unrealizable. Advent of a society founded upon systems with harmonious ideals is then essentially a matter of methodology for the expeditious organization and implementation of a meritorious Islamic Legal System. In the modern nation-states, efforts have been successfully made to organize and reform societies through law, as law is no longer considered simply a means of resolving disputes, but increasingly as the instrument for creating differentiable type of society." The limited perspective notwithstanding, the significance of an Islamic Legal System in the consideration of national security, definable as the capabilities to safeguard the *national sovereignty,* is then obvious.

The *raison detre* of state within the meanings of the universalism of Islam is none other than to provide creative expression to the fundamental principles of Islam, which otherwise would prove elusive. For the principles of Islam as religio-legal paradigms necessitate the framework of political state for their practical expression, which is essentially an explanation of the Divine intent underlying the revelation of law. The Islamic concept of "good life" within an Islamic state structure is epitomized in the symbolic meanings of the Garden, which represents an existence of independence in conformity with sublime principles. The Islamic constitutional theory, to propose the political authority in such setting, will envision the ruler as the custodian of the trust reposed voluntarily by the believers in exchange for the maintenance of the supremacy of the Islamic Law and the safeguarding of the Islamic norms of life. The Islamic legal system, as an indispensable instrument for the promulgation and legal integrity of these principles and a repository of the provisions of the Islamic constitutional theory, serves as the primary guarantee. In this background, the Islamic system of law, necessarily inclusive of its instruments for the impartial adjudication, becomes a political precondition for an Islamic society.

Faith : Societal Role

The implication of the designation, the "code of life," that Islam is characterized with, is the claim to a universal value-system. Such a system should be comprehensive in order to accommodate the attainment of multifarious objectives. Religion and philosophy, according to Boyles, are traditionally considered to be the fountain-head of values, but their shortcoming is reflected from the inability of their proponents in making those values operational. This inability, in specific, resides in the lack of elucidation of means in order to provide political expression to those paradigms, which makes these values meaningless from a practical standpoint. By the same token, it makes the systemic potentialities immanent in an evolved religion, as a reflection of its comprehensiveness in essential values, irrelevant.

The lessons of history in respect of the translation of philosophical theories into ideological systematizations are illuminating. As a proximately allied issue, altering of values in the face of demands made by new realism, such as those emanating from Islamic resurgence, is the restandardization of the acquired and operational values. The extent of this alteration may be of wide scope in which a transformation from fatalism to meritocracy, from asceticism to self-reliance and from mysticism to rationalism are involved. Implicit in the act of choice from among the alternatives is preference, which is contingent upon values. Accordingly, a preference for a legal system will entail the subscription either to tradition, that is, a static situation definable as status quo, or to the essentials of the value-system corresponding to the legal system, that is, an aspiration to improvement, which is expressible as reformation. Now a "consummate value" is so designated because it lays claim to a consensus in preference, and it can also function as a standard for the assessment of all other values in terms of implementation. The Islamic preference of "best community," comprising of human, political and religious excellence, relies upon the value premise of Islamic ascendancy. Without Islamic Legal System, moral and social ideals of Islam, which is essentially a religion of norms, will be de-Islamized due to shift in the emphasis upon value-premises.

Law Supreme

The mandatory nature of the Islamic legal system is a requirement of the Islamic Law, which in the latter day legal parlance is also notable as the rule of law. A matter of remarkable legal history, this "obligation" for the observance of law that exists in Islam is a "supraconstitutional" guarantee provided for the rule of law, which is comprehensible according to the modern terminology of the hierarchical view of law. According to Dicey, a constitutionalist of repute, in Common Law the rights of individuals were secured not by guarantees set down in the formal document, but by the ordinary remedies of private law available against those who unlawfully interfered with his liberty. The law extended protection against the interference of private citizens or officials. The citizens, whose freedoms were infringed thus, did not need to rely upon formal constitutional guarantees before seeking remedies. In this view, Common Law offered a better protection to the citizen than a written constitution and, moreover, these remedies were preserved in the event of suspension of the constitution.

The Islamic obligation to the observance of law is of fundamental value. This Supreme Fundamental Islamic Principle has the following salient features:

(1) Absolute supremacy or predominance of the law as a fundamental Islamic right, whereby the political necessity would not become a justification for a departure from the law.

(2) Equality before the law, as a simple deduction from this fundamental principle, in consonance with the term and obligation of the trust of political rule, should have a vital legal ramification of the power of one man over another not to be substitutive of law.

(3) The political constitution is not the source of this essential Islamic legal principle but its consequence, as the legal validity, in general, of the primary sources of Islamic Law is not dependent upon its constitutional ratification.

(4) The legal principles available from the primary sources of law are extendable to determine the requirements of the political constitution relevant to the powers of state and political authority.

(5) As a derivative of the Islamic legal concept of fundamental right to the rule of law, where such a right is definable is not accessible to abridgement, temporary suspension or abrogation, and the right is availed equally by all, hence, all laws shall advance the welfare of all individuals alike.

(6) The religious law and moral principles are coterminous, with the implication of any legal obligation not existing in the instance of morally condemnable law.

The absolute supremacy of law is an issue intricately related to the possession by the state of coercive powers that may be used to oppress individuals and it presents fundamental problem both for legal and political theory. Since the age of Greek Civilization, law was thought as a means of extending judicious control over governmental powers, and Aristotle upheld the superiority of government by laws as compared with men. In Islam, state or ruler is not of equal rank with the law which exists as a preponderant entity and is not dependent on either for its existence or legal validity. The Islamic conception of the rule of law furnishes a replacement for the constitutional notion of political sovereignty. Legal development, related to this particular area of Islamic Law, is identifiable as the historic factor in the unsatisfactory making of Islamic Constitutional Law and political theory of state and society.

Concurrence with Plato is due in respect of the supremacy of law, that success or failure of a state hinges on this point more than on anything else. The occasion deserves that the eminent Greek thinker should be quoted on this point at some length: "Where the law is subject to some other authority and has none of its own, the collapse of the state, in my view, is not far off; but if law is the master of the government and the government is its slave, then the situation is full of promise and men enjoy all the blessings that the gods shower on a state. As a matter of coincidence, the suitability of this observation is singularly assignable to Islamic Law. The Islamic conception of the rule of law as a broad political doctrine, and the moral contribution towards the role of law, are compromised once the legal prerogatives are made available to the political authority, for then personal arbitrariness becomes inexcludable. As a matter of comparative legal evaluation, the political and economic systems under Islamic set-up exist within the context of Islamic legal system, for the Islamic rule of law also incorporates the political and socio-economic aspects, which provide contrast with other constitutions." The consideration of the afore-outlined essential requirements for the Islamic rule of law in the light of Ihring's famous definition of law—the form of the guarantee of the conditions of the life of society, assured by the state's power of constraint—emphasizes the necessity for Islamic legal system in a Muslim society, provided "the state's power of constraint" is meant as requirements of the Islamic rule of law.

Functioning Side

Ideology and Theory : The substantive issue of the practicability of Islamic legal system entails the consideration for ascendant social order and, as a proximately related issue, the comparability of the envisaged Islamic legal system with the other major legal systems functioning in the world. In Islamic legal theory, revelational precepts determine the philosophical and political outlook. Religion is from among the sources, such as ethics, economics and science, which have served as the determinants of a particular legal theory. Ethical principles were formative in the Kantian legal philosophy, economics was the underpinning in the Marxian legal thought and scientific facts inspired the functional approach of the realist movement. Islamic response to Man's reflection on his position in the universe furnishes the seminal elements of philosophy, and the Islamic ideas entertained on the best form of society nourish the political outlook, in the Islamic legal theory. In the opinion of Friedmann as well, all the systematic thinking about legal theory is linked at one end with philosophy and on the other end with political theory. The preponderating influence of one or the other in a legal theory is its characteristic feature. As can be seen, the reallocation of requisite emphasis in Islamic legal theory will exercise a critical influence upon the envisioned legal system. The ordaining of Islam as the "best community" entails a political outlook that requires for its benefit the comparative evaluation of the political constitutions from the historical past.

Is Islamic Law a Legal System? According to Fuller, law is the enterprise of subjecting human conduct to the governance of rules. Unlike most modern theories of law, this view treats law as the product of a sustained purposive effort. In another view, a law constitutes a system if it satisfied certain requirements of a criterion. The use of a vocabulary to express concepts, the arrangement of rules into categories, techniques for the expression and interpretation of rules are such requirements. But the most important of all these requirements is the linkage of the law to a view of the social order itself, which determines the way in which the law is applied and shapes the very function of the law in that society. In Hart's concept of law, a combination of the union of primary and secondary rules, minimal content of natural law, and four special features of morality constitute a set of necessary and sufficient conditions for the existence of a legal system. The characteristics of a system, Rene David maintains, are the fundamental elements through which the rules to be applied are themselves discovered, interpreted and evaluated. In this perspective, all the outlined legal attributes are demonstrably contained in the Islamic Law to an extent as to be considered a legal system. The view of the universe, man and society, entertained in the original source of Islamic Law, produces a characteristic vision of a social order in which law performs a preeminent role. However, from an internal viewpoint, the antecedents of the Islamic legal system are its comparable attributes with other leading legal systems in the world, and the potential immanent in the legal system to become the instrument of an ascendant society. Confession is due to the fact that these features represent a futuristic view of the legal system, with the inference that such a system does not exist at the present. Therefore, notwithstanding the existence of original sources of Islamic Law, a formulation comprising of legal methodology for the founding and development of futuristic Islamic legal system essentially remains an invaluable quest, which indeed is the onerous task of this discourse.

The issue of the basis of Shariah notwithstanding, as in the opinion of Gibb it is ethical and not legal, the juristic acumen of the Muslim legists will reflect from the legal edifice constructed upon it. Although Shariah is based upon revelation, however, the actual law is not the text of the communication, but it is framed according to the underlying legal values in Shariah. These legal values can be established directly or indirectly from the revealed communication as an indication of acts, rights and obligations of mankind.

The criterion of public interest or "Masla" was emphasized by Shatibi as the objective underlying Shariah and this is a prominent constituent of his legal thought which imparts legal theory the dimension of consideration for society. This view was an indication of significant development in Muslim legal thought and, as its derivative, legal obligation acquired the important new aspect of social obligation as well. An inference became available that, ensuing from the individual contribution towards the common interest, the overall community, as a requirement of the societal obligation, is to pay attention to the weal of individual. Marked material deprivation posing a threat to individual sustenance and survival, so as to become a cause of moral depravity and to result in a possible incitement to theft, does not fall within the Islamic meanings of legal offence. The principle that offers itself for evolvement through the method of induction from the preceding legal situation is none other than the contingencies of legal obligation, so that, the adjunct consideration of social obligation has its dual aspects. The obligation of the society towards the individual is an undeveloped legal concept even in otherwise evolved laws. This particular aspect of social obligation is in need of juristic recognition as a part of public interest. Convenience in the administration of law should not become an impediment in the development of law and dispensation of justice, and not to forget that law itself is a means to social reformation. To say that the socio-political benefits in this legal notion are still vagrant is a testimony to Shatibi's legal genius.

The legal connotation of the principle of "public interest" or "Masla" included its usefulness as a doctrine of adaptability in law, while its revelational justification resided in the injunction concerning with the revealed purpose of Prophethood in Islam, which is none other than the welfare of mankind. In an intimate relationship to the doctrine was the problem of legal change in Shariah. According to its demands, the universal principles functioning as the basis of Shariah, included in the Meccan part of the revelation, and viewed as its objectives, are external to the considerations of adaptability. At the same time, the juristic tradition had established that the more specific and concrete rules of revealed law did not accommodate alterations. However, the vital legal issue of the contradiction between the universal principles and concrete rules arises and, without its satisfactory resolution, the important jurisprudential consideration of the interrelationship of rules related to the uniforrnity of law, as a criterion of a legal system, remains without a legal resolution. The fore-mentioned issue of public interest as the objective of the doctrine of adaptability in Shariah is translatable in the terms of modern knowledge as the needs of social institutions. This interrelationship between Shariah and the social institutions, that can function according to selective conformity, imparts Shariah the possibility of legal continuity, and lasting usage. This responsiveness of Shariah to social change ensures the stability of law and that of the social system, and Shariah furnishes general guidelines in this respect. As its logical deduction, any legal formulation which equips Shariah law with the capability of responding to the emerging needs of social institutions in a far more comprehensive way than Shatibi's conception of Masla, is a proposition for adoption. The realization is due that elaborate conceptions of social and legal systems can be derived from the analysis of Shariah, and this treatise provides the direction.

Valuable Aspects

Rational principles are emphasized in the revelation, particularly in its portion which corresponds with the advent of Islam. Observation made by Robinson is then appreciable that the Quran accords a much larger place to reason than do the sacred books of Judaism and Christianity. On the other hand, reason and law have intimate correlation, to the extent that one has been designated as the life of the other. The common denominator of reason that exists between Islam and law, thus, should provide compatibility and complementarity between the two. There are constant elements in the life of every system, which is a maxim that finds equal pertinence in the instance of Islamic Law. Among these constant elements are ideals which include the rational spirit of Islam. But viewed in the light of history, this particular maxim appears to be less of a poignant fact than a theoretical enunciation. Irrespective of the explanation for this divergence, to quote Gibb provides an insight in this regard: "Islam being an autonomous expression of religious thought and experience, must be viewed in and through itself and its own principles and standards, and that an exposition of Islam should lay more emphasis on its ideals rather than the failings of its followers." The ideal of freedom is evolved from the conviction of monotheism. As its testimonial, notwithstanding that Quran is a code of life, the Scripture omits to provide any guidelines in the event of loss of political independence for believing community. The ideal of "best community" constitutes the purpose and substance of law in its original source of revelation while, for the sake of comparison, the substance of law in other legal systems is based upon the vision of justice and makes its evident impact upon the Common Law and Romano-Germanic families of law.

Availability of legal and moral ideals, fundamental principles and values in the primary sources of Islamic Law, contain a framework sufficient for the development of a self-reliant and ascendant legal system. The giving of institutional form to Islam is an aspiring enterprise whose attainment is an illusion without the instrumentality of legal system. It is obvious, the expression of the source of law into the formal law is an activity dependent upon the techniques of law-making, a fact which is in want of full appreciation due to its conceptual and practical significance, and it substantiates Fuller's definition of law. In legal parlance, the concept of law embodies the will of the sovereign to create conditions of social order and progress among other things, as also the conditions of the individual and social liberties. Aristotle described law as the enactment of the ruling part of the state, while Aquinas viewed it as an ordinance of reason for the common good. Among other definitions of law, "good as defined by reason" by Hooker, "sum total of conditions for the reconcilement of personal wishes" by Kant, "system of rights and obligations as enforced by state" according to Green are noticeworthy.

But some other descriptions like "the definition and limitation of the security and freedom of individuals" in the opinion of Savigny, "rules of action" in the view of Blackstone, "formulated public opinion or that of the ruling body" in the assessment of Holland, "a binding rule of conduct" in the definition by Pollock are illuminating. And yet some more definitions of law such as "set of rules for the conduct of social and political relations" in the words of Holland, "body of principles in the administration of justice" in the judgment of Salmond and "a system of hierarchy of norms as a prescription for necessary outcome in given circumstances" in the analysis of Kelsen are insightful. These varieties of juristic definitions are indicative of the attempts to encompass the concept of law in a befitting manner. The Islamic concept of law is the enactment of the revealed precepts according to the dictates of reason for the "success" of individual in a social setting of "best community". This description of law offers the prospects of overcoming the inconveniences in the way of embodying suitable concept of law, against the preceding perspective and that of the history of legal development.

Overall penal policy of Islamic Law is corrective and reformatory, and less often it is deterrent and retributive. Material compensation, offered to the relations of the deceased in a capital case, is an illustrative instance. An extrapolation of this legal principle of compensation for the loss in Islamic Law brings into limelight the issue at the centre of justice as a legal conception. In no instance of loss the state takes upon itself to duly compensate the aggrieved party. It is within the scope of Islamic jurisprudence to redefine the legal concept of justice within the meanings of the legal axiom of "giving due to the deserving" as exemplified by the cases of violent offences or illicit loss of property. A human issue of moral improvement after the legal penalty engages the intellect, and Islamic jurisprudence, due to its religious origin, has the antecedents for the successful acceptance of such a juristic challenge.

As a distinguishing attribute of Muslim Law, sexual immorality is held in extreme censor and no compensation is available in contrast with capital offences. However, the fact remains, the deterrent penalty is only reserved for criminal sexual offence of public indecency. In this particular legal setting alone, sexual offences are weighed in the scales of justice without compensation. The standard of proof in such an offence is exceptionally high, because no less than four eye-witnesses, adult Muslims of established integrity of character, are a legal prerequisite for establishing the offence. Anyone with a functional knowledge of the subtleties involved in law, will not fail to appreciate the due recognition granted and proper value attached to the legal notions of defamation, human dignity and right to privacy in the particular instance of Islamic laws concerning sexual offences, and the juridical development of the indicated legal notions provides a noticeable source of law in the relevant and allied areas.

Ethical Aspects

Adoption of the definition of law as the prescriptions for the social coexistence of individuals would necessitate common subscription to certain set of values for the code of conduct. And law in order to secure its objectives of maintaining order and justice, and to provide maximum welfare, requires a delicate synthesis of legal and moral principles. A relationship of "existential interdependence" is viewed to exist between law and morals. The Muslim scholar Fazal-ur-Rahman maintained that Avicenna's account of the moral order in the society is based on the conception of the kind of social contract which is operative in it. It then is a matter of inference that the moral order is directly related to the vision of a society it entertains about itself. Law and morals in this sense have come to share the common attribute of normative propositions which refer to standards of conduct. The differentiation between the two is ascertainable, for the morals have the connotation of individual conscience as the underlying principle in their observance, but in distinction with morals, law contains a certain measure for the regularity of its observance.

The search for a standard to provide the means of judging between right and wrong, as a substitute for natural law, led Kant to the identification of "categorical imperative" which was held to contain the absolute rule of morality. Describable as the state of desirable perfection in accordance with rational assessment, the Kantian principle was not considered to be devoid of difficulties in its proof and as an effective test for the actual solution of particular problems. These difficulties in relation to the principle are likely to be observable in association with the "functional view" of law which, in the opinion of Allen, pays less attention to the ethical content and aim of law than the actual sociological circumstances. In this consideration, view about individual as the rational being is superseded with the notion of human being as a component part of totality inspired by a common purpose. However, "interests" were viewed as the chief subject-matter of law by Roscoe Pound whose contribution towards the development of legal institutions cannot be underestimated. In the legal history, accepted morality of the dominant group has been utilized as the standard to conform law on innumerable instances. On the contrary, Islamic Law has the standards available that can best be described as belonging to "high morality." And it is for this simple reason that law in Islamic society is always deemed to be in advance of accepted morality. Islamic code of morality accepts all human beings as entitled to equal consideration and respect. The legal expression of the standard of morality is reflected in a legal system which extends equal treatment to all human beings within its scope, as entitled to the equal protection and obligation in the observance of law. This fundamental right of all human beings, without any exception, to equal consideration of law has constitutional merits whose legal sinews can lend socio-political stability to the society.

The Explanation

In describing eight ways in failing to make law, Fuller mentions that a total failure in anyone of these directions not only results in a defective system of law, but it also results in something that is not properly called a legal system. The failure of congruence between rules as announced and their administration, and the enactment of contradictory rules are two such ways. The implications of the former way are the misinterpretation or misapplication of law. A modality for the evaluation of these faulty implications can be the empirical results of law. As a matter of general acknowledgment, Islamic Law of divorce or repudiation leads to appalling lack of security in marital life. In recent past, an attempt at improved lawmaking in the relevant area was undertaken by the Syrian jurists. In order to discourage a capricious and unjustifiable repudiation of wife, and giving concession to public weal, in the event of repudiation without "reasonable" cause whereby the wife has suffered material damage, the provision in law was made available to demand a compensation from the husband. From the viewpoint of those not acquainted with the subject of law-making, noticeworthy is the making use of the original provisions in the Quran whereby the option of repudiation is to be exercised "with consideration" alongwith the making of a "fair provision" for the spouse so repudiated. The elegance in law-making in this instance is reflected from the contextual reliance upon the original source, non-literal or logical interpretation of law and the proper focus upon the objectives of law. The exercise of "Ijtihad" in comparison with the retention of, and, in this respect, the assimilation of the empirical results of, the traditional Islamic Law, is also evident. In the Tunisian Law of Personal Status 1957, repudiation was declared a judicial process whereby it became devoid of any legal effect if transpired outside the court of law. The reliance was placed upon the authority of the revealed verse wherein the arbitration is advised in case of the surfacing of discord between spouses. The requirement of arbitration was adopted as the basis for judicial evaluation, and discord as a wide-meaning term was specifically interpreted to include repudiation. And, importantly, the parity of legal status was granted to both spouses in the matter of repudiation, and the authority of the revealed verse wherein the equality of "rights" between men and women is stipulated, was relied upon.

Against the afore-outlined perspective, it evokes surprise to consider traditional Islamic Law of repudiation that prevailed over the last many centuries and indeed holds legal sway in the present time in many a Muslim society.

At once an exemplification of misconceptions about, and an instance of erroneous, law-making in Islam, the law of repudiation should serve as a prototypical example for the "reinterpretation" of the original sources of law in Islam. The philosophy of the Islamic Law of repudiation is the availability of divorce in the face of breakdown of marriage. The revealed provisions for the placement of authoritative reliance would include the juristic values of the use of "consideration" in the matter of repudiation, the apportioning of "fair provision" for the female spouse after repudiation, the equality of legal status in the exercise of "right" to repudiation between both the spouses, and the exercise of judicial "arbitration" to attempt reconciliation or, in the event of no other alternative, to impart legal effect to repudiation.

The revealed injunctions concerning the repudiation are thus numerous, and in conjunction with the rules related to the general subject of women, are in consonance with the general objectives of the revealed law for the improvement of women's status. This general objective, effected in the original source of Islamic Law, represents some of the most revolutionary reformation of the Arabian customary law prevalent prior to the advent of Islam.

The Scriptural legal concept of "waiting period" or "idda," after the formal repudiation and before it takes effect, is essentially meant for the purpose of bringing about social justice and reconciliation during the stipulated period. Thus, it is an evidence of the typical misconception that ironically persists concerning the Islamic laws whereby the repudiation of marriage in Islam is held to be of instantaneous effect.

The repeated injunction to "retain wives honourably or release them with kindness," ought to find its practical implementation in the legal corpus. Therein the rules should be designed for women in general, keeping in view their "honour" as spouses, which is surely unattainable without the acquisition of a corresponding or dignifying social status, and the granting of recourse in the attainment of "equal rights" for women, in society.

An intimately related area in Islamic Law, which had proximate bearing upon the subject of "honourable" status, or equality of rights of women in society, is the general perception of polygamy being expressly permitted according to traditional Islamic Law. Now there is nothing more contrary to the readily ascertainable facts than this long-standing misapplication of law, derived from its original source. The unwholesome impact this particular law left upon the status of women in Islamic society, and the misperceptions it created about the Muslim culture in the view of other civilization, were ironically avoidable for being baseless. To leave the issue of "unattainable equality" of treatment for plural wives, according to the revealed injunction, to the conscience of individual husband, without transforming it into legal condition in Islamic Law, was an obvious misinterpretation of the relevant primary source of law. This becomes manifest from the perusal of the revealed verse even to those who are not initiated into the subtle demands of law-making. Islamic Law about polygamy is amply instructive; it is also demonstrative of the continuing force of the customary law. Wise nature reserves ridicule for erring in religious laws, besides exacting a retribution of sorts. In the final analysis, the epithet of polygamy is incorrect for being unsustainable on legal grounds and, literally it is the mistaken substitute of polygyny.

The Islamic penal policy is censured for prescribing amputation of hands as a legal penalty for the crime of theft. Astonishingly, no period in Islamic history is recognizable for the adoption of this legal punishment. The explanation resides in the immediately next revealed verse wherein the essential Islamic principle of repentance is invoked for the mitigation of the penalty under review...... The inductive reasoning discloses the invaluable principle of equity, described by Aristotle as a superior form of justice. Distinctions are an indispensable function of law and the making of distinctions between retribution and deterrent penalties in Islamic Law is its salient legal feature.

The participation in holy defensive war in Islam is composite of the twin "rights of God and man." The latter is an individual "obligation" towards the preparedness of society for an Islamic defensive war." The right of God ensues from the requirement of participation in defensive war in the event of general proclamation of Jihad, as a religious obligation enunciated in several revealed injunctions. Islam is a religion of peace and the title itself is its indication, but due to the fact that Islamic religious precepts emphasize life as a constant striving or Jihad, Islamic philosophy of war is a natural culmination of this ideological view. The characteristic universality of Islam, according to which the gamut of rights and responsibilities are in principle availed and borne equally by all the faith-abiding individuals, is an additional foundational principle of that philosophy. Another such principle is derived from the title Islam in its sense of peace, and the essentially "defensive" outlook of the religious war is its resultant. However, the intricateness of the science of war prescribes deterrent and preemptive considerations as inalienable components of the defensive outlook. The evident advantages accruing from this Islamic philosophy of self-defence are axiomatic in latter-day literature concerning military defence, such as the concepts of national war, total preparedness and ensured peace. The benefits of individualism are combined with those of disciplined formations, as a distinction of Islamic defensive organization. The bane of idolization of armaments, the self-destructive proportions of economic expenditure on national scale, incurred on present-day defence preparations, will be mitigated by the adoption of Islamic philosophy of war. Noticeworthy is the fact, legal obligation has intimate correlation with the vital issue of individual capacity in its fulfillment and, therefore, obligations and corresponding rights have indissoluble linkage. The obligation of holy defensive war earns the individual a right to the ownership of firearm, whose detail comes within the jurisdiction of national consensus, as well as right of the access to a framework of defensive training, available at the national level.

An irony of history, inability or unwillingness to transform religious obligations into legal relationships in the sphere of holy defensive war or Jihad must have transfigured itself into sin incurred in religious terms, into missing the contribution towards excellence of ideas in ideological terms, and into neglecting the ascendancy of society in political terms. Censure is assignable either to the benign piety of religious scholars, or to the law-making genius of the jurists, that the obligation of Jihad is not included in the five proverbial pillars or obligations of Islam. The invaluable instruction deducible from the allegory of Fall as a part of the Islamic Scripture or from the versified description provided by Milton, howsoever the incident is viewed, it is the lamentable outcome of the disobedience to "high injunction".

The foremost task in relation to "Islamic Nomocracy" is the translation of religious and ethical duties in terms of legal relationships. In order to retain its ascendancy, the great belief-system lays obligation of expertise in the framing and formulation of laws, founded upon its primary sources. The "retribution for sin" and the telling disadvantage due to erroneous law-making are nowhere else more evident, perhaps, than in the area of the doctrine of the separation of powers, to describe it in current terminology, and emphasized by Montesquieu. The ideological translation for the religion of Islam is Nomocracy, with the understanding of the term ideology in the easily apprehensible meanings of the systematization of ideals for the organization of social systems and institutions. The common denominator in both is law; in the one it is constituted by the revealed tenets, and in the other, it is derived through the exercise and exertion of juristic acumen from the original sources of Islamic Law. A matter of common appreciation, involvement of rules necessitates arbitration, which is effective to the extent it is judicious and impartial-prerequisites which can be illusive unless the process is uninfluenced and uninterfered. A rational justification for the scriptural requirement of upholding justice during adjudication is available, if any is needed, whereby the justness is conscientious adherence to the revealed law." The judicial independence in Islam would have reflected from the development of constitutional law, or in more specific terms, from the definition and limitation of political authority in traditional Islam. This key-measure would have gone a long way in harnessing the benefits of ample juristic genius that existed in traditional Islam, and a remarkably evolved polity with an original constitution would have been its rewards.

The Comparison : The socialist laws adopted a revolutionary character in order to accommodate the objectives of overturning the society and creating the conditions of a new social order in which the concepts of state and law would cease to exist. However, the law was considered secondary to the purpose of creating new economic structure, which was an explanation for the collectivization of all means of production. Economic infrastructure was deemed to condition and determine the legal system, thus, the framing of rules by the legislature, as its sole means, was of subsidiary significance as a source. The Civil Code of Egypt 1949 represented a compromise between traditional Islamic Law and adopted Western Systems, wherein the elements drawn from other contemporary codes were selected on the basis of their general consonance with Shariah Law.

A brief comparison among Islamic Law, Common Law and Romano-Germanic Law is provided in other parts of this discourse.

The Islamic Law will be identified with evolutionary character in its objective of organizing the "best community." Social control will be effected with the purpose of facilitating the individual attainment of success ("falah"). From the fundamental legal concept of the sovereignty of law, the definition and limitation of political authority, the fundamental individual right to the rule of Islamic Law, and socio-political system with the designation of nomocracy will be the natural derivations. For the reasons of comparison solely, the obvious is reiterated that due to the primal status of law in the Islamic social order, the political and economic systems are to be determined by the legal system. Due to the universalism of Islam, in the sense of being the evolutionary culmination representing the long duration of time in the memorable history of mankind, an expanded base can be envisaged for the source of its law. The comparability with the prominent systems of law in the contemporary era is a consideration in which the issues of the practicability and originality of the system are necessarily implicit, and it is a prerequisite for the organization of Islamic legal system, which cannot be left unheeded.

Role of Law

The value of legal concepts in law-making is of basic importance, which serve as the means of interpretation, legal reasoning and grounds for legal decisions. Moreover, adherence to law is facilitated as the reverence for law in society is enhanced. Besides, those concepts become the source of actual and derived principles for social organization. As vital considerations for the legal relationships involving interpersonal relations, and association between the state and citizens, are the added functions of the legal concepts.

In religion reliance is reposed in various ideas, while several of them are synonymous with legal conception and others can find ready accommodation and legal utilization in that category. As a matter of common knowledge, Islam is the result of religious evolutionary process, wherein evolutionary change is not to be understood as a necessary deviation from the immutable ideal standards, but as an improvement upon the previous stage of existence. A natural requirement of monotheism, the fundamental belief in the unity of God is a fecund source for the logical derivation of the legal concepts such as human equality, freedom from another source of submission, and social cohesion. The objectives of Shariah law coincide with the legal ideas of public interest, justice and equity, which have been briefly described in the previous sections. Implicit in the religious concept of the vicegerency of man are the deductible legal concepts of human equality, dignity of man, and recognition of individual's status in society. The importance accorded to the "right of man" in Islam, is a testimonial to these legal values, which acts as an additional dimension of social obligation to the basic concept of legal obligation, which has already been dwelt upon. The religious requirements for the participation in religious defensive war or Jihad explicitly accord precedence to individual self-determination over any external imposition upon the option to fulfill the obligation.

This revealed value is exclusive of any impelling interference in the decision for participation in Jihad, and allows complete freedom to individual conscience. The legal development of this value has immanent ideological benefits to impart the society an ascendant and distinctive institutional attribute.

The essential Islamic doctrine of accountability as a prelude to the reward and retribution is the practical expression of the underlying functional idea of the independence and right of informed choice. Without the exercise of this individual prerogative, justification for religious responsibility and availability of moral code does not arise. The adoption of this fundamental Islamic doctrine of accountability as a legal conception has the capacity to impart new dimensions to the political constitution. To hold the political authority accountable, any time in future for the decisions which adversely influenced the social order, will be a positive step towards the development of constitutional law and towards tangible improvement in the quality of statesmanship as well as public service.

A religion in which conversion to Islamic faith is dependent upon an affirmation, the simplest in its prerequisites and ceremony among all such requirements of other faiths in the world, and wherein the followers of other revealed religions are described as "people of the Book," and their prophets are accorded utmost reverence as a matter of religious belief, cannot but lay claim to the distinction of religious tolerance. In relation to this vital truth that lends identity to the universality of Islam-the revealed tenet of the "unity of revelation" has been left unheeded and unavailed—Kalam Azad made this laconic observation: "In fact no other truth of the Quran has been kept so deliberately out of sight." Hence, the legal conception of religious freedom as an individual right is likely to influence the substantive legal issues of political and economical emancipation within the meanings of that right, which will also serve as a test of the legal expression of the conception.

This rewarding and challenging subject, which affords new vistas in the sphere of law-making, is concluded with the suggestion that several other religious and humanitarian principles are available for adoption as legal conceptions to benefit the legal development immeasurably.

Adoption and Improvement

Islamic Jurisprudence : The Quranic legislation is not a legal code nor there is an attempt to deal with any legal topic comprehensively. Within the meanings of the code of life, however, the revelation contains certain universal principles, doctrines and injunctions utilizable in the making of law. The fact of remarkable value nevertheless remains, the Quran as the source of law is of much profounder legal import than it has so far been realized, and this point has already been elucidated.

In this perspective, the extraordinary belief in the Scripture, to contain the principles and guidelines to resolve the practical issues in life, appears to be suited to the genius of a master mind in law-making in order to fathom its juristic value and harness its legal potentials.

Islamic jurisprudence is to be defined as the science of law, or systematized knowledge, that concerns with the fundamental principles underlying the revealed precepts of legal value, and their use in the interpretation and development of law. Its additional function is to consider the ultimate effect which would be produced if each rule is applied to an indefinite number of similar cases, and to provide such selectivity in that application as to produce the greatest advantages to the society and to the Islamic objectives of law. Hence, it can be viewed as the science of ascertaining, understanding and systematic application of the fundamental principles of law towards the completion of the outlined jurisprudential functions. It is a part of the evolvement of systematic approach to the "finding" of laws, consistent with the demands of its original sources and, therefore, to establish a consistency of principles and methodology, in contrast with juristic convenience. Its concern naturally then devolves upon the "ought" of law signifying an obligation towards the Islamic "rightness" of law. In this context, the past of traditional Islamic Law or "fiqh" is relevant to the extent of drawing valuable lessons in the legal development, as a possible source of law, and in the ascertainment of causative factors involved in the coming of "fiqh" to a disuse. In addition, the definition, elucidation and further development of the legal concepts and values in relation to the Quranic concept of "best community" is a function of Islamic jurisprudence. In comparison, according to Coulson, Islamic jurisprudence in the past was the science of understanding and ascertaining the preordained law of Shariah. On the other hand, Kelsen's definition of jurisprudence reflected his theoretical concern with the legal task of rational reconstruction in the distinction of law and jurisprudence. In this regard, the following observation made by Kelsen is pertinent: "It is the task of the science of law to represent the law of a community, that is, the material produced by the legal authority in the law-making procedure, in the form of statements to the effect that if such and such conditions are fulfilled, then such and such sanction shall follow." The term "represent" is a substitute for rational reconstruction, and to construct the representation of the legal material produced by the law-making authority is the function of jurisprudence or the science of law.

The Rules : Legal rules are not accepted as a determinant factor in the characterization of a law, and constitute an inappropriate criteria in the ascertaining of essentially salient features of identification for a legal system. However, rules in themselves have their own significance, and they are not to be viewed as merely legal measures appropriate to the solution of concrete cases. The orientation of society towards certain aims is facilitated by legal rules through the formation of public opinion. Within the meanings of the function of law, rule acts as a model of social organization and, therefore, it is considered of assistance in the building of a new society. With these properties of legal rule in view, in the opinion of Rene David, it should be the product of reflection based upon the consideration of justice, morality, policy and consonance of the system. The rules, as an expression of law which is to be deemed as the main instrument for the realization of Islamic objectives, are means for the organization of a society with distinguishable characteristics. The significance of the legal techniques, to develop or define rules, as a source of law is self-evident. Thus the method for the deduction of rules from the revealed sources, in particular, such as would evaluate the text in account with the whole context, and the principles distinctly guiding the policy of the revealed injunction to impart it the real meanings, has its fundamental importance in Islamic legal system.

Vision, World-View and Law : In the understanding of life and universe resides the solution to the "practical problems of existence."

Hence, the comprehension of the sublime wisdom and substantive practical meanings of the scriptural precept about the revelation actually intended for those in possession of "understanding" is facilitated. The adoption of that view as a guiding principle for the resolution of practical Islamic issues has rational justification. Such a coherent understanding comprises the world-view, the rationale of being, and man's place in the universe, for these are the partial constituents of the purpose underlying the creation of universe and life. Indeed, the vision that is nurtured by that understanding is the reason for the existence of Islamic society, and the warning of the Hebrew sage that without a vision the people perish, has its historical and revelational basis. Any philosophy of the law, that does not take into account these vital considerations, cannot become the sound foundation of a universal legal system. The establishment of such a system will prove elusive without the intellectual apprehension of the attitude of original Muslim jurists. The vision and clarity of legal perception attributable to Shafii and the juristic originality ascribable to Hanifa can serve as the paradigms for the evolution of Islamic Law in its new age.

Fundamental Elements in Islamic Law : The view of social order determines the way in which the law is applied and shapes the very functions of the law in that society. The Islamic social context conforms to the characteristic scriptural conception of the Muslim community and serves as a "given factor" in law, which must be operative in the construction and the definition of its function. The realization of the significance of this observation is a vital factor in the formulation of legal methodology founded upon the Supreme Fundamental Islamic Principles, described in the ensuing sections of this treatise. Such an approach desirably maintains the distinction between law and legal concepts and it provides full expression to law in the administration of justice, as an Islamic legal distinction. The need to reconcile the various functions of the state with the cherished principles derived from the Islamic fundamental of monotheism, or "Tauhid," is also fulfilled. The Supreme Fundamental Principle of the beneficence of mankind as the underlying purpose of the institution of Prophethood in Islam is translatable in juristic terms to be the public interest, with the added meanings of public welfare, and associated legal concept of equity. Augmentation of the judicial independence as a prerequisite for the citizenship-characterized by "equal" citizens and not subjects-is in accordance with the essential requirements of the Quranic rule of law. This accords the benefit of Islamic Law within the meanings of essential Islamic right, with the important implication of adjudication under the provisions of Islamic Law and, in the present circumstances, it becomes a judicial responsibility. A juristic formulation, that provides satisfactory expression to the fulfillment of these legal requirements ensuing from the fundamental Islamic principles, ensures the practicability of law according to actual Islamic demands.

The Legal Formulation : In Islam the opportunistic proclivities of society cannot be the exclusive determinant of law which only operates within the boundaries of the norms and principles, irrevocably established in the revelation. The justification for legal reforms on the grounds of social necessity *per se* demands the furnishing of a juristic basis in, and sustenance from, the revealed principles in order for the reforms to retain the verifiable validity of Islamic Law. Therefore, a formulation for the purpose of definition and limitation of the juristic basis is indicated. For such a framework to function as a formative instrument of the law, and as the enabling means for the juristic expression of legal concepts which are pivotal in the performance of social functions, assignable to the legal system, is meritorious. The legal emphasis upon the humanitarian principles, enshrined in the Islamic sources of law, and to impart the juristic direction to the "ought" of law with the Islamic connotations, will be desirable features of such a legal formulation. The non-repugnancy to the injunctions of the original sources of law as a constitutional provision is not adequate as a feasible legal formulation for the reasons of giving full expression to Islamic Law, for it neither provides full expression to Islamic Law, nor it is a convincing schematic plan for the organization of a comparable Islamic legal system suited to the contemporary requirements. The denouement of such a constitutional requirement is law that only accepts the adjudication of its violation, and the evolved belief-system of Islam is expected to be a precursor of any, but an artless law suited to its genius.

7

Ethical Values

Ethics of Treatment

The character of the Muslim community is not determined by the acceptance of the rituals alone. Acceptance has to be translated into action. All acts of devotion manifested in Salat (Prayer), Som (Fasting), Zakat (Charity), and Hajj (Pilgrimage) are rigid and compulsory, not so much because they ensure a better place in heaven, but because they provide social harmony in the society and engender self-discipline. They give to the community an ethical 'steel frame' within which it can earn rewards on this earth. The ethics in Islam, however, is revealed. It is not the product of philosophical speculations or rational interpretation of the events resulting from man's social and political life. It has its counterpart in Christianity in the form of Protestant Ethics, but the religious ethics in Islam is more compulsive and comprehensive, and there is greater emphasis on the revelational aspect. Gibb has expressed the following views on the religious nature of Islamic ethics.

Source of Ethics : "The fact that the source of Muslim ethics was religious intuition transmitting a divine revelation to mankind, was important also for the structure of Muslim society. Viewed in the light of the ultimate principle which regulates human existence, all human institutions take a new significance. They are not immaterial to the religious life; they either express or do not-express the Will of God for men, and they either conduce or do not conduce to a life of true submission to God."

To fortify the ethical basis of a Muslim society, Hadith (the tradition of the Prophet) has been made the most important supplementary force with the Quran. The Prophet in his life articulated moral connotations of a variety of human situation's. The Traditions of the Prophet constitute a massive and valuable store house of ethical principles, which can make Quranic precepts and ideals more realistic. Even the vast compendium of Islamic law is deeply rooted in ethics. There is no such thing called the dichotomy of law and morality In Islam. The Quran, the Traditions of the Prophet, and Fiqh (Jurisprudence) form an ethical reservoir for all occasions which saves the Muslim community from dwindling into moral anarchy.

For acts of omission or commission, there are certain specified penalties, which cannot be increased, decreased or cancelled by any state authority. Taking into consideration the inherent foibles of human character, and permanent moral infirmities, which crowd the life of an average man. Muslim thinkers have insisted that state is an indispensable institution, obedience to its commands is essential for the peace and prosperity of the community, but the state is also under eternal obligation to provide its citizens with an ethical climate, which would enable them to realize the moral purpose of human existence.

The Quran and the history of Islam furnish an eloquent testimony that right action is the only yardstick by which value or worth of human character could be judged. The Quran says:

> "And those who strive in our (cause) we will certainly guide them to our Paths: for verily God is with those who do right."

Constant Struggle : Life in Islam is a constant struggle to overcome satanic propensities which run in human blood. Believers have been instructed to keep a strict watch over their thoughts and actions. Inner purity of soul is as important as the external manifestation of rites and rituals. It is also laid down that every possible step should be taken to make human life in an organization positive and constructive. In other words, mystical morality of self-abnegation, penance and seclusion is against the spirit of Islam. Goodness is valuable only if it is practiced in society and is used as an instrument for the welfare of the community as a whole. In order to perform a righteous action, and acquire eligibility for membership in the commonwealth of believers, one is expected to practice certain fundamentals in the form of *Ibadat* (prayers). These prayers are basically meant to purify the heart and soul of man, but their true meanings are realized only when this purity in the form of goodness and virtue is reflected in the social interaction among the members of the Muslim community. T. J. DeBoer has summed up the nature of Islamic ethics as follows:

> "The ethics of the Quran might be summed up in the trite formula: 'Believe and do right.' Belief of course is the primary obligation, since without belief all works are vain—a mere mirage in the waste."

In other words religion is the basic source of social ethics. Belief takes precedence over actions, no doubt, but if it is only an embellishment of soul, and actions of men do not synchronize with its substance, it becomes only a hollow spiritual exercise.

Thus in every code of ethics in Islam, belief and action must always go together. According to an authentic religious text *hadith* (saying of the Prophet), morally rewarding works or actions are as follows:

(1) Honour towards parents.
(2) Not to take a niece in marriage against her will.
(3) To pay one's day-labourers well.

A tradition of quite another cast, which had its source among the devout gives the following list of precepts:

(1) Love the poor, and be accessible to them.
(2) Look always at those who are beneath you and gaze not at those who are above you.
(3) Never solicit anything from anyone.
(4) Be loyal to thy kinsfolk, even if they should vex you.
(5) Always speak the truth, even when it is unpalatable.
(6) Be not overawed in the paths of Allah by the reviling of the reviler.

(7) Frequently cry aloud, "There is no might or power save by Allah," for this comes forth from the treasure which is hidden under God's throne."

The Pragmatism : Islamic ethics is pragmatic and is an integral part of the faith. The spread of Islam, however, beyond the frontiers of Arabian peninsula brought it into contact with other ethical disciplines, and in due course, comparative study of different ethical systems became a very important part of the traditional philosophy of education in Islam. Later, out of this synthesis, a science of morals, called Ilm ul-Akhlaq was developed, which attracted the attention of some of the greatest scholars in Islam. But in spite of countless alien influences, in essence, the ethics in Islam remained Quranic. As long as the Muslims were firmly anchored to this morality, Islam remained a dynamic and forward-looking movement. It opened flood-gates of revolutionary forces, and Muslims became the torch-bearers of civilization in every land they inhabited. But the moment they disengaged themselves from the moral moorings of the Quran, their civilization collapsed like a house of cards. To attribute the downfall of Islamic civilization to a single factor would be a sacrilegious oversimplification, but this much is certain that lack of ethical basis in politics and administration was one of the major causes of the downfall of Muslim kingdoms.

Corruption, tyranny, backwardness and exploitation completely eroded their foundations. Political and administrative life of the community became a playground for the nefarious activities of self-seekers and king-makers. Most of the cherished excellencies were sacrificed at the altar of expediency and self-interest. Therefore, it should be a matter of serious interest for a student of Islamic civilization to assess those moral qualities of administration, which constituted the basis of its earlier glories and achievements.

The Honesty : This is a moral quality which refrains individuals from inflicting injury on others by way of cheating, or misappropriation of their possessions. Dishonesty breeds aversion, pollutes social life, degenerates politics, and corrupts administration. All religious and ethical philosophies have emphasized that, honesty ensures stability and happiness for mankind, while dishonesty, they point out, is a sign of moral decadence. Honesty safeguards men against temptations which one finds at every step and gives richness and dignity to human character. Dishonesty, on the other hand, denigrates character, multiplies distrust and suspicion. It is baneful in all areas of life, but its impact is particularly ruinous if a dishonest person happens to occupy a position of authority. As such, honesty has deep relevance to administration, where most of the authority of the state is concentrated.

According to Islam, corruption is a sin for which there is no atonement. The Quran has clearly pointed out, that corrupters will be subjected to divine chastisement. It is an irreligious act which deserves severe condemnation. It says :

> "Not to consume each other's wealth unjustly, nor offer it to judges as a bribe, so that, with their aid you might seize other men's property dishonestly."
>
> "Give just measure and be not of those who diminish and weigh (things) with an exact and right balance. And defraud not the substance of any people, and do not act corruptly in the earth making mischief. And guard yourself against the punishment of God for all sorts of corruption."

Another verse of the Quran says:

> "But seek the abode of the Hereafter in that which Allah hath given thee and neglect not thy portion of the world, and be thou kind even as Allah hath been kind to thee and seek not corruption in the earth lo ! Allah loveth not corrupters."

It is a matter of common knowledge that corruption is universal in human life. In every period of history, sages and reformers have waged unending crusades against tendencies, which produce corruption. The Holy Prophet in his administrative reforms gave highest priority to honesty and moral integrity of officers. His instrument of instructions to officers always highlighted right action and honest conduct in unmistakable terms. Officers were disallowed to have anything beyond their salaries and allowances, and even gifts of all kinds were forbidden. Umar A. Farrukh has summed up the Prophet's views on nepotism or favouritism in the following words :

> "If the man in authority left the better and the fitter (Man) in favour of another because of relationship between them, or because the other man happened to have emancipated him from slavery or because of friendship or of being from the same locality, the same nationality, Arab, Persian, Turk, or Greek, or because of a bribe received in kind or service or for any other cause, or because of a grudge against the more capable man or of an animosity between them; he who does this is a cheater of Allah of His Messenger and of the Faithful (Muslims)."

Accumulation of worldly riches for ostentatious living or for the benefit of one's children are common and universal foibles of human character. Men tend to fall victims to these temptations very easily. Men who are susceptible to these foibles do not deserve any public office. The Quran says, "And know that your wealth and your children are a temptation and that Allah is He with whom there is a mighty reward." The Prophet took special care in allocating offices of the state. A tradition has been narrated by Bukhari from Huraira in which the Prophet pointed out that if the offices were assigned to unworthy people that would mean the end of this world.

The principles of honesty enunciated by the Prophet were strictly adhered to by his four successors in organizing and administering the affairs of the Pious Caliphate. Although historical evidence is meagre, but whatever is left of their official correspondence, is an eloquent testimony that honesty was insisted and advocated for all administrators in all areas of governmental activity. Officers were repeatedly reminded of their duty to God and the people, and anybody found corrupt or dishonest was promptly reprimanded and punished. Umar I, under whom the city state of Medina became a vast empire, is credited with the creation of an effective and efficient machinery of government in Islamic history.

The organization of administration was simple, but he set very high ethical standards for public servants of the state. Civil and military officers found guilty of corruption were always subjected to severe reprimand, and very often they were given exemplary punishment. In 17 A.H., Umar I dismissed Khalid-bin-Walid on charges of bribery. In his dismissal order he wrote that corruption in any form was a naked tyranny. In another letter to Umaro-bin-As, the governor of Egypt, the Caliph made serious inquiries about the ways and means, by which he had accumulated wealth and property, which he did not possess before his appointment as governor. This is a clear indication, that in Islam, rank, status or services to the state would not help an administrator to escape the punishment, which he deserves for his dishonest deeds. In an official circular addressed to the governors of the provinces, Umar I forbade acceptance of even gifts, which in his opinion were also a form of corruption.

Imperishable Impact : Hadrat Ali, the last of the Pious Caliphs, has left an imperishable impact on Islamic thought. Among the companions of the Holy Prophet he was known for his courage, foresight and prudence. He ruled during one of the most stormy periods of early Muslim history, but he did not allow the moral climate of his administration to deteriorate. Even in the midst of growing political restlessness in the realm, he maintained high ethical ideals of Islamic administration. A letter written to Malik-bin-Ashtar, when he was appointed governor of Egypt, has been considered by historians as Hadrat Ali's great contribution to the growth of administrative ethics in Islam. The document is of immeasurable significance.

The caliph expressed his views on official honesty in the following words: "Then come officers of your state. You must supervise their work. They must be appointed after a careful scrutiny of their capabilities and characters. These appointments must be made originally on probation without any kind of favouritism being shown or influence being accepted. Otherwise tyranny, corruption and misrule will reign in your state. While selecting your officers, take care to select experienced and honourable persons, members of respectable families who had served Islam during its early days, because these are usually of noble character and good repute. They are not greedy and cannot be easily corrupted. They mostly have before them the ultimate result of their thoughts and their deeds. Keep them also well paid, so that they may not be tempted to lower their standards of morality and may not misappropriate the cash of the state which they hold in their trust; and even if after being paid handsomely they prove dishonest, then you will be right to punish them. Therefore, keep a careful watch over their system of work and rule. You may also appoint trustworthy and honest men to watch over the activities of these officers.

The knowledge that they are being watched secretly will keep them from dishonesty, misrule, malpractices and tyrannizing the subject. Protect your government from dishonest officers. If you find any of them dishonest and your confidential intelligence service submits acceptable proofs of his dishonesty then you must punish him. This may be physical punishment, dismissal from service and taking back from him all, which he has dishonestly collected. He must be humiliated and must be made to realize the infamy of his crooked deeds. His humiliation and punishment must be given publicity so that it may act as a lesson and a deterrent example to others."

In another letter, Hadrat Ali condemned officers, who had the habit of attending parties arranged in their honour by interested people. This he thought was also corruption, though of a subtle nature. The letter was addressed to Osman-ibn-Haneef, the governor of Basra and read as follows :

> "Ibne-Haneef! I have received information that a person of Basra invited you to a dinner and you immediately accepted the invitation. And very sumptuous meals were served there, finest varieties of viands were placed before you—I am sorry to hear the news. I never expected that you would accept invitation of person who invite big officers and rich people and from whose doors people and hungry paupers are turned away rudely."

Similarly, in another letter to a collector of taxes, Hadrat Ali condemned misappropriation of government money. In his opinion, it was a disgrace of the highest order and should not be tolerated. He pointed out that an officer, who was guilty of such an act had sold his conscience to the devil. He said :

> "Be it known to you that the person who mis-appropriates the poor rate fund, who fills his stomach

> with such amounts and who harms his religion and injures his conscience with such deeds will be punished and disgraced in this world as well as the next. The worst form of dishonesty is the breach of trust of the public funds and the despicable example of maladministration is that the Imam (ruler) should tolerate such forms of dishonesty."

The perusal of the official correspondence of the pious Caliphs shows that acts of dishonesty were not tolerated in administration, and complaints against dishonest officers were handled speedily. They believed that if the rulers want to retain the confidence of the people they must check dishonesty promptly. In order to eliminate nepotism they made every possible effort to curb clannish affinities among administrators; Nepotism in their opinion forbids the available talent in the community to fructify in its fullness. People will not repose confidence in a government where jobs and positions are distributed through favouritism. They emphasized that faith and trust of the masses is the best guarantee against maladministration and political Insecurity. Hadrat Ali in one of his letters said :

> "Let your attitude be such that they do not lose faith in you because a good faith on their part will reduce many troubles of administration and will relieve you of many worries and anxieties."

To further ensure honesty in administration, officers were debarred from pursuing other vocations in life. Moreover, several other practical steps were taken to inculcate propriety and honesty among officers. They were provided all possible amenities and comforts, because it was believed that inadequate salaries and absence of reasonable facilities could be one of the factors, which compel public servants to be corrupt. The Holy Prophet felt that if the officers are debarred from sources of additional income, justice demands that they should be provided with enough funds, so that they could lead a respectable existence. He had laid down special instruction for their salaries, and housing accommodations. But at the same time he insisted that an officer, who seeks more than what is legally sanctioned for him is guilty of the breach of trust. In Abu Saad a tradition of the Holy Prophet has been recorded as follows :

> "Mustaored bin Shahdud reported : I heard the messenger of Allah say who is an officer of ours, let him take a wife, and if he has got no servant let him take a servant and if he has got no house let him take a house; who so takes besides that is one who commits breach of trust."

Corrupt officers have a tendency to be secretive about their ill-gotten fortunes. In Islam this is a sinful act. All employees of the state are obliged by religion to give an honest account of their possessions to the public. Each official is accountable to God and the people. The Prophet once said :

> "O you men! who ever of you is appointed to work for us and then conceals from us even a needle there from or what is above it, is a treacherous man."

In short, Islam has condemned dishonesty in public affairs in the strongest possible terms. A dishonest official has been warned against all kinds of evil consequences, the greatest of them being the chagrin of God.

State-crafts : Later Muslim writers on political ethics and states-craft have also emphasized honesty in government in unequivocal terms. Kaikaus, the author of *Qabus Nama,* has pointed out that bribery is as bad as usury. He has expressed his opinion on the dishonesty of the officials in the following words:

> "Money gained from office under the sultan resembles roses and jasmine, which in a single day make themselves beautiful, sweet-scented and highly reputed. But also it is as ephemeral as the flowers, and like them the profits derived from office cannot be hidden away. Money acquired in the service of the sultan is more easily dissipated than the dust on the surface of the world, and although the honour of service of royal masters is the best form of capital, the money which accrues from it is no better than usury."

Emphasis on honesty in administration increased in later Islamic history because unfettered personal rule of despots in various dynasties had made administration in a Muslim kingdom extremely susceptible to corruption. The original concept that all functionaries including the Head of State were servants of God, holding authority from Him to serve the common good of mankind, had disappeared from the practical politics of Islam. The result was that greed, avarice, and dishonesty had become common features of Muslim administration. Lust for power, and desire to amass worldly fortunes were noticeable in all areas of administrative activity.

Despotic rulers and unscrupulous civil servants, free from the fear of God and the Day of Judgement, completely wrecked the spirit of Islamic administration. Ibn-e-Taimiyya has summed up their characteristics as follows :

> "A class dominated by desire for power and doing mischief having no consideration whatsoever of the Day of Judgement. They realize that they can only attain domination with (various kinds of) payments, and those are not possible except by extorting money illegally. Consequently they become plunderers (from some people, conferrers of favours on some other people). Those say, no one can obtain to domination unless he be one, who eats and lets others eat. If an upright man, who neither eats nor lets others eat. attained to power, the higher officials would detest him and finish by deposing him. Sometimes they are not satisfied with that; they may cause him bodily and financial harm. Those people consider only their immediate (interests) in this world and neglect the future good of this life and the life to come."

Piety, the Yardstick : Ibn Taimiyya insists that in Islam piety is the only yardstick to determine the competence of an individual to hold a seat of authority in government and administration. Any other criteria of personnel recruitment is a stark dishonesty. In his opinion assigning positions in government on the basis of caste, cult or kinship, denigrates the very mission of Islam. He says :

> "It is the duty for any one, who directs any part of the public affairs of the Muslims—to employ the most suitable person he can find in each position, which is under his control—if he rejects the worthiest and most proper candidate in favour of another, because the

> other is his relation, friend, or freedman, or because they belong to the same country, legal sect, religious order, or ethnic group—Arab, Persian Turkish, Anatolian — or because he has accepted a bribe or service for this man, or for other reason, or because of some personal animosity towards the worthier candidate or some enmity between them, he cheats God and His Prophet and the Faithful."

The reason for which piety is advocated as a measure of honesty is that there is no other way of determining precisely the honest intentions of an individual. Rigorous psychological tests and written examination of modern times can uncover instincts like aggression, sentimentality, and sobriety to some extent, but they fail to provide reliable indicators regarding qualities such as honesty, sympathy and a sense of justice. Piety which means fear of God, simple and austere life, and purity of thought and action, was therefore considered a better touchstone for honesty. Later in Islamic history as piety declined among the Muslims, writers on politics and administrative ethics started suggesting other means for scouting honest people for government service. Family, wealth, and sectarian affiliations were advocated as pertinent instruments to determine ability of an individual to be honest. The philosophy behind this approach was that people with pecuniary conditions should not be elevated to positions of authority in government, because poverty of the position holder could be a factor in making corrupt.

Kaikaus has made the following remarks :

> "Never grant office to impecunious or impoverished men, especially if it is important office, because they will not concern themselves with provision for you until they have provided for themselves. Those on the other hand, who have means and possessions of their own, will not immediately busy themselves on their own account. It is like the irrigation of fields and gardens. If the canal supplying the field or garden is moist and well-soaked, it conveys water quickly to field and garden; but if the earth in the canal is dry, and water has not for a long time passed through it, then when

> water is admitted, until it itself is saturated with moisture, it will not deliver water to the field or garden. The impecunious tax-gatherer resembles the dry canal, in first satisfying his own needs and then turning to yours."

Ibn Taimiyya says that in popular Arabic vocabulary bribery is also called *bartil* which originally meant that the mouth of the briber is closed from the truth. A tradition of the Prophet has highlighted this fact by pointing out that "when the bribes enter through the door, honesty flies through the skylight."

In pursuit of honesty, however officers are not allowed to become insufferably arrogant. Honesty should be supplemented with graces like civility and courtesy. Particularly officers, who have constant public dealings—like tax or revenue collectors—are instructed to be honest as well as accommodating and courteous. Without these additional qualities honesty cannot make any significant contribution to public good. Ibn Khaldun has added austerity as another factor to strengthen honesty in human character. Luxuriant living makes an individual indolent and increases his chances of becoming corrupt or dishonest. In his opinion, if public officials are habituated to ease and luxury, the social system as a whole will fall on evil days.

Ibn Khaldun, in his discussion of the rise and fall of a sedentary culture, has given an insightful account of the causes which in his opinion lead to corruption of civilized communities. Sedentary culture he believes originates in cities and adversely affects all areas of social and economic life. Addiction to elegance and pageantry become common. Fads and fashions, the natural accompaniments of luxuriant existence, consume most of the creative energies of the people. Limited means, high taxes, and extravagant living compel people to indulge in immoral practices. Cheating, fraud, theft, perjury, and usury paralyze the framework of social life. Nobody remains immune from this morally polluted climate and even esteemed persons and members of noble families are corrupted, and this ultimately is the sign of degeneration and disappearance of civilization.

The Justice : In religion and philosophy, justice has been emphasised as one of the greatest manifestations of nobility. It gives luster, richness, and dignity to affairs of men, and saves humanity from the evil consequences of force, fraud and aggression. Justice has two distinct meanings. Firstly, it is a quality of the human mind, which helps an individual to distinguish between right and wrong in life.

Secondly, it is an administration of codified legal rules and procedures in a regular law court. Impartiality, objectivity, and rigidity are the chief characteristics of formal legal codes, while graciousness, ability to curb ambitions, and desire to control appetites are the properties of justice, when it is understood as an ethical quality.

Islam has made provision for both kinds of justice. An administrator in a Muslim state is subject to both kinds of regimentation. In the religious literature, and the books on law and administration, however, justice is emphasized as a quality which mostly pertains to mind and thought. The Quran has elucidated the importance of justice as follows:

> "O ye who believe: Be steadfast witness for Allah in equity, and let not enmity of any people seduce you that ye deal not justly. Deal justly— that is nearer to your duty. Observe your duty to Allah."

> "O ye who believe: Be ye staunch in justice witness for Allah even though it be against your ownselves, or your parents or your kindred."

A socio-political climate, in which sense of justice is high among people, is most conducive to ethical development. The Holy Prophet laid great emphasis on this quality. Books of Hadith are replete with traditions of the Prophet indicating his deep and serious concern regarding injustice in life. In his opinion, justice is all-pervading and no area of human existence should be free from its impact. Some of the traditions of the Holy Prophet have been recorded as follows:

> "Abdullah bin Amr reported that the Messenger of Allah said: Verily the just persons near Allah will be upon pulpits of light on the right side of Merciful and both His hands are right hands of those who are just in their orders and in their family and what they are given to rule."

"Abu Sayeed reported that the Prophet said: Verily the dearest of men near Allah on the Resurrection Day and the nearest of them before Him for company will be a just ruler."

"Ibn Umar reported that the Messenger of Allah said: Verily the Sultan is a shade of Allah on earth. Every oppressed man out of His servants takes shelter to him. When he administers justice, there is reward for him and their gratitude on the part of the subjects."

Quality of Justice : There is a saying, "government will continue with unbelief, but not with injustice." According to Ghazzali, the success of any political authority depends on the quality of justice in its jurisdiction. In Islam, an unjust governor of men is threatened with torments reserved for infidels, while a just and righteous ruler has been ensured of unending blessings. According to Ghazzali the Prophet once said, "One day of just rule by an equitable Sultan is more meritorious than sixty years of continual worship." Justice, from the Islamic point of view is a powerful safeguard against arbitrary action. Excessive punishment and excessive compassion, both have been labelled as arbitrary. Writers on administrative ethics in Islam have further elucidated the concept of justice by saying that it entails regimentation of passion and control of aggressive instincts in man.

In another work of outstanding merit called Kimiya-i-Saadat, Ghazzali has given further elucidation of his concept of justice and gives certain definite characteristics which he says can give stability and peace to society. The qualities enumerated are meant for the ruler, but it is understood that they are equally applicable to the rest of the administrators, who are actually governing the people. These characteristics are as follows:

(i) In every case the ruler should mentally put himself in the position of the contending parties.

(ii) He should fulfill the desire of those, who have come to him for justice.

(iii) Justice is possible only when the ruler does not indulge in luxurious food and clothing.

(iv) He should practice leniency, not harshness in his official dealings.

(v) He should try that the subjects should be content with the rule of law.

(vi) He should not attempt any conciliation at the expense of law.

(vii) He should supervise the affairs of the people in the same way as if he were to supervise his own household affairs and should deal with the powerful and the inferior in the same manner.

(viii) He should try to meet the learned as often as he can and should encourage them to have their say.

(ix) He should see that his servants, magistrates and other officers perform their duties diligently and well.

(x) He should not be overpowered by any false sense of pride.

The above characteristics provide a broad and a comprehensive view of those graces of human character which lead to kindness, sympathy, equality, and dignity. Ibn Abi-Rabi defines justice as a condition of correctness in life, dominance of reason over animality in man, and integrity in public affairs. It also means defense of the rights of man with courage and conviction. Weak and inefficient officers have very little chance of performing their duties in a just manner.

Justice in Islam also connotes a sense of balance in conducting affairs of the state and society. The Quran says, "He raised up the heavens and He set the Balance." Another verse says, "Allah it is who sent down the book with truth and the Balance." Imbalance of any kind is against the principle of justice. Islam has not provided any definite framework or procedural code, by which work in government can be conducted in a balanced manner. But an examination of the spiritual values enunciated by Islam leaves no doubt that if they are permanently embedded in human character, chances are that imbalances can be avoided.

Thus, in every discussion of Islamic ethics and administration, justice is highlighted as one of the basic characteristics of good administration. It creates a sense of proportion, encourages ethical behaviour and saves men from impious acts of arrogance, self-glory and self-aggrandizement.

Caliph Ali in one of his sermons, proclaimed that promulgation of justice and truth was the cardinal feature of his mission as a ruler. Impiety and injustice lead to the erosion of societies, and the Prophet's main purpose was to establish a moral climate in which people could be administered in a just manner. Ali said :

> "My mission today is the same as it was at the time of the Prophet. I shall strive till I eradicate impiety and injustice and till I establish a rule of Justice and Truth— a humane and heavenly regime."

In another letter addressed to Muhammad son of Hadrat Abu bakar (the first caliph) whom he appointed governor of Egypt, Ali insisted on just administration in the following words :

> "Be fair, just and impartial in your dealings, so that even the influential persons may not dare take undue advantage of your leniency and the uninfluential and poor may not be disappointed in your justice and fair dealings."

The Veracity : Love for truth and fair-play has been the theme of practically every ethical system. In no other institution is there greater need of veracity than in administration, because decisions being made in it have deep and far-reaching repercussions. Any effort to misrepresent the facts or make a false statement could be extremely hazardous. If veracity is adopted as an integral part of administrative behaviour, and decision makers consciously insist on truthful assessment of every situation, there is every possibility that the climate within an administrative agency would be free from many suspicions which so often plague internal and external environments of complex organizations.

This ethical quality demands that a person in making a decision or providing an information should not be motivated by selfishness. Veracity, in order to be effective, however, has to be spontaneous and should be a continuous habit of mind, rather than an act of expediency resulting from some kind of fear or injury. It has been noticed that men in organizations have the tendency to camouflage realities for self-interest, or withhold information intentionally to harm the interest of someone else. If an empirical investigation is made, ample evidence will be found to how, the inadequate information, a misstatement, and deliberate distortion of facts contribute a great deal in making wrong decisions. All philosophical and ethical systems have emphasized that search for truth should be the continuous professional and intellectual preoccupation of those, who make and execute public policies. The Quran says :

> "The witnesses—among the true believers shall not refuse to present themselves whenever they are summoned to give witness; and conceal not true testimony, for he who conceals it has surely a wicked heart."

> "When you speak a word or pronounce a judgment, be true and just, though the person concerned be your relative, speak not falsely, although the declaration might be against your own interest or against your parents or your near relatives."

In one of his sermons, Hadrat Ali listed faithfulness, truth, and veracity as virtues, which protect mankind against evils. This is in his opinion is the primary object of Islam. Discussing human behaviour in one of his sermons, he said :

> "He is wise who carefully meditates over what he hears (and then accepts only truth) who tries to see things in their real and actual perspectives."

Truth, in Ali's opinion, has precedence even over safety of life and property.

> "A true Muslim is he from whose hands and tongue other Muslims are safe, but not at the cost of truth and justice."

Truth is the foundation of human character and a basic factor which strengthens human faith. The Prophet once said, "No man can attain a firm faith, unless he develops strength of character and that cannot be achieved unless one acquires the habit of speaking truth." Rulers and administrators, who love truth and plain speaking will never become prey to sycophants and courtiers, who are always ready to gather around men of authority.

The Courage : It is by courage alone that individuals in their personal and collective lives can achieve something worthwhile and creative. Cowardice is an ailment of human soul. Courage on the other hand is a spiritual tonic and its value is universally recognized in all areas of organized life. But courage is not to be confused with spontaneous acts of bravery. Bravery is an accident, but courage is a permanent moral virtue. Courageous action is a product of reason and reflection. Rules of propriety and logic play a decisive role in courage, and it does not entail a violation of discipline or decorum. In Islam, control of passions, sublimation of emotions, and curbing of irrational and immoral tendencies are included among courageous deeds. The Quran says :

> "The true brave are those, who lose not their hearts, but stand firmly and behave patiently under ills and hardships and in battles—those are they who are true (to themselves) and those are they who guard themselves against the displeasure of their Lord."

In Islam hierarchical organization is not rigid and excessively formalistic. Distinction among juniors and seniors is maintained, but they are all accountable to God, whose all-embracing sovereignty forms the cornerstone of the Faith. This mitigates formalized subservience of the subordinate to the super ordinate, which is a cardinal feature of all formal hierarchies. The fact that juniors and seniors, irrespective of rank, status, and position are accountable to God for their actions and decisions, changes the climate of human interaction in an organization. Each officer is answerable to God for his own trust.

It is the religious duty of a junior to point out any omission on the part of his senior, which is contrary to religion and morality. Healthy criticism is a sign of courage and shows that the system is stable, tolerant, and progressive. Hadrat Abu Bakr, the first Pious Caliph, in his inaugural address, clearly impressed upon the people that, they were free to exercise strict vigilance on his affairs and if and when he deviated from the path of righteousness, they were under no obligation to obey his commands.

Courage to criticize and large heartedness to accept criticism are certainly counted among the salient features of Islamic administration. There are instances in Islamic history when caliphs and kings were openly castigated for their policies. The critics in doing so always felt that they were performing a religious duty and had not the slightest apprehension about reprisal or punishment. Hadrat Umar I, once while preaching, said, "O, people let him among you, who sees any deviation in me set it right." A man stood up from the congregation and said, "By God if we saw in you deviation we would rectify it with our swords." Umar I answered, "Praise God who created in this Umma him who would rectify with his sword my deviation."

Similarly, Al-Ghazzali in his Ihya has narrated an incident when Muawiya did not pay allowances to the people. Abu Muslim al Khawlani openly told him that royal possessions were not a part of his patrimony. Muawiya, it is said, did not fly into rage and instead said, "Abu Muslim is right. This is not the result of my toil nor my father's. Come forward for your allowances." Authority which is not restricted by certain built-in moral restrictions turns into a naked aggression and forfeits its right to govern people. Ibn-i-Khaldun in his discussion of the incident says :

> "Since kingship is an expression of the essential grouping together of humans and its basic characteristic is domination and force, both of which stem from eradicable strength rooted in mankind, the judgments of the holder of authority usually turns aside from the right and are unjust to whoever is under him, for he usually demands of them that, which is not within his power. This is because of his appetites. For this reason it is difficult to obey him."

Ibn Khaldun not only preached courage and sagacity, but also practiced it during his stay in Egypt. He was one of the signatories of the Fatwa which the Qadi's and scholars of Egypt drafted against the Mamuluk ruler Barquq on the 11th of November, 1389. In this fetwa, the ruler was declared guilty of unlawful appropriation of people's property, murder and several other charges of misconduct. He did so in spite of the fact that Barquq was one of his greatest benefactors from whom he had received all kinds of favours. For a healthy and constructive use of authority, its good and bad attributes should be exposed. Exposition of good that has been accomplished by a man in authority, will mobilize support for him and strengthen and increase his effectiveness, while uncovering of wrongs committed by him, will put him on the path of rectitude. There is more courage involved in blaming a man of authority than praising him, but the criticism should be free from malice and ought to be based on proper assessment of the whole situation. Similarly, in-appreciating good, one ought to be watchful, that he is doing so not as a sycophant, but as a person fully convinced of the righteousness of the acts performed by the decision maker.

The Politeness : This is a quality which has been universally acclaimed as a sign of culture and refinement. It engenders confidence and ensures peace and unity. In organized life where chances of friction are so frequent, politeness helps individuals to save themselves from many ugly situations. All religions and ethical disciplines have vigorously advocated politeness as an essential characteristic of human behaviour. The Quran applauds this quality as follows :

> "They are most honoured by God, who are the best in conduct those, who are most dutiful to God and are fraternally polite with one another."

Arrogance and attitudes of exultance are forbidden in Islam.

> "To walk not in the earth exultantly or arrogantly."

This is a quality particularly useful for those, who exercise authority over others and have the power to be rude or harmful. Authority in itself is a blessing, provided it is used with benevolence for the perpetuation of right and avoidance of wrong. Al-Ghazzali is of the opinion that authority is essential for all organizations in a state, but one who holds it should be watchful that his decisions and actions do not betray malice or callousness.

In Akhlaq-i-Jalaly, the author, has quoted a tradition in which the Prophet is said to have prayed the following :

> "O Lord God, the officer who is benevolent to my followers in the exercise of authority connected to him, be then benevolent to him, and the officer who is severe with my followers in the exercise of authority committed to him, with him thou be severe."

Hadrat Ali in the instrument of instructions issued to Malik-e-Ashter on the latter's appointment as governor of Egypt said,

"Malike, you must create in your mind kindness, compassion and love of your subjects. Do not behave with them as if you are voracious and ravenous beast."

Ibn-Khaldun has listed harshness as one of the fundamental causes of the decline of political systems. He points out that masses in general are not interested in the personality, fame and figure of their rulers. Their primary interest lies in how generous, good and benevolent they are in catering the needs of the subjects. He says :

> "Good rulership is equivalent to mildness. If the ruler uses force and is ready to met out punishment and eager to expose the faults of people and to count their sins (his subjects) become fearful and depressed and seek to protect themselves against him through lies, ruses and deceit. This becomes a character trait of theirs. Their minds and character become corrupted. They often abandon the ruler on the battlefield and (fail to support him) in defensive enterprises. The decay of sincere intentions causes the decay of military protection. Thus the dynasty decays and fences that protect it lie in ruin."

Politeness helps men in authority to win confidence, disarm resistance, and win support for government. It rescues rulers from excesses so commonly associated with power. Politeness, however, is to be exercised with caution and in a discrete manner. Indiscriminate use of it is likely to be understood as weakness of character. Islam has emphasized *modus vivendi* in this matter as the best course of action. Ibn Khaldun has elucidated this principle as follows :

> "In the case of all human qualities, the extremes are reprehensible, and middle road is praiseworthy. This for instance is the case with generosity in relation to waste and stinginess, and bravery in relation to foolhardiness and cowardice."

The Forgiveness : A forgiving man is always held in high esteem in a group. It is a manifestation of one's large-heartedness, and saves individuals from the corrupting influence of power. It cements social ties and ensures group cohesion. In all human situations this moral quality can help to create an atmosphere of fraternity. It is a quality which makes leadership effective, spacious and dignified. A leader who is magnanimous and forgiving is always respected and people render compliance to his commands willingly. The Quranic views on the subject are as follows :

> "Praised are they who restrain their anger and pardon the faults of others; and God loves those who do good to others."

> "God loves those who shun transgressions and indecencies, and whenever they get angry they forgive."

In understanding the ethical connotations of forgiveness in Islam, one important point should always be kept in mmd. Islam avoids extremes like "tooth for tooth" or "turning the left check when the right is smitten" because both are contrary to justice. Muslims are asked to practice a middle course avoiding everything which is impractical. The object is to create a climate of thought and action in society in which maximum good of the largest number of people can be ensured. Indiscriminate use of forgiveness can be as ruinous as stubborness, or excessive sternness. Forgiveness as a trait of politics and administration has to be exercised in the light of logic and rationality. The Quran says :

> "The recompense of an evil deed is punishment proportionate to it, but whoever forgives and amends he shall have his reward from Allah."

> "Take to forgiveness and enjoin good and turn away from the ignorant."

The Holy prophet once said, "There may well be persons, who through forbearance and forgiveness get the same degree (of merit) as those, who keep the fast and perform the prayer." Vengeance and pride are against Islamic ethics. The tendency to lose one's temper quickly, and the inability to forgive people for their minor lapses, creates an atmosphere of awe and despair and brings disrepute to administration and government. Therefore, Muslim statesmen and writers have frequently referred to forgiveness as an indispensable quality of a good administrator. Hadrat Ali said :

> "Do not feel ashamed to forgive and forget. Do not hurry over punishments and do not be pleased and proud of your power to punish. Do not get angry and lose your temper quickly over the mistakes and failures of those over whom you rule. On the contrary, be patient and sympathetic with them. Anger and desire of vengeance are not going to be of much help to you in your administration."

The Patience : Many evils in society stem out of hasty and miscalculated decisions. Errors of judgment and faults in policy-making can be reduced considerably if the decision makers have the habit of patiently investigating and reflecting over the issues in hand. Without entering into its psychological ramifications, one can say with some kind of certainty that patience as a characteristic of human behaviour has been preached by nearly all religious and ethical codes. Islam has also applauded patience, as one of the noble qualities of human character. In the words of the Quran :

> "We shall prove you, by afflicting you in some measure with fear, and hunger, and decrease of wealth, and loss of lives and fruit. Those who prove patient under such misfortunes are to be given good tidings of God's reward—to those who, when a misfortune befalls them."

Ibn Taimiyya has pointed out that patience includes "fortitude, restraint on anger, willingness to pardon people, check on evil desire and abstention from indulgence (in luxury), and from frowning." Because of its significant and vital role, in the formulation of human character, Quran has bracketed patience with prayer. It says :

> "And seek assistance through patience and prayer."

> "So hear patiently what they say, and celebrate the praises of thy Lord before the rising of the sun and before the setting."

A tradition of the Prophet has been narrated by Abdullah bin Abbas which says :

> "When God wishes the welfare of a community he blesses it with officers, who are patient and large-hearted."

In one of his sermons, Umar I condemned ignorance and impatience among officers as despicable public sins." So did Ali in one of his letters said :

> "This virtue of patience is one of high values of morality and nobility of character and is the best habit which one can develop."

The Peacefulness : Aggression has been condemned because it disrupts normal and peaceful conduct of human affairs. Peace has been advocated as a great blessing and a cherished asset for fruitful social evolution. It is a natural inclination, and if human beings do not cultivate this quality, society would be under constant threat of dislocation and anarchy. According to Islam, love for peace is a great embellishment of human character and individuals and communities get dignity and respect through it. The Quran is very eloquent and emphatic on this issue. It says :

> "Live peacefully with one another. If they (the other party) incline to peace, do you also incline to it ? There is much good in coming to agreeable reconciliation, i.e., to live peacefully. And the servants of the Compassionate (God) are those, who walk peacefully on earth."

It has also been pointed out that, men tend to practice violence on many trivial matters. This tendency is extremely detrimental to peace, stability, and general welfare of the community. Unless the material injury is heavy and stakes exceptionally high, the Muslims are ordered to adjust their claims by peaceful and conciliatory means. This quality of ignoring trivialities for the larger good of the society has been praised by the Quran in the following words :

> "And when they hear frivolous discourse, which they fear might lead to some quarrel, they do not listen to it, but pass on with dignity, and do not pick up quarrels on trifling matters."

> "Repel the evil deed which is vain or frivolous with such a better answer, as to make the person between whom and ourselves there was enmity or discord to become as though he was a bosom friend."

There is a general complaint against bureaucracy that its members tend to isolate themselves from people. They are not readily available to the members of the public. There are procedural and psychological barriers, and very often inaccessibility is paraded as a status symbol. With this attitude civil servants can never have the awareness of the needs of the masses, and this ignorance can make public policy hollow and ineffectual. A closer and constant contact between the public servant and the public can breed an atmosphere of trust and confidence, which is so essential for the success of governmental policies.

A cloistered bureaucrat with no awareness of the needs of the people is certainly a misfit Public servants who are self-opinionated, secluded and arrogant can never implement public policies effectively. An administrator, who is easily accessible gets a greater fund of information and better perspectives for his decisions and avoids temptations. A life of seclusion makes an administrator extremely vulnerable to corruption. An officer who meets people readily, sits in a goldfish bowl. His activities are so transparent that he cannot indulge in any dishonest deal. An officer who is constantly interacting with members of the public, has to be extremely watchful about his reputation and performance.

Free and Easy Access : According to Islamic traditions of administration, officers at all levels and in all circumstances have to provide free and easy access to the public. During the Pious Caliphate, special emphasis was laid on this aspect of administrative behaviour. Umar I, in a letter to Muawiyya bin Abu Sufyan, gave special instructions that, he should not isolate himself from the people. He was ordered to maintain easy and facile communication with the masses. Knowing fully the evils that stem out of inaccessibility, Umar I warned his public servants to watch their behaviour continuously so that it did not smack of isolation or arrogance. In this connection his letter to Saad bin Abi Waqas deserves special consideration in which this high-ranking official of the state was administered a severe warning by the Caliph for his inaccessibility to the public.

> "I have come to know that you have built a place for yourself which looks like a fortress wherein you live

> in complete isolation from the people. The doors of this place are closed to the public, and I assure you this place is an edifice of your foolishness, demolish its gates because it hampers peoples access to you and they cannot bring their needs directly to you."

The relationship between civil servants and the public is extremely crucial for social and political stability. If the people know that decision-makers in government are prepared to listen to them, the bonds between the governors and governed would be cemented with trust and confidence. Any political system where the relationship between the subjects and the rulers are polluted with suspicion cannot last very long. In the literature on administration repeated discussions have been unrolled regarding the causes of inaccessibility of the bureaucrats. According to Umar I, inefficiency is one of the major causes of inaccessibility. With arrears piling up every day, an officer does not have enough time to receive people as they flock to his office with complaints or petitions. Umar I, in a letter to Abu Musa, wrote as follows:

> "Let there be no doubt about it that efficiency depends on not postponing todays work until tomorrow. If you do that it will create confusion in work; you will mix priorities and nothing will be accomplished; shun as much as you can from worldly love and lust and imbibe deep-seated interest in the affairs of the masses. Give them audience for justice, even if it be only for one hour daily."

Similarly, Hadrat Ali in his famous letter to Malike-bin-Ashtar emphasized in unequivocal terms that officers must provide every possible facility to the public to vindicate their grievances freely. He wrote:

> "Out of your hours of work find a time for complainants and for those, who want to approach you with their grievances. During this time you should do no other work, but hear them and pay attention to their complaints and grievances. For this purpose you must arrange public audiences for them. During these audiences, for the sake of God, treat them with

> kindness, courtesy and respect—do not place a prestige curtain between you and those over whom you rule."

According to Nizam-ul-Mulk, accessibility should be a universal characteristic of administration in a country. In his opinions, every officer from the Head of the State to the functionaries working at the lowest level must cordially welcome people, who come to them in connection with some official work. If the highest officers are willing to communicate with people freely their subordinates in his opinion refrain from practicing oppression. Rank, status and position of a functionary should not tend to isolate him from the community, whose interest he is supposed to serve. In certain quarters, genuine apprehensions have been expressed that, if the people are endowed with the privilege of visiting officers at will, it might become an excruciating burden on the time of the officers. But a careful examination of the issue, however, will prove that this apprehension is ill-founded.

Accessibility does not mean unending flow of people in offices all the time. Its primary purpose is to inculcate among officials awareness about public needs and willingness to serve the masses. To this end, proper procedures can be adopted, which without impeding the efficient working of administration would provide the public easy access to the officials. Islam has not laid down any operational framework for this vital aspect of public administration. The emphasis is mostly on the attitudes of the administrators. Officers can organize any machinery, which in their opinion would reduce their isolation from the people. In other words the climate, within the political system should be such that strong and weak, confident and timid, all could have access to public authorities. The Holy Prophet once said, "Tell me always of the needs of those, who cannot reach me with their needs, he who transmits to the man in authority an account of the needy of those, who cannot satisfy their needs by themselves, Allah will render firm his feet on the bridge to Paradise on a day when most feet are never firm."

Akhlak-i-Jalali has also maintained that social systems get additional stability if the rulers take personal interest in the affairs of their subjects. Equity, in the opinion of the author of this treatise, depends on the frequency of interaction between the members of the community and public servants. He says:

> "The maintenance of equity is to be methodically conducted only where the prince himself inquires into his subject's circumstances, and conducts each of them to his due share of provision and dignity. And this object can only be realized where subjects and complainants have access to their prince in time of need."

It was a common practice among kings of ancient Persia and rulers of Muslim dynasties to fix a specific day and time when common men, irrespective of rank, status, and privilege could have direct access to them. Akhlak-i-Jalali refers to a tradition which mentions that Pharaoh, in spite of his unbelief and tyranny, had two good qualities. Firstly, he was easily accessible to the people and secondly, he was generous and large-hearted to his subjects. The tradition further points out that there came a time when he discarded these qualities and "he made his "dwelling entirely in seclusion, or rather it may be said like the sulking bat in the den of aversion and repugnance, where none but Eblis (devil) and his attendant demons could obtain an interview." This was the time when the wrath of God descended upon him and this ultimately led to the disintegration of his empire.

Ibn Khaldun is also of the opinion that social organizations move very fast towards decay and dismemberment if the men in authority work in seclusion. He points out that inaccessibility of the rulers is symptomatic of their indolence and incompetence. A ruler of this kind, he says :

> "Seeks to keep away from the common people as much as possible. He employs someone at his door to admit (only) those of his friends and of the people of the dynasty whom he cannot avoid, and to prevent people (in general) from having access to him."

A weak and indolent ruler establishes court etiquette in a manner that only a limited number of people can have an access to him. Very often the members of the Inner circles, in order to perpetuate their own domination, contrive means to withhold information from the rulers about the actual state of affairs in the kingdom. All these are signs of political decay and inefficiency of the administrators.

A frustrated individual, who does not get a chance to unburden his grievances before the proper authorities, loses all interest in the welfare of the government. As this frustration multiplies, the system is bound to decline and deteriorate in efficiency.

The Sympathy : Philosophers and sages have labelled sympathy as one of the sterling excellencies of human character. Fellow feeling is considered to be a natural element of man's nature. Sympathy stems out of several factors. It can be due to residence in a common territory, similarity of religious views, loyalty to the same profession, ideological and intellectual affinity, similarity of objectives and membership of a caste or a cult. There is also something called human sympathy in which the above elements are not involved. It is a sentiment which rises above all personal affiliations and is a manifestation of simple love for humanity. Sympathy can be instinctive as well as moral. As an instinctive passion, it is common to men and animals, but as a moral quality, it is a particularity of the human race alone. This quality, however, is not to be expended on sinners and wrong doers. The Quran explains this point as follows:

> "Sympathy and cooperation are enjoined upon you towards deeds of goodness and piety, but you must not cooperate towards sinful or transgressive deeds."
>
> "And plead not on behalf of any people who deceive themselves; God does not love anyone who is treacherous and sinful."

Importance of Morality

This shows that in Islam sympathy as a moral quality is subject to fundamental condition, that the one to whom sympathy is being extended is not a sinner or evil-minded person. Its indiscriminate use is disallowed because it is likely to encourage sin and crime in society.

In government and administration, it is not the individual act of sympathy which is so important. Emphasis here is on the general climate of thought and practice in which people can satisfy their needs without generating acrimony or hostility. If the government functionaries are unsympathetic and callous in their attitudes, a social system will remain unstable. Frustrated masses will be reluctant to provide the required fund of loyalty which in essence is the main support of healthy politics. Hadrat Ali, in one of his sermons, said, "The greatest of these reciprocal rights is that of a ruler on the ruled and that of the governed on the governing authority, but remember that no subject will be happy and contented unless the system of government is sympathetic, humane and congenial."

Sympathy, in order to be effective, has to be universal, and free from racial and sectarian prejudices. All sections of the population, even the religious minorities, have a right to receive sympathy from administration. Islam has accorded a special and privileged status to minorities in a Muslim kingdom. Their life, property, honour and privileges should be of special concern to the rulers. They should be recipient of the same kindness and sympathy which are reserved for the Muslims in an Islamic state, Hadrat Ali administered a severe warning to a governor who maltreated a religious minority. He wrote:

> "Remember Malik that, among your subjects there are two kinds of people : those having the same religion as yours and they are brothers unto you and those who have other religions than yours and yet are human-beings like you. Men of either category suffer from the same weaknesses and disabilities that human flesh is their to; they commit sins, indulge in vices either intentionally or foolishly or unitentionally without realising the enormity of their deeds. Let your mercy and compassion come to their rescue and help in the same way and to the same extent that you expect God to show mercy and foregiveness to you."

8

Progressive Attitude

Approach to Science

Exploration of the mysteries buried deep in the bosom of nature, is an endless activity of human mind. Science and religion are generally considered to be the two major contenders in this eternal endeavour of man. Religious and scientific views in most cases are irreconcilable. Scientists ridicule the theologians as irrational and mythical and the theologians in turn castigate the scientists as atheists or materialists. Both tend to claim the monopoly of truth. In Islam however, the struggle between science and religion was never so acute or critical. In fact during most of the Islamic history science and religion remained in a very healthy combination in uncovering the secrets of the universe and in fortifying the beliefs and ideals of the Muslims. There is a general consensus among historians of Islamic civilization, that religion in Islam instead of being a barrier to scientific investigation provided a powerful thrust for greater and wider inquiry into the unresolved mysteries of the relationship between man and nature.

Islam and Scientific Knowledge : The Quran in very clear terms has brought home this message to every believer. A passage in the fourth chapter reads as follows :

> He it is Who sendeth down water from the sky, and therewith We bring forth buds of every kind; We bring forth the green blade from which We bring forth the

> thick-clustered grain; and from the date-palm, from the pollen thereof, spring pendant bunches ; and (We bring forth) gardens of grapes, and the olive and the pomegranate, alike and unlike. Look upon the fruit thereof, when they bear fruit, and upon its ripening. Lo ! herein verily are portents for a people who believe.

Floods, rains, clouds, insects, are all God's creations. He is the sole Provider and Protector. He enjoins upon every believer to understand these manifold manifestations of nature, as Ayats (signs) of the Creator. There are numerous verses in the Quran which repeatedly emphasise this theme. Some of them can be reproduced as follows :

> So We sent against them the flood and the locusts and the vermin and the frogs and the blood—a succession of clear signs. But they were arrogant and became a guilty folk.

And He it is Who sendeth the winds as tidings heralding His mercy, till, when they bear a cloud heavy (with rain), We lead it to a dead land, and then cause water to descend thereon and thereby bring forth fruits of every kind. Thus bring We forth the dead. Happily ye may remember.

He sendeth down water from the sky, so that valleys flow according to their measure, and the flood beareth (on its surface) swelling foam—from that which they smelt in the fire in order to make ornaments and tools riseth a foam like unto it— thus Allah coineth (the similitude of) the true and the false. Then, as for the foam, it passeth away as scum upon the banks; while, as for that which is of use to mankind, it remaineth in the earth. Thus Allah coineth the similitudes. What, have they not beheld heaven above them, how We have built it, and decked it out fair, and it has no cracks ? And the earth—We stretched it forth and cast on it firm mountains, and We caused to grow therein of every joyous kind for an insight and a reminder to every penitent servant. We sent down out of heaven water blessed, and caused to grow thereby gardens and grain of harvest and tall palm-trees with spathes compact, a provision for the servants, and thereby We revived a land that was dead. Even so is the coming forth.

All commentators of these verses agree that uncovering the secrets of nature is a religious duty of every believer. Scientific and philosophic explorations and the results derived out of them should help the believer to fortify his faith in God. In order to facilitate rational enquiry and save human knowledge from stagnation, Quran allows intellectual and ideological disputations among the learned because that is the only way one can sort out truth from falsehood. The Quranic verse in this regard is as follows :

> Call thou to the way of thy Lord With wisdom and good admonition, and dispute with them in the better way.

The Muslim scientists used this verse to demonstrate that knowledge acquired through research is valid and does not in any way contradict the revealed word of God. Arberry has given the following interpretation of the verse :

> When the Quranic term 'hikma' (wisdom) came to be used loosely to signify philosophy, this text fortified the philosophers in their contest with the obscurantists. The verbal noun derived from 'jadalhum' (dispute with them) was to acquire the technical meaning of 'reasoned debate.' As for 'mauiza' (admonition) that was the chosen method of the preachers. This verse would be taken to confirm Aristotle's threefold differentiation of proof into demonstrative, rhetorical and dialectical.'

There is ample evidence in the Traditions of the Prophet that he too believed that life without intellectual activity is fruitless. He once pointed out that intellect was the first thing created by God. Therefore, effective and gainful use of intellect was a kind of prayer which would be pleasing to God.

In spite of the clear indications in the Quran and the Traditions of the Prophet that scientific and rational investigation in human life, and natural phenomena was a religious duty, the relationship between scientific knowledge and religious learning in Islam was often very uncomfortable. Suspicions between the protagonists of the two increased after the Greek thought under the patronage of the early Abbasides became almost an official doctrine in the Muslim kingdom.

The clash between the knowledge based on reason and the one derived through revelation kept on mounting, until it became a permanent feature of the world of scholarship in Islam. Such a clash was natural because the Semetic mind for ages had made revealed knowledge the chief pillar of human life, while the Hellenic thinking had relied solely on rational and logical enquiry. The theological circles were disturbed particularly when the rationalists started questioning some of the fundamental principles of Islam. Attributes of God, the nature and character of prophesy, the authenticity of revelation, and numerous other issues relating to miracles, angels and life hereafter were subjected to very critical examination by the rationalist thinkers.

The increasing popularity of such concepts created widespread fears among religious scholars about the future of the religion. Seeds of dissension sown between secular and religious knowledge early in Islamic history persisted for along time. In this controversy the scientists unquestionably were at a disadvantage. The hold of religion on the masses was so strong that they would easily be rallied in defence of any religious cause. Moreover, their contact with the religious leaders was constant. In each mosque, five times during the day, hundreds of them congregated for prayers and listened to the learned theologians with reverence.

Scientists and philosophers on the other hand were mostly cloistered in their ivory towers; and their technical and abstruse writings could not be comprehended by the vast majority of the illiterate people. Another point which needs to be kept in mind is that learning in Islam to a large extent depended on royal patronage, and the kind of knowledge that would be encouraged and developed was determined by the outlook of the ruler. Even a cursory glance at the Islamic history would reveal that, although not practicing Muslims in the true sense of the term, most of the Muslim rulers proclaimed themselves to be defenders of the faith. A large number of theologians held powerful positions in government and exercised deep influence on all aspects of public policy. Even under the most rationalist of the rulers, Shariah was the law of the land, and religious scholars held the monopoly of interpreting its principles.

Judgements given in the religious courts could not be contested in any other court of law, and opinion pronounced by Qadis and Muftis, in most cases used to become precedents for later decisions. From this however, it should not be construed that theologians had an absolute veto in the affairs of the government. There is no question that as an elitist group they wielded considerable power in a Muslim state, but their decisions could be vetoed by the rulers.

Scientists and philosophers were also consulted very often by the rulers but since their advice had no religious backing it lacked the impact of a Mufti's fatwa (religious pronouncement of a Juro-consult). In extreme cases, the theologians used to declare rationalists as Kafirs (infidels), which could be extremely detrimental to their reputation.

The result of this prepondering influence of religion was that secularism as it is understood in the West, never flourished in the Muslim civilization. Irrespective of their private opinions and intellectual proclivities, all public officials in a Muslim state had to show some deference to the word of God.

Even the renowned scientists of Islam, with all their undiminished commitment to reason, never thought that religion in any way was a barrier to their scientific researches. They remained firmly anchored to the religious faith, and there is no evidence that they ever felt intellectually thwarted by the laws of the Shariah. George DeSantillana has made the following remarks on the approach of the Muslim scientists to religion :

> One wishes only at times that he had not drawn so tight the web of orthodox piety as to leave in an uncomfortable and slightly alien position, along the course of time, men who stand out more clearly as representing the scientific temper. These men do not belong to the phase of withdrawal, but to the phase of world leadership; they are good Muslims and true, and a glory of their civilization. Therefore, since this is a history centered on science, I feel they should have been presented in bolder relief. In Al-Beruni, the

> greatest scientist of Islam, we meet a mind in no way different from the Western lay scientific mind at its best. His religious faith is secure but carried lightly, without protestations. It does not impede his freedom of judgement, his love of fact, his free-wheeling curiosity, his easy sarcasm, his strict and watchful cult of intellectual integrity. We recognize soon, in Al-Beruni, the scientist without qualifications as we mean him, as he has been understood again and again, and the same may be said of the other great men of his ilk-observers, experimenters, analysts, such men as Rhazes, Alhazen, Al-Battani, Averroes. This is what the Islamic intellect was able to bring forth during the golden age, as well as later, and they surely need no apologies for their perhaps-a-shade-too-secular attitude, nor deserve the hint that they were out of step with their own culture.

Wider Perspective : In order to get broader perspectives on the relationship between science and religion in Islam it would be in the fitness of things to make a synoptic survey of the views held by some of the leading Muslim scientists. Scientists selected are those whose achievements and contributions are always highlighted in the history of science. It is difficult to say with certainty what were their private opinions on religion, but in their writings and public pronouncements, they always professed un-deviating adherence to religion. On the whole they seemed to believe that Is!am encouraged scientific research and favoured creative endeavours which opened new pathways to human understanding. In their opinion scientific findings provided support and strength to the believers faith in the eternal wisdom and truthfulness of the Quran.

Abu-Yusuf Yaqubi-ibn-Ishaqal Kindi ranks among the greatest scientists of Islam. Attached to the court of Caliph-al-Mamun, he had the opportunity to read and assimilate the latest Greek works which were being translated in large numbers at that time. To attain richness in philosophy and scholarship he had laid down the following six prerequisites :

> For a seeder of learning aspiring to be a philosopher six prerequisites are essential, a superior mind, uninterrupted passion, gracious patience, a free-from-worry heart, a competent introducer and a long time, should one of these prerequisites be lacking, the student is bound to fail.

Al-Kindi was fully equipped with these qualities of head and heart, and his genius under the royal patronage of Al-Mamun who was a great lover of free thought, got every possible chance to develop. He was deeply impressed by the logic and reasoning of the Hellenic thought and spared no efforts to convince his contemporaries that search for divine truth would be strengthened if reason was kept in close companionship with religion. Knowledge, in his opinion, should be accepted from all sources. It is not a monopoly of any one region or religion. He said : We should never be ashamed to approve truth and acquire it no matter what its source might be, even if it might have come from foreign people and alien nations far removed from us.

In his opinion reason and revelation are the two main streams of knowledge in human life. True knowledge always stems out only when ideas flowing out of two sources are cross-fertilized. Hitti has summed up Al-Kindi's tireless zeal to harmoniously blend philosophy and theology, and dispel thickening clouds of suspicions from the minds of the theologians regarding secular learning, as follows:

> He argued that theology was a branch of philosophy, one depends on revelation, the other on reason, one employs logic, the other faith, but the truth attained by theology is not in conflict with that attained by philosophy. As a Mutazilite thinker, Al-Kindi had a special fascination for non-Arab sciences. His sympathetic attitude towards knowledge acquired through foreign sources, and the gusto with which he tried to integrate it with basic theological views and opinions, introduced a patently new approach to the religious researches in Islam. His writings created a tremendous impact on the religious circles of the day

> and mitigated considerably the built-in antipathy of the theologians towards scientific inquiry. He typified the new trend among Muslim scholars to synthesise traditional theological knowledge with the latest findings of scientific studies. In this way he increased the prestige of the secular learning without diminishing the reverence for religious scholarship.

Not Contrary : In other words Al-Kindi was, convinced that the wisdom of the Greek philosophers, as he had been able to construe from the translations of their writings, was not contrary to the spirit of Islam. He found perfect harmony between the revelations of the Quran, and the reasoning of the Greek texts regarding life and society. All that one needed was to establish a working relationship between the two.

Abu Rihan-al-Beruni, who ranks among the greatest scientists of Islam includes his classic work Kitab-ul-Hind (India) with the following words :

> We ask God to pardon us for every statement of ours which is not true. We ask Him to help us that we may adhere to that which yields Him satisfaction. We ask Him to lead us to a proper insight into the nature of that which is false and idle, that we may sift it so as to distinguish the chaff from the wheat. All good comes from Him and it is He who is clement towards his slaves. Praise be to God, the Lord of the worlds and His blessings be upon the Prophet Muhammad and his whole family.

Al-Beruni, like most Muslim scientists, believed that all knowledge was inherently religious. It was difficult for him to disbelieve that the universe was the creation of God, and that all the material glories of life on earth, including the blessings of human reason and intelligence were diverse manifestations of His eternal and universal benediction. All learning and every enquiry was sacred because with every new discovery, man's faith in God was strengthened and it proved the truth of the Holy Prophet's message. He believed that the universe was the handiwork of God and its study constituted the noblest pursuit of human mind. Labels given to various sciences were immaterial, physical sciences, history, or studies relating to man and society, all had religious character. Al-Beruni in all his writings continued to emphasize that examination of visible phenomena, provided a clue to the invisible world, and this reconciliation between the secular and the spiritual knowledge, in his opinion constituted the hall-mark of Islamic civilization !

Ibn Sina (Avecena) another outstanding figure in the history of science in Islam, also insisted that the motions in heavens and movements on earth were due to the will of God. Life with all its trials and tribulations was devoted entirely to the search of Supreme Truth, which directed the multifarious activities in the universe.

Mastery over Science : Ibn Sina worked very hard in the acquisition of knowledge and even before he was twenty, he had mastered practically all the sciences. In his autobiography he proudly refers to the fact that at eighteen he had reached the acme of his intellectual attainments. Most accounts agree that his education was thorough and comprehensive and included both religious and secular sciences. Ibn Khallikan in his Kitab Fafayat Ayan (Biographical Dictionary) says :

> Abu Ali (Ibn Sina) laboured in the acquisition of natural philosophy, divinity and other sciences, he reads the texts with the commentaries, and God opened for him the gates of knowledge. Several contemporary scholars criticized him for his philosophical ideas, thinking that his writings were deeply influenced by Hellenic thought. But there is ample evidence in his encyclopaedic compilations that he continued to adhere to the fundamentals of Islam. His faith in the ultimate power of God remained unshaken and he never questioned the indisputable competence of the prophet to produce knowledge through revelation. Ibn Khallikan has mentioned his overwhelming devotion to ..... in the following words :
>
> And when he met with an obscure point-he used to perform a total ablution and proceed to the great

> mosque, where he would pray to Almighty God to facilitate its comprehension to him, and unlock the gate of difficulty.

In his Aqsam-al-ulum, Ibn Sina said that "through this part of practical philosophy we know the existence of prophecy (as something necessary) and that the human race needs the Shariah for its existence, preservation and future life."

To his critics he replied that "if there is in the world a man like me and that man should not be a Muslim, then there is no Muslim at all in the entire world." He also believed in the immortality of the human soul and life hereafter which brought rewards and punishment for deeds done on this earth. This view was strictly in consonance with the orthodox interpretation of the Quranic injunctions.

Ikhawan-al-Safa wal Khullam-al-Wafa (Brethren of Purity) is another classic of cosmological knowledge which has earned tremendous popularity among scholarly circles of the Muslim lands for several centuries. These Rassails (Treatises) are known traditionally for many of their excessively rationalistic views on religio-political and spiritual aspects of life in a Muslim community. But in spite of their deep interest in Aristotalian logic the authors have abstained from preaching anything which would throw doubt on basic principles which constitute the corner-stone of Islamic ideology. The authors main purpose was to emancipate the human mind from the captivity of ignorance, and enable it to grasp the realities of life in a scientific and rational manner.

J. H. Kramers has made the following estimate of the "Brethren of Purity." Parallel with the fixation of orthodox theology there appeared in Iraq a philosophical movement that was equally unfavourable to the free development of unprejudiced scientific research.. We know this movement through the encyclopaedic writings of the so-called "Brethren of Purity" or "Brethren of Basra." These writings were composed about 950. In the fifty-two treatises of which they consist all the sciences known at that time are placed in a general scheme. Its system, as far as there is any system is mainly influenced by neo-Platonic views, which consider the world as the result of a series of emanations from the divine unity. This philosophy is outwardly Islamic in that it makes use of allegorical interpretations of the Quran. In its application to the sciences this system points to the hidden meaning of connections between various phenomena in nature, as expressed in numbers. On the whole the theories of the "Brethren of Purity" are scientifically less important than the work of Al-Kindi and his contemporaries.

The treatises consist of epistles or long essays which were written during the Buwayhid period and had the support and patronage of the rulers who being Shiate were comparatively more tolerant of free thinking. The essays deal with all varieties of subjects from magic and mythology to mathematics and metaphysics. There are also detailed discussions about theology and astrology, and on matters relating to reason, revelation and prophecy. DeLacy O'Learey has made the following comments on the contents of the epistles of the Brotherhood of Purity :

> The doctrine contained in these letters is eclectic, the world is described as an emanation from God, the human soul as of celestial origin and striving to return to God and to be absorbed in Him, a consummation to be attained by wisdom, the Gnosis of Gnostic and neo-Platonic writers. The rationalism of the authors, and their excessive reliance on reason in resolving the mysteries of life, however, did not minimize in their estimate of importance of the revealed word of God. In one of the epistles the importance of divine knowledge is depicted as follows :
>
> Know, my brother, that the prime support of faith and its most powerful pillar is subservience to the bearers of the divine Laws (nawamis) in that which they command of obedience and that which they forbid of rebellion; it consists of harkening to them and obedience to them. This is so because the noblest works of mankind, the most delightful deeds of humanity and the highest rank to which the wise may attain next to the rank of angels is the establishment of the divine laws.

Fakhr-ad-Din Razi, who had a very questioning mind and seemed to disagree with many of the precepts of Islam, professed publicly that religion was a repository of immeasurable knowledge. His lectures at Herat were attended both by theologians and philosophers and earned him the title of Sheikh-al-Islam (Chief Interpreter of Islam). It is said that he had memorized by heart the whole of Imamal-Haramains treatise on fundamental theology entitled al Shamil. In the same manner, Ibn Rushd who ranks among the greatest physicians and philosophers of Islam, was vehemently criticized among the orthodox circles for many of his views which were deemed to be heretical.

But there is ample evidence in his writings that even he never denigrated the importance of religion in the moral, spiritual, and material welfare of the Muslim community. He once said, "he who studies anatomy increases his belief in God." A common belief has been established among commentators of Muslim philosophy that Ibn Rushd was a staunch rationalist, and that his expressions of religiosity were only an expediency to avoid annoyance of his royal patrons who in spite of their enlightened view were strict believers in Orthodox Sunni doctrine. W.J.J. Rosen that however, is of the opinion that in the absence of any definite evidence, it is wrong to contend that Ibn Rushd was guilty of intellectual dishonesty.

Enriching Knowledge : Like the rest of the philosopher-theologians of Islam, Ibn Rushd was convinced that Islam as a religion had to contribute a great deal towards the enrichment of every branch of knowledge. The knowledge of God, soul and spirit can only be acquired through prophecy, and whatever other insights one acquired through philosophy, logic and ethics, were secondary in character. He believed that religion alone can ensure material welfare and moral health of the society. Any knowledge which ensured happiness of mankind in one form or another, could never be contrary to Islam. Ibn Rushd once said that "philosophy is the companion and the foster-sister of the Shariah." He made a powerful case for the unification of revelation and reason. Truth in his opinion was not a monopoly of any particular race or nationality. He was convinced that the Quran and the Hadith did not debar the believers from accumulating knowledge from pre-Islamic sources.

Ordinance itself requires us to look into the books of the ancients, since their intention and goal in what they wrote was the same goal as that towards which Divine Ordinance has urged us. Any man forbidding the study of these books to anyone properly qualified to look into them—anyone that is, who combines sagacity of spirit with religious uprightness and moral virtue—thereby bars mankind from the very door whereby Divine ordinance calls men to get to know God, the door of speculation, leading to the true knowledge of Him.

In other words, he believed cosmological knowledge as found in the books of the ancients provided powerful crutches to the understanding of the word of God. He points out that it is the duty of every ardent believer to understand the universe around him because it testifies to the greatness of the Creator. Blossoms in the oasis of the desert and the stars in distant heavens, earth and water, plants and change of seasons, rain, rivers and oceans, floods, storms and the entire cyclones, and the entire cycle of life and death, are signs meant to speak eloquently for the boundless authority, control, as well as mercy and benediction of God. Exploration of the mysteries buried in the bosom of the universe is a legitimate activity of the human mind.

Numerous other instances could be collected from the writings of other Muslim scientists, to prove that the dichotomy between science and religion which highlights the Western Civilization did not exist in Islam. Most scientists were devout Muslims, and in their books and public statements, they professed undeviating confidence in the truth and wisdom of the religious doctrines. They did not have to be atheists or agnostics, in order to perform creative experiments in various sciences. In most cases they believed that by uncovering the mysteries of nature, they were serving the cause of religion. In the religion they found a permanent source of inspiration for their innovative endeavours.

There were constant intellectual skirmishes between strictly orthodox circles, and scholars who believed in free will and indulged in liberal interpretation of the Quranic principles, but in the world of Islamic scientific thought atheism was never accepted as prerequisite for enquiry into the realm of sciences. A question is always raised that if religion was such a powerful source of inspiration in Islam for scientific studies, then why after a certain period of time, the scientific activity was abruptly brought to an end. A careful examination of the history of Muslim scholarship will show that the decline in the study of mathematical and natural sciences was not due to religious barriers. It was the result of many causes.

Creative Period : It is true that the creative period of Islamic scholarship was very short lived. It touched the meridian of its achievement with lightening speed, and then suddenly due to certain religio-political reasons it became stagnant and declined. But even during the short time that it led the world, its achievements left an imperishable mark on the later development of scientific knowledge in human history. To everything that Muslim scientists and scholars borrowed from other sources they gave a stamp of their own originality. They clarified many ambiguities of the ancient knowledge, corrected numerous discrepancies in scientific thinking, and through many innovative experiments and verifications they opened countless new vistas in human understanding. For centuries religious prejudices of the Western historians always degenerated the contributions of the Muslim men of science, but in recent years there has been growing realization that the history of learning would have been very poor without the depth and originality of the Muslim scholars. Philip Hitti has made the following comments:

> The question has often been raised, how creative was the thinking of his co-religionist colleagues? Some have claimed that Arab philosophy was a series of footnotes to Plato and Aristotle. But creativity based on nothing takes place only in theology. The creative process presupposes the existence of old elements which when combined in new ways or with new elements yield a new and useful product. In this case Arab creativity consisted in combining old philosophic and theologic ideas to produce original and useful ones.

George Sarton's classic work on the history of science has made the following remarks on the contributions of the Muslim scientists.

Some of the giants of medieval times belonged to the Arabic culture, mathematicians and astronomers like Al-Khwarizmi (IX-1), Al-Farghani (IX-1), Al-Battani (IX-2), Abul-Wafa (X-2), Umar Khayyam (XI-I), Al-Ghazzali (XI-2), Ibn Rushd (XII-2), Ibn Khaldun (XIV-2) physicians like Al-Razi (IX-2), Ishaq-al-Israeli (X-I), Ali Ibn 'Abbas (X-2), Abu-l-Qasim (-2), Ibn Sina (XI-I), Maimonides (XII-2). This enumeration could be greatly extended. Few of these men were Arabs and not all of them were Muslims, but they all belonged essentially to the same cultural group, and their language was Arabic. This illustrates the absurdity of trying to appraise medieval thought on the basis of Latin writings alone. For centuries the Latin scientific books hardly counted; they were out-of-date and out-landish. Arabic was the international language of science to a degree which had never been equalled by another language before (except Greek) and has never been repeated since. It was the language not of one people, one nation, one faith, but of many peoples, many nations, many faiths.

The Arabic culture is of a singular interest to the student of human traditions in general, to those whose greatest task it seems to them is the rebuilding of human integrity in the face of national and international disasters, because it was, and to some extent still is, a bridge, the bridge between East and West.

Range of Scholarship : Richard Sullivan has made these comments on the range of Muslim scholarship.

The range of Muslim scholarship was immense. Theology and religious law commanded primary attention, but other fields of scholarship were also extremely active. In the realm of the natural sciences, Muslim scholars, building on their encyclopaedic collection of ancient knowledge, created scientific manuals that were superior to any found elsewhere in the contemporary world. It is possible to detect in these works the origins of our modern scientific knowledge and spirit.

Scientific Miracle in Holy Quran : There may seem to be an inherent contradiction in the term "scientific miracle" , because when a miracle can be explained in scientific terms, it no longer remains a miracle. Yet under another shade of meaning, even a scientifically explained phenomenon can be a wondrous occurrence and thus a miracle.

The Quran, the whole of it, is a miracle in many ways. But as yet it can only be partly explained in scientific terms. Of course, as our knowledge increases more and more of the Quran will be explained in scientific terms. The Quran has layers upon layers of meanings, which are being gradually revealed to us as our knowledge increases:

> Say: If all the Sea were ink for my Lord's words, The sea would indeed be exhausted before my Lord's Words are exhausted! And [thus it would be] if we Were to add to it sea upon sea. (Quran 18:109)

In other words indeed all miracles are scientific phenomena. Simply because on the basis of our current state of knowledge, we are unable to comprehend their true scientific foundation, we call them miracles. Allah had created the Universe according to a Plan and all knowledge flows from Him. Therefore, there is an underlying unity in all knowledge, whether ethical, scientific or spiritual. For example, just ponder over the concepts of straight line and equality; how they pervade through all branches of knowledge.

Reasoned Thinking

There is no blind faith in Islam. The Quran continuously invites you to observe, think and reflect.

Allow me to digress here a little to present to you the central framework of Islam, which is based on three fundamental concepts of Al-iman, Al-Islam and Al-ihsan. Al-iman (faith), which is based on transcendent intelligence; Al-Islam (the law: submission) which reflects certainty (Yaqin) reflects equilibrium is based on free will and Al-ihsan (the way : virtue) which reflects remembrance (dhikr) is based on the gift of speech. Thus, Islam is the religion of Certainty, Equilibrium and remembrance is based on the three deform faculties of transcendent intelligence, free will and gift of speech. Thus, in Islam the prayer and of course the remembrance of God must be done with free will and intelligence; only then will these be acceptable to Him.

Turning now, to the other side of the coin, we should clearly appreciate that the current 'state of art' of the scientific method is constrained by severe limitations. At a lower level these limitations pertain to the direct verification of an occurrence (null hypothesis) and at a higher level to the fragility of human observation (the Hisenburg principle of uncertainty) and to the relativity of observation (Einstein). The Quran has emphasised the importance of firm observation in the following verses:

> The (Prophet's) (mind and) heart
>
> In no way falsified
>
> That which he saw
>
> Will ye then dispute
>
> WIth him concerning
>
> What he saw?
>
> Behold, the Lote-tree
>
> Was shrouded
>
> (In mystery unspeakable)
>
> (His) sight never swerved,
>
> Nor did it go wrong! (Quran, 53 : 11, 12 & 16, 17).

In view of the above-mentioned limitations of the scientific method, it will indeed be presumptuous on our part if we tried to comprehend Quran strictly in the context of the current framework of the scientific method. It is indeed in the recognition of this human limitation that the Islamic faith ('Iman) also extends to things which are beyond the reach of human perception (Al-Ghayb) :

> This is the Book;
>
> In it is guidance, sure, without doubt,
>
> To those who fear Allah:
>
> Who believe in the Unseen,

Are steadfast in prayer,

And spend out of what We

Have provided for them; (Quran 2 : 2, 3)

You have to accept Islam in totality or reject it is in totality, there is no partial acceptance or rejection.

"Accept Islam is its entirety" (Quran 2:208)

You cannot say that we will accept only that part of Quran which falls within the reach of our scientific percepts:

Then is it only a part of

The Book That Ye believe in

And do Ye reject the rest? (Quran 2:85)

Accepted Principle : This Quranic injunction is also an accepted principle in the scientific method, whereby "either all or none" of the results of an experiment are accepted.

I hope, that this is not in conflict with the Quranic emphasis on reason, is self-evident to you. The Quran beseeches you to strive with reason to understand it but at the same time the Quran asks you to believe in the Unseen (Al-Ghayb).

The Quran asks you not only to use reason, but also to reflect, because it is reflection which will guide us towards layers upon layers of its meanings and its remarkable internal logic. The reason should lead you to ask the question ; Why the "Unseen" or "beyond perception"? The Quran's international logic will lead you to the answer that as the Quran is the book for all times, with human progress over time curtain after curtain will be lifted to reveal the Unseen. Anyway, if the Unseen was never to be revealed, Allah logically would not have talked about it.

Proof of Unseen : The proof of the Unseen for the mankind was provided by Allah through Al-Isra, the night journey of the Prophet (Blessings of Allah and Peace be upon him), which in scientific terms may be at least partly explained by the concept of 'pure time', as discussed by Iqbal in his The Reconstruction of Religious Thought in Islam. But, one miracle of the Quran is that it caries its own proof. While the Quran gives a great importance to reason or logic, it does not consider it as the sole means of gaining knowledge and the only criterion for judging the truth.

The Intellect (al-aql-al-kulli), the instrument through which Divine Knowledge is obtained, must not be mistaken for reason alone (al-aql-al-juzi). In the Quran the aql is at once both intellect and reason. But if the 'aql is obscured by the worldly passions, then it can become the veil that hides man from the Divine and leads him astray. Thus, the reason can be both an instrument for reaching the divine truths, truths which are super-rational but not irrational, and a veil which hides these very truths from man. We should, therefore, be wary of this two - edged nature of the "sword of reason".

The Quran describes three distinct levels of knowledge: first ilm-al-Yaqin, knowledge through information; second ayn-al-yaqin, knowledge through experience and third and highest haqq-al-yaqin, true knowledge through being:

> Nay, were ye to know
> With certainty of mind,
> Ye would beware!
> Ye shall certainly see
> Hell-Fire!
> Again, ye shall see it
> With certainly of sight! (Quran 102:5, 6,7)
> But verily it is Truth
> Of assured certainly. (Quran 69:51)

A Muslim sage had explained these three stages of knowledge more picturesquely with the analogy of fire. If you had not seen fire; only heard about it, that is 'ilm-al-yaqin. When you saw it before you, that is ayn-al-yaqin. But only when you jump into it, you really know what fire is and that is the high stage of haqq-al-yaqin.

It was through beseeching Allah for ayn-al-yaqin that Prophet Ibrahim (on him be peace) strengthened his faith:

Behold! Ibrahim said:
"My Lord! Show me how
Thou givest life to the dead,"
He said: "Dost thou not
Then believe?" He said:
"Ye but to satisfy
My own understanding."
He said: "Take four birds;
Tame them to turn to thee;
Put a portion of them
on every hill, and call to them;
They will come to thee
(Flying) with speed.
Then know that Allah
Is Exalted in Power, Wise". (Quran 2:260)

Once you have attained ayn-al-yaqin there remains no need for you to speculate about many things or creatures of the Unseen such as the Jinn. Then you know with certainty what they are. The source of ayn-al-yaqin or being a sahib-al-nazar is available to all of us by purification of our hearts and minds through a constant recitation of the specific verses of the Quran and the dhikr-Allah, the remembrance of God.

Miracle of the Prophet : The miracle of Prophet Muhammad (Blessings of Allah and Peace be upon him) is the Quran. After God, the most powerful instrument in the Universe are neither the Angels nor the forces of the nature but the Word-the Word of God.

The Quran being the spoken Word of God is thus a repository of His Power. Each Word of the Quran has a secret power, which when you learn that Word become yours and can lead you to wondrous things and space-time dimensions. The power of the Word is verified by the Quran among others in the following verses:

He said (to his own men):
"Ye Chiefs! which of you
Can bring me here throne
Before they come to me
In submission?"
Said a bold one of the Jinns:
"I will bring it to thee
Before thou rise from thy
Council : indeed I have
Full strength for the purpose,
And may be trusted."
Said one who had knowledge
Of the Book: "I will
Bring it to thee within
The twinkling of an eye!"
Then when (Solomon) saw it
Placed firmly before him,
He said: "This is
By the grace of my Lord!
To test me whether I am
Grateful or ungrateful
And if any is grateful,
Truly his gratitude is (a gain)
For his own soul; but if
Any is ungrateful, truly
My Lord is Free of all Needs,
Most generous in giving!" (Quran 27: 38, 39, 40)

The status of such persons who rise to this power is described clearly by the following Hadith-al-Qudsi:

....And My slave keeps coming
closer to Me by performing
extra prayers until I love him.
And when I love him, I become his ears
with which he listens; his eyes with
which he sees; his hands with which
he hits; his legs with which he
walks and if he asks Me anything
I will give it to him and if he comes
to Me for My protection I will
Protect him (Al-Bukhari)

The most wonderful among these, however, seek not the powers but only him. Please remember that the miracle is the strength of your faith.

9

Impact of Materialism

"Verily, we created you of a male and female, and made you into nations and tribes, so that ye may know each other". Quran (49:13)

Since time immemorial, the Europeans has sought their nourishment from the soil. This vital necessity helped them to develop the bases of an agrarian, or as a French sociologist puts it, of a "civilisation de P herbage". The original synthesis of men and soil having been realised at an early stage, the latter found themselves disciplined in terms of very close neighbourly relations that created the notion of property, strictly delimiting it as the fixed space of a human life, of a hearth and a family. Internally this space of life, this "vital space" is essentially conditioned by regular seasonal activities that engender a very precise notion, that of the daily work. The social notion of time, in its turn, incorporated itself in the original synthesis. The climate would lead man to adopt fire as an essential element of his life, and to furnish his interior in terms of his daily work, climate and fire. The table and chairs became the conditions of a very intimate family life wherein the individuals gathered at fixed hours for the common meal.

First Phase

Externally, this family space necessarily articulated on neighbouring spaces similarly conditioned. The church spirit born of these local agglomerations would little by little give birth to communal life, thus realising the integration of the individuals to an order responding to the conditions and aspirations of a static life.

Neither Roman imperialism, nor Germanic nomadism succeeded, in the course of centuries, in modifying this original canvas of European life. Christianism and Cartesianism came to complete the physiognomy of this society, profoundly, perhaps excessively, penetrated with the sense of utility. The former brought to it the sense of the universal, and through it the dynamism that its static temperament lacked; the latter tailored its fundamental activities for efficiently integrating them in the industrial vitality that was going to surge from its evolution. In this society of centripetal virtues that practised mutual aid, but did not know hospitability. Christianism also deposited the ferment of moral expansionism that would serve as a justification for the Crusades and the colonial enterprise.

The Crusades offered the European civilization an opportunity to turn towards the exterior, and to reap a profitable harvest in the Muslim civilization. The same tendencies pushed it to the discovery of America, and one could here discern the beginning of a profound rupture between a dominating Europe and the rest of humanity, that explains the politics of the world for the last four centuries as well as its present disequilibrium. Howsoever it may be, it was this society marked with the genius of the soil, but where the possibilities of inter-human relationships were almost completely stifled that, towards the 18th century, discovered the Muslim world.

In this world, the individual did not originally seek his nourishment from the soil-which could not furnish it, but obtained it from the beast. He was a shepherd, a nomad or a warrior. The space of his life, his vital space, was as indefinite as the zone, the nearest to his habitat, where the last rain had fallen. This habitation itself was mobile by necessity and could dispense with furniture.

Why settle on a soil that did not give food? The man thus on the move, did not have regular activities, and though he well knew the effort, at times exhausting, that his profession of shepherd and warrior demanded, he had no idea at all of an organized, daily work, which only the soil teaches to those who work on it during the seasons. Content with the warmth of the sun, he did not adopt fire as an accessory of his life. Moreover, this errant life did not impose relations of orderly neighbourhood since the individual did not own landed property. As his nurture did not depend on such relations, his gregarious instinct was little developed, and he did not seek to integrate himself to a social order. The tribe of which he formed a part, was not an order determined by social reasons, but rather by biological causes. The relations of the individual outside the tribe, that is, his properly social relations were non-existent.

Divided World : A world divided in the extreme and atomised into individuals, a world of centrifugal virtues that did not know mutual aid, just as it ignored the efficacy of the matter, but practised hospitality, honoured generosity, loved vanity and poetry. Its dynamism explains the extreme rapidity of Islamic expansion, the cause of which the historians have vainly sought in the external conditions. On this canvas Islam came to embroider its admirable civilization, giving to a world dominated by individualism a cohesion and a sense of the collective that determined its historical orientation. The Quran transformed the Beduin into a sedentary, who left in Spain and the south of France, the evidence of a perfect agricultural science. This fixation of the man to the soil immediately produced its effect. Science and art appeared and developed in a disciplined society where the individual no longer obeyed his vagrant humour, but submitted to an order and to the laws.

In the 18th century, this civilization had long finished the cycle of its civilization, and the individual found himself once again in the conditions of life offered by an atomised society of abolished activities, save for certain enclaves such as Fez, Qayruwan and Damascus, prestigious vestiges that alone bore witness to a finished past since in general the post-al-Muwahhid man preferred a return to the nomadic life of his ancestors to a sedentary life. Just as a European engineer or artist once seeing the cycle of his civilization nearing its end, would again become a cultivator or a gardener, the Muslim world had reverted to a tribal, nomadic state when the West made its discovery, more than a century ago.

It would be convenient not to forget that Europe which looked upon itself as the sole depositary of the human destinies had already, since the age of Boccaccio-even while its cradling civilisation still drew its first nourishment from the Arabs, disowned purely and simply the Arab civilisation. On this point, it would be doubtless more fitting to quote a European himself. Here are, for example the melancholy reflections of D. Gustave Lebon that conclude his study on the *Arab Civilisation:*

> The reader would ask himself why under these conditions, the influence of the Arabs is so ignored today by the scholars whose spirit would seem to place them above all religious prejudices.... In reality, this independence of opinion is much more apparent than real and we are by no means free to think as we wish on certain subjects. The hereditary prejudices that we profess against Islam and its disciples have been accumulated over so many centuries, that they have become part of our organism.

This text indirectly, but clearly illuminates the position of the European civilisation vis-a-vis the Muslim, at the debut of the colonial era, position to which corresponded the attitude of this Muslim world towards the "things" and "notions" of Europe which it, in general; covered with a sovereign scorn-pretending as it did, to be the sole depositary of Divine grace. From these given facts, one could easily imagine the internal contradictions which the modern West was going to introduce in the archaic world of the post-al-Muwahhid man.

> ***Reformist Movement :*** "Verily, God will not change the condition of men, till they change what is in themselves." Quran (13:11)

While implanting himself in the Muslim world towards the beginning of the last century, the European presented of his Christian morality, only certain dispositions of his soul—a beautiful soul if one viewed it from the interior, from the point of the convergence of his centripetal virtues, but which would remain closed and impermeable to the Muslims.

In fact, from the exterior, that is to say, in its actual contacts with the Muslim world, the Christian soul was, above all, that of a coloniser who, before embarking for the Barbary coast, the Indies or the Islands of Java, had heard, in the course of evening family re-unions by the fireside, of the fabulous Eldorados. In his turn, he had parted in search of Peru, and never was the thirst for gold so violent as after the discovery of the "Colony".

If one views it as a sociologist and not as a moralist, the salutary role of the Europeans in the history of the world since the last two centuries, becomes apparent. However detached he was from the rest of the humanity that he disdained, viewing it only as a sort of stepping stone - the European did, nonetheless, pulled the Muslim world out of the chaos of the occult forces, wherein every society that substitutes for the spirit, its simple function, founders, shadow deformed by the imagination of the visionaries who have lost, along with their sense of the real, the very genius of the soil. By causing the social order, wherein the post-al-Muwahhid man peaceably vegetated, crack on all sides, the activism of the European would give him a new revelation of his social worth. The man from Europe unknowingly played the role of the dynamite that explodes in a camp of silence and contemplation. The post-al-Muwahhid man, like the Buddhist of China and the Brahmana of India, felt himself jolted and finally awoken.

He found himself thus in a new order that was not of his making, and before two imperative necessities. Despite his bankruptcy, he must assure himself of the minimum of dignity that Islam demands of all his adepts, even in the primitive societies of central Africa; and he must assure himself of a vital minimum in an implacable social order that no longer nourished either the plunderer living on the razzias, or the hermit living on public charity, or the son of the family living on familial patrimony all possibilities of vegetating were henceforth abolished. On the moral, as on the social plane, the Muslim was thus obliged to seek a *modus vivendi* compatible with the conditions of a new life. From this obscure groping that grafted itself on a lingering uneasiness that Ibn Taymiyyah had left in the Muslim consciousness a few centuries before, stemmed the historical movements that would give the Muslim world its present physiognomy.

These movements issued from two currents; the Reformist linked to Muslim consciousness, and the Modernist, less profound, more fortuitous, and more particularly connected with the aspirations of a new social category, the issue of the Western school, as would be the Aligarh University movement.

The first of these two currents seems to find its way in the Muslim consciousness somewhat like a course of subterranean water, spouting here and there on the surface, from time to time since the days of Ibn Taymiyyah who was neither an alim like the *Sheikhs*, nor a mystic like Ghazzali, but a militant crusader for the revival of the Muslim world, both social and spiritual. It was the same current that with Ibn Tumart had surged into the powerful Al-Muwahhid empire in the West, and with Ibn Abd-al-Wahhab into the Wahhabi empire in the East, which was crushed towards 1820 by Muhammad Ali at the instigation of the Sublime Porte and the Western Powers. But it preserved therein, its doctrinal vigour that allowed it to reappear once again in 1925 under the temporal form of the present Wahhabi empire.

But it was particularly after the disappearance of the first Wahhabi empire in 1820 that this current found a consciousness that was reflect into the modern Muslim world: Jamal-al-Din-al-Afghani who had managed to escape, in his isolated mountains, the degrading stigmas of the post-al-Muwahhid society that turned the individual into a victim or a fawning courtier. To his essential quality of the "natural" man, he brought a unique culture that precisely inaugurated the era of the *homo sapiens* in the modern Muslim world. This culture would attract in its wake the cultured youth of Istanbul, Cairo and Tehran who would furnish the leadership of the Reformist movement. This man whose intellectual capacities Professor Gibb seems to put in doubt, dared talk, a century ago, in the decayed post-al-Muwahhid world, of the "social function of the prophets."

Al-Afghani found himself, by an accident of history, the incorruptible witness and the implacable judge of a society that slowly attained its decomposition, while colonialism installed itself on its soil. It was the sepoy revolt and its bloody ending that seems to have catalysed in the conscience of this man, the will to reform his milieu. He saw in this drama the moral and material bankruptcy of the Muslim society, as implied, in the failure of the revolt and confirmed, in a way, by the Aligarh movement that appeared in the wake of these bloody events and, in the eyes of Al-Afghani, took on the character of a betrayal of Islam. He forthwith launched an offensive against antiquated institutions and fatal ideas.

Powers Undermined : On the first plane he sought to undermine the existing powers in order to realize a political re-composition of the Muslim world, founded on "Islamic fraternity" that was breached at Siffin and finally destroyed by colonial regimes. On the second plane, he led the struggle against "naturism", the term under which he denounced the materialism that he allegedly detected in the teaching of Sir Syed Ahmad Khan at Aligarh and attributed it to the occult influences of the West. Al-Afghani's attitude appears reactionary, the more so since the University movement later proved to be an eminent factor of Muslim renaissance in India. However, it supplied the necessary corrective to the future orientation of teaching at Aligarh, just as a century later, the opposition of Azharite scholars, notably of Rashid Rida, to the thesis of Taha Hussain, far from proving merely negative, exercised a salutary influence not only on the future orientation of Egyptian culture, but also on the writings of Taha Hussain himself.

Anyhow, Al-Afghani's impetuous temperament made of him a militant rather than a thinker who would carefully examine problems and work out solutions. His extraordinary culture was only a dialectical, even demagogic, means of revolutionary action that had a psychological and intellectual, rather than political, impact on a still totally apathetic Muslim world. It must needs make the Muslim drama manifest in the Muslim conscience itself. It does not seem that this recall to the Muslim conscience of the drama that it carried within itself formed part of a systematic plan: his quite rare written work, mostly polemics directed against the naturalists or against Renan, do not allow any affirmation in this regard. But if he was neither the leader, nor the doctrinaire of modern Reformist movement, he was its initiator, at the same time gathering and transmitting, all along his life of a pilgrim, this anxious inquietude to which one owes the modest efforts of the present renaissance.

Fully conscious of the rottenness of his milieu, Al-Afghani sought to cure it through a suppression of its institutional framework rather than through a reformation of the post-Al- Muwahhid man.

He might have achieved his objective if such a revolution was accomplished, for every revolution is creative of new values, and, as a result, susceptible of transforming the man. But the lever of this revolution was ill-forged; it could be efficacious only if the sentiment of "Islamic fraternity" was transformed into an act: "the Islamic fraternisation", such as it once had existed in the days of Ansars and Muhajirin—the first constitutional act that laid the foundation of early Muslim society.

So, while Al-Afghani had been the promoter of the Reformist movement and remains the legendary hero of the modern epic, he was not himself a "reformer" in the exact sense of the term. That role was reserved for Sheikh Abduh, an Egyptian Azharite. Immemorially attached to the soil, Egypt has always been a society, that is to say, a milieu where the individual is constantly merged into a collectivity, and endowed thereby with the instinct of social realities; Al-Azhar has always furnished dogmatic spirits. Having taken cognizance of the Muslim drama Abduh was obliged to transform it into a social problem, whereas his master with his tribal and empirical spirit had seen it from a political angle.

The Disposition : These original dispositions of the Egyptian Sheikh explain the entire genesis and orientation of the Reformist school. Yet, it appears, that the instinct of the soil-which is the quintessence of social sense—and the Azharite spirit separately suggested their solution, perhaps even due to what Gibb calls "the atomism". Abduh knew that for realising a reform of Muslim Society, one must first of all reform the individual. He found for this concept an important reference in the Quran: "God does not make any change in the condition of a people, till the latter has not previously changed what there is in its soul" (Quran, 13:10). In this verse, that became the watchword of the school, notably in North African Islamism there is a vigorous statement of the entire social problem 'which is essentially linked to the soul of the individual. But how to transform this soul? Here the dogmatic spirit of Abduh intervened. He thought, as Sir Muhammad Iqbal thought that a reformulation of Muslim theology was indispensable.

But the word "theology" became the fatality of the Reformist movement resulting in a partial deviation, and devaluation of certain of its leading principles, such as the "Salafiyah" or a return to the original purity of Islam. For theology touches the problem of the soul only in the realm of credo or dogma. Now the Muslim, even the post-al-Muwahhid Muslim, had never abandoned his credo. He had remained a believer or more exactly a devotee; his faith had become inefficacious because it had lost its social radiation, becoming centripetal, individualist: the faith of the individual disintegrated from his social milieu.

Consequently it was not a question of teaching him a faith that he already possessed, but of restoring to this faith its efficacy. In a word, it was less a question of "proving" God to him than of "manifesting" Him to his consciousness, filling his soul with it as with a source of energy. Transforming the soul is to make it surpass its ordinary bounds. This task did not lie in the domain of theology, but in that of a mysticism, or more exactly of a science that still has no name, but what may be termed, the renewal of alliance or union. In an effort of renaissance, mysticism that has led to Marabutic mystification—could not furnish the necessary basis for Reformist action. The mystic did, in fact, aim only at the spiritual condition of certain souls of the elite, while it was a question of general reform, of providing an internal impulsion to the masses thirsting for a (call of) sursum corda (Lift up your hearts) for vanquishing their own inertia.

These considerations would not have failed to appear to the Reformist school if it could have achieved a synthesis of its ideas by establishing a link between the dogmatic views of Abduh and the political and social views of Al-Afghani. It would have indicated quite another path than that of a simple reformulation of theological principles. Moses, Jesus and Muhammad were not the theologian constructors of abstract propositions, but essentially the accumulators of this moral energy which they communicated to simple souls.

Theology restored respectability to discussion and exchange of ideas, but at the same time it de-naturalised the Muslim problem by transforming the "Salafite" principle even in the spirit of the reformers. This unconscious transgression substituted for the psychological problem of renaissance, a scholastic problem. For with theology the "social function" of religion is not posed, as the believing man does not learn anything from a school that teaches him solely the existence of God, and does not, in any case, teach the return to the Salaf.

Reformist Deviation : To explain fully the Reformist deviation, one must, perhaps, add to the reasons already enumerated what Gibb calls the "superimposition". It existed in European culture in the epoch of Thomas Acquinas under the form of a purge of Muslim influences. Today the same phenomenon is evident in the traditional Muslim culture in the form of a resistance to Western ideas: the theological work of Abduh is finally apologetic because of the 'superimposition'.

A sum-up of this criticism would risk to show us only the lacunae of the Reformist movement, so that the latter would lose in our eyes, if not its historical value, at least its social value. However, the present Muslim world, with all its realisations and virtualities, is, for a great part, the other being that of the Modernist current that we would examine later on the work of Sheikh Abduh and his school. Even if the great Egyptian Azharite failed to place the problem exactly in the Muslim conscience, he succeeded in posing it on the intellectual plane, provoking an intellectual ferment not only in Egypt, but almost in the entire Muslim world. For theology was, in fact, the first effort of Muslim intelligence to disengage itself from its secular lethargy. One must not underestimate the significance of the appearance of Risalat-al-Tawhid in a field where nothing had happened since Ibn Khaldun. For the first time since many centuries, a Muslim brain had fathered a thoughtful work.

For the first time discussions broke the silence that had reigned in the old universities of the Muslim world. One of them, Al-Azhar, where the debates opened by Al-Afghani and Abduh had come to resound, was to show itself particularly sensitive to the new mood—not in its programmes and methods which, despite certain superficial tentatives, still await their re-statement, but in its spirit. Al-Azhar, that is to say, the intellectual centre of the Muslim world had at last admitted the law of movement and progress and realised that there was no such thing as an immutable perfection, but only a state of perfectible things, even under its imposing domes.

Thus, the modern Muslim thought set itself to work in the immense field that the Reformist action had opened before it.

However this field, left fallow for centuries, was overrun entirely by parasitic vegetation, and a thorough clean-up was necessary in the spiritual as much, if not more, as in the intellectual domain. To the lacunae inherent in the post-al-Muwahhid man, there came to be added the lacunae attaching to the institution. An institution has its life, its history and traditions; in a word, its own inertia that at times defies the will of man. To the atomism, dogmatism and the apologetic tendency-that the Reformist spirit could not spontaneously shake off-were added the blemishes of an institutional order: the *mujadalah,* literalism, hysterics and poetism peculiar to the post-al-Muwahhid culture. How could one move under the weight of centuries and the burden of traditions that had pell-mell accumulated themselves. For building anew, one needed either a revolutionary spirit like Jamal-al-Din, partisan of the "clean slate" or a systematic spirit that would have methodically proceeded towards the necessary ruptures to liberate the institution from its traditional shackles.

One must have first of all, made a balance-sheet of these indispensable ruptures by a discrimination of the traditions. The word "tradition" *(taqlid)* is a magical Arabic word that could cover up all sorts of superstitions and mystifications under the prestigious varnish of Islamism. 'By a methodical confrontation of tradition with Islam, Muslim culture would have been rid of a great number of sacrosanct *taqlids.* Sheikh Abd-al-Hamid ibn Badis would thus succeed in extirpating the false tradition of *"Marabutism"* from Algeria. But this task of detection could hardly be the work of an isolated individual, and in his time Sheikh Abduh was alone. As a thinker, he had furnished the example of intellectual work to a world unaccustomed to thinking; as the rector of a university, he had given to his institution the movement that made it amenable to new ideas.

In addition to the ruptures that he operated in the Islamic culture, he had revealed Western culture to the Muslim world by introducing it in the re-organization of his university and in his written work which thus bore its first reflection. From all these initiatives must need gush forth the intellectual upsurge of renaissance. But while the "Meiji" upsurge oriented Japan towards the sciences, Muslim renaissance remained confined for a long time to the domain where the natural inclinations of the post-al-Muwahhid man, who cared little for efficiency, and the notions attached to cultural institutions that had since long lost their social objective, helped to maintain it.

The reformers-I am talking of the continuers-themselves contributed to maintain this state of affairs. The *mujadalah* would subsist for a long time in literary debates. One did not look for verities, but for arguments: one did not listen to his interlocutor, but flooded him with a verbal deluge. The *mujadalah* was all the more dangerous since it depended, in general, on a senseless love for words, leading to another lacunae of post-al-Muwahhid spirit "literalism". The Arab genius that had created the most beautiful of languages, resembled a sculptor who becomes amorous of the statue that his chisel has created. Unfortunately the passion for words is more dangerous than that for bronze, marble or stone.

It commences by making one lose the sense of proportion indispensable for all positive constructive effort. The least headline of an Arabic journal is edifying in this regard. Recently, a Tunisian journal announcing the arrival of a leader from abroad, greeted him with five or six laudative epithets- *karim, jalil, zaim,* etc. It betokened, doubtless, an apologetic bouquet, but Arabic words carry an irresistible attraction for the postal-Muwahhid spirit. The Arabic language thus divinised could no longer evolve. The adoration of its adepts has rendered intangible a syntax irrevocably reduced to a dozen of forms, and it has become sacrilegious to constitute new forms through adapted prefixes-something that would be in accord with the very spirit of this language.

Defying Time : In the independent Muslim educational institutions, the syllabi and methods of instruction also seem to defy time; the principles have remained the same since the Christian Middle Ages. For all that these principles constitute the mental canvas of action, the activities remain in the periphery and at the rhythm of a world that has gone by. One believes sometimes to have changed an entire world of ideas by certain superficial retouches, such as the introduction of chairs and tables in independent Algerian schools. It was, of course, the first step to take, but it would be naive to stop at that.

In the circumstances, it is not astonishing that modern Arab thought has still not acquired the sense of efficacy. The despotism of words and forms impresses a superficial character on every translation of renaissance. One could witness it at the Congress of Islamic Culture at Tunis where a Sheikh, while making a discourse consecrated to the Traditions on "clemency", spent more than an hour in counting out the chain of narrators. Needless to specify that its content remained finally unperceived while the listeners yawned-with admiration. Here one comes across an important aspect of post-al-Muwahhid psychology: all is still more grave while the orator and the audience are in accord over the inefficacy. So much so that the living verities that had once fashioned the visage of Muslim civilization are henceforth but dead verities, buried under beautiful phrases and a vast erudition.

It seems that the idea remains the same as it has been since the decadence; the famous "well of science" wherein science is swallowed up and loses the sense of its social role. Just any discourse on Commentary could furnish the occasion for ascertaining the inconsequences of our present culture which, subjugated by the verb, does not express a concern for *acting,* but the simple pleasure of *talking.*

Civilization and Threat

There is another reason for this orientation that the apologetic tendency has impressed on the intellectual effort. In its pre-occupation with the apology of the past, the culture takes on a character of archeology where the intellectual effort is directed not forward but backwards. This retrograde tendency imprints on the entire teaching a retrospective character, incompatible with the exigencies of the present and the future. There results therefrom, in the ideas a sort of the phenomenon of "hysteresis", of a constant obsession with the past.

Two other lacunae would complete this picture of the deficiencies of the post-al-Muwahhid culture: a puerile "quanti-tatism" evident even in the element bearing a "polish" of Western culture, and a "poetism" that is the particular apanage of Zaytunian youth of purely maternal culture. Quantitatism consists in estimating efficacy and value in terms of a book by the quantity of paper written. As for poetism, it is the aesthetics or rather the coquettishness of literalism and the apologetic tendency. It is the means, more or less elegant according to the case, of masking the imperfections and insufficiencies, of gilding the errors and placing before the incompetences the screen of rhetoric.

It is clear that all these lacunae, we have analysed, were not of a nature to favour the efforts of the Reformist school that did not or could not know how to eliminate them, systematically, thus leaving intact the problem of post-al-Muwahhid, residues in the Muslim renaissance. Moreover, since the disappearance of its last two great figures, Rashid Rida in the East, and Ben Badis in North Africa, the movement as a whole, finds itself at a new turning. In Egypt, the fundamental idea of creating a new moral basis for Muslim life finds itself transformed and deepened in a new movement, that of Muslim Brotherhood, which would be treated further on. In North Africa, it has been more and more superseded by a very important institution, that of independent education, that has timely fulfilled the enormous gap of official instruction. On this path the Islamist idea more or less subsists. Certain young teachers are animated with a salafite zeal, but some others are already no more than simple functionaries. This instruction has the merit of attacking the mortal defect of the post-al-Muwahhid world-illiteracy. But in the absence of a doctrine on culture, Islamism propagates a complacent alphabetism that dreams of transforming the conditions of life by communicating, above all, the taste for "Muslim things" and Arab "belles-lettres".

Translation into Reality : It appears from this balance-sheet, that the Reformist movement did not know how to transform the Muslim soul or to translate into reality the "social function" of the religion. All the same, it did succeed in breaking the static equilibrium of the post-al-Muwahhid epoch by introducing in the Muslim conscience partially and on the intellectual plane only the notion of its secular drama. But there remained the task of posing the problem of culture in its generality if the renaissance were to emerge from its embryonic state.

As already noted, the development that goes under the name of "Muslim civilization" was only an accommodation of doctrinal Islam to the state of facts that followed Siffin. The juridical schools were put hard to realise such an accommodation in face of a dynastic hence extra, Muslim power that was exclusive and tyrannical. So much so, that it is not the Muslim civilization that is the issue of Islamic doctrine, but on the contrary, the doctrines that have accommodated themselves to an imposed temporal order.

Any attempt for the reconstruction of Muslim culture must begin with the re-establishment of pure doctrine over the le fait de prince (political power) that has stemmed from Siffin. This reconstruction implies a return to Islam, that is to say, in particular the extrication of the Quranic text from its triple matrix of theology, jurisprudence and philosophy.

But the Modernists seek to drag the Muslim world in quite another direction by breaking-sometimes violently as Kamalism did in Turkey with a "tradition" that is often no more than a cover for the post-al-Muwahhid myth.

> ***Modernist Movement :*** "Would'nt I have been, moreover, flagrantly inconsistent, if wishing to ameliorate the country, I would have balked before the idea of ameliorating man?" H. De Balzac

Far from bringing its entire soul to the Muslim world, Europe brought there only that much of its civilization as concerned the immediate commodities of the colonist. On the "native"' plane, however, it had brought what one calls the "native school". It is from this very small contribution that the Modernist movement of the Muslim world had started.

The school, on the plane of Modernism formed a counterpart to the *Madrasa* on the plane of reform. While the *Madrasa* presented a relatively rejuvenated Islamic thought, the school introduced new cultural elements in the Muslim world. The former would operate a rupture with the post-al-Muwahhid past, the latter would establish a contact with Western thought. Envisaging this new fact, Iqbal remarked that "the most remarkable phenomenon of modern history... is the enormous rapidity with which the world of Islam is spiritually moving towards the West". But was this really the case ?

It could have been so only if Europe had brought its soul and its civilization to the world of Islam, or the latter would itself have gone to discover it on the spot. It does not seem that many Muslims, have gone in search of the West. Instead, Europe came to the East not as the bearer of a, civilization but as a coloniser, and the young bourgeois Muslim went to Europe only for getting a university diploma or for satisfying a wholly superficial curiosity. A Zaytunian student, who after finishing his Islamic studies asked for a scholarship to complete his education in Europe, was told by the concerned cultural organisation that "for studying the French language one need not go to France." That is how the Muslim milieu envisages the role of a student who is going to the West. It is just a question of studying a language or learning a profession, not of discovering a culture. Only the aspect of immediate utility counts.

But this way of looking at things must not be exclusively imputed to the indifference of the Muslim vis-a-vis the West. The "native" school did not disperse elements of European culture, but only certain rudiments susceptible of rendering the "native" fit for European economy. There was no question of detecting and stimulating intelligences, but of forming auxiliaries, of a capacity at once sufficient and limited.

Despite all this, the conscious being-student or simply a governed, even when treated as an "object" did nevertheless remain a "subject". And it is as a "subject" that the Muslim judges the European order that he sees around him or squeezes from his insufficient readings. His ideas on European "civilization" must need flow from this rudimentary judgement and from the superficial contact, administrative or commercial, that he has had with it.

On the other hand, the little Musalman who goes to the native school, is the brother of the one who goes to the *Madrasa*. Consequently, the same mental habits, the same sociological heredity that marked the Reformist movement have come to mark also the Modernist movement, intermingled with the new elements, bookish or empirical borrowings from European life as viewed from the exterior.

Muslim Spirit : For centuries the Muslim spirit has been incapable of delving beneath the surface of the phenomena; the Muslim no longer understood, but only learnt the Quran. Now, having judged grosso modo the utility of European products, he was not going to criticise them! He did not bother himself to find out how they were created, but how they could be acquired. Thus the first stage of modernisation of the Muslim world that would adopt the forms without their content, took shape. This disposition would inaugurate an entropic evolution that did not accumulate its means but solely its needs. And the infatuation for the things "modern" went to absurd length in all social classes, among both men and women. One could see towards 1925, during the years of prosperity, motor cars parked under the tents where the fowls were kept. The ceramic wash-basin made its appearance in bourgeois homes where it adorned the "modern" bed-rooms. A significant clumsiness, 'obviously inspired by the hotel style, that is to say, by a way of looking at the European from the exterior. The woman also partook in this euphoria. Instead of acquiring the art and the taste for a 'bit of frippery', she was content to buy it, according to her condition, from needlework parlours or ready-made garments stores run by shrewd and gracious European saleswomen. Apparent evolution, that often masks a simple transformation of post-al-Muwahhid content from an archaic to a modern form. This tendency seems to develop in Muslim society as the elite, the offspring of Western school, grows more numerous at the top.

Later Developments

This elite has gradually passed beyond the stage of native school, a certain number of young intellectuals have now spent a term in the Western universities. Naturally, it is in this new stage that the Modernist movement approaches its perfection, if this expression could possibly be used-and its moral and social content becomes quite significant.

Because of the psychology of his maternal post-al-Muwahhid milieu where one passes from the sacred to the profane without stopping at the sublime, from Islamic ilm to modern education without pausing at the notion of culture, the Muslim student starts with blinkers that prevent him from contemplating the civilization otherwise than from an abstract or futile side in accordance with his disposition for the serious. He generally registers himself in the university of a capital. The Quarters Latin are the same everywhere: one finds there the bookish and controversial or the superficial aspect of culture, its distractions and its pleasures. From one side as from the other, he can see only the culmination and not the evolution of a society. He does not see the woman who is picking a wild flower, but the one who colours her nails and hair and sits smoking on the cafe terraces. He does not see the artist or the artisan bending over his work to translate an idea into matter. Oriented, from the start, with the sense of utility, he does not remark the energies, obscure, but creative and creative, above all, of moral and social values that render a civilized man superior to the primitive man culture commences when the intellectual effort goes beyond the objective of individual need. Nor would he have the chance to seize the generous aspect of the civilization, that which nourishes the affectivity of the civilised man and gives the creative impulsion to his genius so true it is that "the great thoughts come from the heart".

Descendant of a world that has sold its relics and manuscripts to the American tourist, he would not discern, besides, the healthy cult of the "old thing" that links the past with the future. He will not see the child learning the sense and respect of life as he caresses a cat or cultivates a flower, nor the labourer stopping at the edge of a furrow for judging his work, in communion with the soil which is the embryo of the synthesis of every civilisation. He would not draw, any more, the lesson of certain follies as that of Bernard Palissy burning his last piece of furniture and his floor for obtaining the enamel.

His unconscious materialism and obsession with the "utile" would not let him see, either, the horrible aspect of this civilization that holds in bondage men, whom the machine commands, exhausts and wears out and transforms into "robots of human flesh". He will not see the woman forced to leave her hearth to gain laboriously a loaf of bread in a debasing atmosphere that masculineness women and emasculates men. He will not see this odious side that makes even the degraded post-al-Muwahhid society appear in certain respects frequently superior to a civilization that has lost the sense of the human.

Generally speaking the Muslim student has not experienced Europe, but has been content to read it, that is to say, to learn rather than to understand. He thus remains ignorant of the history of its civilization; he cannot know how it was formed and how it is in the process of disintegrating itself, by its internal contradictions and its incompatibility with the laws of human order, and because its culture is no longer that of a civilization, but has been transformed by colonialism and racism into the "culture of the empire". Even if sometimes guided by curiosity he sets out in search of reality, he finds himself in contact only with the twentieth century Europe, shorn of its secular tradition, nickled, chromited and polished; the modern Europe and the practical materialism of its bourgeoisie and the dialectical materialism of its labouring class. And the intellectual who has not even acquired sufficiently the sense of real efficacy at the European school, by which a Christian still distinguishes himself from a Muslim, would more readily borrow from the materialism of Europe its bourgeois tendency—that is to say, the materialist tastes, rather than its proletarian tendency, that is to say, a dialectical discipline. Having never considered the ontological liaison of European "products" with the natural framework of Europe, he would not care to bother if these tastes had any relation with Muslim life, thus encumbering the latter with a thousand borrowings that possess no raison d'etre whatsoever.

This disposition for accumulating indiscriminate borrowings denounces the rudimentary aspect of the Modernist movement. Civilization is not an accumulation, but a construction, an architecture. Concentrating only on its products, one overlooked the structure of Western society, and did not seize its positive symbol at the level of its virtues, incarnated equally by the artisan, the scholar or a simple labourer, but of its temporary signs such as the aeroplane and the bank. One does not see them any more clearly in the structure of the Muslim world, being content in the one case as in the other, to regard what appears the most easily.

It is not astonishing in these circumstances, that the words themselves have been drained of all the contents that form their social value. Certainly the "parole is divine", but only so far as it is an act and not a simple collection of words as happens during election campaigns. For exercising its seduction, this literalism has at its command an entirely new terminology, favourably received in a society, under strain of an effort of recovery. The parole here betrays its mission: instead of directing this "effort" in the direction of over-effort, necessary for confronting the tasks of the present, it degrades it to an under-effort into gestures barely sufficient for securing a seat or an honourable position. The man who pretends to direct public life does not conceive things for doing them, but only for saying them, and talking about them eloquently. This word is purely a verbal act without social potential or moral "tension".

However, it is this moral tension that essentially characterises all efficacious intellectual, moral and physical attitudes. It is the man in his plenitude who "strains" himself, goes beyond his nature because he constantly modifies it. In such a case, his word is a will, an act that expresses a just relationship between words and realities. But when this relation between word and the act makes default, the former is no more than mere talk. If the liaison between the word as an expression of thought—and the act—as its concretisation does not exist in our spirit, we would - no more seize the reverse relationship of act to thought, and will miss this perpetual dialectic that goes from new conquests to new words and by these words to still new conquests.

If with the Reformists (particularly since the disappearance of its last great representatives) the word is not founded on a social imperative, with the Modernists it does not aim at efficiency or implicate the practical tension of words towards acts. The common cause of the error of the two movements is that neither went to the very source of its inspiration. The Reformists have not in reality gone back to the origins of Islamic thought, any more than the Modernists to the origins of Western thought. However, on the psychological plane, a discrimination between the two is altogether indispensable. The "Salafist" individually carries the notion of renaissance. Even if he does not methodically realize therefrom the practical conditions, he at least does not lose sight of the essential objective. He has enough awareness of his milieu to demand only the "duties", leaving "rights" for the Modernist. In performing his work, however naive, he reaches an understanding of his milieu through his own "reformist" effort. With the Modernist, on the contrary, the very notion of renaissance makes default or is relegated to a secondary position. The Modernist engages himself in the life of his country only on the political plane. For him the primary question is not the regeneration of the Muslim world, but of pulling it out of its present embarrassment. It is a borrowed notion that does not, in fact, envisage the Muslim problem of the man, but the European problem of the institution. This results sometimes in distressing scenes. I have seen in the streets of Algiers, a young man bending over a dust bin in search of his pittance, while a wall-poster a little above his head, invited him to demand a "Sovereign Constituent Assembly". It well seems that the inspirers of this sinister inconsistency had never regarded from near the man of the people, for seeking to know exactly what would have really and immediately referred to his sad fate.

Precise Doctrine : The modernist movement does not in fact reflect any precise doctrine: It is as indefinite in its means as in its ends. Its only precise path that leads the Musulman to be a client or imitator without originality, of an alien civilization that more readily opens the doors of its shops than of its schools, where the students could perhaps learn to utilize their personal genius for their own benefit. It would suffice, in this regard, to consider the very composition of the student missions that Egypt annually sends to European universities. One of the most recent group consists of some sixty students, none of whom was destined for technical studies, and of whom the majority was, besides, Copt. This example, like so many others, shows that the Modernist movement is not oriented towards acts and means, but towards fashions, tastes, and wants. When its representatives attribute to colonialism their own inefficiency, it seems that it is for them chiefly the question of an alibi and that they wish to run away from their true responsibility. This subterfuge is also employed by the Reformist movement which instead of seeking the internal causes of its insufficiencies, contents itself to impute them to foreign political powers. Neither the one nor the other cares to remedy its own shortcomings, but only to mask them from the eyes of the people.

However, a certain spirit of initiative-sole criterion of the efficacy of the individual has begun to manifest itself in certain intellectual circles, notably in Algeria. In Constantine, for example, a number of doctors have arranged to observe a weekly social day to attend to the poor—an instance of the intellectual seeking to enter the life of his people otherwise than through the customary threshold of elections. The intellectual and the political effort could thus resume normal significance of being the means and not the end.

This does not mean, however, that the political effort of the Modernist movement has always been in vain. It has succeeded in the crystallisation of a collective consciousness that as we have seen-has been missing in the Muslim countries since Siffin, and has constituted in these countries a signpost which designates, if not the essential objective, at least certain, more or less, practical ends capable of drawing the masses from their indifference and apathy. On the intellectual plane, if the movement has not brought-for lack of a real contact with modern civilization and an effective rupture with the post-al-Muwahhid past the elements of a culture, it has, nevertheless, given birth through its borrowings from the West, to a current of ideas which though debatable have nonetheless the merit of bringing into question all the traditional criteria.

10

Negative Aspects

"And they devised and God devised. But of *those who devise is God the Best".* Quran (3:54)

In noting the "enormous rapidity with which the world of Islam was moving towards the West", Iqbal merely referred to a particular aspect of a phenomenon that Ibn Khaldun had seized in its generality. "The conquered people", the great medieval historian wrote, "adopt the forms, the ideas and the manners of the conquering people." It is this same phenomenon, known as the "law of adaptation" in modern phraseology that confronts today the Muslim world. The anguish and hesitation that, as earlier mentioned, had troubled Iqbal in his quest for a solution to the problem of women, point to the general perplexity of the modern Muslim consciousness before two solutions that appear equally deplorable. It seems that in most cases one is searching for a third solution that would be compatible, at the same time, with the spirit of Islam and the demands of modern age.

The hesitation and anguish involved in the search have resulted in a sort of pause in the evolution of ideas, a "historical no man's land", since the Muslim society could neither return to the post-al-Muwahhid stage, nor make a blind thrust forward in its movement "towards the West". For the latter no longer exercises the irresistible fascination and influence it wielded in the epoch of Mustafa Kemal and Iqbal; the West in its turn, represents today the spectacle of but another chaos, wherein the Muslim spirit in its search for an "order", does not find a model to imitate or the source of external inspiration that could guide its progressive march. It is thus forced to fall back on its own values, and so one remarks in the writings and discourse of young Muslim intelligentsia a renewed interest in Islam which is, in no sense, a withdrawal. Indeed the Muslim world seems to open itself in a more conscious manner towards the modern world, with the knowledge that though the West could not provide it with all the solutions, as it had fondly believed in the Kemalist epoch, yet one would find therein the results of a highly edifying experience, that constitutes at once the most perfect achievement and the gravest failure of human genius-prodigious lesson of history for understanding the destiny of peoples and civilisations. This double intelligence of events becomes all the more necessary as the Muslim world in its present pause, since the Palestine affair, seems to strive at a real comprehension of its problem through a more objective evaluation of the factors of its renaissance as well as those of its chaos.

One has remarked already a tendency to try to grasp the sense of the European historical process, rather than to copy it purely and simply. By seizing the relativity of the European phenomena, one would find it easier to understand their imperfections as well as their real grandeur, and the contacts and exchanges would become more fruitful with this Western world which must, for a long time still, provide the canvas of one's thought and action.

International Scene

In fact, it is the universal radiation of the Western culture that makes its present chaos a world problem, that has to be understood and analysed in its liaison with the human problem in general, and by consequence, in its liaison with the Muslim problem. Such an analysis could not fail to give the Muslim a chance a placing himself as man, and not as indigene with regard to the European order, and to the purely material interdependence that at present constitutes the essential relation between a more or less colonial Europe and a more or less colonised Muslim world. Thus, there would succeed a state of mutual esteem and more fruitful association. Such a modification would not be solely beneficial to the

Muslim world, for colonialism weighs as heavily on European life: colonialism that materially kills the colonised, also destroys morally the coloniser.

While one could note a tendency among the colonial nations to modify their political relations with the colonised countries, a sort of fatality seems to neutralise this awareness of the colonial peril. The colonial habit seems to be too deeply ingrained in European society to allow the new turn of mind to modify the psychology and the usages that lie at the basis of its moral chaos. It would suffice here to point out the relation of the latter with the chaos in the Muslim world.

Double Aspect : The European chaos, like the Muslim, presents a double aspect. The first is merely the simple and ineluctable culmination of a historical movement, while the second is an accidental aspect that results from the incidence of the colonial fact on the life, habits and the ideas, for more than a century. These two aspects merge together in a phenomenon common to all the civilisations: the retardation of consciousness over science and the march of thought. Consciousness is, in fact, the psychological resume of the history, the distillation of the past in a human "ME", a crystallisation of habits, prejudices and tastes. All acquisitions of thought, therefore, if they have no direct link with the past, the tradition and habits of a people remain beyond the grasp of its consciousness. Herein lies the origin of the drama of modern civilisation where the consciousness has failed to assimilate most of the realisations of science.

The same retardation had caused the rupture of Siffin in the Muslim world. The Quran as a philosophical system was a science singularly beyond the horizon of the Jahili consciousness. This resulted in a rupture between those who had assimilated the new thinking and those who remained attached to their old conceptions and conditions of life that the Quran sought to abolish. This has been the underlying phenomenon of Muslim history for thirteen centuries. Masked by historical trappings, it has nevertheless been periodically surfacing in one crisis or the other, through internecine struggles. The Kharijism and the Mutazilism were but-the one on the political and the other on the intellectual plane, the tentatives to catch up with the Quranic thought that still escaped from a retarding consciousness. In all these conflicts, it was always a question of divorce between the temporal Muslim world and the Quranic thought. If the decadence denoted an imbalance between the temporal Muslim world and the Quranic thought, the renaissance marks the effort of the Muslim consciousness to regain its retardation over the Quranic and modern scientific thought.

The same process could be observed in the history of Europe. The first rupture therein, took place on the moral plane in the name of Reformation, but various schisms as that of Al bigenis had already indicated that the Christian consciousness could no longer span the gulf that divided it from a rationalism derived from scientific development. The second, on the political plane, appeared with the French Revolution; it shattered the traditional social structure and replaced it with a statute founded on the equality of individuals. However, this theoretical equality merely established a precarious equilibrium, and one could already discern in the bosom of the third Estate, champion of the new order, 'a working class tendency among the Jacobins, opposed to a bourgeoise tendency. The execution of Robespierre, and the liquidation of the First Commune of Paris resulted in a bourgeoise triumph. However, the conflict remained latent between the two wings of the new society, the bourgeoise who inaugurated the new era of capitalism, and the workers who prepared the advent of a new class: the proletariat.

But the world born out of this double development is full of all the contradictions and ready for all ruptures. In fact, the Third Estate eventually found itself definitely split, when in face of the practical materialism of the European bourgeoisie, the proletariat would set up its "dialectical materialism".

For the moment the conflict was confined on the summit, between the economists of the bourgeoise tradition, mainly Adam Smith and Ricardo and the economists of the new school, Engels and Marx-without taking account of the doctrinaire anarchist-syndicalists, like Bakunin. But with the set up of the First International, after the preparatory congresses at Brussels and London, and the Paris Commune in 1871, the disputes between the two opposing forces were carried from the philosophical into the political arena. It was this period in European history marked by a moral, political, and social schism that was contemporaneous with the zenith of the colonial era and the first manifestations of the Muslim renaissance. It was by this double material thrust-bourgeoise and proletarian, that the Muslim world became conscious of European influences in its political and intellectual evolution. It was chaos not civilisation that it discovered in this Europe where the ruptures were going to aggravate in terms of the two growingly preponderant factors: the rapidity of scientific development and colonial expansion. These two factors, scientism and colonialism, joined together to become the "fatality" of Europe, just as theology had become that of the post-al-Muwahhid society. Under their influence the slide of Europe into materialism could not but accelerate with the soaring of a prodigiously innovating science. Each invention, each discovery deepened still more the gulf between an overwhelming science and an overwhelmed traditional consciousness.

Drunk with the new forces that it had unleashed, 'the European "ME" was enticed by its own genius, becoming a slave to the machine that he had created but could not control. Reality became calculable and happiness measurable in quantities of calories and hormones. It was the era of quantity, of "quantitatism" in the consciousness. It was also the era of moral relativism, of the commencement of a century that had for its maxim the famous, "all is relative..." One no longer possessed the sense of the "absolute" since the 20th century positivist like the brain of the machine, no longer understood what went beyond the "relative" perspectives of the matter. The sense of the "absolute" died in the same manner as did the concept of justice, the day it was declared in Europe that a "bad settlement is worth more than a good proceeding", and one dared affirm that "commerce is authorised theft". Thus the quantitatist and relativist Europe killed a good number of moral precepts, stripping them of their title to nobility and transforming them into the pariahs and untouchables of language, banished from usage and from consciousness; and dictionaries became cemeteries of words that no longer made sense since they responded to dead concepts.

Quantitatism Aggravated : In Europe the quantitatism aggravated in terms of the multiplier co-efficient representing technical power on the scale of a tentacular industry that multiplied by tens and hundreds the material appetites of men. It marked the vocation of the child who no longer chose his line for what he could give to society, but for what he could get from it. One sought to obtain a sinecure rather than to satisfy his natural inclination-an excellent preparation for the colonial administrator, who did not even need to maintain the relative "dignity" that prevented him going to the end of his moral relativism at home. On the colonial level, the moral relativist found an excellent pretext in "national sovereignty", and the mask of "dignity" that he managed to preserve at home, melted in the heat of the colonial sun and the passion of unchained appetites: one simply got what one desired.

Within Europe itself one came to acclimatise oneself to the habits, tastes and ideas imported from colonial life. All social articulations became numerical: one produced so much, one paid so much, one bought so much and ate so much; the life revolved solely around "how much". In the technical and mechanical society being edified since the beginning of the twentieth century, the number reigns supreme and statistics are unquestionable. The human nature, that is, the conscience itself, does not enter into count, since it could not be deciphered or quantified. The human condition becomes a simple numerical function. The machines tick off, calculate, and drag the man to work in their steel meshes. Even human wants are dehumanised and commercialised, and admitted only so far as they are solvent. The general wants of humanity, more particularly those of the "widows and the orphans", the old and the sick are not solvent, and the machines do not make either moral calculation or metaphysical estimates.

The automatism is admirable: the machines turn, the colonies furnish the raw material and cheap labour, the consumers who can pay, consume, the machines calculate the scales, establish dividends, the salaries, the time-table the automatism is admirable, on condition, of course, that not a single grain of sand entered in the motor.

But there entered more than one in the modern machine. In 1914 there was a sinister grating of brakes. The sources of raw material were not sufficient; there were motors that went idle or did not work to their normal rhythm, that is to say, at the scale of an insatiable avidity and voracity. A row broke out among the machine owners. After four years of destruction and millions of dead, a precarious *modus vivendi* was established, and the machines started revolving again. In the consciences, drunk with the money and the champagne, the 1914-1918 rupture did not leave any mark, and the apparent prosperity momentarily masked the reality.

However, since 1930 a new grating was audible in the machines. This time the crisis was going to lay bare the moral canker that devoured the civilisation, and to prove that technique could not alone solve the human problems by simple graphs and equations. The machines stopped turning. The queues lengthened before the unemployment pay-offices, and misery installed itself in homes and hearths. A tragic irony presided over this misery, that for the first time in history, issued, not from a scarcity of riches, but from their superabundance. It is the stroke of genius of the 20th century to have transformed scientifically the conditions of welfare into factors of misery. Wherein lay the mischief? In an excess of the curve of production over that of consumption. A child's play for the technician who knew very well to rectify the calculation by simple arithmetic: One must destroy the surplus, and one destroyed wheat, cotton and coffee, while there existed peoples who totally lacked them. And the civilisation that had invented Malthusianism, undertook to refer no longer to the consumers but to the commodities of consumption.

No Spiritual Authority : No spiritual authority existed to denounce the scandal. Those who could save Europe from its economic chaos did not have "solvent" wants: the colonised people, who were naked and hungry, and could'nt buy anything because in considering them as mere instruments of work, one has overlooked to take account of them as consumers.

In the, genesis of the phenomenon resulting from the simultaneous impact of scienticism and colonialism, the conflagration of 1939 was only a return of the flame: the moment when Machiavelli turns against himself and Satan destroys his own work. It is the moment when destiny breathes in human veil, which unfolds itself, so that the oracles may be fulfilled. Prophet Muhammad, had said in fact: "He who digs a well under the feet of his neighbour shall himself fall into it." And fearing more for a nation the injustice that it commits, than the injustice that it suffers, he added: "The power even of the unbelievers shall endure if it is just, but the power of the believers perishes surely, if it is unjust".

The Oracles : The history of our period tragically illustrates these oracles. Europe that should have used its torch of civilisation to guide the march of humanity, employed it to set aflame the colonial world. But it has harvested therefrom, the same chaos, the same disorientation, and the same fatalism before the evil powers of mythology on its own soil, that it has sown in the rest of the world. Because, the Cartesian, learned, industrialised and polished Europe has also its myths, inhibitive in a different manner: while the paralysis of the post-al-Muwahhid society is apathetic and silent, that of Europe is convulsive and hurling. Its myths are infinitely more dangerous since they hold the power of machine and matter, and thus risk to destroy scientifically the countries and the peoples.

In Europe, the mythology is learned and has its academies, doctors and poets. A little before the Ist World War, a young artilleries officer, Ernest Psichari, felt himself transported by emotion before the simple but profound faith of the Muslims of Mauritania. It was for him a providential opportunity for introspection and meditation. It matters little if the Road of Damascus leads to a temple, a church or a mosque. Transfigured and converted, Psichari took the path of the church, "the party of my ancestors", as he would note later. Nothing more normal, provided he did not turn the back abruptly on him, who had enlightened his path. In the course of a voyage, in fact, he experienced the urge to vaunt before his young Moorish guide, the material power of modern civilisation. The young beduin replied:

— "You have the earth and we have the heavens." Psichari should have smiled at such ingenuity. Instead, he wrote in his diary, this significant exclamation:

— "Ah! that is a word that the Muslims must no longer pronounce!"

Whence came this unwarranted cry from a man recently converted? Psichari, the believer, was the nephew of Renan, and his thinking here strangely accorded with that of his uncle (whom he had renounced because of his atheism) who, after the 1871 war wrote the following lines, that express, in another form, the same racism and contempt for humanity:

> "... A race of masters and soldiers, that is the European race. Compel this noble race to work in the slaves' prison like the negroes and the Chinese, and it will revolt. Each rebel among us is more or less a soldier who has missed his calling, a being made for heroic life.... Now the life that revolts our workers would render happy a Chinese, a fellah, beings not at all martial. Let each do that for which he is made, and all would go well."

Let us overlook the intellcotual mediocrity of these lines-the great erudite has more than once thus let his pen wander. One may ascertain, however, that it errs here right into mythology, incidentally betraying the supreme myth that has hierarchically dominated, since the last century, all other myths of Europe.

The uncle and the nephew had received the sacrament from the same fountain: the superiority of the "race of masters", source of the bloody myth, of the monster that has fathered the anti-human colonialism and anti-European Nazism. This myth has demolished the entire Christian moral philosophy and has committed an outrage against God Himself by striving to supplant Him in the European conscience. It resides in the hearts, dwells in the ideas, animates the wills and untiringly inspires the vocations of the young. History of the past century, is a saga of the colonial spirit. The child born in Europe feels himself predestined for colonialism, Even if he misses his vocation, he continues, nonetheless to feed his spirit on colonialism, just as he feeds himself on colonial products.

But there is the return of the flame. Colonialism undergoes a transformation in the European consciousness. It engenders a hypernationalism, then moves on, passing through philosophical distillations, refining itself carefully, to become finally the myth of the "chosen race" that would justify the last degree of barbarism. Founded on racial contempt, colonialism engenders a super-racism.

The first world war was in reality only an intermediary term between colonialism and Nazism, a stage in the distillation process. At the time, each invoked for the best of his material interests the propitious entities of modern alchemy: God, the Right, the Man, thus found themselves intermingled with the petrol and the tin. History became an incantation of dead concepts, for recalling them from the hereafter where they had been sent by the civilisation of machine and numbers. This fashion of using religion-as of yore, magic and sorcery— for the safeguard of one's interests is, perhaps, the most monstrous aspect of the Cartesian genius.

But when one invokes God for the performance of fraudulent deeds, for plundering, killing and corrupting, God delegates Satan for perfecting the process and for achieving in the institutions what had commenced in the individual.

When Law Failed ?

The habit of "teaching the native to work", has diverted the coloniser from veritable labour and robbed him of the sense of his civilisation. The practice of injustice has made him forget justice and its fundamentals: respect for law and the sense of the right of the other. The facility of colonial life has made him unaccustomed to all effort, even intellectual, to such a degree that in Algeria the intellectual life, of this community which boasts of nearly a million of colonisers, is less intense and less productive than that of a simple town in France.

Thus the coloniser gradually de-civilises, brutalises and degrades himself. He had wished to de-civilise, brutalise and degrade the colonised, but "whosoever digs a pit under the feet of his neighbour" The oracle is fulfilled. The coloniser is himself today isolated from his own civilisation whose problems he no longer comprehends. His "anti-indigene" racism has exacerbated his individualism on the national plane and his chauvinism on the global plane.

Thus, little by little, a colonial administration ceases to be an impersonal institution and an organisation of state, and is transformed into a company of individuals or a "gang". It becomes like the old East India Company, "autonomous" in its internal regulations, having almost nothing in common with the interests of the colonising nation and no relationship at all with those of the colonised people. One no longer countenances an administration but coteries of civil servants. Each wants his share and trims for himself the portion that he pretends to be his. It is thus that the colon who had abandoned all dignity and moral reserve on the colonial plane is thence brought to abandon all scruple on the national plane.

The oracles are fulfilled .... And in its turn, Europe becomes a field wherein the colonial spirit reigns. To recapitulate the slow but sure march of this process, one could not do better than to allow a colonised to speak.

Let us, listen for instance to Aime Cesaire whose very work testifies to the human riches which colonialism must need destroy." One must, first, tell how colonisation works to decivilise the coloniser, to brutalise him in the exact sense of the word, to degrade him, to rouse his latent instincts of lust, violence, racial hatred, moral relativism and show that each time a head is chopped off in Vietnam or an eye gouged, and one accepts it in France, a young girl raped, and one accepts it in France, a Malgache executed, and one accepts it in France, there is an acquisition of civilisation that weighs down with its own dead weight, a universal regression that begins to operate, a gangrene that settles in, a source of infection that spreads out, and at the end of all these broken treaties, propagated falsehoods, tolerated punitive expeditions, bound and 'interrogated prisoners', and tortured patriots, at the end of this encouraged racial arrogance, and boastful display, there is instilled a poison in the veins of Europe and the slow but sure drift of the Continent towards savagery...."

"And then one bright day, one is awakened by a formidable return shock: the gestapos bustle about, the prisons overflow, the executioners invent, refine and discuss around easels. One is indignant, surprised. One says: '... Bah! it is Nazism, it will pass', and one waits and hopes and does not admit even to oneself the truth that it is a barbarity, but the supreme barbarity that crowns and resumes all the day to day barbarities; that this comes from Nazism, yes, but before becoming its victim, one has been its accomplice; one has supported this Nazism before being subjected to it, one had absolved it, one had closed one's eyes to it, one had legitimised it, because up to now, it had only been applied to non-European peoples; one had cultivated it; one is responsible for it, and that it wells, it pierces and it drips, before swallowing in its bloody waters all the fissures of the Western, Christian civilisation...."

And the ruptures, the corruptions, the transgressions and betrayals multiply and amplify each day in Europe. By the force of utilising justice as means of repression in the colonies, one has degraded it even in the metropolis. By the force of rigging the elections in the colonies, one has contracted even in Europe the taste for falsification in the civic life. By the force of bullying the consciences of the colonised, one does not respect any conscience whatsoever. One is engaged in constant struggle, vying with each other.

Ruthless Struggle : This ruthless struggle is carried on even in the scientific arena. In biology, Lyssenko wished to dethrone Mendel, Wiesman and Morgan. The science, no doubt, gains from such disputes, but, at stake, is not merely a better understanding of the laws of heredity. One fights, more often, for demonstrating that one is stronger. It is not the scientific conscience alone that is torn to pieces, but the conscience of humanity, lending itself to all the ruptures, conflicts and apocalypses. Tragic perspectives open up: a return to the troglodyte age is possible. The atom bomb could inspire, tomorrow, a new urbanism, that of the subterranean era. And in the gigantic mole-holes of monstrous Cartesianopolis, would dwell a human race that has substituted a machine for its brain, numbers for its moral concepts and myths for its God.

Howsoever that may be, the Muslim world can no longer seek guidance in the present chaos from a Western world itself on the verge of apocalypse. For discovering its own sources of inspiration, it must look for new paths. But whatever new paths it might borrow, it could not isolate itself within a world driving towards unity. It is not a question, for it, of breaking with a civilisation that represents a great human experience, but of adjusting relations with it.

11

The Polity

The modern concept of state is, that it is an organised institution, which is run by the people through their elected representatives for the collective welfare of the people, residing in a specified territory. The ultimate power vests in the people, who are real sovereign and, therefore, masters of their destinies. They are free to legislate and enact any law, following their own desires. The constitution of the state is moulded according to the history, belief, customs and ideology of its people. All the secular states of the world, whether Democratic or Socialistic are administrated by man-made laws, and institutions, and are based on the theory of material advancement, and utilitarianism.

Basic Perception

The concept of state in Islam is altogether different from the present-day concept of state. In modern times when territorial nationalism is the order of the day and material and economic considerations almost wholly shape peoples' outlook and policies, the making of an Islamic State stands out as the triumph of an ethical concept. But the Western observers may question: firstly, what the character of Islamic State is and, secondly, as to how an Islamic State can be realised in a democracy in the twentieth century. In this context it becomes necessary for us to ascertain as to what the true form, character and nature of an Islamic State is and how far it can be realised in the structural pattern of a modern society.

In this context, it should be kept uppermost in the mind that Islam is not merely a religion in its narrow import. It is not a set of dogmas, mythological beliefs or mere rituals. It does not divide life into water tight compartments. There is no dichotomy in Islam between the temporal and spiritual; the structure of Islam is essentially religio-political. In this system the state forms an integral part at the apex and as Dr. Muhammad Iqbal points out "is only an effort to realise the spiritual in human organisation". *(Lectures on Reconstruction of Religious Thoughts in Islam,* page 155). Thus, Islam presents the whole of reality to man and wants to give him guidance in every walk of life. It requires him to discriminate between the right and wrong and to accept a path because it is right and not because it is secular or non-secular. It attempts to bring the realities of this world in harmony with the ideals that provide security for this world and the Hereafter. It is a complete code of conduct. It is a way of life and a philosophy of life. It is a social, economic and political system. Hence, it is a statecraft.

It is in this context that the whole outlook and effort for raising the edifice of the state has to be different from the lines on which people ordinarily pursue the task of state building. Thus spiritual and ethical values of Islam have played a decisive role in this regard. This has been embodied in the concept of Islamic State—a state patterned on the socio-moral, religio-political principles of Islam. It is not torn by the dualism of state and church whose separation has been deemed an absolute dogma in Western Political Science. The church is not recognized in the genuine Islamic State as an exclusive institution representing religion. The concept of state religion or the Papacy or theocracy cannot give a correct picture of the character of the Islamic State. In a theocracy, the Pope assumes a special intimacy with God and nobody can reach God except his intermediary. This concept is alien to Islam. The criterion of an Islamic State is not union of the ruler and the government, but the principle of justice and religion combined with social action. Thus, in order to understand the concept of state in Islam, let us examine the essentials of the state.

To constitute a state four elements are essential:

(i) territory;

(ii) population;

(iii) organization; and

(iv) sovereignty.

In regard to the fourth element, the Islamic State differs fundamentally from all other states, and in that occupies a unique position.

No state can be termed independent unless it enjoys sovereign power i. e. the absolute right to make laws for people within its jurisdiction. This gives rise to the question, who should possess such right? In ancient times, when *might is right* was the rule the most powerful individual, through sheer brute force, used to conquer certain territories and instal himself as the ruler of the people. He called himself king and arrogated to himself the absolute right of law making and the right to set up any form of government that suited his convenience. Being himself the chief law-giver for his people, he was considered above law, and, as such, not bound by any law, not even his own. And in consequence of the enjoyment of this and other exclusive rights and privileges, he regarded himself as God incarnate. As an obvious corollary of this belief, he had full control over the life and death of his subjects who are required to give him unquestioning and unconditional obedience and to serve him blindly. The people were, thus, reduced to the position of mere serfs and chatties: they enjoyed no fundamental rights, nor could they claim, freedom of expression or liberty of conscience.

Later in history, when feudalism became the order of the day, a few feudal lords joined the monarch in claiming the right to make laws for the country, but the people remained where they were earlier so far as their rights and privileges were concerned. The monarchs along with those few lords enjoyed innumerable exclusive privileges and all that at the cost of those whom they ruled by virtue of being the law-givers for the land.

During the mediaeval period, the ecclesiastical authorities in Christian Europe tried to set up theocracy i.e. the rule based upon divine laws; but as the few Commandments which were regarded as infallible could not cover all aspects of human activities, the priests found an excuse to arrogate to themselves the right of making additional laws for the people. They also put themselves above the law, and as such enjoyed exclusive privileges, depriving the people of their just and inalienable rights.

Following the pattern of theocracy and in order to assert their so-called inalienable hereditary rights and infallibility, the mediaeval English monarchs claimed the 'Divine Right of Kings' the traces of which theory are still to be found in England, the most democratic country in the world. For that matter, the maxim "The King can do no wrong" still holds as good in England today as it was during the mediaeval and post-mediaeval period.

Even in Greek democracy, which is regarded by some as an ideal institution, the people were divided into two classes: the free (men) and the slaves. The latter, in the opinion of Aristotle, were not fit to participate in government. Their position was like that of animals whose only duty was to serve their free masters who owned them. They had none of the rights of citizens. Nor were women given any right and, so much so that Aristotle would confine to more domestic duties. The philosophers who called the Greek democracy into existence because the sole law-makers for the country and their antipathy towards women and healots resulted in social inequality. In other words, Greek democracy assured freedom only for the free, male Greeks, and was confined to Greece.

Rousseau, the well-known French philosopher, was, however, the first to enunciate the idea of popular sovereignty, and it was after the French Revolution that attempts were made to found state on this basis in Europe.

First State : The Islamic State, as is well-known, was founded by the Holy Prophet in the seventh century of Christian era; and continued with full vigour during the period of first four Caliphs *(Khulfa-i-Rashidin).* But soon enough, its complexion changed owing to certain variations in its ideals. However, certain basic ideals like equality, liberty, justice and even toleration remained in force to a certain degree in the post-Rashidin period.

But owing to the existence of institutions like monarchy and feudalism, the fundamentals of Islamic State, could not find a foothold in European countries, although a very energetic, glorious Islamic State was in existence in Spain for several centuries. The abolition of the institutions of monarchy and feudalism in the wake of French Revolution, however, paved the way for the reception of these ideals into Europe.

Even in modern democracies which are based upon popular sovereignty, equality, liberty, justice and toleration are rarely to be found. Strange though it may sound, this contention is nevertheless based on facts. No doubt, in modern state laws are made by the representatives of the people, yet they are made in such a way as to suit the interests of either a class or a party at the cost of the opposition or they remain so defective that different interpretations are put for different sections of the people. They are so nicely twisted that they always favour the "sovereign" class. In all modern democracies, from the President or the King down to the legislature, they are all allowed, in the first instance, to enjoy some sort of exclusive privileges, for instance, exemption from taxation, exemption from appearance in the court or immunity of arrest (while performing their official duties), reservation of seats in trains or planes, or other priorities in several other respects. Secondly, the ruling party makes such laws which could suit and advance its own interest, although it may adversely affect the opposition e.g., if the Labour Government is in power, it will promulgate laws suiting the labourer and normally at the cost of the capitalists and *vice versa*.

The most flagrant example of discrimination in this respect can be found in South Africa where the original, native inhabitants were deprived of their inalienable right to franchise by the foreign ruling class. This racial discrimination was also to be found on another level in one of the most democrative countries of the world viz., the U.S.A.

Even in the most democratic country of the world, viz., England, one finds the same phenomena of inequality although little in comparison to above mentioned countries in operation: For instance, one does find discrimination, though in a lesser degree, so far as the interpretation of law and dispensation of justice are concerned.

Even in the east while communist states which are regarded more advanced in this respect than their capitalist counterparts, the same phenomena of inequality, injustice and intoleration prevails on account of the same defect. The heads of communist states along with their lesser party bosses, were all above the law; nay, they imposed themselves on the people through the force of an election. As there is no check on the sovereign powers of the legislators, they deprived the people even of their liberty of conscience; and by putting an end to private enterprise and initiative, they reduced human beings to the position of an inconsequential part of a huge machine.

This defective system of law-making is primarily due to the fact that the right of sovereignty has been entrusted to human agency without any divine restriction. And it is because of basic human weakness that men when they are entrusted with the law-making power, more often than not misuse it in their own favour or in favour of the party or class which they represent. In other words, unrestricted sovereign powers have been assumed by human beings, in all the states from time immemorial resulting in exclusive privileges for the ruling authorities and deprivation of inalienable human rights of the people as a whole.

In an Islamic State, on the other hand, sovereignty belongs to God, the Almighty Allah. This does not, however, mean that in an Islamic State, all the laws are to be made by God Himself or that the Quran provides all possible positive laws and that people have nothing to do with sovereign functions. On the other hand, the laws, enacted in an Islamic State are, to be made by the people of the state, but in the light of the Quranic fundamentals. Thus, in an Islamic State, the people enjoy a partial and restricted right of law-making. They cannot, of course, make any law which runs contrary to the Quranic instructions, meant for universal application. In this sense, the people who make the laws, are not really law-makers. Nor are they above the law; they are only the executors of law and they stand at par with ordinary citizens.

First Source : There are two kinds of verses in the Holy Quran, namely decisive and allegorical, the latter being those which are capable of different interpretations. The decisive verses are the basis of the Book, and contain the fundamental principles of religion. So that whatever may be the differences of interpretation over allegorical verses, the fundamentals of religion are not affected by them.

Second Source : The *Sunnah* or *Hadith* (the tradition of the Prophet) is the second, and undoubtedly a secondary, source from which the Islamic laws are drawn. *Sunnah* literally means a way, rule or manner of acting. In its original sense, therefore, *Sunnah* indicates the doings, and *Hadith* the sayings of the Holy Prophet, but in effect both cover the same ground and are applicable to his actions, practices and sayings; *Hadith* being the narration and record of the *Sunnah,* but containing, in addition, various Prophetical and historical elements of Islam. As the Holy Quran generally deals with the broad principles or essentials of Islam the details are generally to be supplied by the *Sunnah* of the Holy Prophet. Even for the two important religious institutions of Islam, viz., prayer and *Zakat,* no details are to be found in the Quran.

The details about these injunctions were only supplied by the practice of the Holy Prophet. These are but two examples: but since Islam covered the whole sphere of human activities, hundreds of points had to be explained by the Holy Prophet by his example in word and deed, while the moral side, his was the pattern which every Muslim was required to follow. The persons, who embraced Islam, thus, stood in need of both the Holy Quran and the *Sunnah.* And it was because the *Sunnah* occupied such a tremendous though a secondary place in the super-structure of Islam that the early Muslims devoted themselves so assiduously and so energetically to collecting all traditions with every possible care that was humanly possible. In judging whether a certain *Hadith* was spurious or genuine, the collectors not only made a thorough investigation regarding the trustworthiness of the transmitters but also applied other tests for its acceptance. No *Hadith* was to be accepted, if it was opposed to or was against the plain teachings of the Quran. Being the secondary source of law, *Hadith,* is, however, to be judged by the Quran. If it agrees with the Quran, it should be accepted; if it runs counter to the spirit of a Quranic injunction, it should be rejected.

Third Source : *Ijtihad* is the third source from which the laws are drawn. The word itself is derived from the root *"jehad",* which means exerting oneself to the utmost or to the best of one's ability, and *Ijtihad,* which literally conveys the same significance, is technically applicable to a lawyer's exerting his mental faculties to the utmost for purposes of solving difficult problems. Reasoning or the exercise of judgement, in the theological as well as in legal matters, plays a very important part in Islam. The Quran does recognise revelation as a source of knowledge higher than reason. But it also admits that the truth of the principles established by revelation may be judged by reason, and in doing so, it repeatedly appeals to reason and denounces those who do not use their reasoning faculty. It also recognizes the necessity of the exercise of judgement in the formulation of a decision. *Ijtihad* or the exercise of judgement is expressly recognised in the *Hadith* as the means by which a decision may be arrived at when there is no direction in the Holy Quran or the *Hadith.* The following *Hadith* is regarded as the basis of *Ijtihad* in Islam:

> On being appointed Governor of Yemen, Muadh Bin Jabal was asked by the Holy Prophet as to the rule by which he would adjudicate. He replied "by the law of the Quran". "But if you do not find any direction in the Quran, how would you decide", asked the prophet. He replied, "I will apply the *Hadith* and Sunnah". "But if you don't find any guidance in the *Hadith* as well?" He was again asked. "I will then exercise my judgement and act on that," came the reply. The prophet raised his hands and said, "Praise be to Allah who guides His Messenger as He pleases".

This *Hadith* shows not only that the Holy Prophet approved of the exercise of judgement but also that his companions were well aware of the principles, and that *Ijtihad* was freely resorted to by his followers, when necessary, even in the Prophet's lifetime.

Fourth Source : The fourth source of Islamic law is *Ijma.* The word *Ijma* is derived from *jams* which means collecting or gathering together, and *Ijma* carries the double significance of composing and settling a thing which has been unsettled and hence determining and resolving upon an affair, and of agreeing or uniting in opinion. In the terminology of the Muslim jurists, *Ijma,* means a consensus of opinion of the Mujtahids, or an agreement of the Muslim jurists, of a particular age on a point of law. *Ijma,* however, is not an independent source of law; it is only *Ijtihad* on a wider basis and like *Ijtihad,* it is always open to revision.

In the second century of the *Hejira* arose the famous schools of the great jurists who codified the Islamic law according to the needs of the time; and this codification became, the chief basis of Islamic law at that time. However, owing to the degeneration that presently set in the Muslim society (in consequence of which it could not produce jurists of the calibre of the famous four *Imams),* the community as a whole began to believe that the codification, as done by those great *Imams,* was final; and that there was no scope for further *Ijtihad* in *Shariat.* Whatever may be the justification, this belief was nevertheless contrary to the very teachings of Islam. Since the Islamic laws are to be derived from the Quran which is regarded as a universal guide for all time, it is inevitable that *Ijtihad* should continue to be exercised. It is, therefore, a mistake to suppose that the door of *Ijtihad* was closed after the four *Imams.* It has already been shown that the Quran and the *Hadith* have both directions to the effect that the Muslim world should continue to exercise its judgement in making laws itself. Since the ultimate test of the correctness of *Hadith* is the Quran itself, the conclusion is evident that Islam allows independence of thought, subject only to one thing—that the principles laid down in the Quran are not contravened.

It will thus be seen that the Muslim community possesses the partial and restricted right of law-making. It is this restriction imposed upon the framers of law in an Islamic State which has created a world of difference between this state and all other states. The beauty of the Quranic principles is that they, being of divine in origin, are equally applicable to the whole mankind, irrespective of a person's status, position, colour, race, sex, language or nationality. If a thing is declared legal, it is legal for all in any shape or form. There are to be no exceptions; and even if they are allowed, they are allowed for all under certain conditions and circumstances. We can, therefore, conclude that owing to the restricted right of legislation entrusted to the most learned scholars among the Muslim community, nobody is regarded as a legislator (in the modern sense of the word) in an Islamic State.

The authority or authorities in such a state can only be regarded as the executor.

Brothers in Islam

In accordance with the famous verse of the Holy Quran "The believers are but a single brotherhood". The first characteristic of the Islamic state is fraternity. This verse asserts that Muslims, whatever, be their country, race, colour, or language, are members of a single brotherhood. Among the believers white and black, rich and poor, master and servant, Arab and non-Arab, stand together and enjoy equal rights and bear equal responsibilities in running the state. Such is the force of Islamic brotherhood that even blood relationship counts for nothing. An unbeliever, even if connected with a believer by blood ties, falls into a totally different category of citizenship. As regards the division of the Believers into nations and tribes, the Holy Quran says, "We made you into nations and tribes so that you may recognize each other. Verily the most honoured of you with Allah is he who is the most righteous of you" (XLIX). This verse emphasises that all regional and tribal distinctions are merely for the sake of convenience. Neither can they form the basis for the classification of rights of status of human beings nor should the separation or fusion of nationalities depend upon them. Among the Believers if any distinction is to be made at all, it should be on the basis of *Tuqwa* or piety. The flowering of Islamic fraternity perhaps, reached its climax on the occasion of *Hijrat* when the prophet knitted one *Muhajir* and one *Ansar* together in the brotherhood of Islam and they both lived under the same roof as brothers.

Centre of Power

Since sovereignty in an Islamic State is restricted to the four corners of the *Shariah,* whose principles are universal and equally applicable to all, the obvious resultant characteristic of such a state is equality. It is, however, a mistaken notion that Islam sanctions absolute equality among its votaries. Absolute equality is denied by nature, as no two persons are equal in every respect. Any amount of effort on the part of a state to equalise the mental faculties or even physical gifts of different persons will prove fruitless.

Consequently, a well-known verse of the Quran says: "Verily, We have given preference to some over others". However, the question arises, "What is the concept of equality in Islam"? It means equality before law and in matters of civic rights and obligations to the state. Above all, it means affording of equal opportunities to all, irrespective of caste, colour, race or birth; it also connotes social equality, a principle which even some of the most progressive and democratic states in the world have not been able to enthrone even in the present age. Only merit, character and devotion to the cause of Islam should enable a person to occupy the highest position in the state. A person's worth should not be judged by birth, but by efficiency, character and services to the cause of Islam.

The Freedom

The third characteristic of an Islamic State is liberty, which in its true perspective was, for the first time, presented by Islam to humanity. The greatest character of individual liberty is involved in that very *'Kalimah'.* "There is no god but one God" excluded all other authority but that of God. A Muslim is free as he is not required to obey any other authority, but that of God. In other words, this would mean that he is only free within the limits, prescribed by the *Shariah.* None can encroach upon the rights of others, but at the same time can feel free within his or her own rights. Freedom of expression and liberty of conscience are the two cornerstones of Islamic polity. Even an ordinary citizen of the state can criticise the highest in the state and call him to account. However, licence in the name of liberty is not allowed; none enjoys the right of slandering people or to make fun of the authorities. It is, however, the obligation of the Islamic State not to deprive any citizen of the liberty Islam confers upon him without proving his crime in the court of law and without giving him full opportunity and facilities for his defence.

Social Justice

The fourth characteristic of an Islamic State is justice. Justice in an Islamic State, should be impartial and no respecter of persons, whether high or low, prince or peasant, white or black, Muslim or non-Muslim. The Quran enjoins upon Muslims to decide a case on the basis of equality, justice and upright testimony. As such, the entire Muslim community is to be held responsible for the administration of justice. The following verses of the Holy Quran sum up the conception of justice in an Islamic State: "O ye who believe be (firm) maintainers of justice, bearers of witness for Allah's sake, even though it be against your own selves, or your parents or your kins and whether it be against rich or poor; for Allah can best protect both. Follow not the lusts (of your hearts), lest ye swerve; and if ye distort (justice) or decline to do justice, verily Allah is well-acquainted with all that ye do". (IV: 135). "If (O Muhammad;) thou judges concerning the affairs of non-Muslims, judge in equity between them (however hostile may be the attitude towards thee). For Allah loveth those who judge in equity", (V: 45). Thus the Holy Quran has emphasised again and again that however hostile, mischievous or cruel may be the person with whom the authorities have to deal, it is not permissible for them to deviate even slightly from the path of justice. In the light of the above Quranic injunctions, it becomes incumbent upon the head of the state to provide free impartial justice to all irrespective of caste, creed, colour, nationality, race, status or sex.

According to Islamic notions, the head of the Islamic State has a two-fold judicial function, one positive and the other negative. His positive functions related to the establishment of peace in the state, maintenance of concord among the various sections of the people and the protection of the weak against the strong. His negative functions concern punishment of the evil-doer and the restitution of the rights of the injured. For the dispensation of justice, the head of the state has to appoint *Qadis,* well versed in *Shariah law.* God-fearing and of irreproachable character and sterling piety.

The *Qadis* who apply divine law, consider themselves responsible not only to the head of the state but also to God Almighty and, as such, dispense justice equitably and speedily. Since the *Qadis'* court is regarded as God's court, no preferential treatment is to be given even to the highest in the state. "The King can do no wrong", does not hold good in an Islamic State so far as the dispensation of justice is concerned. No one can claim exemption from appearance in the court or even a preferential seat in the court. Recording of deposition of influential persons through commission is not allowed by Islamic law. The Islamic law lays down easy procedure for the conduct of cases and cheap and speedy justice is to be meted out to rich and poor alike free of cost. However, Islamic State lays greater emphasis on the prevention of crimes than on punishing the culprits after the offences are committed. Seeking legal opinion from well-known scholars has been in vogue since the very inception of Islam. The authorities allowed learned scholars to give free and legal advice to all and sundry. This institution enabled the state to assume that every citizen know the law, for it gives an equal opportunity to every person to know such legal details which he or she did not already know. Often *Qadis* who were not quite sure about some legal point, referred the case to *Mufti* and took a *Fatwa* from him.

Dual Responsibility : The fifth characteristic feature of the Islamic State is that everyone from the Caliph to an ordinary citizen is doubly responsible, viz., to God and to some sort of earthly authority. The fear of God and the punishment in the hereafter being common to all, the people are responsible to the head of the state, who, in turn, is himself responsible to the former. Hence, there is a double check upon the actions of all the citizens in an Islamic State. In public, they do not commit any act of omission or commission for the fear of the state officials, in private, they also abstain from committing any wrong as they are conscious of the presence of Almighty. Thus, the dichotomy of distinction between the public and private life of a citizen in an Islamic State disappears altogether. The absence of the fear of God is the weakest point in all modern states, particularly in a communist state, where people, devoid of moral conscience, as they are, can commit any wrong, unnoticed by the state officials; whereas people in an Islamic State dare not do any such act of omission or commission as they are conscious of the fact that their God is having a vigilant eye over them and they shall not escape punishment.

In accordance with a verse of the Quran "We created believers" and unbelievers, the population in an Islamic State is divided between believers and unbelievers. Among the believers, there are two kinds: first those who believe in all the revealed religions and their prophets and also in Islam as the last religion and Prophet

Muhammad (peace be upon him); and, secondly, those who believe in their own revealed books and prophets, but not in Islam or its Prophet Muhammad (peace be upon him).

Since the Islamic State is an ideological state, it is but natural that its administration should primarily be entrusted to those who believe in its ideology and agree to sacrifice their all in running the state and making it a success. In order to defend the frontiers of the Islamic State and to promote the cause of its ideology, military service is made compulsory upon all the able-bodied•Muslims without any exception; in return, they are guaranteed maintenance allowance from the state. The second group of believers, viz., the followers of the revealed books who believe in the existence of the God but do not believe in Islam or its ideology when such people agree to live within the jurisdiction of an Islamic State, their relations are guided in accordance with the famous verse of the Quran, "No compulsion in matters of faith".

The Islamic State regards them as *Dhimmis* or its own responsibility; and guarantees them full liberty of conscience protection of property, life and freedom of religious belief. Nay, it goes one step further and provides full scope for the growth of their culture and traditions and the administration of their civil affairs in accordance with their own religious laws. An Islamic State does not believe in forcing its own culture and traditions on others or in adopting coercive measures to get the culture of the *Dhimmis* submerged into that of the Muslim, as it is usually seen under a nationalist disposition. As the *Dhimmis* are not obliged to defend the Islamic State, they are required to pay a small tax in return, known as *Jizya:* in case they offer themselves for military service, they are exempted from the tax too. No distinction is made between the Muslims and the followers of other revealed books in matters of the civic rights and the latter could qualify themselves for all offices of the state except the religious ones. Thirdly, the unbelievers are those who either do not believe in the existence of God Almighty and in the Hereafter or associate other partners with God.

The followers of this Godless cult are fundamentally opposed to all the believers of God; and are at the perpetual warfare with them. Islam which believes in the establishment of peace by liberating mankind from all shackles of slavery is the worst enemy of the Godless cult. So long as this cult survives, Islam cannot flourish and will not be able to achieve its ideals; and, therefore, as a moral force, it is directly opposed to this evil force. As such, this Godless cult has been described in the Holy Quran as *fitna* (mischief) which must be rooted out from the Universe so that the faith of God may flourish.

Rules for Governance

As all the guiding principles of the Islamic State are derived from the Quran which, according to Muslim belief, is a divinely revealed book, some people assert that it (the Islamic State) is a religious institution. In reality, the Islamic State is not a religious institution in the sense of medieval Christian theocracy in which certain ecclesiastical authorities claimed for themselves the right of law-making. Others assert that the Islamic State is temporal as it is required to administer affairs which are temporal in character and not spiritual. It is, however, not temporal in the modern sense of the term, since the modern state is not guided by religion, and it usually lacks moral conscience and a moral basis for administration and application of its laws. Since the fundamental ingredients of an Islamic State are derived from the Quran, it becomes a little difficult to separate religion from temporal function. And since its chief function is to protect Islam and to promote its cause, both within and without and to administer both religious and temporal affairs. In accordance with the Quran and the *Sunnah,* this state may be regarded as both religious as well as temporal. It should, however, be made clear that the state religion of Islamic State must be Islam for whose protection and maintenance, it is called into existence and continues to exist.

It will be a fallacy to compare the Islamic State with any modern state, as it fundamentally differs from all of them and stands as a class by itself. Since it is based on Quranic principles and has a definite mission to perform, it may be regarded as an ideological state. It may, however, be termed as theo-democracy, for, in such a state, under the sovereignty and paramountcy of God, a limited popular sovereignty has been conferred on the believers.

Since the Islamic State encompasses both the religious and the temporal spheres, and come into existence through a contract between the (elected) *Ameer* and the general *Ummah* (community), it is nothing if not a devise to fulfil the aspirations of the individuals themselves collectively and, to a certain extent, individually. The state is thus not marked by any suicidal controversy between the state and the individual. According to the Islamic polity, the state, the *Ameer* and the *Millat* are all animated by an ethical ideal, and it is the duty of each one of them to strive after and towards this ideal. Accordingly, the personal liberty of the individual is guaranteed to a very large extent under this system; and political power is not concentrated in the hands of one person.

Yet another feature of the Islamic State is to carry on the administration through mutual consultation. The Quran says, "those who (conduct) their affairs by mutual consultation" *(Amr a him Shura Beina Hum);* and "(O Muhammad) consult these (i.e. in the affair. Then when thou hast taken a decision put the trust in (Him)" (III: 150). Thus, there should exist in an Islamic State a Majlis-i-Shura or Council consisting of representatives of the people, reflecting the total legal wisdom of the entire country. The appointment of this council is made by the *Ameer* himself from among various sections of the people; the only criteria for appointment being their intimate knowledge of the *Shariah,* their character. The Ameer-in-Council is to legislate in consultation with the *Majlis* and administer the state with their consent. Since the final authority is the Quran and the *Sunnah,* pleas should be based on, and in accordance with them. The decision is to be unanimous and the *Shura* feels collective responsibility.

The Islamic State is noted for separation of powers. Although the *Qadis* are to be appointed by the *Ameer,* the highest executive head in the state, in consultation with Shura, yet judiciary is completely independent of the Executive. The fact that *Qadi* can accept a suit against the very person of the *Ameer* without any previous permission and can try him in an open court—this feature of Islamic judiciary is an index to the independence of judiciary in an Islamic State. Nor is the *Ameer* exempted from personal appearance or to be given any preferential seat, in the court. The question of taking deposition of great and prominent personalities by means of commission does not arise in an Islamic State.

The Centralization : Another feature of the Islamic State is centralization in matters of legislation. The nature of the Islamic state which is based on Quranic principles, demands that there should be uniformity in legislation. It is only the Central Legislative Assembly which could legislate in connection with matter touching the religious aspects of life or the common problems of the state for instance, foreign policy, taxation, justice and constitution. However, in matters of temporal administration, much can be left with the provincial authorities. In case of provincial revenues and expenditure, the provincial treasuries can work as independent units; the Provincial *Baitul Mal* is to receive and disburse the amounts realized. In early Islam too, *Zakat* realized from a certain place was used to be spent on the needs of the local people; balance, if any, in the Provincial Treasury used to be deposited with the Central Treasury, whereas deficit, if any, in the Provincial Treasury met from the Central *Baitul Mal.* The whole empire is to be divided into provincial units. The Governors, appointed by the Caliph in consultation with the *Shura* and the local people, could be transferred and dismissed from their posts.

The economic policy of the Islamic State is to be based on some positive injunctions in the Quran. It lays down, "So that the wealth should not circulate only among the rich from among you". Hence, the distribution of wealth among all classes of believers has been emphasised by the institution of property tax, known as *Zakat,* to the extent of 2½ per cent on surplus property, each hoard as well as commercial capital; and restrictions on the process of testamentary disposition, laws of inheritance and the prohibition of usuary.

The Islamic State believes in the imposition of minimum taxation and the provision of maximum comforts for the people. The believers who are supposed to pay less than the *Zimnis* could, however, be required to pay all their surplus wealth to the state in case of emergency. Since the believers have to stake their lives and property for the defence and the maintenance of the state, they are secured due provision for their food, shelter and other necessities of life. Islamic State does not believe in class war nor does it undertake a complete socialization or democrative management of the basic instruments of production and distribution. It does allow the individuals to acquire private property so that their incentive may not be lost; but, on the other hand, it does not allow the concentration of wealth into few hands in order to perpetuate capitalism in its naked form. The economic system in an Islamic State thus stands midway between the two antagonistic systems in the present world capitalism and communism.

The objective of the Islamic State is to "establish prayer and pay *Zakat;* and enjoin good upon the people and to restrain them from committing wrong "(XXII: 41). The Quran also refers to Muslims as the best people sent down to Universe in order to do good and prevent others from committing wrong. These verses are very significant and sum up the chief objectives of the Islamic State regarding the duties of the Muslims. The first part of the first verse relates to prayers and *Zakat* which enable Muslims to practice in actual life the principle of equality, liberty, fraternity, justice and obedience to the *Imam.* The first part of the second verse regard the Muslims as the best people and as such incapable of doing wrong. They are, therefore, required to persuade others to do good as also restrain them from committing wrong. This express Quranic injunction entails enormous responsibilities upon the head of the state as well as its people. This obligates the state not only to carry out these orders within its own jurisdiction but also beyond it if occasion arose.

It is, thus, that the Islamic State is to be at perpetual war with forces of tyranny, wickedness, and godlessness. In order to emancipate mankind from bondage, whether physical or intellectual, the Islamic State is required to wage *Jihad.* But *Jihad* or holy war is not to be fought for personal aggrandisement or national glorification. It is to be waged only for the establishment of the rule of God and for ending man's tyranny over man and man's injustice to, and man's inhumanity to man.

The first Islamic State was set up by the Holy Prophet (peace be upon him) in the city of Yathrib, later named Medina-tun-Nabi, which ultimately became shortened into Medina. This should be our model, because it is our belief that whatever the Holy Prophet (peace be upon him) did was perfect as he was not only a living embodiment of the Holy Quran but also acted under Divine guidance through revelations.

The State came into existence after the *Hijrah* from Mecca, but before that the Holy Prophet had entered into a compact with the leaders of *Banu Aws* and *Banu Khazraj,* two leading tribes of Yathrib who had embraced Islam and invited him to shift to their town. This pact was made at a place called Aqaba and was in the nature of a bilateral treaty under which the Medinites on their part, accepted the Holy Prophet (peace be upon him) as their religious and political leader and undertook to protect him from all his enemies, and in particularly the *Quraish,* and the Holy Prophet (peace be upon him), on his part, bound himself never to forsake them or to return to Mecca. The words used translated into English read:

> "Nay in life and death I am with you and you are with me. I will fight whom you fight and I will make peace with whom you make peace."

The formula adopted for the oath of allegiance taken by the Medinites at the hands of the Holy Prophet (peace be upon him) was to the following effect:

> "We pledge that we will hear and obey you, in times of our distress and in times of our plenty and shall stand by you whatever may befall us of happiness and of anguish, and that we will speak the truth wherever we be not fearing the censure of the censurers in the path of Allah." *(Bayat-i-Aqaba Thani).*

City of the Prophet : The conditions prevailing at Medina at that time were one of utter chaos. Not only was there no administrative machinery to bind the tribes together but they were actually weary of their traditions of unending tribal wars. *Banu Aws* and *Banu Khazraj* were divided into twelve clans and the Jews into ten and each clan was fully autonomous. The first task, therefore, was to teach the new converts the principles of the new faith. Hence, the first thing undertaken was to construct a mosque where the community could be collected and taught the practical lessons of fraternity, equality, liberty and justice. Thus, the new community was welded into a disciplined group with a common ideology.

Having got the followers together, the Holy Prophet (peace be upon him) gave practical shape to the injunction of the Holy Quran that "the believers are but a single brotherhood, so make peace and reconciliation between your (contending) brothers and fear God that ye may receive mercy" (XLIX: 10) by obliterating the distinction between *Quraish, Aws* and *Khazraj* and pairing them together as brothers in Islam. Each of the 150 *Muhajirs* adopted by an *Ansar* as a brother with whom he was even agreeable to share his wealth but, the *Muhajirs,* not wishing to be a burden on their hosts, were content to engage themselves in various trades with the help of their *Ansar* brothers and this brought prosperity to them and really integrated themselves with the *Ansars.*

After organising his followers into a social polity the Holy Prophet (peace be upon him) applied his mind to the essential task of providing protection to the newly formed community from the *Quraish* who were still bent upon destroying the Muslims. To meet this external threat it was found necessary first to consolidate the position of the community within Medina itself which was then in habitated by a large number of Jews also. The hand of friendship was extended to them and treaties of mutual security and defence were entered into guaranteeing them equal civil rights, freedom of religion and mutual protection against external aggression in return for their recognition of the Holy Prophet (peace be upon him) as the paramount executive, military and judicial authority. The Jews willingly accepted this condition and became as a body the allies of the Muslims and thus the city state of Medina came into existence as a political entity.

The Holy Prophet (peace be upon him) was not content to leave all this in a nebulous state; so a charter was drawn up meticulously recording the terms of agreement and the rights and obligations of the respective contracting parties. This became the constitution of Medina and is, perhaps, the first written constitution to be drawn up in the world. It was drawn up in two parts. The first part consisted of 23 articles dealing with matters concerning the *Muhajirs* and *Ansars* and those who were "attached to them and crusaded with them", while the second part dealt with the relationship between the Muslims and the Jews.

The basic concept of this charter was that all would accept the Holy Prophet (peace be upon him) as the Paramount Authority in all matters administrative, judicial and military, and obey his lawful orders. He was to be the commander of the combined army, the executive head of the state and the final court of appeal but not a ruler in any sense of the term as the sovereignty over the universe, according to Islam, vests in Allah alone and all without any exception are subject to His laws.

The next main concept was that the Muslims were to form a single unit of this political community, separate and distinct from the rest, and the Jews as a body were to constitute the other unit. The two together were to form a federation for the purposes of war and peace and the defence of Medina. In all other matters each federating unit was to be completely autonomous but subject to the paramountcy of the Holy Prophet (peace be upon him). Each unit was to enjoy complete freedom of religion and governed by its own laws, customs and traditions except that the practice of blood-revenge and counter-revenge was to be totally banned and no interference on the basis of kinship or tribal affinity was to be permitted in the affairs of the state, and particularly, in the administration of justice.

This compact did not extend to purely religious wars *(jehad)* but the Jews expressly undertook that they would not in any event grant protection to the *Quraish* or their allies.

So far as the Muslims were concerned the number of *Ansar* tribes was fixed at ten and the *Muhajirs* were declared to be one tribe. Each tribe was to be treated on a par with the other in respect of their rights and duties. War and peace and the administration of justice were to be matters of common or federal concern and were to be the concern of the clan, tribe or individual. This put an end to tribal anarchy and gave birth to a sense of collective responsibility. Henceforth, everyone was to be a party to peace and war and, therefore military service was compulsory for all. In the same way, all were collectively responsible to see that no one dared harm or encroach upon the rights of others and that everyone, according to the teachings of the Holy Quran, acted with absolute fairness, free from any bias or partiality, fear and favour, even though it be against one's own interest or the interest of one's parents, kinsmen or tribesmen (IV: I 35). Tribal affiliation was recognised only to the extent that the tribe was saddled with the responsibility of ransoming its own captives from the enemy and the payment of a debt was made obligatory on the debtors' kinsmen as well.

Organised Institution

The right to grant protection was to be enjoyed by everyone, high or low, and the pledge given even by the lowliest was to be binding on the entire community but no Muslim was entitled to grant protection to a *Quraish* to Mecca or to prevent anyone from taking revenge from such a *Quraish* for the cruelties perpetrated by them upon the Muslims in Mecca.

If to these we add that the entire Muslim community was already firmly pledged to believe in one God, accept His sovereignty over the universe, follow His Commandments as revealed to the Holy Prophet (peace be upon him) and to obey the latter's lawful commands, then the pattern that emerges is of a community organised on the basis of the cherished principles of equality, liberty and fraternity in the real sense.

The main characteristics of this state that can be gathered from the above are:

— That it was an institution established through a democratic process namely, the free will and accord of the people desiring to form the same and to accept the Holy Prophet (peace be upon him) as the paramount authority (Pledge of Aqaba Thani and Agreement with the Jews).

— That it was a constitutional organisation set up under a written charter (Charter of Medina).

— That it was a federal structure comprising two communities, the Muslims and non-Muslims, and not two territories.

— That it was an ideological state based on the concepts and fundamental principles embodied in the Holy Quran.

What these fundamental principles are is well-known not only to every Muslim but also to the entire world, for the simple reason that Islam is a living force and a world order. Although the fundamental principles of Islam are universally known, yet it would not be out of place to recount them here.

Concept of Sovereignty: The concept of human sovereignty is completely absent from the political philosophy of Islam. The Holy Quran proclaims: "It is only for Allah to command" (XII: 40) and "to Allah belongeth the dominion of the heavens and the earth (II: 107). This has been repeated often in the Holy Quran: "To Allah alone belongeth the dominion of the heavens and the earth and all lies between" (V: 17); Knowest thou not that Allah hath power over all things" (II: 106). Next to Allah sovereign power resides in the people, as in respect of Adam. Allah announced to the angles that He is going to create a *Khalifa* on the earth (II: 30). Again Allah said: "Oh David, We did indeed make thee a *Khalifa* on earth—so judge thou between men in truth and justice" (XXXVIII: 27). This introduces the concept of *'Niabat-i-Ilahi'* and from this flow the following consequences:

- That next to Allah the sovereign power resides in the people. As Sir Abdur Rahim put it in his book on *'Islamic Jurisprudence'* (p. 62), Islamic law does not admit of "the sovereign power being dissociated from the people howsoever they might choose to exercise it".
- That all are equal before the law.
- That the exercise of power is a trust.
- That power has to be exercised in accordance with the Commandments of Allah and in His name.
- That everyone vested with power is accountable for his actions.
- That no one is above the law; none not even the *Khalifa,* enjoys any immunity.

This puts an end to the concept of divine origin of kings hithertofore adopted by the Hindus, the Pharoahs of Egypt, the Sassanians of Iran and the Christians of Europe. Under this concept, the sovereign was the source of law and it was religious duty to obey his commands; but under the Islamic system, the king was not the source of law and, therefore, not above the law.

Liberty : The Principle of *Tauhid* is the fundamental principle of Islam and the *Kalima-i-Tauhid* is the greatest charter of individual liberty. When a Muslim declares that "there is no god but one God", he at once excludes all other authority but that of God, because this demands "loyalty to God and not to thrones" as Allama Iqbal puts it *'Lectures on the Reconstruction of Religious Thoughts'* (p. 147). This also implies that in Islam there is no room for kingship or dictatorship. There is no ruler and no ruled. Everyone is *free* within the limits of the divine law. Freedom of expression and liberty of conscience are the cornerstones of Islamic polity and even an ordinary citizen could differ from the opinion of the Holy Prophet (peace be upon him) himself and voice his own views. Liberty did not, however, mean anarchy, for one could encroach upon the rights of others or refuse to obey those in authority or revolt if those in authority were acting within the limits of the divine law. Allah ordains:

> "Oh ye who believe: Obey Allah and obey the Apostle and those charged with authority from amongst you. If ye differ in anything among yourselves, refer it to Allah and His Apostle." (IV: 59).

Justice: Islam seeks to set up a just society and, therefore, attaches the highest importance to justice, equity and fair dealing. The Holy Quran says:

> "Oh ye who believe; stand out firmly for justice, as witnesses to Allah, even as against yourselves or your parents or your kin and whether it be against the rich, or poor; for Allah can best protect both. Follow not the lusts of your heart lest ye swerve. If ye distort justice or decline to do justice, verily Allah is well acquainted with all that ye do." (IV: I 35).

Justice is placed next to piety (V: 9). God is also the fountainhead of justice and the doing of justice is a religious duty. The entire community is also made responsible for seeing that none dares harm or encroach upon the rights of others. The entire community was, therefore, involved in the administration of justice. There was no immunity from the law for anyone. The Holy Prophet (peace be upon him) himself never claimed any such immunity. Indeed in his last *Khutba* at the *Hajja-tul-Wida* he publicly declared that if he owed anything to anyone or had deprived anyone of his property or had done any harm to anyone's life or reputation, he was present there to pay his legal dues or recompense any such claimant as he was bound to do under the law. It is reported that of the whole assembly only one person stood up and claimed a few *dirhems* which were promptly paid.

Two important constitutional principles are founded on this:

(i) that everyone is equal before the law and enjoys equal opportunities; and

(ii) that in an Islamic State even the head of the state can be sued not only as a private individual but also in respect of his public acts. The rule of law was a reality under such a system and this is what led German historian Von Hammer to say that under the Islamic system the "law rules through the utterance of justice and the power of the governor carries out the utterance of it" quoted by Syed Ameer Ali in *"A Short History of the Saracens"* (p. 62).

Another consequence of such strict adherence to justice was that all appointments to state offices were made only on the basis of merit and the seeking of office was considered to be a disqualification.

The Holy Prophet (peace be upon him) was always recognised as a truthful, honest and absolutely impartial person, so much so that even non-Muslims used to bring their disputes to him for decision, yet he himself never claimed infallibility. He did not hesitate to point out that he decided the cases brought him on the evidence adduced and that, like any other human being, he was liable to *err* in forming his judgement. Error on his part was, however, unthinkable, because whenever he was in doubt he received a revelation giving him the solution of his doubts. The classical instances of such revelations are the verses of *Surah Nisa* dealing with the inheritance of female heirs and a *Kalalah* (issueless person), and the verse of *Surah Nur* dealing with the punishment for adultery and false imputation of unchastity against a female.

Legal Framework

Under the Charter of Medina, the prophet was the court of final appeal but the services of the savants of Medina, chosen from amongst the senior companions, were also utilised for acting as a court of first instance. In the provinces, however, the judicial power was at first vested in the governors but later the practice grew up of appointing, in addition, a separate *Qadi* as an independent functionary.

The Holy Prophet (peace be upon him) had in his lifetime also introduced a department of *'Al-Mazalim'*, which had a wide and general jurisdiction both correctional and remedial in nature. Under this, persons doing wrong to each other could be compelled to do mutual justice and even litigants could be restrained from falsely refuting just claims by inspiring awe into them. This was the basis on which the criminal jurisdiction later developed.

The procedure was naturally simple but even at that early stage the rules had been laid down that parties must be present at the time of the hearing of the disputes, that the burden of proof lay upon the party asserting a claim and the defendant had to deny the claim on oath. If he did so, then the plaintiff was called upon to adduce his evidence; but if the defendant refused to take the oath, the case could be decreed against him straightaway. The number of witnesses required was usually more than one. In certain cases, however, the number was prescribed in the Holy Quran as in the case of marriage, divorce, theft, imputation of unchastity and adultery.

Concept of Fraternity: Fraternity was the fourth fundamental principle embodied in the Holy Quran on which was based the ideological State of Medina set up by the Holy Prophet (peace be upon him). "The believers are but a single brotherhood" (XLIX:10), declares the Holy Quran and then describes them as "friends and protectors of one another" (VIII: 72), with the warning that unless they protect each other there will be "tumult and oppression on earth" (VIII: 73).

The Holy Prophet (peace be upon him) has explained this concept thus: "The *Ummat* (Community) is a single fold in which each is a shepherd unto the other". This, at once, eliminates all differences and distinctions on the basis of caste, colour, creed, race or birth. All—whether black or white, master or slave, rich or poor, Arab or non-Arab—stand on the same footing and equally share the responsibility of running the affairs of the state. The Holy

Prophet (peace be upon him) himself removed any possibility of doubt or misconception with regard to this when he declared in his last Sermon at the *Hajja-tul-Wida:*

> "Oh people, listen and obey, even though a mangled Abyssinian slave is appointed your *Amir* provided he executes the Book of Allah among you."

This principle of egalitarianism is not only the foundation of the body-politic of Islam but also its greatest strength. It is on this principle that the *Muhajirs* and the *Ansars* were united together in a bond that was stronger than blood relationship and enabled the Muslims to grow from strength to strength.

Another political consequence which flows from this principle is that in an Islamic State the non-believers form a separate category but not necessarily an inferior one. They were guaranteed protection of property, life and honour, granted freedom of religion and liberty of conscience and assured of non-interference with their culture and traditions or their religious laws. Religious tolerance is inbuilt in the teachings of the Holy Quran and the traditions of Islam. Had it been otherwise, there would have been no Jews left in Asia Minor or Hindus in India or Christians in Spain.

The non-Muslim citizens were called *'dhimmis'*. They enjoyed the same rights as the Muslim citizens except that they were exempt from participation in any religious war *(jehad)* and the payment of poor tax *(Zakat)* but they paid a special tax called *Jizya,* for the protection given to them. Their constitutional position can be best gathered from the following declaration made by Hadrat Ali:

> "Their life is my life, their blood is my blood and their honour is my honour. See that none ill-treats them, for they are your *'zimma'*, your responsibility from God."

People's Power

Democracy comes next. The affairs of the state were not only required to be regulated in accordance with the laws of the Holy Quran but had also to be decided by mutual consent. The Holy Prophet (peace be upon him) himself was advised by Allah to "consult them (the believers) in all matters of administration and when thou art resolved, then put thy trust in Allah" (III: 159). This verse and verse 38 of *Surah Al-Shoora* lay down the basic principle which should guide the Muslims in the transaction of their national affairs. This principle was followed by the Holy Prophet (peace be upon him) in all matters not covered by a revelation and he never sought to impose his will upon anyone. It is reported in the *'Fatuhul Bari'* (Vol. 7) that on the occasion of making preparations for the Battle of Uhud there was a difference of opinion between the Muslims on the strategy to be adopted. The Holy Prophet (peace be upon him) accepted to follow the majority view that the Muslims should go out and give battle instead of defending Medina from within.

Last but not least, comes the concept of accountability. Authority or power to rule, according to Islam, is a trust— *'Amanat'*—of the people and not the birth right of anyone. The Quran says: "Verily Allah commands you to give over the trusts to those entitled to them and that when you judge between men, you judge with justice" (IV: 58). The nature of this trust is later indicated thus: "Establish regular prayer, pay *Zakat,* enjoin good upon the people and restrain them from doing wrong" (XXII: 41). These are the objectives of an Islamic State, to achieve which those placed in power or authority must strive. This concept of trust automatically brings in that of accountability, because a trustee is in law liable to account. Under the Islamic system this liability extends to rendering account not only to the people who appoint him but also to God as it is also a Quranic injunction.

In the light of these principles, therefore, the final picture that emerges of this first Islamic State is that it is an ideological state set up by the free will of the people in a constitutional manner and following the democrative principle of decision-making in which every citizen has an equal right to participate. Governance in this state is a trust which has to be discharged with due regard to the principles of justice, equality, liberty and fraternity for the welfare of the entire community and in such a manner that the basic needs of all are satisfied and everyone enjoys equality of opportunity without distinction of race, caste, creed, colour, faith, birth or rank.

This was a unique welfare state for which no parallel can be found in the history of the world. In this state, the Government was really a social service designed for evolving a polity based on social justice under which there was no difference between even the head of the state and an ordinary citizen. They observed same laws, had the same obligations and shared the same simple and frugal life. It would be futile to compare this state with the modern states because it differs fundamentally from all of them. The people in it are not confined to any territory nor is sovereignty vested in any human agency. "Islam is non-territorial in its character," says Allama Iqbal, "and its aim is to furnish a model for the final combination of humanity".

The entire *Ummat* is a nation no matter where located and that is why as the *Ummat* increased territorial limits of the state also expanded. The state was divided into provinces for administrative reasons but Medina remained the capital. The concept of state sovereignty is non-existent as sovereignty in Islam vests in Allah. Similarly, the concept of government is also different because government is a trust from the people and has to be exercised in accordance with law and justice for the welfare of the people. Above all, in this ideological state the bifurcation of the unity of man into temporal and spiritual is done away with. The Christian doctrine of "give unto Caesar what is Caesar's and unto God what is God's" is replaced by the thesis propounded by the Holy Prophet (peace be upon him) that "the whole earth is a Mosque". In Islam, the Church and the state constitute one indissoluble whole and, until the very essence of Islam passes away, this unity cannot be relaxed. The state, according to Islam, is only an effort to realise the spiritual in a human organisation, as Allama Iqbal maintains and it is not an end in itself but only a means to an end.

This was the model given us by the Holy Prophet (peace be upon him) himself and after him the next model for us is the structure of the state prevailing during the period of the *Khulafa-i-Rashi-deen*. The basic structure, of course, remained the same but certain changes had to be introduced to meet the changed circumstances as a result of the expansion of the state for beyond the sandy dunes of Arabia to Palestine, Syria, Iraq, Egypt and even further. The first elated to the selection of a *Khalifa*. According to a *Hadith* (confirmed by both *Bukhari* and *Muslim)*, the Holy Prophet reported to have said:

> "The affairs of the state of the Bani Israel used to be in the hands of their prophets and when one prophet died another succeeded him; but since after me there is no other prophet so in the near future there will be *Khalifas* after me and many of them". When asked if he would like to give any instructions about them, he said: "Take the oath of allegiance at the hands of him who is chosen as the first (the most fit), by the *Jamhoor* (People)."

The method suggested by the Holy Prophet (peace be upon him) was, thus, the democrative method of election by the people. But since the *Khalifa* had to be a person of undisputably high qualifications, the method adopted for the selection of the first *Khalifa* was first to get the approval of the council of senior Companions of the Holy Prophet (peace be upon him) and then to put him up for election by the entire community. In the council, the *Ansars* wanted the *Khalifa* to be chosen from amongst them but after Hadrat Umar pointed out that the community was one and the fittest person is that community was Abu Bakr (the senior most and most venerated among the Companions of the Holy Prophet whom he himself had in his lifetime during his last illness, assigned the task of leading the congregational prayers), the proposal of the *Ansars* was withdrawn.

Thereafter, Hadrat Umar was the first to take the oath of allegiance at the hands of Hadrat Abu Bakr. He was followed by Abdu Ubaidah, the *Ansar* nominee, and the rest of the council. On the next day, the entire community assembled in the mosque at Medina, and unanimously approved the selection with acclamation and took the oath of allegiance. It should be noticed that the method very closely approximates to the modern method of nomination and election, with a salutary variation of nomination by a high-powered select committee of elders. Since the seeking of office was a disqualification, it was necessary that knowledgeable persons should select a man of unimpeachable character and unquestionable capability.

Hadrat Abu Bakr, in turn, during his last illness, proposed the name of Hadrat Umar before the council of prominent Companions. When he found that they unanimously agreed, he convened a general assembly of the people and made known the unanimous view of the prominent Companions. This, too, was accepted with acclamation and all the people present took the oath of allegiance.

Hadrat Umar was stabbed by a slave of Mughaira bin Shaaba and it was felt that he might not survive; he was accordingly approached by the prominent Companions to nominate his successor. He, however, refused to do so. It was actually suggested that he may consider his son, who was duly qualified, as his successor. He replied that he had no power to do so but if he had the power he would have nominated Salim, a manumitted slave, who was no longer alive. He, however, set up a council of regency consisting of the six most important Companions (including his son) and asked them to select one from amongst themselves (but not his son) within three days of his death. The choice fell upon Hadrat Uthman and the people again accepted him unanimously. By this time, the state had spread beyond Arabia and so the oath of allegiance was also taken in each province in the presence of governors.

Hadrat Uthman was murdered by a rebel group and Hadrat Ali was selected as *Khalifa* by the people of Medina, including the rebel group, but the principle of unanimity was unfortunately lacking in his case. There was difference of opinion even among the prominent Companions. The provinces of Syria and Iraq, which were governed by Muawiyyah, did not accept his *Khilafat.* This led to war with the Iraqis and opened the floodgates of dissension. The Iraqis were defeated and forced to accept the *Khilafat.* Some well-meaning Companions then attempted to bring about a reconciliation but their attempts were thwarted by the assassination of Hadrat Ali. On his death-bed Hadrat Ali refused to nominate his son, Hasan, as the next *Khalifa* but, unlike Hadrat Umar, he did not debar him from being elected. The result was that Imam Hasan was, in fact, elected by the people. Muawiyyah, who had earlier refused to take the oath of allegiance to Hadrat Ali, did not accept the *Khilafat* of Hasan as well and proclaimed himself the *Khalifa.* After a brief tussle Hasan abdicated in the interest of general peace, but was soon poisoned to death. Muawiyyah, thereupon became the undisputed ruler of the entire Muslim empire. By nominating his son, Yazid, as the next *Khalifa* during his lifetime he laid the foundations of the Umayyed dynasty. Yazid succeeded his father and imposed his *Khilafat* by force. His armies sacked Medina, laid seize to Mecca and brutally murdered Imam Hussain, the second son of Hadrat Ali, who had been invited by the treacherous Kufans to deliver them from unjust rule of Yazid. The Umayyed dynasty ruled from Damascus till A.D. 749 when they were supplanted by the Abbasids.

It will be futile to delve any further into the tragic history of the succeeding periods as the republican era of Islam ended with Hadrat Ali, except to point that the rulers of the Umayyed and Abbasid periods did not adopt the title of King nor was the hereditary principle of kingship ever fully accepted. Although each nominated his successor from amongst the members of his family the rule of primogeniture was not strictly adhered to. Of the fourteen rulers of the Umayyed dynasty only four had their sons as successors. The practice was to nominate the eldest and fittest member of the royal family.

The principle of election of the *Khalifa* was adhered to right up to the days of the Ottomans even though it had been reduced to mere formality. The Ottomans, even though they had adopted the title of *Sultan,* preserved the idea of free election. Each new Sultan was solemnly elected by the *Ulama* and divines of Constantinople, who claimed to act in the capacity of representatives of the *Ummat.* Thus theoretically, at least, the broad characteristics of free election were all along maintained till the Turks, after the First World War, abolished the institution *of Khilafat.*

The conclusion that emerges from the above is that election of the head of the state is the recognised principle but since he has to be a person of high qualifications the election is preceded by a preliminary selection and nomination by a recognised body of knowledgeable persons. It is for this reason that in the early period only the prominent Companions of the Holy Prophet (peace be upon him) were considered suitable. But this was not an essential condition; had that been so Hadrat Umar would not have mentioned the name of Salim, a liberated slave in connection with this high office.

Muslim jurists like Al-Mawardi, Qadi Baidhawi and Al-Ghazzali have laid down elaborately the qualifications necessary for being eligible for election to the office of *Khalifa*. He was expected to be free from physical infirmities, profoundly knowledgeable both in theology and statecraft, capable not only of leading congregational prayers but also in the field of battle, courageous and, above all, indisputably pious and dedicated to the service of the *Ummat* according to the injunctions of the Holy Quran and the *Sunnah* of the Holy Prophet (peace be upon him).

Al-Mawardi also prescribes qualifications for the electors. He suggests that they must at least be adults, literate, intelligent and of known integrity, because Islam enjoins upon them to exercise their franchise honestly, freely and intelligently in favour of the right person regardless of kinship, tribal affiliation or any other consideration. This is in no way opposed to the practice of general *Baiyat* (allegiance) on the hand of the elected *Khalifa* as the *Baiyat* follows their decision and is its manifestation. If one did not agree to accept a nominated person, he could refuse to take the oath of allegiance as Muawiyyah did in the case of Hadrat Ali.

After the choice of the *Khalifa*, the next important variation introduced in the model state left by the Holy Prophet (peace be upon him) was the establishment of a *Majlis-i-Shoora*, or Advisory Council for meeting the Quranic injunction to act only after consultation. Although the members of the *Shoora* were chosen by the *Khalifa* from amongst both the *Muhajirin* and *Ansars* they did not change with the *Khalifa* as the selection was based on no other consideration but merit. This made the *Shoora* a very important body, more or less of a permanent nature, which was in no way subordinate or subservient to the *Khalifa*.

The *Shoora*, it appears, could initiate proceedings for the impeachment of the *Khalifa*. S. Khuda Buksh, however, in his book 'The *Orient under the Khalifas"* (p. 268) says that "for deposing a Sovereign the people generally met in the chief mosque. Some men of position addressed the assembly when charges were formulated and made against the ruling *Khalifa* and his deposition was declared in the interest of Islam. "History does not record any account of the deposition of any *Khalifa* but the very fact that Muslim jurists unanimously accept that a *Khalifa* could be deposed again affirms the principle that the only and exclusive source of sovereignty and power in Islam was election by the assembled community".

All matters of administration had to be placed before the *Shoora* which decided by a majority of votes after full discussion. The voting was not ón any party basis but each member tried to convince the others by his arguments supported by Quranic injunctions and *Hadith.* The endeavour was always to attain unanimity which was more often than not obtained because all acted with a sense of collective responsibility and with an open mind.

The *Shoora* was in effect also the legislature of Islam. No law could, of course, be made which was opposed to the Quran and the *Sunnah* or not in conformity with the principles that could be deduced therefrom but even within this limit no law-making was possible unless approved by the *Shoora* in coming to a decision the *Shoora* followed the democratic method of majority voting which was based on two *Ahadith* to the following effect: "It is incumbent on you to follow the most numerous body"; and "My followers will never agree upon what is not right". This is the principle that later developed into the doctrine of Ijma which is now unanimously accepted as one of the source of Islamic law. Originally, it was in fact a referendum of the entire Muslim polity; subsequently it came to be confined to the consensus of the juris-consults or *'Faqihs'* after the end of the republican era on the pretext that since the limits of the state had spread far and wide the referendum of the entire polity had become an impossibility. The learned jurists claimed to act as the representatives of the Muslim world.

Maulana Shibli Nomani maintains that under the *Majlis-i-Shoora* there was another body which discussed problems of day-to-day administration while the Shoora deliberated upon policy matters or rather dictated the policy of the *Khalifa.* Be that as it may, the importance attached to it was so great that Hadrat Umar used to say that "the institution of the *Khilafat* is void without the deliberative council (the *Shoora)".*

The third important change introduced was the complete separation of the judiciary by Hadrat Umar. Having regard to the importance Islam attached to the principle of equality before law and its insistence on absolute fairness in the administration of justice this separation of powers was considered essential. He felt this to be necessary from the very nature of things so that power should be a check to power and all power should not be concentrated in one hand. Thus, it was not Montesqueu or Hallam who conceived of the doctrine of separation of powers and the theory of checks and balances in the distribution of the powers of the state considered so necessary by present day political theorists.

In addition to the above, Hadrat Umar also set up the institution of jurisconsults called *Ifta* to advise the executive and assist the judges as well as the lay public. This body consisted of capable and trustworthy scholars of law *(Muftis)* who could give legal opinions *(Fatwas)*. They were not only legal advisors of the state but also a body which gave legal aid to the lay public on the salutary principle that no one should suffer due to ignorance of law. This principle has only in the twentieth century been recognised in the Western World.

Under the *Umayyads* the *Muftis* were permitted to charge a fee for the services rendered by them. They were also permitted to represent lay clients before the judges by filing a *Tawakeel Nama* and from this developed the institution of *vakils* or advocates.

Under the Ottoman Sultans the *Ifta* became a department of state with the *Mufti-i-Azam* as its head. Some idea of the importance of this official can be gathered from the fact that during the days of the Crusades, Sultan Salahuddin Ayubi sought a *Fatwa* from him permitting the killing of a non-Muslim wherever found but the *Mufti-i-Azam* refused to issue such a *Fatwa* as it was opposed to the injunctions of the Quran to the following effect:

> "And fight in the way of Allah against those who fight against you but begin no hostilities. Surely Allah loves not aggressors". (11-91).
>
> "So if they keep aloof and fight you not, and make you an offer of peace, then Allah has allowed you no way of aggression against them". (IV: 91).

Hadrat Umar also divided the administrative functions of the state into the following departments, each under a Companion of the Holy Prophet (peace be upon him) whose position could be likened to that of a Minister of State under the American system:

(i) *Bait-ul-Mal* or Treasury;

(ii) *Mahasil* or Board of Taxes and Revenue;

(iii) *Jund* or Military Department;

(iv) Educational and Religious Instructions Department;

(v) *Dar-ul-Qaza* or Judicial Department;

(vi) *Ahdas* or Police Department;

(vii) *Mazalim* or the Board of Inspection; and

(viii) *Ihtisab* or the Department of Public Censor.

The state, as already mentioned, was divided into Provinces, each headed by a Governor and a *Qadi.* The administrative set-up in the Provinces followed the same republican pattern as in the Centre and enjoyed a considerable amount of autonomy subject to the superintendence of the Centre. Hadrat Umar even gave to the Provinces the power to elect their own governors subject to confirmation by the *Khalifa.*

The sources of revenue at that time were (i) *Zakat,* (ii) *Ghanimat,* (iii) *Jizya*—payable by non-Muslims, (iv) *Khiraj*—share of produce of land left with non-Muslims in conquered territories, (v) *Fey*—income of state lands and (iv) *Sadaqat*—contributions in times of need. To these Hadrat Umar added (vii) *Ushr* or *Zakat* out of agricultural produce payable by Muslims. In addition to the above, there was a levy called *ju'l* or compensation for not being able to participate in *jehad.* It was the duty of every Muslim to provide his own equipment and weapons when taking part in *jehad* and as such if he was unable to do so and had the means to provide the same he had to pay for equipping a substitute.

Lastly, to overcome the difficulty felt for meeting new situations arising out of growing problems now covered by Quranic injunctions or *Hadith.* Hadrat Umar developed the practice of *Ijtihad* or analogical deduction. This became necessary due to the extremely limited legislative powers of the Islamic State. Like *Ijma* the doctrine of *Ijtihad* is also based on Quranic texts and traditions of the Holy Prophet (peace be upon him) particularly, the one who to his conversation with Muaz bin Jabal approving of the latter's proposal to decide cases on the basis of *Qiyas* where neither the Quran nor the *Hadith* provided any direct solution.

This *Hadith* is reported both in Abu Dawood and Tirmidhi. It is on this basis that Hadrat Umar introduced the institution of imprisonment and transportation, banned the sale of a slave girl who had given birth to a child from her master, suspended the *Hadd* punishment for theft in times of scarcity of food, stopped the practice of distribution of lands of non-Muslims in conquered territories, and granted maintenance allowance to an irrevocably divorced woman.

This is comparable to the modern judge-made law. The judges never claim to make law but only to interpret it, yet that interpretation sometimes alters the law itself. The same principle is followed in *Ijtihad* but its importance cannot be minimised if the Islamic law is not to become static. Instances are not wanting of attempts to creatively interpret the Quranic teachings and the *Sunnah* of the Holy Prophet (peace be upon him) to meet the new impacts on the growing Muslim society. But, unfortunately, the introduction of the condition by the *Faqihs* of later periods that *Ijtihad* was only permissible by *Mujtahids* possessing special qualifications led to the misconception that the doors of *Ijtihad* had been closed. Be that as it may, the fact remains that it has not been restored to for more than 700 years now. This is what led Allama Iqbal to lament that the decadence of Islam was largely due to the discontinuance of the practice of *Ijtihad,* which seems to have dulled the capacity of original thinking among the Muslims.

Notwithstanding the separation of the judiciary, the distribution of executive power and the grant of a measure of autonomy to the Provinces, the *Khalifa* retained in his hand the power of superintendence and revision of the work of all authorities through the *Mazalim* jurisdiction. At first during the *Hajj* gathering which was attended by all functionaries, anyone could complain before the *Khalifa* against any authority and the complaint was immediately dealt with in the presence of the person concerned; later such a complaint could be filed at any time. This was a very important jurisdiction which made accountability really effective so far as officials of the state were concerned. This can well be compared to the Writ Jurisdiction of the present times except that it was wider and free from the restrictions with which the modern system is circumscribed.

Under the Islamic system, even the *Khalifa* was responsible to each and every citizen no matter where located and held, himself also equally accountable and open to correction. Two every interesting stories about the first two *Khalifas,* credited to be authentically reported, may give some idea of how these two treated their responsibilities. The first is about a blind widow who had no one to look after her. Seeing her plight, Hadrat Umar thought of helping her by doing her household chores but when he got there the next morning he found her place tidy and done up. The same thing happened the next day and the day after. So he sat watching throughout the next night to find who the mysterious helper was. At break of dawn he saw a person enter the widow's house and clean it up. He waited outside for the person to come out and lo! who should he find coming out? None other than Hadrat Abu Bakr the *Khalifa* himself. On another occasion Hadrat Umar coming to know that a man was dying in one of the bye-lanes of Medina rushed there to find a crowd already collected and an old woman roundly abusing the Khalifa. Finding that he had not been recognised, he tried to plead for the *Khalifa* (himself) and to point out how difficult it was for the *Khalifa,* who was but an individual, to keep information about everyone. The woman replied that if he could not do so, then he should not have become the *Khalifa.* Hadrat Umar admitted his lapse and ordered the man to be removed to the mosque for proper treatment.

Remarkable indeed is the relationship between the nation and the *Khalifa.* The latter never considered himself to be the master but always the servant of everyone in the state and carried on the governance under what Al-Mawardi calls a Bilateral Contract and Rousseau, the modern propounder of the constitutional theory of the state, Contract Sociale. It will be worth reproducing here the words of the Khutba given by the first *Khalifa* immediately after his election. He declared:

> "O people, I swear by Allah that I never coveted the office either by day or night nor had I any inclination towards it. I never prayed to God openly or in secrecy to confer the same on me. But I certainly feared that

> some mischief might arise. In fact, a tremendous amount of work has been assigned to me which is beyond my power to fulfil except with the help and guidance of Almighty Allah. I wished to see the strongest of men in my place. Now, it is beyond doubt that I have been elected your *Amir,* although I am not better than you. Help me if I am right. Set me right if I am in the wrong. Truth is a trust, falsehood a treason. The weak among you shall be strong with me till his rights have been vindicated and the strong among you shall be weak with me till, if God will, I have taken what is due from him. Obey me as long as I obey Allah and his Prophet. When I disobey Him and His Prophet then obey me not."

This is the social contract par excellence to which, authorities maintain, no parallel can be found in the history of the world. It defines the relationship between the *Khalifa* and the people who elect him, lays down the limits of his authority, and gives the people the right to remove him if he departs from the right path. Every subsequent *Khalifa* adopted the same formula in his first *Khutba* after election. Even after the end of the republican period of Islam the formula was adhered to, because it was in accord with the essence of the nature of an Islamic State which in theory never changed.

The concept of Islamic State, as discussed above, reveals that most of the modern theories of constitutional government—like social contract, separation of powers, checks and balances, rule of law, natural justice, equality before law, government as a trust, sovereignty of the people next to God, and welfare of the people—were known to Muslims from the earliest times. It is, therefore, considered that there can be no great difficulty in setting up an Islamic State within the framework of a modern democracy based on political theories of the present-day statecraft. But the difficulties that arise are with regard to the institutions similar to those set up by the Holy Prophet (peace be upon him) and the *Khulafa-i-Rashidin.* Let us now consider how, in what manner and to what extent those institutions can be reconstituted in the present day conditions.

The political theorists will pose the question: Can they be re-introduced in the present changed conditions? Take, for instance, the institution of the *Khilafat.* The unity of the state and the *Ummat* has now, of course, disappeared along with the concept of the *Khilafat* and the Universal State. The Muslim world is now divided into several independent states each claiming separate identity. This happened several hundred years ago when at one and the same time there were three Muslim *Khalifas* in three different regions and each was equally great. During the time of the *Abbasids* there were actually three *Khilafats,* one in Asia *(Abbasid),* another in Africa *(Fatimid)* and a third in Europe *(Umayyads* in Spain). Thereafter, the Ottomans, after the conquest of Egypt, obtained the surrender of the *Khilafat* in their favour from the Fatimid Khalifa Salim and retained it till it was abolished by the Turks after the First World War. Even during this later period, other independent Muslim States existed in the subcontinent, Malaya and Indonesia. The idea of a Universal *Khilafat* having eased to be operative and found unworkable as a living factor in the organisation of modern Islam. Allama Iqbal thought that "for the present every Muslim nation must sink into her own deeper self, temporarily focus her vision on herself alone, until all are strong and powerful to form a living family of republics (Lectures *on Reconstruction of Religious Thoughts in Islam,* p. 159).

If the republican form of government is not inconsistent with the spirit of Islam and the *Khilafat* forms the Islamic system of government, then is it not possible to institutionalise the *Khilafat* by vesting it in a body of persons or even an elected body? This was the view of the Turkish Grand National Assembly after the deposition of Sultan Abdul Hamid, the last *Khalifa.* The Turks argued that after the Holy Prophet (peace be upon him), who was the last Prophet, the concept of *Niabat-i-Ilahi* had ceased to be operative and, therefore, keeping the *Khilafat* indivisible thereafter was purely a matter of expediency. It worked as long as the Empire of Islam was intact, but after the break-up of the Empire its utility had not only disappeared but it had in fact become a hindrance in the way of reunification of independent Muslim States. The fallacy in this reasoning lay in equating the *Khilafat* with *Niabat-i-Ilahi.* The *Khalifas* themselves never claimed this right; they only claimed to act as *Khalifa-i-Rasool.* Indeed, Hadrat Umar considered it presumptuous to even assume this title. He, therefore, introduced the title of *Amir-ul-Momineen* and this was the title adopted by subsequent *Khalifas* right up to the time when the Ottomans adopted the title of *Sultan* and considered themselves to be the Shadow of God on Earth—*Zill-i-Ilahi*—a concept totally opposed to the spirit of Islam.

Notwithstanding the innovations it seems that if we return to the pristine form of Islamic republicanism and institutionalise the concept of Universal *Khilafat* there can be no serious objection, Al-lama Iqbal also took such a view when he said:

> "It seems to me that God is slowly bringing home to us the truth that Islam is neither nationalism nor imperialism but a league of nations which recognises artificial boundaries and social distinctions for facility of reference only and not for restricting the social horizon of its members". *(Lectures* on the *Reconstruction of Religious Thoughts,* p. 159).

However, even if it is not possible to have a Universal *Khilafat* or to vest the *Khilafat* in a Council of an Islamic League of Nations, there can be no serious objection to the head of each independent Muslim State being vested with the attributes of a *Khalifa* provided he fulfils the qualifications required for the post. The important thing is not whether we call the head of a modern Islamic State a *Khalifa* or not but whether he can act like Abu Bakr or Umar.

So far as his election is concerned, the Islamic polity can well adopt the procedure laid down by Hadrat Umar, namely, initial selection or nomination, if the legislators wish to use the modern terminology, by an electoral college or council or regency consisting of highly qualified persons, to be followed by a general election. The qualifications can be prescribed by the Constitution to ensure that only capable persons are elected and the Electoral College itself should consist of both elected and ex-officio members so that all shades of public opinion are represented and, in order to be successfully nominated, the candidate should obtain a majority of votes from each section, namely, elected and ex-officio members.

Let us now discuss the legislature. *Majlis-i-Shoora* can easily be expanded and adopted to become a modern legislature. Of course, it will have no power to legislate in a field or in respect of a subject already occupied by or provided for in the Quran and Sunnah, but it should be capable of exercising the powers of *Ijma's* and *Ijtihad.* It is, therefore, necessary that they should also be persons possessing special qualifications needed for this task and these should also be carefully laid down in the Constitution. Once elected, they should function as independent members and not be tied to any political party or its programme. They should vote on the questions laid before them on the basis of their own honest conviction. No other consideration ought to be allowed to prevail.

The *Shoora* once elected should not be at the mercy of either the Head of the State or the Prime Minister. Once elected, its members should hold office for their full term unless earlier impeached by the *Shoora* by a special majority. The Council of Ministers should be appointed by the Head of the State and be removable by him. They should be members of the *Shoora* but should be appointed purely on the basis of merit. The Head of the State himself should also be removable by impeachment by the *Shoora* and that too only if a special majority of votes is cast in favour of such impeachment. Alternatively, impeachment should be by a vote of censure passed at a joint sitting of the Electoral college and the *Shoora* by a special majority of both.

It will, thus, be observed that there is no scope for the Anglo-Saxon type of democracy or the parliamentary form of government in the Islamic system. The presidential system appears to be more akin to it. For the successful operation of the parliamentary system it is necessary that there should be only two major political parties opposing each other. Whenever this is not so and there are a number of small parties in the field, the parliamentary system has not worked satisfactorily. Even in the United Kingdom, with the emergence of the Liberal Party as the one which can effectively tilt the balance, the British are themselves having a second look at their system. Indeed if we look around we shall find that the parliamentary system has not proved successful in any Muslim country, the main reason being that it is entirely foreign to our concepts.

So far as the judiciary is concerned, there is no difficulty at all in adopting the Islamic pattern because the concept of an independent judiciary, even though appointed by the executive, is our special contribution to the world. It has in fact been prevailing from the very infancy of Islamic State. Our system of administration of justice is far superior to that of any other system. Delay and dilatoriness in the process of administration of justice now prevailing are due largely to the importation of British concepts into it which have resulted in encouraging the giving of false evidence and the adoption of dilatory tactics in litigation. These should be removed and the power should be given, at least to the superior courts to strike down laws repugnant to the Quran and the *Sunnah.* Muslims have from the earliest of times established very high traditions of complete impartiality and equality in the administration of justice and there is no doubt that given the proper facilities the judges in the present-day Islamic State can acquit themselves equally well.

It is, however, suggested that an *Ulama* Council should also be set up in modern times to bring back the old *Ifta* jurisdiction and to assist the judges in solving complicated questions of *Fiqah.* It should be obligatory for judges to consult them before striking down any existing law on the ground of repugnancy to the Quran and the *Sunnah.* The legislature should also have the right to consult them whenever any question arises regarding the validity of law proposed to be passed by it.

Revisional Jurisdiction : The re-introduction of the revisional or correctional jurisdiction of the Head of the State on the pattern of the *Mazalim* jurisdiction on the executive side is also suggested. A Board or *Nazir-ul-Mazalim* can be set up to advice the Head of the State who should be the Chairman of this Board having a number of Ombudsmen under it. The Ombudsmen should act as courts of first instance from whose decisions there should be an appeal to the Board, whose decision should be final. It is only in this way that principle of accountability of the executive can be made meaningful and effective.

Some machinery like that of the *Muhtasib* should also be devised for enforcing religious duties and obligations and preventing encroachments on the rights of others, which come under the category of *Haquq-ul-Ibad.* This will prevent unnecessary litigation by making the people respect each other's rights.

Nothing has been said about sovereignty, because the concept of state in Islam is unique in this respect as the sovereignty over the universe vests in Allah Almighty.

To put it in a nutshell, what has been discussed above is a bare outline of the pattern that it may be possible to adopt in the light of modern conditions to bring the system of government into line, as far as practicable, with the essential characteristics of the Islamic pattern. It should be pointed out that unless we accept the unity of the *Ummat* as a cardinal principle of our faith, the superimposition of a pattern based on this foundation will not be of much use. We must eschew the notions of nationalities within the nation and false concepts of the state as a federation of several nationalities. The Islamic State is a unitary state wherein brothers-in-faith reside and enjoy equal rights without any distinction of caste, colour, creed or race. In unity lies the strength of the Islamic State and in the pursuit of the welfare of the people its greatness. Its aim is to create dynamic social order based on the principle of justice cooperation, brotherhood and self-sacrifice for the welfare of all. In such a society there should be no scope for disharmony or discord and the changes of conflict would be reduced to the minimum, for if everyone behaves in this spirit no one should have any grievance against the other.

12

Ideal State

It is extremely misleading to apply non-Islamic terms to Islamic concepts and institutions. The ideology of Islam has a social orientation peculiar to itself, different in many respects from that of the Modern West, and can be successfully interpreted only within its own context and in its own terminology. Any departure from this principle invariably tends to obscure the attitude of Islamic Law toward many of the burning issues of our time.

Common Prosperity

The concept of "Welfare State" is a quantitative concept and not a qualitative concept. This has important Connotations for Afro-Asian countries, having their own sense of destiny. Also, it is in this context, that we must view the disenchantment or disillusionment which is felt in Britain about the 'Welfare State'. This disillusionment arises primarily from the awareness of the fact that the British system now no longer produces 'Empire Builders.' The ears stands on hearing such words as 'Empire' and 'Empire Building'. But these are used here only as a concept and also perhaps to catch the attention of the reader. The 'Empire' in the modern world is akin to the 'Area of Influence' or a 'Block'. Was it not Allen Dulles who had said:

> "Our conflict is world wide and we must intervene in order to protect our global interests."

We should not, however, blame Mr. Dulles for what he says. Every great power in any time would have had to same interests. In fact in the history of the world, one cannot find a great country which has also not been an empire building country. There are numerous references to this phenomenon in the poetry of Dr. Muhammad Iqbal. It must, however, be understood that the word 'Empire' has a different connotation in Islam, that what this word is commonly understood to imply. The Quran says:

> "You are the best community that has been sent forth unto mankind: you enjoin the Right and forbid the Wrong: and you have faith in the Laws of God"
>
> (Al-Quran 3:110)

Protection of Rights

Allama Muhammad Asad commenting on this issue says:

> "This is the moral justification of the aggressive activism of Islam, a justification of the early Islamic conquests and of its so-called 'imperialism'. For Islam was 'imperialist', if you insist on this term; but this kind of Imperialism was not prompted by love of domination, it had nothing to do with economic or national selfishness, nothing with the greed to increase Muslim comforts at other peoples' cost; nor has it ever meant the coercion of non-believers into the fold of Islam. It has only meant as it means today, the construction of a worldly frame for the best possible spiritual development of man. For, according to the teachings of Islam moral knowledge automatically forces moral responsibility upon man. A mere Platonic discernment between Right and Wrong, without the urge to promote Right and to destroy Wrong, is a gross immorality in itself. In Islam, morality lives and dies with the human endeavour to establish its victory upon earth."

Right to Conquer : If one goes back in history, one finds Aristotle preaching to his disciples, one of whom came to be known to the world as Alexander of Macedon that Greeks as a civilized nation had a right to conquer and civilize the barbarians and, if need be, to destroy them.

The 'State' is nothing but a sum total of the ideology, aspirations and hopes of a people. These act and react to produce (that is, if these actions and reactions occur in the right direction and are of sufficient force) a prototype personality to whom the name of 'Empire Builder' is given. This 'Empire Builder', acts on one hand on the ideology, aspirations and hopes and on the other on the education, culture and religion of his people. This action and reaction produces the needed personality-type i.e. the person which ideally reflects the image of a nation. When a nation has succeeded in producing the needed personality-type in adequate numbers, their actions and reactions on the previous blocks of the model would tend to lead to the fulfillment of a nation. The name 'Empire has been given to this state of fulfillment.

Let us put some flash on our 'Empire Builder'. What type of man is he? To do this, we must first select a 'State'. Let us select Great Britain for this purpose which has been after all most recent of the 'Empires'. In a somewhat lighter vein, we may find a caricature of the Britain 'Empire Builder' in Major Thompson the dynamic impact of the others can be gauged in the following quotations:

> "He (John Jacob) was remarkable man, possessing both physical and moral courage to an extraordinary degree. Whatever he thought was right and just he would do it....I seldom get above three hours sleep in the twenty-four, and the work will kill me which I do not regret, for I have proved and established principles and built foundations on which other will be able to work"

> "In August, as the situation steadily deteriorated, John Nicholson rose from his bed, though in a raging fever, and headed south for Attack with sixty Pathan horsemen, leaving orders for 150 levies to follow him on foot. Riding hard through the night, he reached the Indus with about half his horsemen, in the early hours of the morning, and dashed up to the gate of the fortress. Rousing the garrison from their sleep, he demanded that the gates be opened for him, and when this was done ordered that the men arrest their

> mutinous leaders. For some moments the situation looked ugly, and if the Sikhs had set on him Nicholson could not possibly have escaped with his life. But he was of the stuff that great heroes are made (twenty years later mothers in the Punjab would threaten their naughty children that 'Nikal Seyh' would get them) and his language and presence made a shattering impression. The Sikhs were cowed, and did as they were told; Nicholson took over the fort and prepared it for a siege, then, leaving it under a loyal commander, began scouring the countryside with his cavalry, putting down disorder whenever he found it".

John Nicholson had once written to Henry Lawrence:

> "I feel I am little fit for regulation work, and I can never sacrifice common-sense or justice, or the interest of a people or the country to red-tape"

Empire Builders : Some of these 'Empire Builder' were vain and proud while others were modest and considerate, but all possessed one quality which was their complete devotion to duty, and above all a cultivated sense of self-righteousness. Now we come to the Islamic Empire, the memory of whose glorious past has haunted the Muslims throughout the ages. It is the memory of dynamic Islam which rose like a storm from the wilds of Arabia and enveloped the world in a short span of 125 years, pulling down from their high pedestal gods who had ruled over man since the beginning of history, up-rooting centuries old institutions and superstitions and replacing all civilization that had been built on enslavement of humanity. Who were these people then, who created this greatest of the empires, the Muslim 'Empire Builder' in addition to the above mentioned qualities of the British 'Empire Builder', had one more advantage, that was his devotion was not to man-made ideals but to the concept of 'Tauheed', which enabled him, while remaining fully involved in the affairs of this world, to cultivate a sense of detachment and spirit of sacrifice for other fellow beings. Belief in Tauheed meant that their devotion to Allah was absolutely complete; that is they had no fear but that of Allah and fear of Allah means consciousness of the disadvantages of acting against laws of God given to man through the Quran. These people in the

Muslim terminology are called 'Mumin' and 'Muttaqi' and only these are fit to be the rulers and administrators in an Islamic State.

In the affairs of the nations, it is mot important to maintain a balance between socio-economic ideology and the spiritual ideology. It was in fact this balance which for the first time in the history of world was presented by Islam. It is felt that the present Chinese Cultural Revolution initiated by Mao Tsetung is nothing but an arrangement to fill the gap which has arisen between the great economic ideology of China and the lack of a supporting spiritual ideology. It will not be out of place to mention once again Allama Asad who says:

> "It was the religious teaching of the Quran that gave a solid foundation and the life-example of the Prophet Muhammad (Peace and Blessings be upon him) that became a band of steel around that grand social structure. The Roman Empire had no such spiritual element to keep it together; and therefore it broke down so rapidly."

It is most important to appreciate that imitation — physical or ideological — is a most dangerous course for any nation to follow "and only very superficial people can believe that is possible to imitate a civilization in its external appearance without being at the same time effected by its spirit. A civilization is not an empty form, but a living energy. The moment we begin to accept the form, its inherent currents and dynamic influences set to work in ourselves and mould slowly, imperceptibly, our whole mental attitude."

It is in perfect appreciation of this experience that the Prophet said:

> "Who imitates other people becomes one of them"

Also there is feeling among the intellectuals of the Afro-Asian countries that the ideals of 'Welfare State' are purposely being imposed upon the developing countries by the West. The Western Powers, it is felt, are interested in extending 'Welfare State' to the developing countries, with a view to counteract the popular political reactions in these countries in the overall interests of their 'Global Strategy' and diverting these countries from their drive towards real economic viability based on a sound and self-expanding infrastructure of capital and technology.

It is also feared that Western concept of 'organized welfare' leads to a crisis of identity and that its organized propagation by West aims at creating an 'awareness' leading to general dissatisfaction, frustration and drift. This state of affairs, then naturally diverts the attention of developing countries from nation building tasks of real importance.

Scholars have laid much emphasis on Islamic Charity'. His idea of a 'Modern welfare state' being a heaven of charity, though having some superficial similarity with some limited functions of an Islamic State, is practically an antithesis of Islamic concept, simply for the reason that this idea of charity results in building a makeshift barricade against the emergence of a true Islamic order. The countries of Asia and Africa need a revolutionary concept if they aspire for self-sufficiency and real independence. Only such a concept can extol them to an honourable position in the community of nations. The changes in social structure may be drastic, violent or evolutionary. But makeshift concepts or patchwork ideas simply would serve no real purpose.

The scholars while advancing their ideas of charity so vehemently overlooks the revolutionary concept of Islam in human, economic and social structure. Islam in its pristine ideology, does not envisage society composed of 'haves' and 'have nots', where a vast majority of people are perpetually degraded to the position of beggars, asking for alms from a minority of charitable and benevolent ruling class. This is diametrically opposed to Islamic principles of Akhuwwat and 'Musawat' and hinders any real progress of the society. It is a concept born out of western capitalism and neo-colonialism. Islamic concept, as can be understood from the Quran and authentic hadith, aims at building a classless society obeying the laws of the Quran:

> "And what do you understand what the Era of faith is; again, what do you understand what the Era of faith is? It is the Era in which no man shall have any control over any other man; and the reign in that Era shall be entirely of Allah's Laws." (Al-Quran 82:17,18,19)

Thus a country, aspiring to become an Islamic State, must declare its faith and pledge at the very outset to create such classless society governed by the Laws of Quran, as illustrated by the life of the Last Messenger of Allah (peace and blessings be upon him) and his four closest companions, Khulafa-i-Rashideen. It will be a waste of time and energies for Muslims to grope in the dark labyrinth of Western political and social theories. All charitable activities in an Islamic state are meant to cover the interim period till the conditions of a true Islamic society are reached and to meet exigencies of curing maldistribution of wealth. Allama Muhammad Asad commenting on the following hadith says:

> "The faithful are like one man, if his eye suffers, his whole body suffers; and if his head suffers, his whole body suffers. You will recognise the faithful by their mutual compassion, love and sympathy. They are like one body; if one of its part is ill, the whole body suffers from sleeplessness and fever".

Sociological Lesson : "This, then, is the deepest sociological lesson of Islam; there can be no happiness and strength in a society that permits some of its members to suffer undeserved want, while others have more than they need. If the whole society suffers privations owing to extraordinary circumstances (as, for instance, happened to the Muslim community in the early days of Islam), such privations may become the source of spiritual strength and, through it, of future greatness. But if the available resources of a community are so unevenly distributed that certain groups within it live in affluence while the majority of the people are forced to use up all their energies in search of their daily bread. Poverty becomes the most dangerous enemy of spiritual progress, and occasionally drives whole community away from. God-consciousness and into the arms of soul-destroying materialism. It is undoubtedly this that the Prophet had in mind when he uttered the warning words:

> Poverty may sometimes turn into unbelief (Kufr).
>
> "Poverty in the midst of plenty is a negation of the very principle of brotherhood by which Islam stands and falls."

The scholar have suggested the collection of 'Zakat' by Union Councils. In Islam 'Zakat' is a central responsibility and obligation and must be collected centrally by an Islamic State. Furthermore, if a state is not Islamic in its positive basic concept by virtue of its declarations and actions, it cannot collect 'Zakat' whether centrally or through such agencies as Union Councils, as it no longer remains obligatory on Muslims to pay 'Zakat' to an un-Islamic State, no matter whether it is entirely composed of people paying lip-service to Islam.

In this connection, it is also important to note that:

> "Behold, God has bought of the Faithful their persons and their possessions, offering them Paradise in return".
>
> (Al-Quran 9:111)

Government's Rights : It follows, therefore, that a government ruling in the name of Allah and His Prophet and in obedience to the Law of Islam has the right to call upon all the resources of the citizens —including their personal possessions and even their lives — whenever the interests of the community and the security of the state demand such an effort. In other words, the government is entitled (a) to impose, over and above the Zakat- tax immutably laid down in Quran and Sunnah, any additional taxes and levies that may be deemed necessary for the welfare of the community, (b) to impose, whenever necessary, restrictions on private ownership of certain kinds of properties, means of production, or natural resources with a view to their being administered by the state as public utilities, and (c) to subject all able-bodied citizens to compulsory military service in defence of the state.

It will not be out of place to point out here that most of the present day problems of concept in Muslim world are the outcome of attempts to amalgamate. Western pseudo-social and political theories with wrong notions of Islam. This will lead us nowhere. The absolute truth of Islam does not accept any compromise with man-made fallacies.

> "Accept Islam in its entirety" (Al-Quran 2:208)

Acceptance in Totality : Either we shall have to accept Islam in its full application to our social and political life or reject it totally and be damned. There is no midway. There is a very big difference between a state run by Muslims of today and a true Islamic State. We have to discard many legacies of Muslim Monarchism and Western Imperialism in order to become an Islamic State. The

Quran provides us the required sound basic concept of such a state without hankering after alien and doubtful ideologies.

Faith and Polity

The great scholar of Islam, Allama Muhammad Asad said that : "We should not underestimate the difficulties that will confront us should we decide to give to our polity the contents and forms demanded by Islam. For one thing, it is not an easy task to achieve a truly Islamic polity after the centuries of debasement and slavery which have sapped the strength of the Muslim community and undermined its social morale. During the period of their political decay, the Muslims have lost a good deal of their cultural self-confidence as well, and many of them find it difficult today to avoid thinking in Western terms of 'state and nation' and to think in Islamic terms instead. They blindly follow Western patterns of thought in the naive belief that every thing which comes from the West must be more 'up-to-date' than anything which they, the Muslims, could produce out of themselves; and this conviction leads them to an irresponsible application of Western political concepts to all that happens in their own society. On the other hand, many conservative Muslims who, in word and deed, insist on the maintenance of all traditional forms and, consequently, oppose the Westernization of their community, base their opposition not so much on the real values of Islam as on the social conventions evolved in the centuries of our decadence.

Their minds seem to work on the assumption that Islam and the conventions of Muslim society are one and the same thing (which every thinking person knows is an utterly false assumption) and that, therefore, everything that implies a departure from the conventions evolved in the course of our history — both with regard to our social habits and our approach to the problems of state and government — goes against Islam; and that, therefore, it would be the duty of an Islamic state to give permanence and legal sanction to all the social forms in which we have hitherto been living. In other words, these conservative elements within our society seem to take it for granted that the survival of Islam depends on the maintenance of the very conditions which, because of their sterile rigidity, now make it impossible for Muslims to live in accordance with the true tenets of Islam....Apart from the difficulties arising from our own cultural decadence and the centuries-old stagnation of Muslim thought, any attempt to reorganize our countries on truly Islamic lines invariably arouses apprehensions in the non-Muslim world and causes ;it to place all manner of obstructions, direct and indirect, in our way towards this ideal. Ever since the Crusades, Islam has been misrepresented in the West, and a deep distrust — almost hatred — of all Islamic propositions has become part and parcel of the Western cultural heritage.

The Westerners see in the tenets of Islam not only a denial of many of the fundamental beliefs of their own religion but also a political threat. Under the influence of their historical memories, of the centuries of passionate warfare between the Muslim world and Europe, they attribute to Islam — quite unjustifiably — an inherent hostility towards all non-Muslims; and so they fear that revival of the Islamic spirit, as manifested in the idea of the Islamic state, might revive the slumbering strength of the Muslims and drive them to new aggressive adventures in the direction of the West. To counteract such a possible tendency, the Westerners are doing their utmost to prevent a resurgence of political power in Muslim countries and a restoration of Islam to its erstwhile dominant position in Muslim social and intellectual life.

Their means of combat are not merely political; they are cultural as well. Through the instrumentality of Western Schools and of Western-oriented methods of education in the Muslim world, the distrust of Islam as a social doctrine is being systematically planted in the minds of the younger generation of Muslim men and women; and the principal weapon in this campaign to discredit Islam is being supplied, unconsciously, by the reactionary elements within our own society".

13

Institution of State

The *Ulama*, over the centuries, have developed a structure for determining the entire set of rules and regulations arising from the Quran and the Surma (normative practice) of His messenger, Muhammad (PBUH).[1] This structure is called *fiqh* and is a legal discourse. But this legal discourse has been marginalized and attacked from many quarters, and for that reason few people are aware of the political ideas which the *Ulama* hold. This chapter attempts to convey certain traditionally held political ideas of the *Ulama* which will challenge conventional political notions held by some political scientists and students of Islamic civilization.

The *Ulama* and the Islamic legal discourse *(fiqh)* have been continually and ferociously attacked, even from within the Muslim world, from many quarters from secularists to modernists, reformists to fundamentalists. If these groups have one thing in common, it is a desire for power, and more specifically for state-centred schemes for Muslim progress.

Simply stated, the *Ulama* stand in their way as modern state centralization has historically been shunned by the *Ulama*. In fact, the very essence of the *Ulama* project that edifice erected to determine rules and regulations from the revelation is its decentralization, slow accumulation of positions and argumentation, local dominion, and diffusion. No one person can define and represent the Islamic experience, so the *Ulama* resist Islam being centralized in the person of the nation-state leader, or in any university or institute. And as for state-centred schemes for progress, in accord with traditional religions, the *Ulama* do not see progress as a virtue. As Norbert Wiener remarks. Most of us are too close to the idea of progress to take cognizance either of the fact that this belief belongs only to a small part of recorded history, or of the other fact, that it represents a sharp break with our own religious professions and traditions. The importance of the nation-state and the concept of progress to the dominant voice of politics in and about the Muslim world, helps explain why the *Ulama* are portrayed as the enemy or at least as the obstacle, to necessary 'change' and 'development'. But they are not unique in this respect.

Jerry Mander in his book *In the Absence of the Sacred,* quotes Oren Lyons, describing legal procedures of the Iroquois Nation: 'We meet and just keep talking until there's nothing left but the obvious truth, and both (disputing) families agree on the solution'. I was struck by the similarity between this description and that of Lawrence Rosen of a *qadi* (judge) in a Moroccan town. For rather than being aimed simply at the invocation of state or religious power, rather than being devoted mainly to the creation of a logically consistent body of legal doctrine, the aim of the *qadi is* to put people back in the position of being able to negotiate their own permissible relationships without pre-determining just what the outcome of those negotiations ought to be.

What the *Ulama* share with other traditional knowledge-elites is a desire to preserve a social realm where law is played out in the communal arena with language (or other discursive formats), where not only contention is resolved, but also societal definition and direction is nurtured. This definition and direction comes from the community itself, and not from a media dominated by huge corporations or the government, or from a priestly class of lawyers who design and prosecute laws. In fact, there seems to be no place in their vision for the totalitarian, corporate, legal fiction called the State which we take for granted.

The word *qadi* recalls the Arabic word's meaning of one who settles the affair *(qada),* and Rosen shows how the discretion given to the *gadia* discretion typically criticized by Western observers as laxity allows him to make law a 'metasystem which creates order in a universe that is often experienced in a more disorderly way'.' The disputants are facilitated by the *qadi* to continue defining the situation until the solution is obvious to all. Consensus developed over time and not coercion, is the central product of this legal activity. There is a great chasm between a 'traditional' society, which will mean here a society which organizes itself around divine guidance, and a 'modern' society, which means a society with a state. As we shall see, the concept of state which has fully emerged in the last hundred years or so, and which saturates our field of vision, is alien to many traditional societies and to central activities of Islamic civilization. Yet when we want to investigate politics in Islam, we tend to look for states and at monarchical rulers like caliphs, sultans, and amirs; and when fundamentalists dream, they dream of a powerful, Utopian Islamic State. The fact remains that politics in Islamic civilization is located predominately in quite a different arena, and the *Ulama*, including Ibn Taymiyyah, traditionally resisted all kinds of forces which might have potentially led to the kind of state powers which we have seen recently.

The dream of an Islamic State seems to include visions of sticks taken to rebellious Muslims, timorous non-Muslims citizens, and autocratic rulers on white horses solving all the prevailing problems. But the preoccupation with caliphate seems entirely modern, arising especially in the face of the humiliation suffered at the hands of nineteenth and twentieth century imperialist powers. Historically, Muslim communities throughout the world established the *shariah* by themselves, not *ex cathedra,* as the central focus of their community. Glimpses into daily life, chosen from hagiographic accounts of Sufis and their travels, popular poetry, inscriptions, and accounts of peasant revolts, reveal Muslim communities implementing the *shariah* themselves, striving thereby for a just society. In fact, the very word government *(hukumat)* in Arabic,' as recorded by the lexicographer Ibn Manzur below conveys a negative role for government, not a positive one.

The Arab says *hakam-tu,* I prevented someone and *hakam-tu,* I averted someone with the meaning of I prevented someone and I averted someone. In this category, one says about the *hakim* among people that he is *hakim* because he prevents the oppressor from oppression. Al-Mundhiri reported from Abu Talib that he said about their statement *hakama* Allah among us, that al-Asma'i said the root of *hukumat* (government) is averting the oppressor from oppression.'

Here the government's role is simply to prevent oppression, because positive political benefits arise directly from practising the *shariah.* There is no place in this Arab conception of *hukumat* for massive bureaucracies, governmental spending and taxing, standing armies and governments. This conception suggests that government is quite an incidental affair, necessary only to stop the oppressor, and that the real political activity of the community is to be found elsewhere and I suggest that place is the communal arena of the *fiqh.*

The Fiqh in the Political Realm : The *Ulama* traditionally exercised a distancing from encroaching state power. Indeed, we find great animosity among the *Ulama*, including fundamentalist favourites like Ibn Taymiyyah, for emerging state power." According to Rosen, the law 'provides a context for the peaceable formation by individuals of their own ties,' so in the classical Islamic theory of the state, law and government were kept largely separate from one another ... By remaining resolutely focused on the individual, the legal establishment forsook the politicization of the law; by avoiding inclusion of the law as an instrument of state policy, the political authorities passed up the opportunity to use law as a vehicle of political centralization.

As with primitive people, Muslims traditionally refused state power over their lives. The kind of distinctions we find between 'then' and 'now', between the largely hidden and suppressed alternative political configurations and our contemporary situations, suggest a fundamental dichotomy. This can be variously characterized as the pre-Columbus era, the last five hundred years (for those concentrating on the civilizations of native peoples) and tradition and modernity (for those emphasizing the sacred, such as the perennialists and traditionalists). But state power is almost invisible, as often is modernity, and so the fundamental dichotomy between anything today (government, media, religion) and then is not always perceived. One way to call attention to modern and state contexts is to draw on analyses which trace the radical changes influencing daily life. Writers like Mumford, Berman, Illich, Feyerabend, and Ellul show us a world where everything is called into question, where the questions of 'why do we do this' and 'why do we think this is normal' assume a particularly poignant note. The popular anti-hero Travis McGee meditates:

> I get this crazy feeling. Every once in a while I get it. I get the feeling that this is the last time in history when the offbeats like me will have a chance to live free in the nooks and crannies of the huge and rigid structure of an increasingly codified society. Fifty years from now I would be hunted down in the street. They would drill little holes in my skull and make me sensible and reliable and adjusted."

In Foucault's lecture 'The Political Technology of Individuals'," a fundamental change in politics is seen with the process of defining the 'police' in the seventeenth and eighteenth centuries. He locates a book written in 1779 which is the 'first great systematic program of public health for the modern state'." At the same moment, 'the French Revolution gives the signal for the great national wars of our days ... meeting their conclusion or their climax in huge mass slaughters'.

While for Saint Thomas, the king should imitate God to lead men to the good life, and for Machiavelli, the art of politics is to increase the power of the prince, the aim of the modern state is to 'reinforce the state itself'." This gives rise to a political arithmetic, a statistics which creates a calculus of power, where 'the individual exists insofar as what he does is able to introduce even a minimal change in the strength of the state, either in a positive or in a negative direction ... And sometimes what he has to do for the state is to live, to work, to produce, to consume; and sometimes what he has to do is to die."

Without a calculus of demography, a statistics of population, what we now call politics—state, power, or government—had little to do with the daily life of traditional societies. With the calculus, the individual becomes the business of the state. From before his birth to after his death, the state is concerned with any increase or decrease the individual might confer on its aggregate power. The state has an interest in monitoring and deciding the fate of infants, educating children, intervening to protect them from parental abuse, immunizing them, and so on. What rational opposition can there be, where one must argue today for 'freedom from state interrogation' over 'health' and 'saving lives'?

The desire of the modern state, which is to endlessly interrogate and govern the subject interminably, with forms that need to be filled out, credit card records, and social security numbers, is contrasted with the reticent 'primitive'. Resistance to development is a resistance to this interrogation.

The very idea of 'naked' truth, and truth 'laid bare' rests in a worldview quite opposite to that of the classical Muslim scholars. Now, the truth of someone is that person's failing, sins, and frailties. In the Islamic world, one did not broadcast shortcomings. In his discussion of the metaphor of rinsing the mouth and sniffing water in the process of *taharah* (ritual purity), Ibn al-Arabi reveals the typical emphasis given to this civilizational value. 'Even if his recompense (for speaking of evil),' Ibn al-Arabi comments, 'is in His statement, *[Allah loves not that evil should be noised abroad in public speech, except where injustice has been done],* [4:148], nevertheless silence about it is most excellent."

The resistance of the primitive is well-illustrated in a passage in Munif's novel about the advent of oil exploration in what is now Saudi Arabia, where the bureaucrats say, 'The information we need is simple and necessary, and it is confidential too.' To their long series of questions about his parents, Ibrahim blurts out 'What do you want with my mothers?' And then after even more questions, 'What's wrong with you—can't you talk about anything but my father and mother?' Finally, he cries out, 'God help me—leave me alone!'"

Communities who refuse statehood and states are found throughout the world, from the Penans in Malaysia to the Aborigines in Australia, from Indian nations throughout North, Central, and South America to Kurds and Pathans in South and Southwest Asia. *Cultural Survival Quarterly* reports that three-fourths of the 120 military conflicts in the world in 1987 were native nations defending themselves against nation-state. The ultimate supremacy of the nation-state is not yet established and many communities throughout the world are struggling against it till death. In a world dominated by state powers, and at least—if not more—as influentially by corporations, it is no wonder that the voice of the *Ulama* is seldom heard.

Polity in Caliph's Time

The classical discussions of caliphate are sparse, overly abstract, and full of hidden agendas. They are not very helpful while questioning how authority is configured in Islamic societies. The voluminous discussions of who is best suited for leadership *(imamah)* during the prayer *(salah),* in contrast, is very helpful.

Should it not then be possible to extrapolate from the discussion of the *salah,* ideas about a larger universe? Is not the ideal leader for the *salah,* the ideal leader for the larger society? Is not the discussion of the criteria for a good leader for the *salah* at the same time a discussion of the good leader of society? If indeed we can examine the *salah* as. a microcosm of the Muslim universe, a number of propitious consequences ensue. What I am proposing here is nothing short of an entire re-evaluation of politics in Islam. The entire fundamentalist discourse on the Islamic state in fact arises from the invisible concealment of a traditional world view having its own kind of politics, by a modern world-view of the sovereign state. Let us therefore delve into this matter of politics, because one of the main reasons of examining the *fiqh* discussion of the *salah* as a microcosm for the larger discourse of Islamic communities, which is so propitious, stems from the reassessment of politics which it occasions.

Historically, there is a noticeable absence of sustained and direct discussion on Islamic leadership. The subject matter of kingship or caliphate tended to create treatises at once highly abstract and overly specific. The works of Mawardi, Nizam al-hulk, al-Ghazali, and Ibn Khaldun, for example, when addressing kingship or caliphate, have quite definite agendas to pursue; attacking amid abstract and idealistic verbiage, a powerful woman behind a would be leader, or simultaneous caliphates, or justifying pinning one's hopes on converting a ravaging Hun. Arkoun lists what Mawardi overlooks:

> Al-Mawardi talks neither of the Shiite theory of the designation of the caliph based on a text, nor of the great conflict *(al-fitna)* between Ali and Muawiya, nor of Yazid who, according to the Shiite version, had Hussain assassinated at Karbala, nor of the conditions of civil war which initiated the fall of the Umayyeds and the ascendance of the Abbasides, nor of the politics

> of Mamun toward the Mutazilites and to Shiism, nor that of Mutawakkil for installing Sunnism, nor of the conquest of power by the Buyides.

The actual caliphate was formally abolished by Ataturk in 1925, and even though it was obvious that the caliphate had been an extremely ineffective system for decades, even centuries, the loss of the caliphate had a tremendous impact on Muslims throughout the world. Muslims in India, for example, spontaneously arose and began walking to Turkey to recover their world. Ali Abd al-Raziq's short treatise, published in Egypt in 1933 on government in Islam, arguing that the caliphate is not essential to the Islamic community, quickly brought him major troubles and seemed to many to be salt thrown on their wounds. To this day, many Muslims have put their hopes in a revived caliphate. We have a situation here where there is a dearth of material on Islamic government, together with an inchoate understanding that, against Abd al-Raziq, politics is essential to Islam.

The problem, as I see it, is that there is no state in Islam-state being understood in the Western sense of a sovereign, corporate institution with a reality across time and space, independent of its human constituents or components. When people talk of the 'Islamic theory of state', Ayubi notes,

> They are addressing themselves specifically to the problem of government and especially to the conduct of the ruler, and not to the state as a generic category or to the body-politic as a social reality and a legal abstraction ... Even when the Islamic bureaucracy developed and became quite complex, officials and other 'public' personnel appointed to certain jobs or dismissed from them, never signed a contract with the 'State' or any other 'moral personality', but simply with a certain individual employer (al-muwalli).

The issue is not one merely of definition. The concept of a sovereign, corporate nation-state entails absolutism and totalitarianism—no matter how much people in liberal democracies want to believe that their freedom and rights are protected. Traditional scholars spoke of this kind of politics as Thoreau did, where the best government is the least government, or none at all. Ayubi writes that neo-fundamentalists 'invoke the text and quote the source, but in doing so they are highly selective and remarkably innovative. Political precedence is of practically no interest to them; neither is the main body of official jurisprudence, apart from a few exceptions such as Ibn Taimiya.

We tend to equate politics with state and government, and thus when we ask about politics in Islam, we are actually asking about states and governments. At that point, we gather the fairly small series of works, like al-Mawardi's, discussing the caliphate and the sultanate, which digress into discussions about intact testicles and other criteria for leadership, and end up with Abd al-Raziq's ultimate destruction of the whole thing, with his persuasive argument that the Prophet left no system of government and Muslim scholarship never actually addressed the entire issue of how people should be governed.

The moment we disengage 'politics' from 'state', an entirely new situation arises. The many Muslims who were appalled at Abd al-Raziq's position, and at all subsequent liberal positions on government, were right but they were inarticulate (the actual official rebuttal to his work seems to have zeroed in on his use of 'Bolshevik' in a long list of possible governmental systems which could be seen as Islamic). If we ask, 'What governmental system did the prophet leave his community?' the answer is 'the *fiqh* of the *shariah*'. If the *shariah* is the politics of the Islamic community, then its entire legal discussion—the *fiqh—is* the expression of politics in Islam. And whereas we have a few hundred pages on the subject matter of caliphate and sultanate, we have perhaps a million pages on the subject matter of *fiqh.*

So if we want to examine Muslim views on leadership, power, relations with the other, differences in communities, structures, and institutions, we would do well to pass over the official statements on caliphates and sultanates and turn instead to the actual arena of political contention and discussion—the *fiqh.* Taking the selection of a leader for the *salah* to be a microcosm of political leadership in Islam unleashes a torrent of positions, arguments, ideas, and terminologies which begin to reflect the historical realities of politics in Islam. At the same time, it offers Muslims an authentic discursive format which allows for an Islamic assessment of politics today. The basic need, then, is to re-evaluate this *fiqh,* both for historical understandings as well as for contemporary problems.

Law and Justice

What exactly is the *fiqh?* It is perhaps the most concrete and voluminous monument of Islamic civilization, one format of Muslim understanding *(tafaqquh,* f.q.h.) of the *shariah,* the rules and regulations of Islam. Although the *fiqh* can become atrophied and reified, static and full of the weight of authority, it is traditionally the living expression of the Muslim community's commitment to realize the guidance of the *shariah.* For the Muslim, 'right life' is a consequence of right action, and the criterion for right belief is right conduct. Hence the importance of *fiqh.*

The *fiqh* combines concern with both the spiritual and the quotidian, and serves as the arena for political-economic life, regulating activity in the markets, mediating disputes, and determining David Easton's authoritative allocation of value' as well as administering rites of passage (birth, puberty, marriage, death). Its tendency for accumulation means that it preserves centuries of deliberations, discussions, decisions, and debates.

Therefore, the extension of the *fiqh*, and specifically the *fiqh* of *salah*, to the macrocosm allows us to reconstruct a political discourse. The fiqh surrounding the issue of privacy and windows, for example, tells us something about the priorities of Muslim scholars. We can reconstruct that when someone created a window, the neighbour's right of privacy prevailed: the existence of filled-in windows in traditional Muslim cities is the physical sign of the following event. Someone opens up a window to improve his house, and a neighbour begins to worry that the window looks into his house, disturbing his privacy; they take their case to the *qadi* (from the Arabic root q.d.y. as we saw, meaning to settle or resolve). The *qadi* seeks *sulh*, harmony among disputants, and so he brings along a builder to the site. If indeed the window 'harms'—from the axiomatic *hadith* 'There shall be no harming, nor being harmed', *la darar wa la darar*—the window is boarded up. I suggest that in this process, the traditional politics for Muslim societies is seen. In this process, obedience to the revelation is manifested within community relationships. This is why a break between spirituality, as expressed in obedience to the revelation, and politics, as depicted in interactions in communities, is inconceivable in traditional Islam. Let us look now explicitly at spirituality and politics.

14

Rules for Governance

Moral Aspects

In an imperfect world, it has been man's eternal yearning to create perfect institutions. The ideal of the Caliph-Imam as a vice regent of the Prophet, and the head of the newly formed community of believers, was one of such efforts. It was meant to create a political institution, which would be free from moral bankruptcies commonly associated with politics. The institution in its original spirit did not last for long time. Its failure could be attributed to the fact that the Arabs before the inception of Islam had very little experience in the political organization of a large community. Tribal organization to which they had been accustomed from times immemorial was not suited to the centralized governmental machinery of a territorially integrated state. But even a bigger cause could be that the moral ideals, which supported the Caliphal edifice were difficult to attain in practical politics. The result was the office of the Caliph became a subject of acute controversy, and Muslim scholars of various schools of thought wrote almost a library of literature on the subject. The hold of the ideal over the popular imagination was however such, that in spite of repeated setbacks, people's faith in it was never shaken. This glaring incompatibility between the ideal and the reality kept gnawing at the soul of the Muslim community. Muslims in many lands suffered from the crisis of the conscience throughout their history.

Recession of Ideals : After the Pious Caliphate, the ideal receded from the field of practical politics, and the Muslim state was modeled on the pre-Islamic political and administrative practices of the newly conquered non-Arab lands. Religious and moral aspects of the Caliphate were reduced merely to a superficial embellishment, and political and administrative behaviour of the Muslim rulers was completely denuded of the spirit which had motivated the immediate successors of the Prophet on the seat of Caliphate-Imamate. In every Muslim dynasty, with a few exceptions, majority of the rulers were corrupt and incompetent. Most of them were guilty of moral turpitude, and under their rule public life in a Muslim community was thoroughly contaminated with vices of despotism, oppression and ethical irregularities. Widespread exploitation of the masses was a common feature, monarchs and state functionaries indulged in ethical lawlessness without any compunction of the soul.

There were some great rulers, no doubt, who lived up to the great religious ideals of Islam, but such periods in Islamic history were always short-lived. The general tenor of the government and administration in a Muslim state remained far removed from the pristine values and beliefs of the doctrine. Shariah was the law of the land, but the functionaries who administered it were so utterly subservient to the will of the rulers that no independent judgement or interpretation could be expected of them. *Ulamas* (religious scholar) who in theory were the custodians of the high ethical standards in public life, were corrupted and majority of them lived as spineless minions of the state. The Caliphate was changed into sûltanate, which was another name for military dictatorship. The society became a loose confederation of feudal estates, wherein the feudal lord and the tax collector were always on the rampage. So far as welfare of the masses was concerned, the spectacle of government and administration was depressing and disheartening.

It was in these circumstances that Muslim statesmen and scholars turned to "wisdom literature" and wrote some of the classics, which have enthralled students of Islamic studies for centuries. That most of the writers were statesmen and administrators should not surprise anybody, because the cream of talent in a Muslim kingdom always gravitated towards the court of the ruling prince. Attachment to the retinue of the ruler of the day was the highest certificate of merit that a scholar or a professional in any trade could have. Their primary responsibility was to ensure the welfare of the prince in all walks of life. The court was the nerve center of the realm and for an observant eye there was enough material to draw a comprehensive picture of the prevalent moral and political climate in the kingdom. Not all, but some of them used this accumulated knowledge to compile books on counsels for the kings, or general dissertations on the art of governing men. Some of these works have won permanent place in Islamic culture and literature. There is always something refreshing in them, although the expression might not be so absorbing and cultivated. According to Reuben Levy, these works constituted the Islamic version of the Eastern tradition of "wisdom literature manifested in such scriptural books as Job, and Proverbs, and frequently also in Sanskrit literature."

Wide Canvass : These statesmen-scholars used a very wide canvas to portray the dynamics of socio-political and religious issues with which they wrestled their mind and soul. Their approach was both diagnostic and prescriptive. They explored in depth the causes of the malaise, which had hit the Islamic civilization, and then in the light of precepts enunciated by the Quran, the Traditions of the Prophet, and the lives of great kings of the past, they drew certain guidelines which in their opinion could open vistas of rectitude for a world which had been so badly corrupted and demoralized. To explain their point of view they also made extensive use of anecdotal literature of many cultures. Each one of these works is a harmonious blend of facts and fables, out of which the authors have drawn shrewd and insightful conclusions. To dispel the tedium and monotony of their ethical sermons, they also make a frequent use of Persian and Arabic verses which are relevant to a principle or situation being examined. Stylistically these books lack the elegance and beauty of a good prose work, but they are remarkable for the breadth of wisdom, and depth of human insight.

But more than anything else they provide a lucid account of the religio-political conditions of the Muslim society in which their authors lived. Moral and political failures of the rulers, and the inertia and helplessness of the people are depicted in a frank and candid manner. The range of topics discussed is also very wide.

Justice, probity, duties and responsibilities of kingship, public morality, princely manners, statescraft, religious sects, political factions, dynastic squabbles, administrative failures, social foibles, economic problems, military matters, are all fit subjects for such works. Very often authors unroll detailed exposition of human nature, and relate it to the discrepancies and fallacies they notice in social life and political organization. They are also an immeasurable storehouse of wit and wisdom. Their pages glitter with social maxims, spicy half-truths, and brilliantly spun anecdotes. At appropriate occasion people's habits, customs and eccentricities are also uncovered with great perspicacity. In short, everything which has bearing on human behaviour is examined in one form or another.

In spite of the exuberance of their wisdom, however, note of caution is warranted for a student who approaches them for critical appreciation. Firstly it is to be understood that these works were not written by historians with a keen and anxious eye on the authenticity of fact. They were written by statesmen and administrators, out of their life long experiences, observations and hearsay, and very little care was expended to verify the historicity of the details. One has to be particularly careful about the anecdotes attributed to great personages of the past, because most of them seem to have been derived from untrustworthy sources. The integration of the materials also at various points is unscientific, and a reader tends to feel the strain of monotony as he goes through certain portions. But these deficiencies do not delete anything from the tremendous value they have for a student of government and administration in Islam, and the amount of pleasure they have afforded generation after generation of readers in many Muslim lands. They are free from rhetoric and abstruse constructions, commonly associated with Arabic or Persian prose. The beauty of diction is not there, but the style is simple and direct.

In this book nine classic books of the Islamic wisdom literature have been reviewed, but only those portions have been subjected to review which specifically pertain to the issues relating to ethical behaviour in politics and administration of a Muslim state. As mentioned earlier these works, though small, have an encyclopaedic range of subjects. But for our purpose only those elements have been skimmed which either portray the degeneration in which the

Muslim society had sunk, or provide guidelines to understand the ethical contours of administrative machinery in a Muslim state.

Civility and Morality : There are two treatises with the same title written by two different scholars. The first was written by Ibn Adi (d 976 A.D.) a Syrian Christian scholar. Ibn Adi's book is basically a collection of ideas borrowed from the Greek ethical thought. There is nothing specific relating to rulers and administrators, but from his narrative an impressive list can be prepared to indicate virtues of good disposition and vices of corrupt behaviour. The list is as follows:

I. Virtues of Good Dispositions

1. Continence
2. Self-control
3. Dignity
4. Mercy
5. Trustworthiness
6. Humility
7. Truth of speech
8. Generosity
9. Aspiration
10. Steadfastness in adversity
11. Frugality
12. Tranquility
13. Love
14. Fulfillment of promise
15. Keeping a secret
16. Cheerfulness
17. Good intention
18. Courage
19. Great ambition

II. Vices in Corrupt Behaviour

1. Dissoluteness
2. Greediness
3. Shabbiness
4. Levity
5. Awkwardness
6. Excessive love
7. Pitilessness
8. Sternness
9. Falsehood
10. Deceit
11. Secret hate
12. Avarice
13. Cowardice
14. Envy
15. Treachery
16. Perfidy
17. Divulging a secret
18. Impatience in misfortune
19. Smallness of ambition
20. Injustice

The virtues listed above according to Ibn Adi are essential for the perfection of human character. They are cultivated by rigorous training of mind and soul and depend to a large extent on the depth and comprehension, that one possesses about the world. Self-discipline and abstinence from harmful pleasures of life are advocated as instruments of moral rectitude.

The second treatise was written by Abu Ali Ahmad Ibn Muhammad ibn Maskawaiha (d. 1030 A.D.). The author of this treatise lived during the military dictatorship of the Buwaihid who had put Abbaside Caliphs under their forced protection. They captured Baghdad in 945 A.D. and remained the indisputable rulers of the Eastern Caliphate for 110 years. Ibn Maskawaiha was secretary of Al-Muhallabi, the Prime Minister of Muizz-al-Dawla the Buwaihid prince who conquered Baghdad. *Tahzih-al-Akhlaq* (The Correction of Disposition) is considered to be an outstanding work on the philosophy of ethics in Islam. The author believed that human conduct is built by restraint, courage and judiciousness. The fruit of righteousness stems out of integrity.

In other words, integrity connotes translation of worthiness, truth, and goodness into human action. They constitute a moral conquest over falsehood and evil. At another place Ibn Maskawaiha has listed four fundamental qualities which are vital for higher ethical standards and has contrasted them with four evils which constitute the bane of morality.

(i)	wisdom	——	ignorance
(ii)	purity	——	greed
(iii)	courage	——	cowardice
(iv)	righteousness	——	violence

Wisdom, a Virtue : Wisdom is a virtue of human soul by which men comprehend the existing things in the light of the words of God. It is a quality by which distinction is made between desirable and undesirable actions. Purity is an instrument of self-discipline. It is a thoughtful use of human desires and soundness of judgment. Righteousness is a sense of justice by which excesses and deficiencies are eliminated and a fair course of action is adopted. Anger, conceit, vanity, jesting, boastfulness, perfidy, unfairness, laying up treasures, are counted among the diseases of the human soul. Courage and judiciousness are advocated as antidotes to these evils. He pleads for restraint on desires and appetites. Courage is not merely a weapon to defend one's body and material possession, it is also a strength of mind by which evil propensities of self have to be conquered. Judiciousness stems out of wisdom cultivated through study and reflection. It is therefore incumbent upon all right-thinking people and seekers of truth and righteousness to search for knowledge in all directions. A person who has decided to discipline his soul, and wishes to avoid risks of moral defilement must, according to Ibn Maskawaiha, set before himself the following objectives :

1. He had striven to maintain what we would call personal integrity. This he defined as the preference (ithar) for what is worthy (al-haqq) over what is futile in beliefs; for what is true (al-sidq) over what is false in statements; and for what is good (al khair) over what is evil (al-sharr) in actions.
2. He had emphasized the continuous struggle that he needed to keep up between his essential manhood (al-mar) and his animal nature.
3. He had felt the importance of adhering to the Law (al-Shariah) and of recognizing the necessity of its functions.
4. He had endeavoured to remember agreements and to fulfill them, particularly any agreement that he had made with Allah.
5. He had shown little confidence in men, and this he accomplished by avoiding familiarity with them.
6. He had cultivated the love of the beautiful for its own sake and for no other reason.
7. He had appreciated the value of silence in times of agitation, until reason would direct him.
8. He had striven to continue any state of mind that was beneficial until it would become a habit.
9. He had approved taking the initiative in things that were creditable.
10. He had found that whole-hearted sympathy was necessary

in order to work on any important undertaking without distraction.

11. He had felt that the fear of death and of poverty could be counteracted by doing what was still possible and by not being indolent.
12. He had casted out from his mind such anxieties as were aroused by sayings of the base, and he had tried to suppress his desire at night to plan something against them.
13. He had come to realize that he must be inured to wealth or to poverty, and to liberality or to contempt.
14. He had tried to remember times of sickness when he was in health, and occasions of joy and pleasure when anger was apt to arise, so that there might be less injustice and transgression.
15. He had rejoiced in times of trust, appreciating the goodness of hope and confidence in Allah, turning his whole heart to him.

He further points out that greatest happiness of man depends on the manifestation of the innate excellencies of the human soul. The happiness of one man is linked with the happiness of the rest. Mutual assistance in other words is the essence of social health and stability. In pursuit of happiness, each individual should be a torch-bearer for the perfection of others. It is for this reason that Ibn Maskawiha points out that virtue cannot be practiced in isolation. Asceticism, in his opinion is wrong and inimical to individual and social happiness. In essence ethics is an instrument of self-discipline and a method for character-building.

Books for Counselling

Qabusnamh (Book of Qabus) or Andarz-nama (Book of Counsel)

It was composed by Kay Kaus ibn Iskandar ibn Qabis in 375/ 1082 A.D. The author was the Ziyarid ruler of Tabristan. He was endowed with profound wisdom and literary attainments which are amply manifested in the said treatise. At the age of sixty-three Kay Kaus thought to capture in book form his life-long experiences as a ruler and administrator for the guidance of his son Gilanshah.

The purpose was to outline eventualities which are likely to befall rulers of men, and to suggest ways and means to tide over difficulties which so often crop up due to the chronic uncertainty of political conditions. John Alden Williams has given the following sketch of the purpose with which Kay Kaus decided to write his experiences in the form of a book of counsel for the rulers.

In the advice of Kay Kaus ibn Iskandar the Ziyari ruler of a little kingdom in the Caspian provinces of Persia, to his son, Gilanshah, we have a valuable insight into Islamic kingship as it appeared to a Muslim king in the eleventh century. Kay Kaus is a professional member of the ruling class, and an affectionate father, who wishes to pass his knowledge to his sons. He is very conscious that even if a king cannot have lordly morals, he must appear to have them. He knows that a king must sometimes tell lies and kill, but it is not expedient to get a name for it. Virtue, or its appearance, is useful; it is one of the means by which a king in his civilization must try to secure his power.

Kay Kaus had the ability to wield sword and pen with equal dexterity. The book has enjoyed great popularity in the annals of Persian literature. Wit, wisdom, frankness, conviction, directness of expression, and richness of experience constitute the highlights of the work.

The *Qabus-nama* consists of forty-four chapters and a preface. The contents of the book provide ample evidence that the royal author was deeply concerned about the growing malpractices in the administration of the country. The first thirty-four chapters are related to the general principles of moral life. They range from obedience to God to the uses of astrology, mathematics, and poetic arts. It is in the later chapters that Kay Kaus turns his attention to the affairs of kingship and administration. Chapter thirty seven deals with services of the kings. Thirty eight is on the qualities of the courtier, the thirty ninth deals with the secretaries of the state and secretarial art; the fortieth chapter is on the qualities of the wazir ; the forty first on the duties and responsibilities of generals; the forty second on the qualifications and duties of the king; forty third deals with farmers and agriculture, and forty fourth discusses generosity. The pervading spirit of all his analyses is emphasis on the cultivation of virtues and excellencies which have been preached by Islam, Kay Kaus is of the opinion that rational and practical side of religion should be a vital element in understanding Islam. Browne remarks :

"The author's ideas display a curious mixture of craft and simplicity, of scepticism and piety. Thus he dwells on the ethical, as apart from the spiritual value of prayer, fasting, and other religious exercises as means to cleanliness, humility, and temperance; and advocates conformity with the laws of Islam, because there is no stronger bond than the Commonwealth of Islam."

The whole of the work is replete with worldly wisdom some of which at least has great relevance even to our own times. The book throws a flood of light on the state of affairs in the Muslim civilization as it existed during the Middle Ages. It advocates lofty ethical principles, which would be above greed and expediency. He is convinced that human society cannot exist without some kind of governmental organization, because man's bewildering propensities for evil need an effective machinery of control. "Now man has need of government and regulation; without direction he is brutal (uncivilized)." Government in turn depends upon authority, the way it is organized, the manner in which it is used in decision-making, and the image which people hold about it. Kay Kaus has laid down certain principles which must be strictly adhered to if authority has to make any impact on affairs of men. A person making authoritative decisions should "be neither harsh, nor sharp tempered, nor devoid of clemency (yet be not so entirely yielding as to be swallowed upon on account of your softness) and never be so morose that you are not to be won over."

Worldly Wisdom : Browne has summarized the worldly wisdom of *Qabus-nama* in these words:

> His worldly maxims are shrewd, and wonderfully modern at times. He expatiates on the advantages of a smooth tongue, bids his son learn wisdom from fools, and cautions him against over-modesty, "for," says he 'many men fail of their objects through bashfulness.' His remarks on truthfulness are delightful. But do thou, O son, says he, 'be specious, but not a liar*:* make thyself famous as a speaker of truth, so that

> if at some time thou shoudst tell a lie, men may accept it as true from thee.' He also cautions his son against making statements which, though true, are likely to be disbelieved, and cannot be easily proved; for, says he, 'why should one make a statement, even if it be true, which it needs four months and the testimony of two hundred respectable witnesses to prove?

He is also of the opinion that in adopting a particular course of action, a man on the seat of authority should not act arbitrarily. Even with the maximum of learning and knowledge, it is always desirable to consult someone. Over-confidence in one's own abilities and judgment is symptomatic of arrogance, a quality quite unbecoming of those who have been entrusted with authority to preside over the destiny of human organizations. He says :

> Therefore, be not puffed up with your own learning, however learned you may be. And if any task befalls you, even if you have the capacity to perform it, do not rely entirely on your own judgment, for he who relies entirely on his own judgment ever regrets it. Never be ashamed of asking advice, consulting old men of understanding and well-disposed friends. Even Muhammad despite his wisdom and his prophethood, after becoming the exemplifier and agent of God's work was told by him 'Consult them in the matter, O Muhammad'. (Quran 3, V, 153).

He further adds that it does not behoove a man in authority to be "any degree careless over the duties of justice and governmental control and from treating overlightly anything essential to these matters." One must also be watchful that offices are not bestowed on "impecunious or impoverished men," and he compares such appointments to a dry canal which will not water fields and gardens until it is saturated with moisture. Meaning that a poverty-stricken man, if installed to a position of power, is most susceptible to dishonest dealings. Probably knowing that such a rule cannot be meticulously followed, Kai Kaus mentions that authority should be maintained with firmness and spiteful disregard of it, should not be tolerated. Those who willfully disobey legitimate commands deserve exemplary punishment. But in order to avoid an ugly situation, those who wield authority have certain professional and ethical obligations. Their commands should be precise, clear and decisive. Their tone and intention should be firm and unambiguous. Their reputation should be such that people will not hesitate to repose confidence in their decision. Men of authority are custodians of the realm and it would be ridiculous to have someone take custody of the custodians or to have a guard for the guardians. He says :

> "The orders, then, of both kings and viziers must be unequivocal and their commands decisive, if their authority is to remain firmly established and their interest to prosper. Next, drink no intoxicant liquor, out of such drinking there arise carelessness, laxity and injustice Allah protect us from a wine-bibling vizier and wanton governor ! If it is the king who indulges in wine, decay soon pervades the realm. Therefore keep a watch on yourself and conform to what I have told you; the vizier is the custodian of realm and it would be a very ugly matter if the custodian should need another to have a custody of him."

Kai Kaus, in order to substantiate his contention narrates an anecdote, relating to a confrontation between an old woman and King Masud of Ghazni. The woman had lodged a complaint against a governor, who had refused to pay heed to the King's letter, which the woman had taken to him. The King decided to write a second letter, but the woman refused to carry it saying that such a letter had already been taken to the governor which had failed to redress her grievance. The King said "What am I to do?" The woman replied, "Your course of action here is simple. Maintain your authority in such a fashion that your instructions will be acted upon or else resign your authority and let another possess it leaving you to occupy yourself with your pleasures. Thus mankind will cease to be held fettered in the miseries of tyranny." In other words, an ineffectual authority is a gateway to tyranny, and a state where authority fails to get compliance forfeits its right to exist. Therefore authority requires strict control and vigilance from one who holds it. In other words an authority which is not used effectively is worse than anarchy because under cover of law officers will indulge in illegal extortions and the time would come when the country would be depopulated. An oppressive authority leads to decay and desolation and it is therefore extremely inexpedient to show any negligence in this matter.

Political Authority : After having established the necessity of political and administrative authority, our author goes on to elucidate ethical equipment of those who govern men. These ethical principles are spread over all the forty four chapters of the book. They are more or less the ones which have universally been applauded as pertinent guidelines for righteous action. In his opinion wisdom and virtue should be in inseparable partnership in life. If a person is wise, but the moral side of his character is tainted, he cannot be a success in life. He says :

> If you have wisdom, therefore acquire virtue for wisdom without virtue is like a man without clothes or a person without a face or a body without a soul. Indeed there is a proverb to the effect that 'virtue is the visage of the mind.'

The world is not meant for fools although they are in abundance, but nor are the wise of any good if their wisdom is denuded of ethical lustre and dignity. Kai Kaus gives primacy to wisdom and virtue, because both are qualities, which are acquired and not inherited. He quotes an Arabic proverb which says, "Honour lies in the mind and in acquired worth, not in origin and noble birth," and then mentions Socrates, who in his opinion, once said "that there is no treasure better than virtue, no honour more glorious than knowledge, no ornament more beautiful than modesty and no enemy worse than an evil disposition."

An accomplished person is judged by his frank and fair disposition. Duplicity destroys trust, and if trust is gone other qualities can be of no avail. Profession, must synchronize with action. Any incongruity between the two can have a damaging effect on individual's integrity. Kai Kaus says :

> "Once having made a profession of your beneficence, however, let not your actions contradict it. Do not say one thing with your tongue and harbor a contrary thought in your heart, lest you reveal yourself to be one who displays wheat but sells barley."

He maintains that it is a great virtue to be generous and benevolent, and believes that malice is a bane of the human soul, and it leads to spiritual impoverishment and social humiliation. He is however not very sure about modesty which according to an Arabic saying is bracketed with faith. He believes that modesty may be good, but "yet it may frequently happen that bashfulness is a misfortune to men. Do not therefore be so shamefaced as to cause failure or injury to your own interests. There are many occasions when boldness must be exercised to ensure that your purposes may be achieved."

It is through speech that most of the qualities of human character are manifested for the rest of the world. It behooves, therefore of those who make public policies and issue statements to be watchful of what they say. Language helps understanding, facilitates communication, and is the one and only effective carrier of information. Wrong choice of words can infuriate another person, inflict unnecessary humiliation, and damage human relations. Command over words is a powerful weapon, but one ought to be discrete in their use. Kai Kaus has divided words and their uses into the following four categories: those neither to be understood nor uttered, those to be both understood and uttered, those to be understood though not uttered. Those which are neither to be uttered nor understood are they that contain some peril to the faith.

Noblest Category : The noblest category from the point of view of our author is the one "which contains those words which can be both understood and uttered." It is a matter of common knowledge that loose or sharp-tongued persons could be a source of great social and organizational tensions. They can breed resentment, and considerable apprehension and dissatisfaction both for superordinates and subordinates. Therefore one who is discrete in the choice of words is ethically fortified against many evils. Words should not be used for uttering falsehood, because lying according to our author "is a form of madness."

Another quality which can morally strengthen a decision-maker is to abstain from action unless the matter has been subjected to reflection and deliberation. Haste breeds waste—wastage of time, wastage of energies and wastage of resources. For some ignorant persons haste is synonymous with efficiency. This in reality is a sign of imprudence and irrationality. Many ills have befallen administrators and men of authority, who pronounced their judgements in haste. More often than not it can lead to injustice and tyranny. Anything which is done in a hurry carries an element of uncertainty; it reduces precision and determination which give authority in a state its effectiveness. He says :

"Both in speech and action, be weighty and deliberate."

According to Kai-Kaus, quarrelsome and contentious persons are also ethically weak. They are mostly stubborn and irreconcilable in their attitudes. No group or organization can tolerate such members for a long time. It is extremely unbecoming of a man of authority shouldering vast responsibilities for decision-making to quarrel frequently. In this way he will not only lose respect, but become a source of many petty squabbles which lead to stress and tension. Quarrelsomeness very often stems from arrogance, which as all accounts agree, is a reprehensible quality from any ethical standard. He has depicted the evil consequences of such an attitude as follows : quarrelling is not indulged in by men of dignity, but rather by women and children. If a quarrel should on any occasion break out between you and another, do not utter all that you could say, but so conduct your quarrel as to leave a loophole for reconciliation. Don't be completely irreconcilable and stubborn; considering stubbornness and irreconcilability as the characteristics of persons of little worth. Realize that humility is the best of qualities, one of God's blessing which no one envies. Do not with every word you address to others say 'O man'; this repetition of 'O Man without reason detracts from a person's dignity as a man, Extravagance and excess have also been listed as evils which ruin the moral fiber of human beings. According to Kai Kaus, extravagance is the cause of poverty and all misguided persons, who tread this path have suffered in the long run. Anybody indulging in it is an enemy of his own interests. He uses the term with its widest connotations. Extravagance in his opinion does not merely mean indiscrete spending and thoughtless disbursement of funds. Excess in all spheres—eating, drinking, speaking and working—is bad because it makes one deviate from the path of moderation and rectitude. In his opinion one who indulges in excess "harms the spirit and deadens the living mind." He says :

> "You observe that the life of a lamp is generated by oil; if you pour oil into the lamp without measure and limit, so that it overflows the spout of the container and passes beyond the tip of the wick, it immediately extinguishes the lamp. Oil itself then becomes the cause of lamp's extinction, although had it been present in moderate quantity it would have been the means of keeping it alight once there was an excess of it, it became the means of lamp's extinction.

Man in charge of public affairs is supposed to have a good reputation. According to our author ill-repute begets shame, disgust and frustration. One should not be swearer of oath because people tend to lose faith in a person, who takes oath frequently. Riches and power cannot safeguard an incumbent of high office from evils of bad reputation. The best course is to create an image of trustworthiness because all right-thinking people shun the company of a liar. One should abstain from misleading others, and also be watchful that he himself is not misled. A person who has acquired this characteristic is certainly going to win the trust and confidence of those around him. A good reputation, particularly for trustworthiness is the Philosopher's Stone, which would make an individual an embodiment of sterling qualities. Unbridled appetites also spoil reputation.

Generosity of Mind : Generosity of mind is a quality, which mitigates the rigidities of law. It is true that without law political systems and administrative organizations cannot exist. But obsessively legalistic views could also be extremely detrimental to peace and harmony in the affairs of men. One should be an administrator of law and not its captive, and in administering rules, according to Kai-Kaus, the most dignified thing is not to punish people for trivial mistakes, and if a petitioner comes the best course would be to forgive him. If at all a person is to be punished and there is no escape from it, the penalty should be strictly in proportion to the gravity of the offense, and if possible may be a little less than what is entailed by law. Clemency and mercy are virtues of high merit. An officer who is not generous in his attitude creates tension and ill-feelings among persons subjected to his jurisdiction. A person who holds money higher than honour is doomed to ignominy. Avarice and insatiable lust for wealth are enemies of honourable conduct, and one who indulges in dishonourable deeds brings destruction on those who are held in esteem and honour.

It is a common characteristic of men working in governmental hierarchies, or may be it is a common feature of human endeavors in all avenues of life, that they want to have accelerated promotions. They want to attain highest rank overnight, and impatience is writ large over all their activities. Subordination is galling to them, and by swiftest means they want to get the highest position available. Kai Kaus thinks it is unethical and he says : "Until you have borne the drudgery of subordinate position, you will never attain to the comforts of high ranks." There is considerable truth in the remarks of our author because many ills in human organizations stem from ambivalent behaviour of overambitious persons. They make life for others irksome, have no peace and equanimity in their own lives, and very often intrigues and frictions which lead to the disenchantment of the participants can easily be attributed to them.

In Chapter VIII, Kai Kaus has listed forty two counsels which Nushirwan (the just) gave to his son. Some of those which are relevant for men in authority and who hold in custody the welfare of the people can be listed as follows :

1. The great man who looks upon himself as small is the great man of the age.
2. There is no meaner person in the world than he to whom appeal is made for help and though able to grant it refuses.
3. If you desire to remain free of unhappiness be not envious.
4. If you desire to command men's respect then exercise justice.
5. If you want not to be disillusioned, do not regard an undone task as having been done.
6. If you do not wish to be stricken with shame do not remove what you have not yourself deposited; and if you desire not to be mocked behind your back, respect them that are subordinate to you.

7. If you desire to be included in the numbers of honourable men, give covetousness no place in your heart.
8. If you desire to be a man of justice be generous as far as lies in your power towards them that are subordinate to you; and if you desire your heart never to be stricken a blow which no remedy can heal, never engage in agreement with fools.
9. If you wish to retain men's esteem, learn how to esteem other men.
10. If you wish for effectiveness in your tongue then restrain the rapacity of your hand.

The *Qabus-nama* was written at a time when the political authority of the Abbaside Caliphate had almost been extinguished. The Commanders of the faithful still wielded a supranational spiritual authority, but it was facing growing challenges from new sects and heretical cults. The author makes a strong and stirring advocacy of Sunni Islam. Therefore there are a wide ranging discussions on theological matters which point out that a ruler in order to cultivate wisdom must follow the word of God meticulously. He made a fervent plea for effective governmental authority, but at the same time pointed out that it could only be established if the people living under its jurisdiction were happy and prosperous. Extortion and recklessness in his opinion perpetuate tyranny, seal the wellspring of justice and would ultimately spell ruin and desolation for the kingdom. Authority should not be an intoxicant, and rulers of men should be equipped with six qualities, "awesomeness, justice, generosity, respect for law, gravity and truthfulness" The four basic factors which maintain peace, order and stability in a kingdom, according to Kai Kaus are authority, army, finance, and prosperity, and they are all interdependent.

Tradition Politics

Siyasat-nama : Nizam-al-Mulk (d. 685/1090), the author of this treatise was Prime Minister for more than thirty years of two Seljuq monarchs, Alp Arslan (d, A.D.-1072) and Malik Shah (d. A.D.-1092). This was a period of acute ideological stress and political lawlessness in the Muslim world. In this stormy climate the Seljuqs had been able to establish a stable kingdom by conquering

Khwarizm, Tabaristan and Persian Iraq. Their rule touched the highest watermark of economic prosperity, political stability, and intellectual development during the reign of Nizam-al-Mulk. He enjoyed unlimited power and through his prudence, sagacity and diplomacy was able to maintain peace and tranquility in the kingdom. His role as a statesman and administrator in one of the most critical periods of Islamic history has been summed up as follows :

> "As a great Iranian Vizir he conspicuously exemplifies the chief minister's role of mediator between a despot, in this instance, an alien Turk and his Persian subjects—he enhanced the dignity and prestige of the Seljuqs by inculcating canons of royal behaviour and etiquette, and he tempered military harshness with lessons in judicious clemency and conciliation. He built up Seljuq powers with the Sultan as the keystone in an integrated administration."

Hitti calls him "one of the ornaments of the political history of Islam. His political and administrative achievements were great, no doubt, but in Islamic history his reputation primarily rests' on scholarship and his generous patronage of art and letters. He was particularly anxious to encourage scholars and theologians, for whom he established *madrasas* (Institutes of Studies) in all the major cities of the kingdom. Nizamiyah colleges, named after him were built in Nishapur and Baghdad between 1065-67. At these institutions instruction was imparted by leading intellectual and religious luminaries of the day. Al-Ghazzali, one of the greatest theological thinkers of Islam, taught at both the academies. The Nizamiyah college in Baghdad was a rendezvous for famous preachers; for nearly two centuries, and disappeared only when it was merged in a new college founded by Caliph Mustansir (A.D. 1226-62). According to Goldziher the foundation of Nizamiyah college was an "epoch-making advance" in the development of higher learning in Islam. Nizam-al-Mulk was not only a patron of scholars, he was himself endowed with scholarly qualities of very high order which have earned for his *Siyasat-nama* a place of eminence among the great prose works of Persian literature. E. G. Browne has summed up the significance of this book in the following words:

> The *Siyasat-nama* is, in my opinion, one of the most valuable and interesting prose works which exist in Persia, both because of the quantity of historical anecdotes which it contains, and because it embodies the views on government of one of the greatest Prime Ministers whom the East has produced—a Minister whose strength and wisdom is no way better proved than by the chaos and internecine strife which succeeded his death."

The work was written at the behest of Malikshah. It is divided into fifty chapters, thirty nine of which were completed at the time of its original submission to the king, but later eleven more chapters were added on subjects relating to government and religious controversies, which were threatening the unity and solidarity of Islam. The declining years of the great statesmen when he made up his mind to revise and enlarge his work were beclouded with gloom and distress. He had become a victim of court and *harem* intrigues, which ultimately cost him his life. John Alden Williams has depicted the last years of the aged and shaken Prime Minister in the following words:

> About 1091 the aged minister began to write again, and now his words had an urgent note. Times had changed. Much of his earlier advice had not been heeded, and Malik Shah's favourite wife was his enemy. The Sultan was engaged in a quarrel with the Caliph, and had also come under the influence of adventurers and heretics. The elder statesman outlined the dangers that particularly threatened the Seljuq empire, and the states like it. Before the addition to his book could be presented to Malik Shah, however, Nizam-al-Mulk was dismissed from office. In A.H. 485/A.D. 1092 he was murdered by Ismaili assassins in circumstances suggesting that they may have been sent with the knowledge of the Sultan or his queen.

The author's main purpose was to write a basic source book on the art of governing men. It was an effort to examine the political and administrative dimensions of a despotic form of government, a system which was extremely susceptible to abuse of authority and corruption.

Rich Scholarship : Muslim scholarship has always been very rich in religious literature and history. Scholars have always found in religion and history an immeasurable reservoir of wisdom and human experience. Religion was the revealed word of God, while history was a resplendent stockroom of events which if intelligently and objectively analyzed could be a tremendous source of guidance and enlightenment. Nizam-al-Mulk's knowledge of both these sources was deep and profound and in collecting the substance of *Siyasat-nama*, he relied heavily upon them. At the conclusion of his work he has made the following remark:

> So ends this book of the Rules for Kings. Your humble servant was previously commanded to compile a volume on this subject, and he carried out the command. At the time he composed thirty nine chapters extempore, and submitted them to the Lofty Throne (may Allah exalt it.) They were found acceptable. However, that was merely an epitome. Later he expounded at his leisure, and wrote chapters and related stories on a variety of subjects, expounding everything in the clearest and simplest language. Let him not listen to what others say, but read this book constantly; he will never be wearied by reading this book, for it contains advice, wisdom, proverbs, interpretation of the Quran, tradition of the Prophet (upon him be peace; stories of prophets, memoirs of saints, and tales of just kings, it tells of the lives of the departed and deeds of the living.

The instrument of instructions from the king which commanded the author to compile this work pointed out that the administration of the kingdom was decaying, and that he should find out reasons for that sorry state of affairs, and search out remedies against evils which had destroyed peace and harmony in the working of the government.

The purpose of commissioning the seasoned statesman to write such a treatise was that out of his long administrative experience and knowledge of history and religion he should produce a manual, which would ensure stability in politics and honesty in administration. In short, the book was to be a digest of political wisdom and knowledge about administration so that decision-makers in both fields could make ethical and rational judgments. As he proceeded with his compilation, Nizam-al-Mulk widened the scope of his assignment, and made frequent comments on the state of affairs of Muslim societies in his own time. Whenever opportunity arose he unhesitatingly uncovered the evils of contemporary government and administration. There is, however, a basic deficiency in the book that it only makes comments, but does not give any clue about the actual machinery of the government. The book also gives an impression of having been written in a hurry. As the author himself confesses, the first thirty nine chapters were written extempore, as such, in spite of his experience, wisdom and breadth of comprehension, which are abundantly reflected in every chapter, they lack the depth and authenticity of historical research. Pieces of advice and anecdotes relating to noble qualities of the past rulers have not been coherently organized.

The scope of the book, however, is fairly wide. The writer has collected large numbers of maxims on good government, and discusses in reasonable detail duties and responsibilities of state functionaries, both at the center and in the field. In analyzing various issues he draws extensively on the storehouse of experiences, which he had accumulated during thirty years of service as a leading administrator of the Muslim world. In his opinion a Muslim ruler should be physically handsome, his character good and untainted, courage undiminished, justice perineal, and warlike qualities unquestioned. Nizam-al-Mulk's advocacy of absolute monarchical rule is understandable, because that was the accepted ideology of the day, but he repeatedly insists that all authority should be exercised within the boundaries of Shariah (religion). He firmly believes that religion is a powerful antidote against those corrupting elements which are rooted in human nature. Since the rule in most cases are not conversant with religious law, he insists that while making public policies they should show special deference to the opinions of the doctors of law. Companionship of the learned assures sound judgment and rulers can fulfil their religious, moral and temporal obligations effectively. He says:

> It is incumbent upon the king to inquire into religious matters, to be acquainted with the divine precepts and prohibitions and put them into practice, and to obey the commands of God (be he exalted) ; it is his duty to respect doctors of religion and pay their salaries out of the treasury, and he should honour pious and abstentious men. Furthermore, it is fitting that once or twice a week he should invite religious elders to his presence and hear from them the commands of the Truth, he should listen for the interpretations of the Quran and traditions of the Prophet (may Allah pray for him and give him peace) and he should hear stories about just kings and tales of the Prophets (upon them be peace). During that time he should free his mind from worldly cares and give his ears and attention to them . . . then the way of prudence and rectitude in both spiritual and temporal affairs will be opened to him.

Knowledge of Religion : Knowledge of religion has always been considered an essential quality for rulers in Islam. It is deemed to be a remedy against vanity, jealousy and numerous other kinds of evil. It insures equity, probity, and justice. Nizam-al-Mulk had to insist more on religion because he lived during one of the most critical periods of the religious history of Islam. All kinds of heretical doctrines were trying to sap the original simplicity and purity of Islam. In *Siyasat-nama* he has devoted six chapters to these heretical doctrines. He examines their origin, principles, practices, and undesirable consequences, which result from them in the body politic. He had deep-seated hatred for Ismailes, and Batnis, and bitterly opposed the employment of Jews, Christians, and Zoroastrians in government service. He argues, representatives of these communities, because of their affluence formed a great source of corruption in the realm. In his opinion, since the non-Muslim minorities were rich, they could easily buy public offices. Probably the chain of his famous Nizamiya colleges in the kingdom was meant to remedy this defect. Graduates of these institutions were religious scholars, but they were primarily trained to fill administrative positions in the government. They were expected to keep the people on the "Straight Path" Vladimir Minorsky says:

> In the *Siyasat-nama* of Nizam-al-Mulk we have a document of first importance setting forth the program which combined the force of the Turks with the administrative methods of the Sassanids and the great Abbasid Caliphs. The system of spies, of messengers, and of troops skilfully assorted from different elements was harmonized with the founding of the religious colleges, those nurseries of administrators who were to watch over the rectitude of the path followed by their flocks.

He was convinced that if the rulers and officials do not conform to the same religion, administration suffers from chronic distrust and unrest.

Heavy Responsibility : Nizam-al-Mulk feels that governing of men is a very heavy responsibility ; particularly personal rule of despotic kings entails special obligation. Any ruler who has usurped despotic powers must exercise constant vigilance over the conduct of his functionaries otherwise the state would be under permanent threat of dissolution. Rulers must have proper machinery to collect information about the activities of public officials and they should have the courage and honesty to punish them for all omissions and abuse of authority. He recommends an effective network of central intelligence, which would keep a watch over the actions and affairs of all senior officers. He relates a story of Nushirwan (The Just) the pre-Islamic Iranian king, who attributed financial and moral degeneration of his kingdom to the negligence of his father who had failed to keep himself well-informed about the shameless embezzlements of his civil servants. A king should appoint informers in every part of the country, because that is the only way to safeguard people against oppression. Information received from such sources should reach the king directly.

The author is fully aware of the delicate nature of such spying and reporting on public officials and would therefore advise the rulers that agents of central intelligence should be persons of unimpeachable integrity and honesty so that what they report is not subject to any suspicion. An arrangement of this kind would enable the king "to know every event that takes place and will be able to give his orders as appropriate, meeting out unexpected reward, punishment or commendation to the persons concerned." Nizam-al-Mulk is of the opinion however, that information culled out of the secret reports of the informants should be anxiously examined, before any decision is based on it. Every report needs to be dissected with patience and understood with care. The Quran says: "O you who believe, if a wicked man brings you tidings, verify it lest you smite some people in ignorance and then repent of what you did.'

After giving the above citation from the Holy Book, Nizam-al-Mulk says:

> "So one should not be precipitate for precipitancy brings regret, and regret is of no avail. . . . Elders of religion have said, 'Haste is from Satan, deliberation is from the Merciful. Works undone can be done, but that which is done cannot be retrieved."

Like other writers on ethics and administration, Nizam-al-Mulk has emphasized justice, honesty, accessibility to complainants and generosity of mind as the best moral equipment for rulers of men. Justice in his opinion is the corner-stone of political and administrative stability. Injustice wrecks state and ruins peace and prosperity of the people. He deems that it is the personal responsibility of the head of the government to see that the legal institutions are strong and not discriminatory in the administration of justice. Law should not make any distinction between high and low, and the entire official world should give ungrudging support to judges in their daily work. If anything contrary to this principle happens it is symptomatic of decadence. He says:

Dignity of Judiciary : All other officers must strengthen the hand of the judge and uphold the dignity of the courts. If anyone makes excesses and fails to appear in court, however exalted he may be, he must be forcibly compelled to be present. For in the time of The Companions of the Prophet (upon him be peace and blessings) justice was dispensed in person and not delegated to anyone else, so that there could be no scope for injustice. In every age from the time of Adam (peace be upon him) until now, in every nation and every country men have practiced equity, justice and striven after righteousness, and when this has been so, dynasties have endured the generations.

Justice bridles the evil intentions of the oppressors, and protects and preserves the rights of the oppressed. Governments are judged by the means they adopt to eradicate evildoers and the remedies they provide to victims of injustice. He believes that "sound judgment is a better thing to have than a powerful army."

Honesty is universally recognized as a vital requirement for good, effective and efficient administration. Corruption has been a cause of ruin of many establishments. Nizam-al-Mulk has not made a scientific or psychological inquiry into its causes, but he emphatically points out that unchecked corruption is a sign of political ailment. In a climate of distrust; effective implementation of public policy is simply impossible. Nizam-al-Mulk has suggested special watchfulness on tax collectors, who in his opinion are the biggest source of corruption. Every tax collector who is in charge of a revenue district should be given strict instructions not to harass the peasantry by untimely demands and additional extortions. In his dealings with the public he should be guided by civility and courtesy. If a tax collector has taken a bribe, the best course would be to reclaim the money from him, deprive him of his office and ban all future government employments to him. In view of the universality of corruption, he recommends exemplary punishment for the culprits. He narrates the story of an officer who was beheaded by King Altiginm because he took some hay and a chicken from a peasant. Honesty among senior officers is of particular significance because juniors are very likely to be influenced by their behavior. He points out that if an officer of the rank of wazir is corrupt, the other officials will behave likewise or may be worse.

Accessibility of common people to the chambers of administrative decision-making to complain against wrongs suffered at the hand of public servants has been acclaimed as one of the cardinal characteristics of Islamic code of ethics for administrators. It is a virtue which insures rectitude in administration, and generates popular trust and confidence in government. Even the most despotic governments require the cooperation of the people, but if the latter do not have the right to complain against administrative decisions, no cooperation will be forthcoming. It is for this reason that Nizam-al-Mulk at several places in his treatise has warned the rulers against inaccessibility of government functionaries to aggrieved persons. He says:

> "It is absolutely necessary that on two days in the week the king should sit for the redress of wrongs, to extract recompense from the oppressor, to give justice and to listen to the words of the subjects with his own ears, without any intermediary. ... I have read in the books of the ancients the most of the non-Arab (Persian) kings used to put up a high platform and sit up there on horseback so that they could see all the complainants gathered about, and they would redress the grievances of everyone. The reason for this was that where the king sits in a place protected by gates, locks, vestibules and screens, self-interested and oppressive persons can keep people back and not let them go before the King."

He cites the example of Nushirwan, who, in order to save the people from palace guards and other officers had hung a chain with bells, which any complainant could pull and seek redress of grievances. If the people have no access to the rulers, the only other alternative under despotic rule for people to undo wrongs is to strive through conspiracies and revolts.

Generosity and large-heartedness are also advocated as essential characteristics for those who wield political or administrative authority in a state. They eliminate fear from the mind of a common man and enable him to give maximum compliance and loyalty to the state.

Significant Features : Nizam-al-Mulk has listed certain other features of good administration, which in his opinion, ensure peace and stability in a kingdom. He feels that collectors and other field officers should be transferred every two or three years. He does not want officers to be entrenched at one place for a long time, because the longer they stay at one place, greater the chances of their becoming a source of tyranny and maladministration. They are likely to become corrupt and indifferent to the interest of the masses. He further recommends that the King should not appoint his personal friends as officials of the state, nor should the officers be included in the circle of his intimate friends. By virtue of their closeness and friendship with the ruler, they become arrogant and practice oppression and high-handedness. He also believes that the best way to avoid abuse of administrative authority is to introduce participative approach in decision-making.

Holding consultations on affairs is a sign of sound judgment, high intelligence, and foresight. Every person has some knowledge and in every branch of knowledge one knows more and others less. One may have knowledge and never have put it into practice or tested it. Everybody in the world agrees that there has never been any mortal wiser than the Prophet . . . and Gabriel (upon him be peace) often used to visit him, bringing inspiration and giving news of things past and things to come ... in spite of all this perfection, in spite of all his miracles, God (be He exalted) said to him (in the Quran 3:153) (Consult them in affairs) 'O Muhammad, where you do any work, or when you are confronted with an important matter, confer with your companions.'

Some Advises : At another place he has mentioned that it is very unbecoming of seniors to reprimand their juniors publicly. Loss of honour leaves a dent in one's ego and an individual with a damaged self-respect can never be honest and efficient. It diminishes goodwill in organizations; as such the best course according to our author is to overlook a mistake, if it is committed for the first time. Administration is an onerous job. It taxes all human faculties, therefore, those who are involved in it deserve every possible encouragement. Their achievements and services should be properly rewarded. A disgruntled bureaucracy can do a lot of damage to the peace and security of a country. There should be no wastage of talent in society. Each capable person has a right to ask for appointment according to his abilities, so that he could earn his livelihood. Another fallacy which continuously erodes administration, is lopsided distribution of work. He warns against assignment of two or more positions to one person or one position to two persons. In both cases performance is bound to be faulty and inefficient. He says :

> Enlightened monarchs and clever ministers have never in any age given two appointments to one man or one appointment to two men, with the result that their affairs were always conducted with efficiency and lustre. When two appointments are given to one man, one of the tasks is always inefficiently and faultily performed;

> and in fact, you will usually find that the man who has two functions fails in both of them, and is constantly suffering censure and uneasiness on account of his shortcomings. And further, whenever two men are given a single post each transfers (his responsibility) to the other and the work remains for forever undone.

Counselling the Rulers

Kitab Nasihat-al-Muluk : This book was written by Abu Hamid Muhammad-al-Ghazzali (d. 505/1111) who ranks among the greatest theologians of Islamic history. The work was originally composed in Persian and later translated into Arabic. Scholars have claimed that several popular writings attributed to Ghazzali are spurious, but none has contested the authenticity of Nasihat-al-Muluk. The treatise was written at the behest of Sultan ibn Malik Shah sometime between 499/1105 and 505/1111. Ghazzali lived during he Seljuq period and his thought and mind were greatly influenced by the state of affairs prevailing at that timo in thc Muslim world. After complete mastery of the canon law theology, and mysticism, Ghazzali studied critically the writings of those, who vehemently opposed the orthodox view of Islam. He also read Batinite and rationalist philosophers with special interest and anxiety. In this way he kept the spectrum of his philosophical and spiritual inquiries very wide and whatever he wrote or discussed was always imbued with precision and profundity. He considered *aql* (intelligence or reason) as one of the supreme graces of man and included it among the greatest gifts of God. It was his belief that all religious doctrines except the fundamentals like the existence of God, revelation and prophethood could be substantiated through basic reason. In religion his greatest work was *Ihya Ulum al Din.* (Revivification of the Sciences of Religion). In 1106 he was asked by Sultan Sanjar of Khurasan to resume teaching in the Nizamiyah College at Nishapur. In 1109 he retired to Tus and spent the rest of his life as a mystic. He died on the 18th of December 1111 at the age of 53. It is said that *Nasihat-al-Muluk* was compiled during his retirement shortly before death.

In all his ethical writings, al Ghazzali preaches that men become perfect only by emulating attributes of God in their character. He wrote:

> "The perfection of the worshipper as well as his happiness lies in imitating the qualities of Allah the Most High and in adorning himself with the meanings of His attributes and of His names ... in that measure of course that may be considered within his right."

He contends that there are all kinds of failures and frailties associated with human character, but most evils result when ambition and anger dominate man's disposition. Ambition in his opinion is a source of "shamelessness, wickedness, extravagance, stinginess, hypocrisy, defamation, impudence, folly, greed cupidity, flattery, envy, rancour, gluttony, and lewdness. Anger induces men to indulge in rashness, excessive spending, haughtiness, boasting, arrogance, self-admiration, derision, making light of others, disdain, mischief, abuse." In order to mitigate the effect of these vices, al Ghazzali has mentioned qualities like "chastity, contentment, abstinence, fear of God, piety cheerfulness, a comely appearance, modesty, ingenuity, courage, generosity, self-control, fortitude, clemency, endurance, forgiveness, stability, genius, bravery and gravity" which in his opinion if harmoniously blended can produce an ideal human character.

"Al-Ghazzali was a keen and anxious student of human behaviour and tried to explore psychological and social causes of men's actions in organized society. In his opinion each action is composed of four factors, i.e., *Khawatir* (affections of mind), *raghbia* (inclination), *itiqad* (intellectual conviction), and *irada* (will). In other words:

Khawatir, (Affections of the mind)		*Raghbia,* (inclination)
ad, Irada, (intellectual conviction)	(will produce)	*Amal,* (action)

In his Ihya-al-Ulum-al-Din, Al-Ghazzali compares human heart to a fortress, which has to be guarded against satanic intrusions. Anger, desire, envy, and greed are the main gates through which Shaitan (Satan) leads his hordes of evil to attack this fortress. Religion and reason are the primary defences against such inroads. If they are weak, Satan and his evil forces have every chance of being triumphant in human life. So far as moral accomplishments are concerned, he has divided humanity into four groups :

(1) "The first are those who are heedless who do not distinguish truth, from folly and beautiful from the base."

(2) "Those who know well enough the baseness of what is base, but they do not become habituated to good conduct because they consider that their evil conduct is something enjoyable."

(3) "Those (who) actually approve of base dispositions maintaining that they are necessary, right and beautiful."

(4) "The fourth kind are those, who along with what accompanies corrupt belief and practise, see also a sort of virtue in their very excess of evil and the destruction of lives."

Moral Values and Precepts : Moral values and precepts constitute a universal antidote against error and evil, but men belonging to the fourth category are so wicked that no amount of persuasion could convince them about the aims and objectives of righteous action. Morality in his opinion is a skill or a habit of mind which can be cultivated only by conscious efforts. It consumes time, and requires absorbing interest, but once an aptitude for ethical conduct is developed then it flows effortlessly into all channels of human affairs. In his Ihya, Al-Ghazzali has made the following remarks:

> "This question of moral progress is precisely like progress in the arts, for if anyone wishes to acquire skill in calligraphy, for instance, he must exercise the necessary mental perseverance. He must engage in what the skillful writer gives him to do, which is the production of a well-written line. At first this will be a matter of requirement and of imitation. And afterwards he must not cease to give his attention to making this well-written line until his aptitude in doing so is established, and until his skill becomes actually a mental quality. In the end he will do naturally and easily what was at first an arduous effort. The time however, will be good which he had made good, first

> with conscious effort, but in the end quite naturally. This is all because of mental capacity to receive an impression"

Nasihat-al-Muluk, which is strictly a treatise on administrative ethics, is replete with Al-Ghazzali's depth of understanding about human character and behaviour. It also shows the sad spectacle of political lawlessness and administrative anarchy which was rampant all over the Muslim world at that time. There are nostalgic references to glories of Muslim and non-Muslim past when justice and equity reigned supreme in human affairs. He complained bitterly of the wickedness of the people and the luxuriant and comfort-seeking existence of rulers. He was convinced that Islamic society was unhinged because unethical character of politics and administration had destroyed its moral moorings. Another reason which in his opinion had wrecked peace and order was that political authority was either too weak or too lenient. He was convinced that wickedness could only be eradicated by firmness. He says:

> "The reason why we are saying so much on this subject is that our present age is an exceedingly wicked one. The people are wicked and the Sultans are preoccupied with the lower world. With wicked people things cannot be set right through tolerance and indulgence . . . power to inspire awe and maintain discipline are essential, if the individual is to be able to go about his business and if the people are to have security from one another, peoples' outlook has been corrupted and in which they have all grown wicked in both deed and intention."

Bitter Experience : The wickedness of the people, the torn fabric of once powerful Caliphal authority of the Abbasides, deep ideological frictions which plagued the Muslim world, and worries of his declining years, made Al-Ghazzali a mystic during the last phase of his life. The *batinis* under the leadership of their teacher the Fatimide-al-Mustansir (1035-1094 A.D.) and Nazarites led by Hassan-al-Sabbah (d. 1129) with his spiritual and military headquarters at Almout, challenged the righteousness of Sunnite doctrine which was the official creed of the Abbasides and the Seljuks, and used all subversive means to dismantle their political hegemony. There was chronic insecurity of life and property, and anarchy and lawlessness were almost endemic. In such a socio-political climate, mysticism with its negative approach to worldly gains, and human ambitions, had every chance of capturing the imagination of scholars and intellectuals. Therefore it is not surprising that Al-Ghazzali in his retirement preached mystical ethics. Nasihat-al-Muluk is replete with admonitions, anecdotes, aphorisms, which furnish an eloquent testimony to the deep-seated mystical proclivities of its author. He believed that ghoulish enticements of the world hamper man's salvation. It was common among mystics to believe that lust for worldly gains and insatiable appetites grievously injure the welfare of mankind. Al-Ghazzali says :

> "You should understand that a stopping place is not a fixed abode, and that man is in this world in the role of a traveller, the mother's womb being his first stop and the grave his last stop." In order to substantiate his contention about the transitory nature of human life and treacherous ways of the world he has given ten analogies to create awareness about them :

1. This is to explain the spell of this World. God's Apostle said, "Hold aloof from the world for she is a worse spellbinder than Harut and Marut. The beginning of her spell is that appears to you in such a way that you suppose her to be stationary and fixed in relations to you; for you look at her, and she is the universe itself yet she is continually fleeting from you.
2. She resembles a worthless woman who is vicious and importunate and lures men to her in order to make them her loves, then takes them to her house and destroys them.
3. She is like an ugly old hag who masks her face, but has put on fine clothes and done herself up ornately. Men see her from afar and are enchanted with her, but when they remove her veil they are dismayed to find such ugliness.
4. He will then understand that this world resembles the route of a traveller, starting from the cradle ending at the grave, and with a given number of stages in between.

5. You should understand that this world, in the pleasures which her sons get from her and again in the disgrace which in the after-life they suffer because of her, is like a person who eats rich and sweet food in such excess as to ruin the stomach.
6. Jesus declared that the seeker of this world is like the drinker of sea-water, the more he consumes the thirstier he becomes and he will continue drinking until he perishes and he will never be cured of that thirst.
7. This is that a person who comes into this world resembles one who goes as a guest to a home of a host, whose custom is to keep his mansion always adorned for guests and to invite them in parties. The host places before them a tray of jewels and gold, and a silver censor with aloes wood and incense for giving fragrance, but they leave, the tray and censor for the next party when it arrives.
8. This world's inhabitants, in their preoccupation with its affairs and forgetfulness of the world to come, resemble a ship's passengers, who on reaching an island go ashore to perform the natural functions and rituals ablutions. The ship's officers call out "Let nobody take too long or get busy with anything except the ablutions as the ship is to sail soon."

Thoughts embodied in the above analogies form the crux of Iranian and Arabic mystical literature. Many of their connotations are inimical to the basic principles of Islam. Mystical ethics is vastly different from Islamic ethics in the sense that Islam insists on purity of thought and action, preaches that, life of sin and vice is destructive, enjoins virtue and righteousness, but does not advocate asceticism. Its approach is positive and activates the believers to appreciate and enjoy the fruits of this world, but in doing so they should abstain from excesses and injustice which lead to immoral acts. The frame of reference of Nasihat-al-Muluk is predominantly mystical. Moreover the treatise has focused most of its attention on the kings. There are only passing references to administrators and other state functionaries. Some pages have been devoted to the role and qualities of Wazirs (Prime Ministers) and Dabirs

(Secretaries), but the author does not provide a comprehensive picture of the ethical basis of these offices.

For instance, in his chapter on secretaries, Al-Ghazzali has put more emphasis on the shape and form of a pen to be used by a secretary than on the qualities of head and heart which would mold his character as an administrator. The chapter on Wazirate, however, though short, has some references to the ethical foundation of this office. His exposition of the moral qualities of kingship are detailed and exhaustive and this has accorded the book a respectable place in Islamic literature. From this material a student of administrative ethics in Islam, can glean valuable guidelines to crystalize moral basis of government and administration in an Islamic society. The qualities depicted no doubt were meant for the princes, but they could be equally relevant to the character and behaviour of the functionaries who executed their policies.

Foundation Rock : According to Al-Ghazzali, authority is the foundation rock over which the super-structure of a politically organized society is built. Authority ensures stability and prosperity for the realm, but it is a delicate instrument. It is both a bane and a bliss. If exercised righteously and with care, wisdom and prudence it can be a source of eternal blessings, but abuse or misuse of authority can damage peace and order in a country. He says:

> "This is that (the ruler) should first of all understand the importance and also the danger of authority entrusted to him. In authority there is a great blessing, since he who "exercises it righteously obtains unsurpassed happiness, but if any (ruler) fails to do so he incurs torment unsurpassed only by the torment for unbelief, ... Such being the case there is no greater blessing than God's grant to a person of the office of ruler and Sultan, whereby an hour of his life is raised (to be equivalent) to the whole life of any other persons, but if he shows no appreciation of this blessing and gives himself over to tyranny and passion, there is a terrible wish that God on High will count him as an enemy."

He makes reference to the two traditions of the Holy Prophet in which a serious warning has been administered to those who have been given the responsibility to preside over the destiny of a Muslim community. The Prophet said "If any man is granted authority over the Muslims and does not look upon them as he would look upon members of his own household, tell him he will get his place in Hell." "Two persons in my community will be denied my intercession; the tyrant and the innovator, who practices such exaggeration in religion that it goes beyond the limit." There is, however, a slight contradiction in Al-Ghazzali's approach to authority. He begins his analysis by pointing out that exercise of authority within the boundaries of ethics and religion is the greatest benediction of God. An hour spent in the righteous use of authority is equal to the whole life of other human beings, but a little later in the same chapter, he takes considerable pains to explain that all authority, just or unjust is subject to divine admonishment. He says:

> "Hudhayfah (ibu-al-Yaman) used to say: 'I never praise any holder of authority. Whether virtuous or wicked. When asked why, he replied that it was because he had heard God's Apostle declare : "On the Resurrection Day, all holders of authority will be brought in: whether unjust or just.' All will be stationed on the (bridge called) Sirat, and God on High will inspire the Sirat to shake them off in one sharp shake; for there will not be a single one among, them who has not judged unjustly taken a bribe when trying a case, or lent his ear overmuch to one contestant. All will fall off the Sirat, and all will go down the Hell for seventy years, at the end of which they will reach their final resting place."

Mystical Suspicion : Mystical suspicion and derision of worldly possessions could be the reason for this outright condemnation of all kinds of authority. Whatever might have been the reason, Al-Ghazzali's earlier statement that righteous use of authority brings unsurpassed happiness and ensures salvation hereafter is the true ethical basis of authority of Islam.

Justice and equity according to Al-Ghazzali constitute prominent branches of the true Faith. Injustice and inequity are vices for which there is no atonement. The unjust Sultan is warned against severe torments, and a prince who collects taxes from his subjects and does not practice impartiality between the strong and the weak, and is arbitrary in his judgments will have to pocket odium of God. Justice in his opinion entails strict adherence to the laws of God. A ruler, whether he inflicts punishment or shows compassion must exercise discretion. Excessive compassion is as bad as excessive punishment because both are contrary to principles of justice. He quotes the following tradition of the Holy Prophet:

> "God's Apostle stated that on the Resurrection Day, holders of authority will be brought in and told 'You were shepherds of my sheep', (One will be asked) 'Why did you award a penalty and inflict a punishment on so-and-so in excess of what I bade you?' He will reply: 'O Lord God, in wrath because they were offending against you and he will be told, Why should your wrath exceed Mine?' Another will be asked 'Why did you inflict a punishment falling short of what I bade you?' He will reply 'O Lord God I did so out of compassion' and he will be told 'Why should you be more compassionate than I am? Their God on High will order them to be shown the corners of Hell."

A ruler should refrain from injustice and it is incumbent upon him to exercise constant vigilance over the behaviour of his soldiers and civil servants. If he is just, and his employees are unjust, the conditions of society will never improve and he would be held responsible for their misdeeds. Justice becomes effective and meaningful only if the entire governmental machinery is pervaded with judiciousness and all state employees make justice a permanent feature of their professional ethics. Al-Ghazzali is of the opinion that if the chief holder of authority is just and endowed with excellencies of character, there is every possibility that these traits will be emulated by his subordinates. He points out that Shaqiq-al-Balkhi, a learned ascetic once told Harun-al-Rashid the Abbaside Caliph, "You are a fountain and the other officials (who help you to govern) the world are the streams (which flow from it). If the fountain is clear, there can be no damage from silt in the channels; if the fountain is turbid, there will be no hope (of maintaining) the channels." Unjust officials have a tendency to hoodwink the rulers and more often than not they indulge in tactics and use strategies by which injustice is portrayed as justice. Such functionaries are the greatest enemies of state and their evil intentions spell destructions of the realm.

Passion and Anger : Passion and anger render the prospects of justice bleak, and it therefore befits a ruler who is in search of just laws to avoid them as much as he can. Intellect should be the guardian of those passions which blur human vision, and hamper perception of reality in its true perspective. Outward appearances are often deceptive and in order to do justice men are advised to comprehend things as they really are Al-Ghazzali sums up his views on this subject as follows :

> "To sum up (the ruler) must act justly towards his subjects and (at the same time) keep his staff, household, and sons on the path of justice. Nobody, however, can do this unless he first observes justice inside himself. Now justice consists of restraining tyrannous instincts, passions and anger in order to make them the prisoners of reason and religion, and not letting reason become the prisoner of tyrannous instincts, passions and anger .... reason is the army of God on High, and that passion and anger are the army of the Devil. How can a man who keeps God's army captive in the hands of the Devil's army act justly towards others .... you should understand and be assured of this, O Sultan, that justice springs from perfection of the intellect and that perfection of the intellect means that you see things as they really are and perceive the facts of their inner reality without being deceived by their outward appearance."

After justice Al-Ghazzali expects men of authority to be humble in disposition. He is conscious of the fact that authority has the tendency to become a narcotic of human mind. It makes people proud and arrogant and pride and arrogance impel holders of authority to become angry and revengeful very fast. These undesirable characteristics deprive human personality of that eternal lustre that stems out of humility and modesty. Anger which in his opinion is a manifestation of pride is a "blight of the intellect". As an antidote to the natural inclination of pride among men of authority, Al-Ghazzali advocates forgiveness, generosity and forbearance. These qualities in his opinion distinguish men from beasts. In this connection he makes a reference to the tradition of the Holy Prophet in which he mentioned three things for the perfection of faith. They are : "not to form a wrong intention when angered, not to set aside what is right when pleased, and not to take more than what is right when powerful." In order to further support his contention he mentions another saying of God's Apostle in which forbearance and forgiveness have been considered as good as fasting and prayer for the purity of human mind and soul.

Significant Principles : Redress of the grievances of the masses is another principle of governmental ethics, which has been emphasized by Al-Ghazzali in a great deal. He insists that if a ruler disregards public petitions; he is treading a dangerous path which can pose immeasurable hazards. He brackets redress of people's complaints with religious duties. For a healthy polity a ruler must have a network of effective espionage by which he can uncover people's reactions to governmental policies. Accessibility of officials to complainants has always been considered one of the fundamental principles of administrative ethics in Islam. Practically all writers on the subject have accorded this quality a high place in the professional and moral equipment of public officials, Al-Ghazzali says:

> "The Arabs (have a saying); that nothing is more damaging to the subjects and more prejudicial and sinister for the king than royal insensibility and seclusion; and that nothing impresses the hearts of the subjects and officials more, than ease of access to the king. For when the subjects know that the king is easily approachable it will be impossible for the officials to oppress one another. Through making himself readily accessible, the king will acquire information about all the affairs of which he must never be heedless of the prestige of the monarchy is to be maintained and if he himself is to reign undisturbed."

Oppressive rule of inaccessible officials destroys peace and prosperity and ultimately political fabric is torn into shreds.

In Islam religion and politics are inseparably integrated. It is essential for a political authority to safeguard interests of religion from internal and external attacks, and watch the conduct of the subjects so that sanctity of religion is not tainted by eccentric distortions and heretical practices. As has been noticed earlier Al-Ghazzali lived at a time when Muslim lands were plagued with religious dissensions and established Sunnite doctrine was being virulently questioned by many new sects in Islam. Therefore safety of religion was a matter of deep concern for Al-Ghazzali. In Nasihat-ul-Muluk he repeatedly emphasizes that kings must take special care to eradicate heresies from their jurisdictions. A ruler under all circumstances, in his opinion, should abide strictly to laws of *sharia,* and his image among masses should be that of a devout and conscientious adherent of religion. He must adopt stern measures against those, who deviate from the established order, because this is the only way by which he can acquire reputation as a defender of the faith. He says :

> "The quality which kings most need is correct religion because monarchy and religion are like brothers. (The king) needs it equally whether he be healthy or sick. He must be diligent in matters of religion, performing the duties at the proper times avoiding eccentricity and heretical innovation and shunning unjust and immoral actions. If he hears that any person in his territory is suspect as regards religion, he must summon him and interrogate him until he repents or else punish him or exile him from the territory; in this way the kingdom will be purged of eccentrics and heretical innovators, and Islam will be strong. He must keep the border lands populated by sending garrisons, strive to increase the power of Islam, and keep the Prophets Sunnah fresh and vigorous."

Evil Traits : All human beings have certain evil traits like envy, ambition, spite, cupidity, and love of pleasure and it is one of the primary duties of a ruler to adopt such effective measures by which these vices can be contained. This is a vital service which can be done by men presiding over socially organized entities for the cause of human welfare. A weak authority can as much be a cause of ruin as tyrannous authority, and a competent ruler always avoids both extremes from his actions. Piety, equity, and awareness of the interests of the people are advocated as essential characteristics of those who administer human affairs. Since rulers don't have divine vision, they are advised to exercise special vigilance over behaviour of their administrators. This would minimize chances of corruption and other baneful practices commonly associated with administration. Umar I, the Second Caliph after the Holy Prophet, in one of his sermons said :

> "O People! In the time of the Prophet the divine inspiration used to come down, and through that inspiration he used to know men's outward acts and inward thoughts, both good and bad. Now the inspiration has ceased and we view every person by his public behaviour; but God the Strong and Glorious is well aware of men's secret motives. I try to ensure that neither I nor my assistants and revenue officers ever take anything from the people (wrongfully) nor ever give (anything to anybody wrongfully)."

Al-Ghazzali is convinced that corruption, nepotism, and favouritism result from negligence, irrational mildness and constant slackness of rulers. If a ruler personally supervises administration and anxiously looks into affairs relating to the welfare of his people the impact of these vices could be reduced considerably. If the king is upright, his subjects and officials will be upright, but if he is dishonest, negligent and comfort-seeking, people living under his jurisdiction and officers implementing his policies will soon become slothful and corrupt.

Al-Ghazzali has devoted a separate chapter on magnanimity which in his opinion is a sterling quality for rulers and administrators. Magnanimity is an antithesis of low-mindedness. He defines the term as "self-restraint and courage and self-respect and self-knowledge, but the numerous anecdotes that follow these definitions, show that the term is used to connote large-heartedness and generosity. Particularly if a person is blessed with munificence, he should not hesitate to provide financial and material succour to others. He quotes the saying of Umar ibn al Khattab who said, "Take good care not to be mean-minded, for I have seen nothing more degrading in men than low-mindedness." Reference is also made to aphormism of a sage who said, "The essence of greatness is taking pains and the essence of error is haste ; the essence of depravity is miserliness". Another sage said, "If men open their hands to give generously their faces will shine luminously".

Divine Gift : According to Al-Ghazzali, political authority as embodied in kings and governors is a divine gift and a trust. Application of this gift for the general good requires cultivation of certain graces such as intelligence, knowledge, sharpness of mind, ability to perceive things, perfect physique, literary taste, horsemanship application to work and courage, together with boldness, deliberation, good temper, impartiality towards the weak and the strong, friendliness, magnanimity, maintaining toleration and moderation, judgement and, foresight in business, frequent reading of the reports of early Muslims, and constant attention to the biographies of the kings, and inquiry concerning the activities of the kings of old, because the present world is the continuation of the empire of the forerunners. He further refers to the letter which Yuman the Dastur wrote to Anushirvan in which he advised the king to promulgate justice, use intelligence, exercise patience, and practice modesty and to abstain from envy, arrogance, narrow-mindedness, and malice. At another place he mentions Sufyan (al-) Thawri who said that permanent happiness of men depends on intelligence and knowledge and cultivation of such excellencies as "chastity, courtesy, absteniousness, honesty, truthfulness, modesty, compassion, kind-heartedness, fidelity, patience, tact and equanimity."

Divine Politics

Akhlaq-i-Nasiri : Its author Nasiruddin-Tusi (1201-1276 A.D.) was born ninety years after the death of Al-Ghazzali. He was attached to the court of Assasins Chief Ala-al-Din (1220-1255) at Alamut. Like the rest of the writers who preceded him, Tusi was convinced that salvation of mankind lies in establishing a political system which is divine in origin. He calls it Siyasat-i-Rabbani, (Divine Politics). He elaborated his views on this point as follows:

> "There is no state more ruinous than that which means the abandonment of the divine administration (siyasat-i-rabbani) and the wasting of his favours. That is the very essence of unrighteousness, for it is ingratitude for his benefits and a denial of which is the equivalent of unbelief. For the true content of oppression is the placing of things at wrong places. Thus the manager becomes the managed, the King becomes the subject and the lord becomes the slave."

Al-Tusi lists absent-mindedness, rashness, cupidity, and oppression as the bane of human conduct. In his opinion human soul is motivated in all actions by three faculties, i.e., reason, appetite, and temper. Reason distinguishes between good and evil, appetite helps acquisition of goods and physical pleasures and temper helps man to defend himself against injury. Man in his opinion can be reasonable, but he has also the tendency to succumb to a very low level of irrationality also. In order to attain high level of perfection, it is essential to curb appetite and discipline one's temper. Al-Tusi believes that men have many things in common with animals, and morality is meant to minimize the role of animality in human affairs. Lust and unbridled aspirations to satisfy bodily desires reduce man to the level of a beast. They hinder healthy development of human personality and as such it is essential to safeguard oneself against such a degradation. He says :

> "It may be said in regard to what man has in common with animals and other forms of life, that if his animal nature prevails over him and his inclination is in that direction, he will be degraded from his proper rank to that of the order of beasts or even lower. For the Quran says "They are like the brutes. Yea, they go more astray." (VII : 178). He reaches the place, for example, where he longs to gain the pleasures and the desires of the body, those for which the bodily sense and powers are eager and have a craving—such as things to eat, things to drink, things to wear, and marriages. The result is that the power of beast soon gets the upper hand. Or his development is similarly curtailed if he takes to violence and assault and vengeance, which are the fruits of anger having sway."

Sole Objective : Al-Tusi, following other moral philosophers in Islam insists that the sole objective of human existence is the perfection of man's soul. *Nafs-i-natiqa* (soul) in his opinion has two powers—the power of knowledge and the power of action. Knowledge entails comprehension of the known world and mastery of arts and sciences relating to it. Action relates to human capacity to harmonize— variegated powers of self in a manner that they do not try to dominate each other. Everything good or bad has been entrusted to the custody of man. Preferences are all his own, and if he is careful and vigilant he can control evil propensities, and through his watchfulness he can direct them for personal and social goodness. If his control is casual or relaxed, or his powers deficient, he will be left destitute of moral purpose in life. He has illustrated his point as follows :

> "Others said that the situation of mankind with reference to these selves is more like that of a man mounted on a powerful horse, when with a dog he goes out to hunt. If the authority is with the man he will employ his riding animal and his hunting animal with discretion. He will be attentive to what is necessary for the well-being of all of them in time of danger, and he will make arrangements for what food is needed for them all in just measure. Thus as companions in eating and drinking and in other matters of subsistence, they will be maintained according to the needs of their respective natures. But if the riding beast has his own way and does not recognize the authority of the rider, then he will start to run wherever he sees the best grass. In roughness of gait, in straying from the road, and in making speed at the wrong place, he will give great annoyance to himself and his companions . . . Also if the hunting animal has its own way, at the time when it sees the prey it will lead the riding animal and its rider in that direction as fast as it can, with resultant hardship and fear of destruction, as has been mentioned. It is even probable that in the course of the encounter, when fighting with the animal that is hunted, it will itself be wounded and worn out that it will perish.

> But if the two beasts are subject to the rider who knows what is best and who has the right to command, they will be saved from these misfortunes and accidents."

Al-Tusi warns against excesses. In his opinion any deviation from accepted standard can unhinge a situation. Overdoing is one way of excess and neglecting the other. Men, in order to live a healthy, moral existence must avoid both. Virtue is moderation, while evil resides on both extremes. Wisdom, bravery, purity and righteousness are midway virtues in his opinion, and their extremes on both sides he has analyzed as follows :

> "To be absent-minded is on the side of excess, for it is the employing of powers of thought on what is not necessary, or to a greater extent than is fitting. Some call this self-deception or being like a large over-ripe cucumber. To be ignorant or stupid is to err on the side of carelessness or neglect, in voluntarily failing to make use of the power of thought, not because of any physical limitation."
>
> "Rashness, which is from excess, is always ready to start something which it is not seemly to start, whereas cowardice, which is on the side of insufficiency, is avoiding things which it is not commendable to avoid."
>
> "Cupidity, which is on the side of excess, is greed for pleasures beyond measures that is proper, whereas the abating of passion which is on the side of deficiency, is lack of initiative in seeking necessary pleasures, or such as reason and law permit—when this indifference is voluntary and is not due to physical limitation."
>
> "Oppression, which is on the side of excess, is the acquirement of the means of living by methods that are reprehensible, whereas living oppressed, which is on the side of deficiency, consists in affording opportunity to anyone who is seeking the means of living by methods of violence and plunder, i.e., in submitting to their being taken without justification and merely because they are themselves object."

Reputed Treatise

Al Fakhri : The author of the book Muhammad Ali son of Tabataba (Rapid Talker) wrote this book in 1302 A.D. in honour of Prince Fakhr-ad-din Isa son of Ibrahim. The treatise enjoyed wide reputation for authenticity and scholarship among the later Muslim scholars. It was first translated into French in 1910 and later the Arabic text was published in 1921. The English translation of the work was done by C.E.J. Whitting in 1947.

The author in his introduction has given reasons for the compilation of this book. His main purpose was to provide a compendium of knowledge for kings and rulers because their ignorance, lack of historical perspectives and indifference to the interest of the subjects, in his opinion, constituted one of the fundamental causes of the ruin of kingdoms. The ministers, he points out, always felt happy under a prince who was not knowledgeable, because that would facilitate their monopoly of power in the state. A monarch with knowledge and will of his own was always considered a threat to the prerogatives of a minister. The immediate cause for writing this treatise was the desire on the part of the author to furnish a manual of statecraft to his patron from whom he received kindness and hospitality.

Major Dimensions

The book has been divided into two parts. In the first part he has listed certain special characteristics which form an indisputable, moral and intellectual equipment of a ruler and establish his superiority over his subjects. The second part gives a chronological account of dynasties which ruled the Muslim empire during different periods of history. It is the first part of the book which is relevant for our purpose because in it the author has elucidated his ideals about the ethical foundations of a Muslim polity. The narrative, like other books on the same subject, is embellished with verses from the Quran. Traditions of the Holy Prophet, anecdotes from the lives of rulers, who were just and generous in their attitudes towards the subject. The author has abstained from theoretical discussions regarding the origin of power, and the nature of religious and temporal authority in Islam. He says, "it (book) has been composed only to deal with systems of government and conventions useful in current affairs and in conflicts which occur, in the rule of subjects, safety of the realm and improvement of manners and conduct."

Knowledge, intelligence and justice are the first set of qualities which according to Al Fakhri, can help a ruler or administrator to escape from errors of judgment. To be governed by an ignorant ruler in his opinion is the worst tragedy that could happen in a society. Knowledge that he envisions for just and efficient and kind-hearted rulers is not a specialized knowledge of arts and sciences. What he expects of them is a general familiarity with different areas of learning, so that they can coordinate matters of public policy with insight. Specialization in his opinion leads to obscurity of thought and narrowness of mind, both of which are detrimental to efficiency and comprehension.

They must have enough understanding so that they can enter into dialogue with experts. A ruler or administrator must have breadth of vision and sufficient understanding so that his subordinates will not be able to deceive him. Knowledge, however, in his view is culture-bound, because polities derive their strength or weakness from the socio-religious and philosophical climate in which they are nurtured. Knowledge imbibed by men in authority will also differ according to their personal proclivities, but the author of Al Fakhri believes that over a period of time each social system develops its own ethos and ethical principles which are always deemed to be essential for intelligent and effective administration of the realm. He says :

> "The studies of the rulers of Persia were laws, moral precepts, literature, history, geometry and the like. The studies of the rulers of Islam were philology, grammar, lexicography, poetry and history, so much so that an error in speech was one of the most objectionable faults in the royal dignity, and man's rank might be advanced with them by a single anecdote, a single verse of poetry nay a single idiomatic word. As for Mongols, all these studies were rejected and other studies were popular with them—economics, accountancy, for balancing the budget and the estimates of revenue and expenditure, medicines, and astrology to choose occasions."

Fear of God : Like other Muslim thinkers Al Fakhri advocates that fear of God is the foundation-rock for a stable moral character and most of the sterling qualities of human behaviour, and other ethical excellencies stem from it. He believes that rulers tend to be irate and full of hatred. But in his opinion these are ignoble qualities which lead to moral degeneration. A ruler should show love and concern for his subjects rather than pity. If a ruler or administrator has nothing but pity for his people, the society will be full of disenchantment and bitterness. In a population which is alienated a ruler will, never be able to get proper affection and cooperation. He says :

> How can a ruler attain his desire in major affairs of state, and achieve his intended objects, save through the willing cooperation of his subjects? What wisdom is there in that ? Is there aught in it some embitterment of the ruler's life, the decerebrating of his subjects against him and the estrangement of them from him?

Feelings of Conciliation : Bonds of the rulers and the subjects have to be cemented by feelings of conciliation. These feelings in his opinion, are cultivated only through clemency and forgiving attitude of the administrators. Generosity of mind, spaciousness of thought are qualities which are of invaluable significance in winning the hearts of people. Al Fakhri has enumerated ten basic qualities which could insure peace, order, and prosperity of the kingdom. They are, (1) to spare bloodshed, (2) to guard property, (3) to protect morals, (4) to prevent disasters, (5) to restrain evil-doers and troublemakers, (6) to check the extortion which follows from civil war and unrest, (7) to study the affairs of the subjects in depth and detail, (8) to reward good and punish evil, (9) to exercise constant vigilance and (10) to manifest unending care. These prerequisites are vital determinants of legitimacy in a political system. A ruler who entirely relies on his independent judgment, will miss the depth of understanding and richness of information and alternatives which are produced by-consultation. The author mentions that if the Prophet used to consult his companions so often in handling the affairs of the community, he sees no reasons why the rest of the Muslim rulers should claim immunity from.it. On the question of consultation enjoined upon the Prophet by God,

Al Fakhri has summed up the views of the various schools of thought in Islam as follows:

> The theologians disagree as to whether God, Most High, commanded his messenger to seek advice despite the help and advice given to him by Him. On that there are four views. First, that he was ordered to consult the companions to win their loyalty and secure their willing cooperation. Secondly, that he was ordered to consult them in war, so that the correct view might be confirmed for him, and he act accordingly. Thirdly, that he was ordered to consult them because of the useful and advantageous (counsel) they possessed. Fourthly, that he was only ordered to consult them in order that people might copy him and this I hold, is the best view and the most correct.

Thus, according to Al Fakhri, consultation in decision-making creates confidence, disarms resistance, and once the people are convinced of the integrity of the ruler they develop the natural tendency to emulate him.

Impetuosity, and ennui are very unbecoming characteristics in a ruler. They bring nothing but humiliation. It is one of the supreme ethical responsibilities of the ruler to protect people from oppression and strengthen the hands of the weak so that he can fight battles of life with success. "Among the duties of a ruler to his subjects is restraining the stronger from (oppressing) the weaker, giving the lowly justice against the powerful, establishing the rule of law among them, maintaining their rights as they should be maintained, helping the dejected, answering any of them who cries for aid, and holding the scales of justice equal between the most distant of them and the nearest, the lowliest and the mightiest."

It is indisputable that the ethical standards of the government to a large extent depend on the moral values of the administrators who run the affairs of the state. As such recruitment should not be left to chance. It must be based on sound judgement. Al Fakhri mentions the practice of a ruler who used to publicize the name of a person who was a potential candidate for a position of responsibility. In this way he used to feel the pulse of popular reaction to the future appointee. In the light of information thus collected he used to finalize his decision. He had informers who used to mix with the common people in disguise and collect information on such matters.

Firmness and strength of character are qualities which are always applauded in the art of governing men. Firmness, however, has to be based on reason and compassion. Indiscriminate persecution or high-handedness would never be considered as signs of firmness. Such excesses should be distasteful to a ruler, unless they are necessitated by some unavoidable emergency. Obsessive firmness is symptomatic of arrogance which creates a climate of frustration in society. Pride in ones ancestry does not help in politics. One should feel proud of one's own attainments in civility, culture and knowledge.

Faulty View : People tend to take a simple but faulty view of administration. They categorize administration into five kinds: of the home, the village, the city, the army, and the state. They believe that "he who administers his home well, will administer his village well, he who administers his village well, will administer his city well, he who administers his city well, will administer an army well, and he who administers an army well, will administer a state well." Al Fakhri believes this oversimplified analysis deceptive because many whose domestic affairs are well administered are poor administrators of the affairs of the state, and those whose administration of public affairs is superb are weak and inefficient in administering domestic affairs. The role of sword and pen has been a subject of deep controversy among Muslim scholars on politics and administration. Sword symbolizes military establishment and coercive power of the state, while pen stands for civilian machinery which is created to administer affairs of kingdom in peace time. Al Fakhri has summed up this controversy as follows:

> The realm is guarded by the sword and administered with the pen. People disagree about the sword and the pen, as to which of the two is superior, and takes precedence. Some think that the pen has it over the sword, and urge in support of their view that the sword guards the pen, and so stands to it as a guardian and servant. Others think the sword superior, and urge that

> the pen serves the sword because it provides the soldiers with their pay, and so it is a servant to it. Others say that they are equal and that neither of them can function without the other. They say a realm is fertilized by generosity, populated by justice, secured by common sense, protected by courage, and administered by leadership.

The author of Al Fakhri is fully aware of the critical nature of power in politics. He thinks it is a delicate instrument which has to be wielded with care and utmost anxiety. He says that "the practice of power is more difficult than (to obtain) power itself." Power has to be exercised with patience and fortitude. If power passes into the hands of an impatient person, there is every possibility of its being abused and misused. A seeker of power must also have the ability to discriminate and should also be endowed with talent and insight to make sound judgement. It would be better if he is aware of the vicissitudes of life, and the ebb and flow of human fortunes during different eras of history. Power without tact and grace is a crude weapon which can be extremely dangerous for civilization. A person holding power must be able to cajole his enemy with tact and hide his secret with grace. Power corrupts where an individual becomes over-confident, and refuses to seek advise from others. One's own commonsense alone cannot resolve complexities of politics and administration. It requires constant reinforcement from the genius of others, in the form of consultation.

The most competent ruler according to Al Fakhri is one "whose work rules his play, and whose judgement overrides his desire, whose deeds express his intentions, whose will does not counter his luck, nor anger his cunning." One of the qualities of a competent ruler is, his ability for self-examination. It is a common frailty among rulers that they always try to camouflage their failures. A ruler with a high ethical standard would readily subject himself to public scrutiny and speedily accept his failures and deficiencies. Self-assessment and self-realization are characteristics which clarify vision. A ruler ought to be a personification of affability, his kindness proverbial and manners exemplary. If the attitude and habits of the governors and the governed synchronize, systems tend to be stable and prosperous. People cannot blame the acts of rulers if their own life and character are imbued with the same spirit. It is also essential for administrative efficiency that the decision-maker be in a position to anticipate dangers. An administrator who lacks these qualities is patently incompetent.

Another matter which requires special consideration of rulers is the verification of information received from government informants. It is a matter of common knowledge that kingdoms have suffered grievous wrongs at the hands of corrupt and selfish spies. Rulers have committed egregious blunders in relying for their judgements on wrong information.

For you have to judge that which appears (in the open) while God judges the hidden. Dislike on behalf of your subjects, what you dislike for yourself. Conceal the shame of others and God will conceal for you that which you wish concealed. Be not in a hurry to believe the informer, for he is dishonest even though he may give good advice.

Since there were long periods of anarchy in Islamic history Muslim political thinkers had always deep concerned about peace and stability. Many of them concluded that only a strong and powerful ruler could provide security of life and property to his people. They unhesitatingly acknowledged that even if the ruler was unjust, his rule should be preferred to one who was just but weak. The latter in ·their opinion was unable to protect the fundamental rights of his subjects because his weakness made him susceptible to exploitations by self-seeking nobles and other vested interests in the realm. People were victimized by overambitious and unscrupulous fortune-hunters, and instead of suffering the despotic rule of one they would be subjected to many despots. Al Fakhri has made the following remarks on this controversy:

> They have disagreed as to the unjust ruler and the weak just ruler. They (mostly) prefer the strong unjust, arguing that the unjust powerful (ruler) guards his subjects against "vested interests" (and protects them by his power) from others than himself. His pride preserves them from being damaged by others than

> himself. So his subjects are in the position of who one is spared damage by all men but suffer damage by one. The weak just (ruler) neglects (the interest of) his subjects, and everyone has authority over them, and every hoof tramples them, so that they are in the position of one who is spared damage by one and suffers damage by all.

Compendium of History, Philosophy and Sociology

Muqaddima : Ibn Khaldun, the author of the *Muqaddima,* ranks among the greatest historians of the world. The book is basically on the philosophy of history, and has never been included in the literature on political or administrative ethics. It is a compendium of history, philosophy and sociology, and unquestionably the greatest work of Muslim scholarship which has won universal recognition for depth, comprehension, and creative insight into all organized affairs of men. Ibn Khaldun dealt at length on all theoretical and practical aspects of government and administration, and in doing so he has not failed to uncover ethical dimensions of the art of governing men. He emphasized that human life is a playground of good and evil, and evil propensities in organized moral communities are manifested, in the form of aggression and injustice. Governmental authority, in his opinion, is the only force which can save social systems from evil consequences of injustice and aggression. He says :

> Mutual aggression of people in towns and cities is averted by the authorities and the government, which hold back the masses under their control from attacks and aggression upon each other. They are thus prevented by the influence of force and governmental authority from mutual injustice, save much injustice as comes from the ruler himself.

Ibn Khaldun is perceptive enough to know that governmental authority equipped with the coercive power of the state is necessary to ward off dangers of subversion from within and destruction from outside. But at the same time he is fully aware that all bureaucratic structures have a built-in tendency to abuse this authority. It is not uncommon for guardians of justice and equity to commit brazen acts of injustice and inequity. How to guard against the guardians is a prominent theme of Ibn Khaldun's great work, and it is in this connection that he has unrolled the discussion on administrative ethics. His feelings are that although evil is ingrained in human nature, but still more often than not, men prefer doing good than pursuing actions which are morally reprehensible. Politics and public morality in his opinion should be inseparable from the affairs of organized communities. He says :

> "The existence of (royal authority without the simultaneous existence of) the perfecting details would be like the existence of a person with his limbs cut off, or it would be like appearing naked before people."

The Perfection : The emphasis all along in his great work is on perfection of Islamic principles of ethics. Prudence, wisdom, kindness, justice, fortitude, and honesty are repeatedly mentioned as glories of human conduct which give continuity and stability to moral communities. They ensure peace and order in kingdoms and give moral legitimacy to governmental authority. He says that 'politics is concerned with the administration of home or city in accordance with ethical and philosophical requirements, for the purpose of directing the masses toward a behaviour that will result in the preservation and permanence of the human species.' He insists that lawgivers must live up to the spirit of the religious laws because they are good for both here and hereafter, and they are free from foibles and frailities so commonly associated, with man-made laws.

To articulate his views still further Ibn Khaldun has reproduced a long letter written by an Abbaside general Tahir ibn-al Hussayan to his son Abdallah b. Tahir when the latter was appointed governor of ar-Raqqah Egypt by Al-Mamun. He speaks admiringly of the contents of this letter and mentions that Al-Mamun was so impressed by the depth and wisdom of the subject matter that he ordered that the letter be circulated among all officials stationed in various regions of the empire. Tahir starts this letter with usual exhortations of a devout Muslim, impressing upon his son the need to cultivate the fear of God and never to be forgetful of the fact that ultimately he would be accountable to Him for all his deeds and misdeeds, and one who holds authority over people, shoulders a grave responsibility. One of the primary duties of a God-fearing administrator is to preserve law and order, avoid brutality, protect the life and property of his subjects and to see that God's laws are not violated. It is also incumbent upon rulers of men not to allow their prejudices to interfere in the administration, and that they should set an example of moral rectitude so that people can repose confidence in their leadership. He says :

> "Do not be swayed from Justice according to your likes and dislikes, either on behalf of a person close to you or on behalf of one remote to you—In addition when people notice your (religious attitude) they will have respect for your rule and reverence for your government."

Those who are charged with the authority to govern men, have primary responsibility to exercise constant vigilance over the behaviour of their subordinates. A negligence in this direction has been the cause of ruin for many a ruler. It is a universal phenomenon that delegated authority, which is not investigated and supervised constantly, has a tendency to exploit people, and once a situation like that arises, kingdoms tumble very fast towards decadence. Tahir is unequivocal in his statement that this is the most important task of one who has been entrusted with the sole responsibility of governing and guiding the masses.

This is the only way to preserve the spirit of the religion in the life and character of a polity. At the same time it is essential that the wrong-doers should not go without punishment which should be according to principles ordained by God. Rank and status of culprits should not interfere in the dispensation of justice. Even postponement of punishment can have an impairing effect on public opinion. Justice deferred is no justice. Anger, deceit and levity are some of the evils which administrators must avoid in their actions. Tahir makes significant remarks about arrogance which is common vice among those whose authority is unchecked. An authority which has no ethical base is unislamic. Authority according to Islam is only a means to an end and not an end in itself. The ultimate authority belongs to God. Human beings hold it only as a trust. This accountability to the ultimate source is a recognized principle of Quranic law. He says:

> Beware of saying: "I am in authority. I may do what I want to do. This soon reveals a lack of sense on your part and little certainty of the one and only God. Let your intention with regard to (God) and your certainty of Him be sincere. You should know that royal authority belongs to God. He gives it to whomever he wants to give, and takes it away from whomever he wants to take it away."

Divine Retribution : According to Tahir, men occupying high positions in government are subject to divine retribution more than anybody else, because their actions can make or mar the fortunes of millions living in their jurisdiction. They probably don't know that by not using authority in a righteous manner they are being guilty of stark ingratitude to God who confers power as a special privilege on a selected few. The only way one can repay this gratitude is by dispensing justice and working ceaselessly for the welfare of the subjects and curbing greed and lust which inhibit ethical performance. He administers a special note of warning against extravagance and ostentatious living of state functionaries. Avarice and insincerity of officers, always have a disenchanting effect on social life in a community. Generosity, he preaches, is a balmy quality and its constant practice ensures trust and confidence in administration. Tahir has depicted the relationship between the ruler and his subjects in the following words:

> "You should know that by your appointment, you were made treasurer, guardian and shepherd. The people under your jurisdiction are called subjects (raiyah flock) because you are their shepherd and overseer. Therefore accept from them what they give you of their affluence, and use it for the administration of their affairs, for their welfare and for providing for their needs. Employ for them understanding skilled and experienced men, who have theoretical knowledge of, and are able to act with, political wisdom and moderation. Give them good salaries. This is one of the duties incumbent upon you in connection with the task from which you have been entrusted."

The above remarks show that the writer was fully aware of the significant role which the selection of personnel plays in creating a healthy administrative climate. Understanding, experience, knowledge, political wisdom and moderation are some of the salient qualities, which he thinks are essential for good administrators. On the other hand it is the responsibility of the government to see that salary structure is rational so that administrators can have adequate income to maintain a certain respectable standard of living. Financially dissatisfied public service can play havoc with the fortunes of the people. Adequate salary is not an absolute safeguard against corruption or dishonesty, but it can certainly reduce its intensity considerably. Tahir also advocates effective intelligence service as another safeguard against excesses of officials. This would keep the government well-informed about the behaviour, style of life and other activities of officers working in the field.

Another theme which Tahir has developed at length is the accessibility of the ruler to his subjects, particularly the poor ones who don't have the means to find ready access to the regular law courts. If these simmering grievances of the people are not corrected, they can ruin the stability of the kingdom. He says :

> Devote yourself to looking after the affairs of the poor and indigent, those who are not able to bring before you complaints about injustices they have suffered, and other lowly persons, who do not know that they may ask for their rights. Inquire about these people in all secrecy, and put good men among your subjects in charge of them. Command them to report to you their needs and conditions, so that you will be able to look into the measures through which God might improve their affairs.

Even if officials are legally accessible to the public, many of them have the tendency to adopt such measures which would discourage a visitor from visiting public offices. Either there are restrictions on the number of interviews one can have with an official or there are so many barriers of security and secrecy, that petitioners have neither the courage nor the means to surmount them. In order to make accessibility meaningful Tahir suggests that, 'let people frequently come to see you and show them your face. Let not your guards hinder them. Be humble towards them. Show them your smiling countenance. 'Be lenient with them when (you put) questions and speak to them, Be benevolent to them in your generosity and bounty.' And lastly it is the duty of the government to keep a constant watch on the accumulation of wealth and property by state officers and no effort should be spared in exercising vigilance on their faithfulness, straightforwardness and support for the government. Very often, it also happens that one has an access to an officer, but the latter's attitude would be so scowling and arrogant,' that the complainant would never be able to unburden all his grievances. It is unbecoming of an officer to give an interview to an aggrieved person, and then to give such a shabby treatment, that he may not turn up again with any complaint.

Perfect Diplomacy

Akhlak-i-Jalali : Muhammad ibn Asad Jalal-al-Din-al-Bawwani (1627-1501 A. D.) the author of this book was attached to the court of Turkoman ruler Uzun Hassan, who at the meridian of his power, had diplomatic relations with Venice and Constantinople, in the West, and Samarqand and Herat in the East. The period of his rule was crowded with political turmoil and administrative anarchy. The character of the people had been adversely affected by lawlessness, and the ethical standards of the rulers and administrators were painfully low. The main purpose of the writer was to find causes of the prevalent stresses and tensions which had so completely polluted the moral climate in administration, Muhammad ibn Asad was a prolific writer and he wrote on variety of philosophical and mystical subjects in Arabic, but his most famous work is *Lawamie al-Ishraq fi Makarim-al-Akhlaq* popularly known as Akhlaq-i-Jalali. The book has been frequently printed and widely read in Iran and Indo-Pakistan sub-continent. In 1839 it was translated in English by W. F. Thompson under the title *Practical Philosophy of the Muhammadan People.*

The author has made extensive use of the ethical writings of the Greek philosophers and Muslim scholars who preceded him, but every discussion carries a deep stamp of his own genius. His analysis of human nature and character is unquestionably very rich and profound, and constitute a meaningful manifesto to guide men in sorting out issues which are morally right. He believes that man is a vice-regent of God on earth and emulation of divine attributes is his ultimate destiny. This is a difficult assignment and he points out that to fulfil the obligations of vice-regency "two things are necessary, (i) mature wisdom which means perfection in knowledge, (ii) and eminent ability which connotes perfection in practice." Muhammad ibn Asad had a firm conviction that knowledge is meant to serve mankind and unless it is put into practice, human affairs will never be smooth and harmonious. He said, "Knowledge without practice is a burden, and practice without knowledge is a mischief."

He has drawn a very comprehensive list of virtues which in his opinion make life socially and morally worth living. These characteristics lend luster, dignity and richness to human behavior and assist human organizations in the realization of their objectives. He has made four broad categories of virtues and labelled them as Wisdom, Courage, Temperance, and Equity, and then under each category he lists certain qualities which ensure the growth of a morally healthy personality.

Wisdom : It means penetration, quickness of intellect, clearness of understanding, facility of acquirement, propriety of discrimination retention, recollection.

Courage : It means magnanimity, collectedness, elevation of purpose, firmness, coolness, stateliness, boldness, endurance, condescension, zeal and mercy.

Temperance Shame : (The author calls it soul's restraint upon itself when aware of intending to commit anything odious, that it may guard against deserving censure. One of the Prophets saying is this, *Shame,* is a compendium of every virtue). Good humour, righteousness, easiness, patience, content, steadiness, piety, regularity, integrity, and liberality.

Equity : It consist of fidelity, union, exactitude, tenderness, brotherhood, gratitude, good fellowship, good faith, cordiality, submission, resignation and devotion.

The above virtues are not merely abstract ethical principles in the opinion of the author. They are meant to be operational instruments for conducting human affairs. For government and administration, Muhammad ibn Asad has added a few other moral responsibilities also. He points out that a free and frequent interaction between governors and governed is essential for justice and cooperation. Any government where people don't have access to rulers is a bureaucratic tyranny. The author of Akhlak-i-Jalali has expressed his opinion on this aspect as follows:

> For this reason intercourse with our fellow creatures in the way of cooperation is incumbent on us all, or else we deviate from the first principle of justice and fall into the path of inequity, like that class of persons who betake themselves to a savage retirement from mankind, and remain altogether aloof from cooperation with their fellow men, loading them however, with the burden of their support and then they call seclusion and consider meritorious in fact it is altogether a state of inequity.

The above statement testifies to the fact that Muhammad ibn Asad feels that meeting people and cooperating with them is an essential characteristic of a good government. In fact this is a quality which can infuse trust, confidence and cooperation in all areas of human relations. He has further clarified the distinction between the righteous and the unrighteous government by saying:

> "He who conducts the righteous government in his rigid adherence to the role of equity, considers his subjects as his children and his friends, placing all covetousness and love of money under the control of judgment. He that conducts the unrighteous government adheres to the principles of force, treats his subjects like beasts of burden, considers them as slaves, and is himself the slave of avarice and passion."

Like other Muslim writers on administrative ethics, Muhammad ibn Asad emphasized in unqualified terms that virtue and rectitude among rulers always have a widespread impact on the subjects. It is a natural tendency among people to emulate their governors. If a ruler is good, his goodness would be a source of inspiration, but if he is bad, the people unhesitatingly follow the same course. It is therefore vital for the moral uplift of society that administrators should set an example of honesty, justice and integrity. This will give dignity, poise, and solidity to the character of the masses. In Akhlak-i-Jalali this problem of the image of the ruler or administrator has been explained as follows:

> "We are told in holy writ, 'Men resemble their contemporaries even more than their progenitors', and 'Men are of the same religion as their princes.' Hence when the age's guidance is in the hands of a just king everyone directs his course towards equity and the attainment of virtue, on the contrary, the people likewise incline to falsehood, covetousness, and vice of every description."

The qualities which would endear the rulers to the subjects are, seriousness of purpose, rational decision, resolution, endurance, hardwork and incorruptibility. Moreover, authorities in a kingdom are expected to be anxiously concerned about three fundamental principles for the welfare of the state: (i) Financial stability, (ii) kindness and compassion to the people, (iii) and ability to keep away petty-minded people from government offices. Employment in a state, according to the author, should be reserved for people who are talented by nature, and prudent in thought and action. Ibn Asad compiled a code of ten articles, which in his opinion could ensure a sound moral base for administrative behaviour:

(1) Whatever he holds impossible toward himself he should hold inadmissible towards his people.

(2) Quick justice.

(3) Abstinence from licentious and sensual gratification.

(4) Courtesy and kindness in decision-making.

(5) Faith in the supremacy of the will of God.

(6) Nothing should be done in the opposition to the Message of God.

(7) Mercy and Indulgency.

(8) Should associate with men of righteousness.

(9) Maintaining everyone in the position he deserves.

(10) Officers, soldiers and the people in this relationship should be so balanced that they could not injure each other's interest.

There are many other discussions on morals and manners in Akhlak-i-Jalali, relating to individual and social life, but they don't have such relevance to government and administration. Friendship, family, property, rearing of children, rights and privileges of wives, education of women, rights of parents, meals, etc. are some of the subjects on which the author has dilated in depth. In short, the treatise is a valuable compendium of ethical values both Islamic and pre-Islamic which the author considers, provide richness and dignity to human character. He insists that without positive moral climate, and universal ethical standards social system decay and wither away. In short, the treatise is of indisputable significance for understanding the practical moral standards of the Muslim people and Thompson is right when on the title page of his translation he calls Akhlak-i-Jalali 'the most esteemed ethical work of Middle Asia'.

According to Erwin Rosenthal, *Jalal-al-Din-al-Dawwani* made extensive use of Nasir-al-Din Tusis *Akhlaq-i-Nasiri,* and to a large extent many of his concepts and discussions were only summaries of Tusi. Al-Dawwani, however, being a theologian, jurist and scholar, has put greater emphasis on traditional Islam. His narrative is free from Greek philosophical influences which so conspicuously dominate Tusi's analysis. His examination of ethical, economic and political problems in a Muslim polity is direct, precise and lucid. A ruler who isolates himself from his fellow men is unjust in his opinion. Rulers, he suggests are 'physicians to the temperament of the world' and their main responsibility is to inculcate righteous opinions, mold convictions of the people, and fashion their disposition in a manner so that good actions could be ensured.

In his opinion people are divided into five categories, "good, with good influences on others, good in themselves without influence, bad without bad influence, and finally the opposite of the first group, the bad ones who exert a bad influence." A ruler's most onerous responsibility is to maintain an equilibrium among all these kinds. That in essence is the purpose of authority in a state and following other works on governmental ethics, he insists that those in authority should have kindness, and compassion and that in selecting state functionaries, rulers should not entrust offices to mean people. Moderation, respect for people's rights, devotion to their welfare, justice and close vigilance over the working of the government and fear of God are the other qualities which give strength and stability to kingdoms. Rosenthal has summed up Al-Dawwani's contributions as follows:

> These examples show how Al-Dawwani combines philosophy both ancient and modern with Quran, Hadith and tales as found in the 'Mirrors.' In this way he gives an interesting and colourful account of political thought which is intellectually satisfying and traditionally unobjectionable.

Counselling for Ministers

***Nasaih ul-vuzera vel-Umera** : [The Book of Counsel for Vezirs (Ministers) and Umera (Governors)].*

This small treatise was written by an Ottoman statesman during the later half of the seventeenth century. It's author, Baqqal-Oghlu Sari Hajji Muhammad Pasha was born in Constantinople, but biographical details of his early life are missing from available historical records. In 1671, probably as a teenager, he became an apprentice in the office of the *ruznami je-i-evvel,* an important official of the Treasury department. By hard work, devotion, and knowledge of the financial problems he ultimately became the head of this department. In 1702 Rami Muhammad Pasha, the grand vezir appointed him chief defterdar (Treasurer of the Empire). This was the pinnacle of his professional attainments, but it made the last years of his life extremely uncomfortable. Ottoman administration during this period was a web of unending intrigues, in which all the senior officials of the realm, governors of provinces, courtiers, and members of the royal sergalio were deeply involved. Every senior public servant lived in a state of chronic insecurity. This can be illustrated by the fact that Muhammad Pasha was seven times in and out of his job as a *defterdar* of the empire. His ability and experience were of no consideration to his opponents. Ultimately he fell victim to their jealousy and enmity. By orders of Sultan Ahmad III he was dismissed and imprisoned in the castle of Qavla on the Aegean coast. After sometime in February 1717 he was executed, his head was sent to Constantinople where it was hung on the gate of the Imperial palace.

Writing in Exile : It is assumed that the Book of Counsel for Vezirs and Governors was written during one of the exiles of Muhammad Pasha. The main purpose of the scholar-statesman was to give a detailed account of the political and administrative vicissitudes which had engulfed the empire at that time. Ottoman bureaucracy has always been accorded a place of eminence among the great historical bureaucracies of the world. Its spirit was autocratic, but during the earlier period of the dynasty under capable rulers who presided over an unwieldy empire, which stretched from Constantinople to Egypt and from Algeria to the borders of Persia, it worked efficiently. But this era of territorial expansion and administrative efficiency, ended with the death of Suleyman the Magnificent. After him the fortunes of the empire were in the hands of harem-reared princes who were educated in the cloistered atmosphere of the palace through eunuchs, slave-girls and pages.

War State : The Ottoman empire in essence was a war state. It was one long crusade against the infidel world. As long as the rulers were busy conquering foreign lands administration was efficient and resourceful. Bat once the territorial expansion stopped, there was rapid deterioration in the efficiency and moral standards of the administrators. Revenues which used to flow from booty, ransom, and other spoils of war disappeared, and the empire entered into a period of financial decadence from which it could not recover. While revenues decreased, the luxuries of royalty and its sprawling circles of regal parasites kept on increasing. Ease-loving Sultans, luxuriating courtiers, disgruntled armies, rebellious governors and rapacious bureaucracy completely wrecked the machinery of the government. Bernard Lewis says :

> "The breakdown in the apparatus of government affected not only the supreme instruments of sovereignly, but also the whole of the bureaucratic and religious institutions all over the Empire. These suffered a catastrophic fall in efficiency and integrity which was accentuated by the growing change in methods of recruitment, training, and promotion. This deterioration is clearly discernible in the Ottoman archives, which reflected vividly and precisely the change from the meticulous, conscientious, and strikingly efficient

> bureaucratic government of the sixteenth century to the neglect of the seventeenth and collapse of the eighteenth centuries."

Ottoman administration which under Murad II Muhammad the Conqueror and Salim I, was a source of strength and stability under later weak rulers became an instrument of corruption and exploitation. Sale of public offices became a common feature, and one who paid the highest price would immediately start using his official position unscrupulously for personal gains, because he was not sure when another bidder would replace him. A contemporary western observer of the time remarked that "the frequent changes of the principal ministers saps silently the foundation of the empire, and gives to the government terrible wounds. Those who are elevated to office, for seeing that this will not long be held, preferring their own enrichment to the interest of empire, let it perish in order to assuage their avarice, and being able to enrich themselves only by unjust means they make use of every means." Army, which was once one of the finest fighting machines, was reduced only to a pale shadow of its former strength and character. Janissaries which had played a significant role in the creation of the empire, taking advantage of the weakness of the ruling Sultans, had monopolized all positions of power in the state. Their devotion to the ruling Sultan was only a facade for self-aggrandizement and the non-payment of salaries by the government led them to pillage the land freely and indulge in illegal extortion from the peasantry. The commanders on the frontiers kept false registers to defraud the Treasury at Constantinople. Palace intrigues, corruption, deceit, jealousy and treachery were commonly noticed in every area of politics and administration. Gibb and Bowen have summed up this phase of the Ottoman history in the following words :

> "The ruling institution had thus by the eighteenth century, undergone as complete a transformation as was compatible with the maintenance of most of its original forms. Instead of inspiring its members to earn merit by the exercise of talent and virtue, it taught them they must look to corruption for advancement, and might safely neglect duties that should have been concomitant with their privileges. Finally, instead of

> providing the sultans with an efficient instrument for the preservation and extension of their power, it was now scarcely strong enough to maintain their authority at home, and become an engine of feeble tyranny over those of their subjects that were unable to continue against it."

It was in this depressing climate of moral and material decadence that Muhammad Pasha wrote his "The Book of Counsel". He admired the political wisdom and high moral standards of administration of Ottoman rule during the fifteenth and sixteenth century. But he felt that in his own time the empire had reached the nadir of its ethical standards. His analysis is illustrated with verses from the Quran Traditions of the Prophet and relevant passages from earlier works on the subject. The narrative is an index of author's rich and vast experience which he had accumulated as a high-ranking administrator. As defterdar (Chief Treasurer) and as member of the Imperial Divan (Central Cabinet) he had ample opportunity to observe from very close quarters, every branch of administration. Although Muhammad Pasha's main focus was on the Ottoman administration, but in diagnosing the causes of its decline he has pointed out certain basic ethical principles, which can be relevant for administrators, holding positions of power and prestige in any society. In subject matter, Nasaihul-vuzera vel-umera, resembles a great deal with Siyasat Namah and Qabus-namah, although in breadth and depth of analysis it falls short of the earlier works. The treatise is divided into the following nine chapters :

(1) Explanation regarding the behaviour and habits of the Grand Vezir.

(2) Explanation regarding the official positions and the harmfulness of bribes.

(3) Explanation regarding the behaviour of the Secretary of the Treasury and holders of office.

(4) Explanation regarding the Bektashi Corps.

(5) Explanation regarding the condition of Rayas (the subject peasants and the harmfulness of tyranny and oppression of the poor.

(6) Explanation regarding the state of the Ever-Victorious Frontier and the qualities of commanders.

(7) Explanation concerning avarice and liberality, greed, covetousness, pride, and envy, humility and arrogance, good temper and bad temper and hypocrisy.

(8) Explanation regarding faithful friendship and the harmfulness of calumny and backbiting.

(9) Explanation regarding the state of the Ziamet and Timar (the two principal categories of fiefs in the Ottoman feudal system).

Absence of Facts : Muhammad Pasha, in his narrative does not mention anywhere the moral degeneration of the royal household, or the inexcusable negligence of the Sultans cowards the affairs of the state. As an employee of an autocratic ruler, he probably could not openly criticize the Sultans whose tyranny and pursuits of pleasures had changed the machinery of government into an engine of coercion and exploitation. He opens his first chapter with the following remarks :

> "Since the Lord without equal, who showers down abundant gifts (may His glory be exalted beyond the reach of imagination) has made that firmly founded dynasty, the surpassing Ottoman Sultanate, to be the refuge of the rulers of the times, and has made their court, which pours out on every hand favours from the ocean of abundance, to be distributor of the sustenance decreed by Providence to the people of the world, it has consequently become a necessary responsibility and obvious obligation of the padishah to fulfil the incumbent gratitude due for their Divine Grace in accordance with the precept." "Everyone of you is a shepherd and everyone is responsible for the flock, he should make affluent the condition of the governed and establish good order in the affairs of the citizens."

Muhammad Pasha advocates that officials occupying positions of authority must abstain from illegal practices, avoid injustice and remove weeds and thorns of tyranny and corruption. Administrators in his opinion should be free from the baneful attitude of discriminating among people. Rich and poor, high and low, friend and a stranger, all should be treated strictly according to the principles of law and ethics. They must have the moral courage to speak the truth, because truth alone ensures integrity and emancipates human thinking from deceit and suspicion. Hasty use of power is also detrimental to sound administration. In the application of his authority an officer has moral duty to weigh intelligently and rationally pros and cons of every bit of evidence and information. He says :

> "Throughout their period of authority let them treat with equality the humble and the noble, the wealthy and the poor, the learned and the unlearned, the one from far and the one from nearby, the visitor and the neighbour—let them not make use of their power until the evidence is complete—to the glorious padishah let them speak the word of truth without veiling and concealment. For the Prophet of God has said, "words of truth are the best alms."

The Other Side

The largest portion of the treatise, however, is devoted to the evils which are bred in administration by corruption and worldly greed of public servants. These evils had completely changed the life and character of Ottoman government. A bureaucracy with a legendary reputation for efficiency and uprightness became a playground of internal frictions and squabbles, and in their dealings with the public, its members were always busy in devising means by which they could further their worldly fortunes. The man in the street and the defenseless peasantry were completely disarmed against their deceitful manipulations. According to Muhammad Pasha, lust for wealth is a sign of unhealthy politics. It makes a holder of authority unscrupulous, time-server, haughty and disdainful. While giving advice to the grand vezir, he makes the following remarks :

> "The grand vezir especially must not be a time-server thinking of the benefits of money; let him shun the hope of gathering wealth and treasures and spend his ability in preparing a remedy for the weakness and

> languidness which prevent the good health of the country—nor let him become puffed up with his greatness and exhibit to the people an appearance of haughtiness and disdain—whatever appointed thou mayest receive from among the exalted offices be content with the designated salary and be on the guard against tyranny and cruelty and daring to cause harm to the people through greedy longing to amass wealth."

He has further castigated bribery in the following words :

> "Bribery is the beginning and root of all illegality and tyranny, the source and fountain of every sort of disturbance and sedition, the most vast of evils and the greatest of calamities. It is the ruin of corruption than which there is nothing whatever more calamitious to the people of Islam or more destructive to the foundations of religion and government. Than this there is no more powerful engine of injustice and cruelty, for bribery destroys both faith and state."

The menace of bribery in the seventeenth century Ottoman administration, had increased manifold because administrators were not only getting bribes and gifts from the people, but large scale bribery was practised within the ranks of bureaucracy for promotion, transfer and acquisition of new offices. Such a practice had such degenerating consequences for administration that Muhammad Pasha wrote "to give office to the unfit because of bribery is a very great sin."

The virus of corruption had become so widespread, that even judges were not immune from it. They freely auction their judgments in favour of the highest bidder. He sums up his discussion about the harmful implications of bribery with the remarks that "to government officials the disease of bribery is one whose cure is hard to determine. Perhaps it has no cure, yet there is no disease without remedy. This must be considered in all its aspects and absolutely eschewed and avoided." He is particularly insistent that officials of the treasury who hold in custody the wealth of the state should have an untarnished record of honesty and integrity. They should be men who have full comprehension of the affairs of the realm, and complete awareness of all the dynamics which are shaping the character of a polity at a particular time.

They should be men, who are experienced, righteous and religious. They should be watchful of the 'trustworthiness or contemptibleness of those who follow the rocky and unrighteous road of treachery', because that is the only way to save the country from frauds and misappropriations. Revenue officials, are very susceptible to calumny and derision from jealous persons. This further necessitates that they should be honest and upright. He says that 'those who are defterdars (Treasury Chiefs) should be extremely circumspect in behaviour, upright and devout, devoid of avarice and spite. They should be satisfied with the revenues assigned to them by the Exalted Government and should not desire bribes from anyone or be greedy of amassing wealth and profits.

Army's Responsibility : According to Muhammad Pasha, the responsibility of the army, particularly its commanders, in creating higher standards of public morality is equally important for the health of body politics. The Ottoman army had become one of the most corrupting influences in the state. On the frontiers, commanders used to draw salaries for soldiers who did not exist. Knowing the power and prestige of Janisseries, all kinds of people had joined their ranks either through intercession or bribery. The result was that corps which was once the pride of Ottoman army became an asylum for good-for-nothing fortune-hunters. Many who had never budged out of Istanbul, had not rendered any service in a campaign, were drawing salaries of soldiers, or pensioners.

If the above mentioned evils emerge in a political system the greatest sufferers, according to our author, are the poor raya (subjects). A tradition of the Prophet compares oppression to darkness, and another one says "Guard yourself against the prayer of the poor man, even though he be an unbeliever." After quoting these sayings Muhammad Pasha goes on to prove that in the last analysis, it is the people who are the real benefactors of the rulers. It is through their sweat and blood that nations attain their greatness. Therefore anyone who neglects their comfort and interest is in reality an enemy of the state. He says:

> "The rayas (subjects) are a trust from the Creator of man and Universe. The state exists through them and treasure produced by them. If the subjects be always protected they become not wretched, but increase. Kindness to them and protection of their affairs from the hands of tyrannical oppression is a form of worship."

In support of his contention he quotes a famous Arabic maxim of statecraft which reads as follows :

> "Without men of consequence there is no ruler, and without property there are no men of consequence, and without prosperity there is no wealth, and without justice and good administration there is no prosperity."

Ethical Value

Over and above the qualities of honesty, trustworthiness and integrity, Muhammad Pasha has listed certain other ethical characteristics which he deems essential for men, who have been given the charge of public affairs in a state. Irritable and bad-tempered person can never make a good officer. An officer should be free from jealousy and hypocrisy, and in dealing with people he should avoid pride and arrogance. Generosity of heart and liberality of attitude will strengthen his position, and people will not hesitate to repose confidence in his decisions. Avarice is a positive disqualification because it is a manifestation of man's unregenerate nature. Passion without reason and ill-humor are also accounted as major evils of administrative behaviour. Wrath in the opinion of the author spoils belief just as aloes (a plant which has bitter juice) spoils honey. Humility gives richness and dignity to human character, while haughtiness is a moral debasement. He quotes a tradition of the Prophet in this respect which says "He who has in his heart an atom's weight of arrogance enters not into Heaven."

Vicious Intrigues : The Ottoman governmental machinery during the sixteenth century was crowded with vicious intrigues. Faith and fidelity were conspicuous by their absence from human relations. Our author had full share of this intrabureacratic deceit and treachery which ultimately cost him his life. Therefore, one is not surprised that he has introduced a special chapter on friendship to prove that human interaction should be free from flattery, and it should be based on mutual sympathy, trust and confidence. It should not be an hypocritical facade to hide spite and hatred. A friend should be one to whom you can entrust your secrets and who has the ability to live up to his promises, whose affections are not fleeting and who loves truth. Men have a tendency to gravitate towards and cluster around rulers and men of authority. Not all who do so are trustworthy. Large numbers of them have always some personal axe to grind. The character of such persons has been portrayed by the author in the following words :

> "They desire amicable relations and double-faced friendship in order, purely for their own advantage, to dupe with all sorts of tricks and wiles someone of eminence for a great personage of government and to cause him to commit sins. In the end they become the cause of his suffering. If diligent inquiry be made, they are found to be sinners and wine blabbers. How can good come from such as these ? Such men are boaster and braggarts, liars and bringers of false accusation, contemptible in nature and abominable in character. They are unmixed evil, obstacles to good, exaggerators, flatterers and time servers."

Men in authority are also warned against 'talebearers and backbiters', because they have the evil habit of adding uncalled for comments to information passed on to them. In his opinion, "rulers must expel and drive away such persons from their councils and give them neither pleasantry nor license." And in the end the author advises all men of rank and status in government to be at guard against calumnious persons, because the Quran itself has said, "Slander not one another. Would any of you like to eat the flesh of his dead brother ? If so you would despise him."

Bibliography

Ahmad, Aziz : *Islamic Modernism in India and Pakistan*, Oxford University Press, 1970.

Ahmed, Hasanuddin : *A Handbook of Muslim Belief,* Goodword Books Pvt. Ltd., New Delhi, 1995.

Ahmad, Imtiaz : *Divorce and Remarriage among Muslims in India,* Manohar Publishers, New Delhi, 2003.

Ahmad, Khurshid : *Islam : its Meaning and Message,* Islamic Council of Europe, London, 1976.

Ahmad, Manzooruddin : *Pakistan : the Emerging Islamic State*, Allies Book Corporation, Karachi, 1966.

Akhtar, Hakeem M. : *Remedies to Spiritual Maladies,* Idara Ishaat-e-Diniyat Pvt. Ltd., New Delhi, 1991.

Akhtar, Wazir : *Economics in Islamic Law,* Kitab Bhavan, New Delhi, 1992.

Alfieri, Binaca Maria : *Islamic Architecture of the Indian Subcontinent*, Lawrence King, New York, 1989.

Ali, Akhtar : *Israel and Prophesies of Islam,* Raj & Co., New Delhi, 1997.

Ali, Kattani : *Muslim Minorities in the World Today,* Ashish Publishing House, New Delhi, 2001.

Ali, Adil : *Presidential Addresses on Arab Islamic Studies,* Kitab Bhavan, New Delhi, 2002.

Ali, A. Yusuf : *Message of Islam,* Kitab Bhavan, New Delhi, 2000.

Arnold, Sir Thomas : *The Caliphate,* MacMillan, London, 1965.

Arnold, T. W. : *Preaching of Islam*, Luzac & Co., London, 1913.

Arvind, Sharma : *Women in World Religion,* New York Press, New York, 1990.

Athar, Ali : *Mughal Nobility under Aurangzeb,* Pupular Prakashan, Bombay, 1968.

Barkatullah, M. : *Khilafat,* MacMillan, London,1924.

Basham, A. L. : *A Cultural History of India,* Oxford, New York, 1975.

Basil, King : *The Conquest of Fearm,* Illias Pub., Islamabad, 2000.

Batty and Morgan : *War its Conduct and Legal Results,* Feroz Pub., Lahore, 2000.

Berger, M. : *Islam in Egypt Today : Social and Political Aspects of Popular Religion,* MacMillan, London, 1970.

Bevan, E. R. : *House of Seleucus*, Allen & Unwin, London, 2001.

Bhatia, H. S. : *Studies in Islamic law, Religion and Society*, Deep & Deep Publications, New Delhi, 1997.

Brett, M. : *Northern Africa : Islam and Modernization,* Allen & Unwin, London, 1973.

Brigadier, Gulzar Ahmed : *The Prophets (PBUH) Concept of War,* Aziz Pub., Islamabad, 2000.

Brow, John R. : *Islam, Law, and Equality in Indonesia : an Anthropology of Public,* Cambridge University Press, New Delhi, 1997.

Bukhsh, S. K. : *Contribution to the History of Islamic Civilization,* Kitab Bhavan, New Delhi, 2000.

Burton, Sir Richard : *Sind and Races that Inhabit the Valley of the Indus,* Allen & Unwin, London, 1851.

Campbell, Arnold : *Arabian Medicine,* Oxford, New York, 2002.

Carre, Olivier : *Islam and the State in the World Today,* Manohar Publisher, New Delhi, 1989.

Commissariat, M. S. : *A History of Gujarat,* Longman's Green & Co., Bombay, 1938.

Cook, Michael : *Forbiding Wrong in Islam : an Introduction*, Cambridge University Press, New Delhi, 1985.

Corbin, H. : *Avicenna and the Visionary Recital,* MacMillan, London, 1960.

Dorothy, Vaugham : *Europe and the Turks,* Oxford, New York, 2004.

Drfyer, J. L. E. : *History of the Planetary Systems*, Cambridge, New York, 1903.

Edwards, Beverly Milton : *Islam and Politics in the Contemporary World*, Blackwell, New York, 1987.

Emil, Brunner : *Justice and the Social Order,* Oxford, New York, 2000.

Engineer, Asghar Ali : *Islam : Challenge in Twenty-first Century,* Gyan Books Pvt. Ltd., New Delhi, 2004.

Faris, Nabith A. : *The Foundations of the Articles of Faith,* Feroz Pub., Lahore, 1963.

Fatima, T. : *Islamic Law and Judiciary,* Deep & Deep Publications, New Delhi, 2001.

Fordon, S. : *Preliminary Statement on a General Theory of the Islamization of the Malay-Indonesian Archipelago,* Kuala Lumpur, 1969.

Fordon, S. : *The Origin of Malay Shair*, Kuala Lumpur, 1968.

Foster, W. : *The English Factories in India*, Oxford, New Delhi, 1906.

Francois, Bernier : *Travels in the Mogul Empire*, MacMillan, London, 1916.

Gaborieau, M. : *The Cult of Saints among Muslims in Nepal and North India,* Cambridge University, Press, Cambridge, 1983.

Gellner, E. : *Post-Traditional Forms in Islam : the Turf and Trade*, Oxford, New York, 1982.

Gibb, H.A.R : *Islamic Society and the West,* Luzac & Co., London, 1960.

Hasan, S. Badrul : *Muslim Behaviour,* Kitab Bhavan, New Delhi, 1991.

Hasan, Ibn : *The Central Structure of the Mughal Empire*, Adam Pub., New Delhi, 1980.

Hasan, Mushirul : *Islam and Indian Nationalism : Refection on Abdul Kalam Azad*, Manohar Publishers, New Delhi, 1992.

Iqbal, Muhammad : *The Development of Metaphysics in Persia*, Royal Pub., Lahore, 1964.

Khaduri, M. : *War and Peace in the Law of Islam,* Hopkins Press, Baltimore, 1955.

Levy, Reuben : *The Social Structure of Islam*, Cambridge University Press, New York, 1993.

MacDonald, D.B. : *Development of Muslim Theology*, New Century Pub., London, 1903.

McIver, R.M. and Oage, Charles H. : *The Society,* Macmillan & Co., London, 1959.

Montgomery, Watt : *The Majesty that was Islam,* Oxford, New York, 1973.

Muir, William : *Early Caliphate,* Oxford, New York, 1970.

Muni, S.D. and Kalim Bahadur : *Domestic Conflicts in South Asia,* South Asia Publishers, New Delhi, 1986.

Murata, S. and Others : *The Vision of Islam,* Ashish Publishing House, New Delhi, 1991.

Murthy, T.S. : *Muslim : the Difficult Years,* Himalayan Books, Chandigarh, 1983.

Musil, A. : *The Manners and Customs of the Rwala Bedounis,* Oxford, New York, 1928.

Muslehuddin, M. : *Banking and Islamic Law,* Idara Ishaat-e-Diniyat Pvt. Ltd, New Delhi, 1990.

Nasr, Seyyed H. : *An Introduction to Islamic Cosmological Doctrines,* Cambridge, 1964.

—— : *Ideas and Realities of Islam,* MacMillan & Co., London, 1966.

Nicholson, R.A. : *The Mysteries of Islam,* MacMillan & Co., London, 1914.

Palamer, E.H. : *The Quran,* Atlantic Publishers, New Delhi, 1996.

Pandit, Sneh : *Perspectives in the Philosophy of Culture,* S. Chand & Company Ltd., New Delhi, 1990

Pickthall, M. M. : *Islamic Culture,* Feroz Sons Publishers, Lahore, 1992.

Qureshi, W. : *Selections from the Iqbal Review,* Iqbal Academy Pakistan, Lahore, 1983.

Qureshi, I.H. : *The Administration of the Mughul Empire,* Feroz Pub., Karachi, 1966.

—— : *The Muslim Community of the Indo-Pakistan Subcontinent,* The Hague, New York, 1962.

—— : *The Administration of the Sultanate of Delhi,* Royal Pub., Karachi, 1944.

Rabi, Muhammad Mahmud : *The Political Theory of Ibn Khaldun,* MacMillan & Co., London, 1967.

Rabnson, Chave F. : *Islamic Histroriography,* Cambridge University press, New York, 1990.

Richards, J.F. : *Mughal Administration in Golkonda*, Oxford, New York, 1975.

Rizvi, Hasan Askari : *Islami Reassertion : a Socio Political Study,* Progressive Publishers, Lahore, 1981.

Rizvi, S.A.A. : *A History of Sufism in India*, Ashish Pub., Delhi, 1978.

—— : *Muslim Revivalist Movements in Northern India in the Sixteenth and Seventeenth Centuries*, Neeru Pub., Agra, 1965.

Rumi, Jalaludin : *The Masnavi,* Gyan Books Pvt. Ltd., New Delhi, 2000.

Ruthven, Malise : *Islam : a Very Short Introduction*, Oxford, New York, 1990.

Sabiruddin : *Muslim Husband and Wife : Right and Duties,* Kitab Bhavan, New Delhi, 2000.

Sadiq, M. : *A History of Urdu Poetry*, MacMillan & Co., London, 1964.

Sahai, Surendra : *Indian Architecture : Islamic Period (1192-1857),* Prakash Books, New Delhi, 1967.

Schwartz, E. : *Science and Civilization in Islam,* Cambridge, London, 1966.

Sergeant : *Constitution of Madina,* Feroz Pub., Lahore, 1992.

—— : *The Sunnah Jamia,* Feroz Pub., Lahore, 1992.

Setalvad : *War and Civil Liberties,* Feroz Pub., Lahore, 1992.

Shaikh, N. M. : *Women in Muslim Society,* Kitab Bhavan, New Delhi, 1991.

Sharma, S.R. : *Women's Education in Ancient and Muslim Period,* Discovery Publishing House, New Delhi, 1996.

Shaukat, Ali : *Masters of Muslim Thought,* Deep & Deep Pub., New Delhi, 1992.

Sikandar, bin Manjhu : *Mirat-i Sikandari,* Department of History, Faculty of Arts, M. S. University, Baroda, 1961.

Subhan, J.A. : *Sufism : its Saints and Shrines,* Kitabiyat Pub., Lucknow, 1960.

Suhrawardi, Umar : *Awarif al Maarif bin Muhammad,* Sheikh Ghulam Shahabuddin Ali & Sons, Lahore, 1964.

Syed, Amir Ali : *The Spirit of Islam,* Royal Pub.,Lahore, 1979.

Syed, M. H. : *Islamic Terrorism : Myth or Reality,* Gyan Books Pvt. Ltd., New Delhi, 2002.

—— : *Status of Women in Islamic Society,* Anmol Publications, New Delhi, 2003.

—— : *Impact of Islam,* Anmol Publications, New Delhi, 2003.

—— : *History of Muslims in India,* Anmol Publications, New Delhi, 2003.

—— : *The Mysticism of Hazmali Fansuri,* A. Pub., Kuala Lumpur, 1970.

Syed, Nageeb al-Attas : *Raniri and the Wajudiyyah of 17th Century Acheh,* Century Books, Singapore, 1966.

Temple, R.C. : *The Sufi Path of Love,* MacMillan & Co., London, 1954.

Thomas, W.F. : *Mutual Influence of Muhammedans and Hindus in India,* Cambridge, London, 1892.

Titus, M. : *Indian Islam,* Milford, New Delhi, 1979.

Umaruddin, M. : *The Ethical Philosophy of al-Ghazzali,* Adam Publishers, New Delhi, 1996

Underhill, E. : *Mysticism : a Study in the Nature and Development of Man's Spiritual Consciousness,* Oxford, New York, 1956.

Usmani, J.M. Tariq : *The Authority of Sunnah,* Kitab Bhavan, New Delhi, 1998.

Waheed, Akhtar : *Sufi Approach to the Problem of Alienation,* Wilson & Co., New Delhi, 1975.

—— : *The Early Imamiya Shiite Thinkers,* Ashish Publishing House, New Delhi, 1995.

Waines, Davids : *A Introduction to Islam,* Cambridge University Press, New Delhi, 1995.

Watt, W.M. : *Islam and the Integration of Society,* Routledge, London, 1961.

Wensick, A.E. : *A Handbook of Early Muhammadan Traditions,* Luzac & Co., Leiden, 1960.

Whitting, C.E.J. : *Al-Fakhri,* Oxford, London, 1947.

Yeome, Yezbeck Haddad : *Islamic Values in the United States,* Oxford, New York, 1999.

Yousuf, Abbas Hashmi : *Rasul (PBUH),* Adam Pub., New Delhi, 2001.

Yusuf, Iblish and Peter Lambron Wilson : *Traditional Modes of Contemplation and Action,* University Press, Tehran, 1977.

Zahid, Malik : *Subjects of Quran,* Kitab Bhavan, New Delhi, 1998.

Zaydan, Jurji : *Umayyads and Abbasides,* Luzac & Co., London,1907.